Financialization as Welfare

Philipp Golka

Financialization as Welfare

Social Impact Investing and British Social Policy, 1997-2016

Springer

Philipp Golka
Sociology of Markets, Organizations and Governance
Friedrich Schiller University Jena
Jena, Thüringen, Germany

This work has been accepted as a PhD thesis (dissertation) at the Faculty of Social and Behavioral Sciences, Friedrich-Schiller-University Jena, Germany in 2018, as: Financialization as Welfare – Social Impact Investing and the Resonance of Financial Market Frames in British Social Policy, 1997–2016.

ISBN 978-3-030-06099-2 ISBN 978-3-030-06100-5 (eBook)
https://doi.org/10.1007/978-3-030-06100-5

Library of Congress Control Number: 2018965203

This Springer imprint is published by the registered company Springer Nature Switzerland AG
The registered company address is: Gewerbestrasse 11, 6330 Cham, Switzerland

For my father Jan.
In loving memory.

Foreword

Since the turn of the century, social impact investing (SII) has been emerging as a new branch of sustainable investing. SII investors focus on the impact their investments have—not only the financial return on investment but also the "social impact" their investments entail. Put differently: in what way does the investment indeed improve the situation of the persons concerned? This question is particularly intriguing, as in the case of SII financial market instruments are employed to solve social problems. Ideally, both aspects turn out well: with the investment, the social as well as the financial goals are reached.

While many SII researchers analyze the measurement or analysis of the social impact in question, Philipp Golka focuses on another aspect. He asks, how, and in what way SII as a financial market instrument fits into the existing welfare state institutions, or disrupts, or even replaces them. Is SII a case of financialization in which a normatively "good" endeavor by way of its involvement with and in the financial market becomes financialized and concurrently financializes the welfare state? Or, as Golka puts it: are we living in a world that is increasingly dominated by financial actors?

To address this question, Golka argues, based on a review of empirical research, that a crucial—and often overlooked—tipping point in financialization processes is the emergence of cooperative relations between financial and nonfinancial actors. He uses the empirical material at first to show that his conception of financialization is adequate to describe the empirically observed process but also to find a mechanism capable of explaining the emergence of such ties. Here, he shows an important gap in institutional and financialization theories, namely the structuring role of field-level, background conditions for the acceptance of innovative frames. The solution he proposes draws competently on current and classic views of pragmatism while remaining well-suited for future empirical research.

Golka's book makes manifold contributions on several levels. It contributes to the debate about financialization; it advances our theoretical understanding of fields, frames, and resonance spaces; it offers a unique insight into the financialization of SII and the British welfare state; and it makes a contribution to public sociology by discussing the merits and pitfalls of SII and offers reflexive knowledge for SII proponents and researchers.

Golka's book is a very compelling work of excellent quality. Each part is finely drafted, well-founded in its approach, rich in material, fine-grained in its analysis, rigorous in its argumentation, consistently presented, superbly verbalized, and deeply insightful. It is also a very courageous work as it tackles theories, methods, and empirical objects in an intrepid way. In an excellent manner, Golka not only deeply penetrates theories, methods, and empirical objects, but he also convincingly connects and relates them to each other. Reading the book is both an intellectual joy and satisfying intellectual work.

Jena, Germany
November 2018

Stefanie Hiß

Acknowledgements

This book, and the doctoral dissertation upon which it is based, could never have been written without the generous support from a large number of people for whom my gratitude far exceeds these notions of acknowledgement.

First of all, I am deeply grateful to Stefanie Hiß for giving me the opportunity to embark on this journey by accepting and supervising me as a graduate student. In every step of the process, she was an inexhaustible source of support as well as critical and constructive feedback, without which this book would never have taken shape, let alone seen its publication. Eve Chiapello's invitation to join her workgroup for a semester abroad at EHESS Paris and her generous support at a critical time were of vital importance to this work. It would have been impossible for me to devote the whole book to the study of financialization in the realm of public policy without her intellectual and personal encouragement, as well as her seriousness to discuss my work.

My work furthermore benefited significantly from support and comments by Lisa Knoll and Michael Hutter, as well as by the faculty at Freie Universität Berlin who allowed me to participate in their PhD seminars: Elke Schüssler, Gregory Jackson, and Jörg Sydow. I received very helpful feedback from participants particularly at the Society for the Advancement of Socio-Economics 2016 conference in Berkeley, the 2016 London Social Impact Bonds Workshop, and the 2017 Social Finance, Impact Investing, and the Financialization of the Public Interest conference in Hamburg. I benefited massively from my interviewees, who took the time to answer (or rework) my questions thoroughly, provided me with crucial data, and granted me access to their personal networks for further interviews. In addition, Leslie Huckfield provided me with insights and data I was unable to access elsewhere.

This study would have been impossible without a PhD scholarship from the German Federal Ministry of Education and Research, which has been realized by the Foundation of German Business (sdw). In addition, funding from the Alexander von Humboldt Foundation's Anneliese Maier Research Prize that has been awarded to Eve Chiapello allowed me to spend a year at the University of Hamburg, where Anita Engels and her team provided me with a welcoming and stimulating environment.

Countless discussions with friends and colleagues have propelled my thinking and their results are deeply interwoven with this text. These include the whole team in Jena, as well as Max Heimstädt, Georg Fischer, Lorenz Grünewald-Schukalla, Julia Bartosch, Camille Rivière, and Mehdi Arfaoui. Without the unconditional support and companionship of Jens Bendel, Joscha Enger, Lauren Howe, Hanna Pauls, and Marco Paladines, none of this would have been possible.

My family is the foundation upon which all of this has been built. I have never felt this more strongly than since the tragic loss of my father earlier this year. I would like to dedicate this book to him.

Jena, Germany
November 2018

Philipp Golka

Contents

Abbreviations

ACEVO	Association of the Chief Executives of Voluntary Organisations
BSB/BSC	Big Society Bank/ Big Society Capital
CDFI	Community Development Financial Institution
CEO	Chief Executive Officer
CIC	Community Interest Company
CITR	Community Investment Tax Relief
CoSA	Prime Minister's Council on Social Action
CUA	Commission on Unclaimed Assets
DTI	Department of Trade and Industry
DWP	Department of Work and Pensions
EU	European Union
ICRF	Investment and Contract Readiness Fund
IGU	Internal Governance Unit
IPO	Initial Public Offering
NESTA	National Endowment for Science, Technology and the Arts
NEET	Individual Not in Employment, Education, or Training
NGO	Non-governmental Organization
NHS	National Health Service
NSI	New Sociological Institutionalism
OTS/OCS	Office of the Third Sector/Office for Civil Society
PbR	Payment by Results
PFI	Private Finance Initiative
PSA	Public Service Agreement
SAF	Strategic Action Field
SE	Social Enterprise
SEL	Social Enterprise London
SIFI	Social Investment Finance Intermediary
SII	Social Impact Investing

SITR	Social Investment Tax Relief
UK	United Kingdom
US	United States of America
VAT	Value-Added Tax
VCS	Voluntary and Community Sector

List of Figures

List of Tables

Chapter 1
Introduction

Are we living in a world that is increasingly dominated by financial actors? This question has generated extensive debate across economic sociology, political economy, and organization studies (van der Zwan 2014). Scholars of financialization have strongly supported this claim by showing how in the past forty-or-so years, financial actors have not only extracted and amassed unprecedented amounts of wealth but also profoundly transformed a vast set of objects, ranging from individuals, households, firms, and states, to (formerly) critical discourses such as sustainability, or international development practices. Institutionalist scholars of capitalist variety have been more cautious to attribute such a uniform direction of change. In particular regarding firms, they have argued that institutions on a national level exist that constrain the ability of financial actors to mill through extant social orders and transform them in their favor. Indeed, the question of whether and how financial actors have the capacity to transform social orders seems to be central here. If we are able to find out how and under what conditions financial actors are able to become more dominant, then we will have made a leap forward to understanding not just the current state of the social world, but possibly even demarcating ways out of a potentially one-sided dominance of financial actors.

Understanding through empirical work the change-making capacity of financial actors—or lack thereof—promises to contribute to one of today's key puzzles in sociology: the relation between structure and agency. To what extent are we humans determined by the social structures, such as language, organizations, or institutions, that are around us? How is it possible for us to transcend their conforming pressures to conceive of something new and alter social reality for the people around us? Is this more a question of our individual capabilities, our position vis-à-vis others, the nature of the structures around us, or are other factors more important, and how do they interact?

This book aims to contribute on both the theoretical and empirical level. Though my primary goal is to enhance our understanding of the current state of (mostly Western) capitalism, this phenomenon is inextricably linked to theoretical questions.

P. Golka, *Financialization as Welfare*,
https://doi.org/10.1007/978-3-030-06100-5_1

Thus, it would be impossible to address the former without the latter, and somewhat detached from social reality to do so vice versa.

On an empirical level, I aim to understand how processes of financialization unfold. The scholarly literature has already made important contributions to our understanding of financialization: Debates between financialization and institutionalist scholars have been the most heated regarding the case of corporate governance. Here, the former have argued for a significant and rather uniform transformation of firms according to the interests of shareholders and financial investors (Lazonick and O'Sullivan 2000). By contrast, institutionalists have argued for sets of external, constraining institutions that shape the transformation process of corporate governance and constrain financial actors' ability to affect change (Aguilera and Jackson 2003).

This marks the jacking point of this book. As an empirical case, I select what institutionalists would see as the prototype of an external, market-constraining institution: the welfare state. Here, I study the process through which financial actors have transformed the prevailing social order, creating financial products that operate within—and even *through*—the welfare state and thus transform how organizations in this field act. If financial actors are successful in transforming social orders in this case, then we might have to thoroughly rethink our conception of institutions and their role in constraining economic actors.

More concretely, I investigate the creation of a "social impact investing" capital market within the British welfare state. According to its proponents, social impact investing (SII) denotes the practice of combining financial investments with the pursuit of a measurable "positive social or environmental impact." As SII is a label that investors adhere to themselves, a large variety of subcategories can be identified. The largest group among these investors are those akin to "socially responsible investors" who attempt to change firms in extant markets, such as in the production of material goods, to adhere to some form of social or environmental standard (JP Morgan 2014). These investors are not of concern here. What I am interested in is a much smaller but qualitatively more significant group that attempts to alter the workings of governments, public organizations, and not-for-profit social service providers in order to extract revenues towards their financial intermediary organizations. This group has been particularly successful in the UK, making Britain the most interesting case in this regard. For example, SII actors in the UK have created so-called "Social Impact Bonds" (SIBs), financial products that turn the success of social service providers in altering the social behavior of individuals into a speculative return opportunity for financial intermediaries: If service providers meet predefined "outcome" targets, then public authorities will repay investors who have financed the intervention with a variable rate of return. These SIBs are just one example of how significantly the British government, public organizations, and not-for-profit social service providers altered their way to (inter-)act.

In this book, I argue that these transformations are emblematic for processes of financialization on a more general level. My point is that to understand financialization, we ought to understand how and explain why *nonfinancial* actors change to act. This way, we may understand financialization as the social process through which nonfinancial actors begin to take financial actors into account in such a way that profit opportunities for financial intermediaries are created. Since nonfinancial actors, like all social actors, may principally act otherwise (Forst 2015a), the key question becomes *how it makes sense* for these actors to forge such rather cooperative relations with financial actors. Thus, from this perspective, we understand nonfinancial actors as having a stake in processes of financialization as they hope to materialize some kind of objective in forging such relations. Such a perspective discords with large parts of institutionalist scholarship that tends to see the state as an external referee in such financialization processes. Rather, my perspective follows yet expands the "state-sponsored" view (Belfrage 2008) that understands repeated state interventions as key to financialization processes.

Tracing how financialization makes sense for nonfinancial actors does not imply that they consciously calculate the utility of acting accordingly, nor does it mean that nonfinancial actors are unrestrained to act in whatever fashion they would like to. A vast body of sociological work has shown the limitations of assuming such atomistic, rational actors and therefore making the assumptions of rational choice theory—even for questions of economic exchange—inapplicable (e.g. Beckert 2003). However, noting that actors could principally act otherwise makes us equally careful of an oversocialized view on agency where actors blindly follow scripts provided by their social environment. After all, such a norm-following view of action seems difficult to reconcile with change—or at least change that differs from rigid path-dependencies or functional differentiation.

One way how these tensions between over- and undersocialized views of action have been discharged in the past three to four decades is through social field theories (Martin 2003). In general terms, fields are socially constructed, meso-level social orders. Although a host of field theories exists, most of them are concerned with the question of how actors begin to take each other into account, and what consequences arise from these patterns of interaction. This makes field theories particularly useful for our endeavor as they allow to conceptualize financialization as a process in which financial actors penetrate nonfinancial fields and, by making nonfinancial actors take them into account, alter (or "financialize") the rules of the very field. Yet even at the field level, this is a tremendously complex social process that is, as institutionalist scholarship has shown, bound up with structural conditions.

Thus, if we are to understand financialization from a field perspective, our field theory must be able to account for both financialization and its absence. This is why in the third chapter, I will critically demarcate the explanatory horizon of field theories for the quest at hand. My discussion will focus on comparing two of the most promising field theories, new sociological institutionalism, and strategic action fields (SAF) theory (Fligstein and McAdam 2012). I argue that a key reason for the explanatory advantage of SAF theory is that it provides us with a social ontology that understands society overall as a "dense latticework of interdependent fields" (Fligstein and McAdam 2012, p. 58), rather than as an "inter-institutional system" (Thornton et al. 2012). This means that the same organizing principle, SAFs, holds for all, state, financial, and nonfinancial actors.

Key to SAFs is that actors are theorized to act according to their *position* within their proximate field environment. This is of fundamental importance for my perspective, as it allows to break open actor classes—such as governments or social organizations—into fields of positioned actors. In SAF theory, this is linked with a second key feature: an action theory based on American Pragmatism that sees action as guided by social situations that correspond to actors' positions within the field. Here, actors are conceptualized as skillful in that they understand their own and others' situations and are creative in developing means to cooperate with others to advance their aims.

I argue that this is why SAF theory is particularly well-suited to allow us to understand financialization processes. Based on SAF theory, we may understand financialization as the success of skilled financial actors in developing cooperative ties with nonfinancial fields. The problem, however, is that, while SAF theory is well suited to explain *contentious* field dynamics, it is in its current form not fully equipped with a mechanism that explains how and when new *cooperative* ties across dynamic fields emerge. The reason for this might be that SAF theory is in essence a combination of Fligstein's (2001b) conception of fields and social skill and McAdam's work on contentious social movements (MacAdam et al. 2001). This makes the question of cooperative mobilization across fields fall on the welding seam between both theoretical components—which, due to the novelty of the theory, has not yet been explored. Closing this conceptional void in SAF theory therefore represents the main theoretical contribution of this book.

Together, this study pursues two research questions. On the empirical level, the question is:

1. *How, and under what conditions, do processes of financialization unfold?*

In Chap. 3, I will show that SAF theory provides large parts of the answer to that question but leaves open an undertheorized residual space. This leads to the research question on a theoretical level, which is:

2. *How do skilled actors form new cooperative ties across dynamic fields?*

To answer these questions, I will study the development of social impact investing through an in-depth, qualitative case study. I will follow an abductive methodology that promises to overcome key epistemological problems that arise from qualitative research that follows the "grounded theory" perspective (Tavory and Timmermans 2014). Most generally, advocates of "grounded theory" argue for inductive theory construction that sees theories as emerging exclusively and directly from the empirical data. From an epistemological perspective, the problem with this approach is that the theoretical and the empirical are fundamentally different philosophical realms that cannot be "bridged" through inductive research: any theoretical generalization of empirical material implies at the very least a conception of what theory is that cannot be reduced to the empirical material alone. This is why abductive researchers argue that rather than attempting to artificially reduce theoretical knowledge when conducting empirical research, researchers should use the empirical material to develop hypotheses that become interesting only in the light of theory. Thus, they propose a research process that frequently iterates between the theoretical and empirical levels.

In investigating the case of SII, I have followed this avenue. This is why I will begin by linking the empirical material to the theoretical problem (Chaps. 2, 3, and 5). In a second step, I will use the empirical material to develop a hypothesis regarding the theoretical research question (Chaps. 6 and 7). In a third step, I will relate this hypothesis back to the theoretical level and solidify the empirical findings against the backdrop of SAF theory and sociological theory more generally (Chap. 8).

I find that a collaborative tie between a group of policymakers and impact investors was key to the emergence and development of SII. Through this cooperation, financial intermediaries have been successful in mobilizing approximately £1.3 billion in public subsidies. Using abductive analysis, I find that this tie was established because policymakers increasingly accepted financial intermediaries' strategic action frame (Snow and Benford 1988) that presented field-level financialization as a means to achieve public welfare. Strategic action frames problematize a specific social situation and build on this analysis to develop a vision of an alternative future that motivates an alteration of future action patterns. Key to financialization was thus the success of financial actors to make nonfinancial actors accept their prognostic and motivational framing. However, their ability to do so was fundamentally constrained by their ability to frame their problem *descriptions* according to nonfinancial actors' problem *situations*. Crucially, as problem situations are liked with positions, this is more a question of dynamics in *nonfinancial actors' proximate field environment* rather than financial actors' capabilities. Nonfinancial actors use the interpretation of their position in a dynamic field environment to *test* whether cooperative ties with financial actors make sense. At a theoretical level, this proposed "resonance" mechanism for the emergence of cooperative ties therefore blends the "European Pragmatism" (Boltanski and Thévenot 2006; Habermas 1981) with its American counterpart. On the empirical level, this mechanism shifts our attention to the structured opportunities, or "resonance spaces," that allow for the mobilization of nonfinancial actors.

In addition to this contribution to sociological theorizing, I develop a small contribution to "public sociology" (Burawoy 2005): through an in-depth analysis of the SII field structure, I attempt to show how the reality of impact investing profoundly contradicts the claims of investors. More precisely, I will show in a little more detail than necessary for the theoretical question how SII represents a case of financialization that alters the rules of social service provision first and foremost to the material favor of financial intermediaries. The same is true for my detailed analysis of investors' justifications of SII. I argue that because of these inner contradictions, SII marks a particularly interesting empirical case of financialization in its own right. This is why it appeared sensible and legitimate to me to devote equal attention to both the empirical and theoretical puzzles that SII presents to us.

The structure of this work is somewhat unusual: it roughly takes the shape of a sandwich where a thick layer of empirical findings is encapsulated by two layers of theory. Although those two layers might at times be somewhat dry, they are not only necessary in order to suffice the epistemological demands created by the methodology of abductive analysis, but also to form a coherent object out of what would otherwise be a set of unrelated ingredients.

The book will proceed as follows. The next chapter establishes a link between the debate of financialization and institutionalist scholarship, and the empirical case of SII. To do so, I first introduce this debate and then point to an often-overlooked strand of the financialization literature that is key to understanding the case of SII. This literature studies the role of state and government actors in processes of financialization. In a second step, I establish the link between SII and financialization by contextualizing the phenomenon and linking its development to dynamics in British social policy. Based on this, I show how it makes sense to apply a meso-level perspective to understand the development trajectory of SII.

The third chapter translates these empirical debates and issues to the theoretical level. Here, I introduce the field concept and analyze the explanatory potential of different field theories for the debate between financialization and institutionalist scholarship, as well as for the empirical case of SII. Comparing neo-institutionalist and SAF conceptions of fields, I show the explanatory benefits of the latter over the former. Subsequently, I introduce key concepts of SAF theory and show how these guide the empirical analysis. By doing so, I point to the theory's conceptual void regarding cooperative ties across fields.

In the fourth chapter, I present my methodological approach. Following the abductive approach to empirical research, I first describe the iterative research process as it led me to the "abductive moment" in which I defined my "resonance" hypothesis. In a second step, I describe the empirical research method that I used in order to investigate the case of SII: a qualitative case design in which I conducted two empirical analyses. For both, I present the empirical material and the analytical process, and describe how such a research design relates to the questions at hand.

The fifth chapter represents the first of three empirical chapters. By demonstrating the field structure of SII, I show how it does indeed represent a case of financialization. More concretely, I show how the rules advocated for by investors favor their interests and constrain nonfinancial actors' possibilities to act. Moreover, I show how SII creates profit opportunities for investors by allowing them to extract revenues from social service providers, private foundations, and public organizations.

In the sixth chapter, I present investors' discourse. Based on the strategic action frames perspective, I show how investors' discourse not only legitimates their own actions, but also advances a nuanced role structure for all partaking actors at the field level. To the extent this frame is accepted, an SII field that establishes investors' central position comes into existence. This is why investors' framing takes a central role for the question of financialization and the development of cross-field ties.

In the seventh chapter, I present the most important empirical analysis: the longitudinal case study of the development of SII. Here, I show how investors' framing not only changed according to the ruling party's normative discourse. Moreover, I show that investors' success in altering nonfinancial actors' way to act hinged on a parallel development in the social policy field. Concretely, I show how the increasing dominance of HM Treasury for social policymaking under Gordon

Brown increasingly created a "resonance space" for investors' arguments. Crucially, the Treasury itself relied on the very same mechanism to alter the policy field as it built on its formal role as the safeguard of the public budget to transform social services into the "value for money" delivery of "social outcomes" by social organizations. Thus, dynamics constrained by the structure of the policy field eventually shaped opportunities for financial actors to affect change. To use these opportunities, financial actors benefited from the failure of social organizations to maintain a clear profit/not-for-profit boundary as this allowed them to enter the field of public service delivery. Following these qualitative innovations, investors' large-scale quantitative success came as a shift in policy advisory networks with the 2010 Coalition government expanded the resonance of investors' arguments at the expense of the perspective advocated for by not-for-profit organizations.

In the eighth chapter, I condense the empirical findings into a more fine-grained hypothesis of the resonance mechanism. In a second step, I draw on the notion of "pragmatist mechanisms" (Gross 2009) to show that the resonance mechanism is indeed a *causal* one. Based on this finding, I further qualify the notion of "resonance spaces" and show how it relates to the theory-level research question on the emergence of cooperative ties. Lastly, I translate these findings back to the empirical level to show the use of the concept for the debate between institutionalist and financialization scholarship.

In the final chapter, I discuss and critically evaluate the contribution of this study. To do so, I first point out how this work advances both sociological theorizing as well as empirical research. Then, I show important limitations of this work and suggest ways how future research could address these. Lastly, I attempt to provide "reflexive knowledge" (Burawoy 2005) to stakeholders of social impact investing outside of and within the academic world.

Chapter 2
Financialization and Social Impact Investing

The goal of this chapter is to place the empirical phenomenon into the sociological debate, thus providing a more specific introduction than the first chapter. For this reason, I first introduce the concept of financialization and how it has been debated from a perspective of institutionalist scholarship of capitalism. Then, I point to the ubiquitous and multifarious role of the state in shaping financialization processes, which has often been overlooked both by financialization and institutionalist scholars. Then, I introduce the empirical case of SII in the UK and show its potential for starting a conversation between these different literature streams. By sketching linkages between SII market development and dynamics in British social policy—which will be discussed extensively in Chap. 7—I point towards the explanatory utility of a meso-level perspective for the case of SII, and the outlined academic debate more generally. This meso-level perspective is then developed on a theoretical level in the following chapter.

2.1 What is Financialization?

The academic debate on financialization is large and diverse, including many different definitions, theoretical approaches, levels of analysis, analytical dimensions, and empirical objects. It is therefore neither possible nor useful for our endeavor to provide an exhaustive review of the literature as can be found elsewhere (see e.g. Dore 2008; Van der Zwan 2014). Rather, my goal is to shed light on the academic debate around the *social process* of financialization. In contrast to institutionalist scholars, my goal is to argue that financialization is a rather general social process that may unfold in vastly different organizational set-ups. Key to understanding this process, I argue, are the conditions under and ways in which state actors get involved, and how, by doing so, the state itself is being changed. Based on a literature review, I will develop a working definition of financialization as *a social process in which financial actors acquire a central position in social orders and*

P. Golka, *Financialization as Welfare*,
https://doi.org/10.1007/978-3-030-06100-5_2

change those social orders to their material benefit, critically based on cooperative relations with state actors. The subsequent section then shows how SII is a relevant case from this perspective.

I acknowledge that such an approach is ignorant to more macro-level financialization scholarship such as in the works of Arrighi (1994), Duménil and Lévy (2004), or Stockhammer (2004). This is because rather than ex ante assuming regimes of accumulation that inevitably create increasing economic inequalities, my perspective seeks to understand how processes of financialization—which certainly create more losers than winners—unfold as a product of human agency. This does not mean that I am arguing against the existence of inherent "logics" of capitalism, but I instead attempt to understand how these logics are reproduced, altered, and further entrenched by reflexive, critical, and creative social actors who could, in principle, act otherwise. Likewise, I ignore a second important strand of the literature that focuses on transformations of financial markets and can be named "financialization of finance." Here, scholars have placed great emphasis on the relation between financialization and technological developments (Coombs 2016; MacKenzie 2008; MacKenzie and Millo 2003). Moreover, scholars have studied how financial intermediation has changed following important regulative changes (Chiapello and Walter 2016). However, these studies are mostly concerned with transformations in *speculation* (i.e. circulating financial products), whereas I am mostly interested in transformations regarding *investment*, that is, monetary flows that both enter and exit the circuit of financial intermediation (Knorr-Cetina 2009). The chasm between these two fields of finance is exemplified by the temporal density of financial intermediation activities: while speculative financial actors may trade billions of US Dollars per minute, even the largest investors usually take a year or longer to achieve a similar turnover. Thus, although these fields are related, entirely different infrastructures and strategies are in place, and hence we may suspect different causal ways of how these actors change to act.

2.1.1 Financialization in Markets and Institutionalist Perspectives on Capitalism

Financialization is often understood as the role of finance "beyond its traditional role as provider of capital for the productive economy" (Van der Zwan 2014, p. 99). A large part of the financialization literature studies how financial actors became central actors in markets, and how, in parallel, non-financial actors changed their actions according to financial actors' material interests. *Redistribution towards financial actors* is pointed out both between and within firms. For example, Baud and Durand (2012) study how global retail firms have since 1990 increased their payments to shareholders despite a slowdown in sales growth. Similarly, Crotty (2005) has shown how non-financial firms have increased their payments to financial companies through increased dividend payments, but also through higher payments in fees and the increased purchase of insurances and other financial products. Moreover, non-financial firms have increased share buybacks in order to elevate their stock prices (Crotty 2008; Dünhaupt 2012), at times spending more than their net income on share buybacks (Lazonick 2014). These developments are mirrored at an aggregate level by increased percentages of GDP, as well as corporate profits, comprised by the financial, insurance and real estate industries (Krippner 2005; Milberg 2008).

The redistributive dimension of financialization is furthermore well documented on the intra-firm level. As Godechot (2015) observes, pay in the financial sector is distributed highly unequally, with top earners reaping a significant percentage of the sectors' overall profits—a finding that is in line with ethnographic studies highlighting the strictly hierarchical organizational structures of Wall Street investment banks (Ho 2009). Other studies have focused on how finance-led transformations in corporate governance have seen dramatic rises in executive pay in order to avoid "agency costs" thought to arise, according to Agency Theory of financial economics, from the separation of ownership and control in large corporations (Deutschmann 2008; Lazonick and O'Sullivan 2000).

Thus, many scholars concord in understanding financialization as a social dynamic that creates winners and losers. Tomaskovic-Devey and Lin (2011) have estimated that non-financial firms have in the past decades transferred "between 5.8 and 6.6 trillion 2011 dollars in income into the finance sector, mostly as profits." This is equal to 13% of all increased income generated by the US private sector between 1980 and 2008 (p. 553). By contrast, (often low-skilled) workers are frequently found to have materially lost from financialization dynamics (Dünhaupt 2012; Fligstein and Shin 2004; Lin and Tomaskovic-Devey 2013)—further increasing financial actors' structural bargaining power (Flaherty 2015). The redistributive effects of financialization are further exacerbated in situations of low economic growth (Piketty 2014).

But while most scholars share the understanding of financialization as a redistributive process benefitting (a broad category of) financial actors, there are different views regarding its causes, dynamics, boundary conditions, and empirical significance. Regarding its causes, most scholars see regulative changes as a critical factor. For example, in the US, the demise and repeal of the 1932/33 Glass-Steagall legislation separating commercial and investment banking is often cited as having created enabling conditions for a later transformation of financial actors and corporate governance, respectively (Lazonick and O'Sullivan 2000; Windolf 2005). Likewise, scholars have emphasized the importance of changes to the regulation of financial accounting for processes of financialization (Chiapello and Medjad 2009; Nölke and Perry 2007).

Other work links the rise of institutional investors to the financialization of markets and transformations in corporate governance in particular (Fligstein 1990; Lazonick 2014; Lazonick and O'Sullivan 2000; Morin 2000; Widmer 2011; Windolf 2008). Here, scholars study how "firms responded to the entreaties of institutional investors, putting most of the innovations they lobbied for into place" (Jung and Dobbin 2012, p. 53). According to this perspective, what institutional investors argued for was a restructuring of the firms' strategies from a focus on profit maximization to a focus on increasing share price. Many of these works, again, emphasize the necessity of regulative changes, such as the 1974 US Pension Reform Act for the accumulation of vast amounts of capital in the hands of few investment corporations. In addition, these works often focus on dynamics in the socialization of firms' managers, from more production—towards more finance-oriented managers, stating the ascendancy of institutional investors as one of the factors influencing this development (Jung 2015; Zorn 2004; Zorn et al. 2005). Where these works largely concord, however, is in the emphasis they put on the development of the academic discipline of financial economics and Agency Theory in particular. As Lazonick and O'Sullivan (2000) point out, attempts to establish a "market for corporate control"—a key factor in the entrenchment of shareholder value orientation—failed before Agency Theory was developed and largely accepted in the field of economics. This means that for institutional investors to transform corporate control according to their material interests (share price), not only regulative changes were required.[1] Moreover, these dynamics required a change in managers' cognitive frames, which built on intra-firm power struggles as much as on changes in accepted means and ends in economics and management theory. This dynamic is neatly pointed out by (Khurana 2007, p. 320f, cit. by Dore 2008), comparing statements on corporate governance by the American Business Roundtable, an association of US business executives. While in 1990 they said:

> Some argue that only the interests of the shareholders should be considered by directors. The thrust of history and law supports the broader view of the directors' responsibility to carefully weigh the interests of all stakeholders as part of their responsibility to the corporation or to the long-term interests of its shareholders.

In 1997, the statement was the following:

> [T]he paramount duty of management and of boards of directors is to the corporation's stockholders. [. . .] The notion that the board must somehow balance the interests of other stakeholders fundamentally misconceives the role of directors. It is, moreover, an unworkable notion because it would leave the board with no criterion for resolving the conflict of interests between interests of stockholders and of other stakeholders or among different groups of stakeholders.

Institutionalist scholars of capitalist variety (Jackson and Deeg 2012) have questioned the empirical significance as well as the causal mechanisms identified by these works. In essence, they argue for national institutional compounds that impact investors' agency in transforming corporate governance (Aguilera and Jackson 2003). While they agree upon many of the findings regarding transformations of corporate control in the US, they show that changes in corporate governance in other countries have much more taken the form of path-dependent trajectories, rather than a largely uniform financialization dynamic (Deeg and Jackson 2007). For example,

[1]This resonates with findings from derivatives trading, where it has been shown that a market for derivatives only emerged after the development and spread of Black-Scholes-Merton formula for option pricing (MacKenzie 2008; MacKenzie and Millo 2003).

in the case of Germany, scholars have stressed the importance of networks of interlocking corporate directorates for corporate governance (Mizruchi 1996). Institutionalist scholars have argued that albeit managers increasingly accepted the rhetoric of financialization, their corporate management practices nevertheless remained somewhat decoupled from SVO due to the larger national institutional set-up (Fiss and Zajac 2004; Höpner and Jackson 2006; Vitols 2002). However, in contrast to the statist path-dependencies advocated for by the earlier Varieties of Capitalism approach (Hall and Soskice 2001), these comparative researchers acknowledge that institutional set-ups can be eroded through internal change processes (Streeck and Thelen 2005). Thus, recent institutionalist scholarship does point to distinct national trajectories of change but seems somewhat more open towards processes of financialization (Jackson and Deeg 2012). To understand financialization we thus need to be sensitive to its context.

In summary, these academic streams of work show that financialization is a redistributive social process that materially benefits financial actors. However, to be successful, it needs to be (re)produced by acting individuals and organizations outside of financial markets. As Kädtler (2011, 2015) shows, in a financialized capitalism, drawing on a "financial rationality" becomes a power resource. Yet both, the mixed results of financialization in European countries as well as scholarship on the transformation of US firms show that the change of action patterns and rationalities of managers and non-financial corporations is critically dependent on boundary conditions inside the firm as much as outside markets. At the same time, financialization scholarship shows that investors are indeed often successful in shaping other actors' strategies. This hints to the core theoretical argument of this book: making others act in line with one's own actions not only requires creativity and social skill, but is also critically dependent on the dynamic situations of the targets. If anything, the academic debate between financialization and institutionalist scholars has shown how both investors and managers in corporate governance dynamics are highly capable, creative, and critical social actors. If we are to understand who succeeds, we thus need to study actors' respective situations very carefully.

2.1.2 Financialization Beyond Markets and the Role of the State

According to financialization scholars, financial market actions and dynamics have caused social changes also beyond markets and corporate governance. Indeed, the "financialization of X" literature knows a vast number of non-market objects, ranging from multiple policy fields (Davis and Walsh 2015; Dowling and Harvie 2014; Lake 2015; Mader 2015) to (initially) critical discursive practices such as sustainability (Feist and Fuchs 2014; Hiß 2013, 2014) and everyday life and individual subjectivities (Aitken 2007; Konings 2009; Langley 2006; Martin 2002). As argued above, a large part of the financialization literature studies non-financial economic actors' change of strategies in relation to dynamics in financial markets. Here, I will maintain this perspective but limit my attention to one particular type of non-market economic actors: the state and public organizations.[2]

In its economic functions, the state may use a very large variety of more or less direct policy interventions that can be linked with financialization. As the works I review below suggest, the state may act as (de)regulator (e.g. defining rules of exchange), provider (e.g. pension systems) or owner of services (e.g. social housing), but may also (not) tax, (fully) fund, (partially) subsidize, borrow, lend, guarantee or "bail out" financial actors, create or use financial instruments such as derivatives and securities, or affect monetary policy. Yet scholarship on market financialization is often rather ignorant to the ubiquity and plurality of government interventions—and their dynamics in particular. Most frequently, the state appears as a mere boundary condition, for example by deregulating financial markets (e.g. in Lazonick and O'Sullivan 2000). By contrast, the political economy literature on "state-sponsored" financialization (Belfrage 2008) has provided nuanced insights into how the state is continuously engaged in forging market dynamics. These insights are important both to understand the development of financialization in producer and financial markets, as well as the financialization of non-market fields such as the organizational realms of the welfare state. The following short review focuses on the latter case.

The political economy literature linking finance and social policies emerged in partial opposition to Esping-Andersen's (1990) typology that classifies welfare regimes according to their decommodifying effect on labor. As Schelkle (2012, p. 61) notes, "this dominant tradition thus ignores the commodifying effect that social policies have, notably in allowing unemployed, poor, or discriminated against households to participate in markets other than that for labor" and thereby "misses the point that the welfare state spends vast amounts on tax expenditure" in order to forge capital market development in social policy fields.

Among the best-studied examples of financialization in fields of social welfare is the US, and to an extent the British, social housing "market." Housing is a particularly interesting case as it is, in "asset based welfare" regimes (Finlayson 2009) such as the US and the UK, at the same time a market, as much as a field of social policy with profound and continuous government intervention. Moreover, it is the birthplace and habitat of key financial derivatives, such as mortgage-backed securities (Fligstein and Goldstein 2012; Langley 2008). In the US, the federal government saw the expansion of the mortgage market as an important social policy goal, building on the hope that the increased availability of mortgages would increase the number of homeowners in the country. Yet, due to the "sprawling" nature of the

[2]I acknowledge that dynamics in other non-market economic actors—households in particular—are, too, of critical importance for the study of financialization. See, for example, Schwartz (2012) on the interplay between the shift from defined benefit to defined contribution pension systems in the US, individuals' increased house price speculation, and regulation. That being said, my research question focuses more on the relation between finance, policy and public organizations.

US government, the ability of the federal executive to establish policy means to expand the availability of credit is severely constrained (Quinn 2010). As a consequence, federal policymakers during the Johnson administration were required to find a way to expand the provision of capital without affecting the federal budget. To make a long story short, federal government created the "government-sponsored enterprises" Fannie Mae and Freddie Mac to stimulate the growth of the mortgage market, while pioneering mortgage-backed securities in order to sell off these mortgages from those semi-public entities (Fligstein and Goldstein 2012).

In the UK, by contrast, the development of a mortgage market was advanced particularly by the Thatcher administration in the late 1980s. As a result of granting social housing tenants a "right to buy", government allowed financial actors to lend rather large sums to low-income populations, thereby creating an early "variant of highly leveraged subprime lending" (Schelkle 2012, p. 64). As a consequence of this and other deregulations, the UK developed a very large mortgage market (with unusually high levels of variable interest mortgages)—despite the lack of more direct subsidies as in the US case (Schelkle 2012, p. 70).

Together, this literature points to the active role played by states in shaping financial actors into central figures for the achievement of public policy goals. In contrast to critical scholarship on neo-liberalism (Blyth 2013; Crouch 2011; Harvey 2005; Streeck 2013), these works point towards the "strange non-death" *of the state* during constrained public budgets and welfare state retrenchment. Nevertheless, both literatures share the empirical insight that financial actors have become key actors in public policy far exceeding the realm of financial, economic and industrial policy.

Indeed, the introduction of financial actors into policy fields and the subsequent repercussions to policymaking have been studied in multiple other contexts. For example, Mader (2015) studies how through the ascendancy of microfinance, financial actors have become increasingly central figures in international development policy, extracting and redistributing at least $125 billion of surpluses generated in the Global South (p. 117) with hardly any positive impact on poverty alleviation (p. 14). Moreover, financial actors have increasingly been able to set the international development policy agenda through the label of "financial inclusion" (Mader 2016).

In refocusing the interaction between financial actors and policymakers, scholars of the "state-sponsored" view have emphasized the dynamics of state-finance relations in contrast to more statist-institutionalist views such as the varieties of capitalism approach (Hall and Soskice 2001) as well as its more dynamist reformulations that emphasize transformative incremental change (Jackson and Deeg 2012; Streeck and Thelen 2005). More precisely, they differ in the independence they grant discursive or ideational processes from institutions.

The link between finance dynamics and ideas has been studied extensively in the "cultural political economy" (Du Gay and Pryke 2002; Jessop 2010, 2011) and "financialization of the everyday" (Aitken 2007; Martin 2002) literatures. Despite differences, these literatures converge in emphasizing the importance of discourse, particularly on the level of non-elite "everyday" actors, for the expansion of financial markets (Seabrooke 2007, 2010). By doing so, they have received criticism from scholars who—although acknowledging the importance of discourse and everyday practices—emphasized that due to high levels of stratification in Western capitalisms, both everyday and elite dynamics need to be taken into account (Konings 2009).

In their study on the transformation of housing in Denmark, Mortensen and Seabrooke (2008) pointed towards the interaction of these two levels by acknowledging how electoral strategies changed as a result of a shift in everyday discourse that was triggered by a change in financial market regulation. Concretely, they showed how a deregulation of mortgage finance led to an increase in flexible rate interest mortgages that fostered a significant property boom between the mid 1990s and the early 2000s. This boom has seen a surge in property prices that made property in Denmark more expensive than in its Nordic neighbors. As a result, the authors argue, the dominant conception of housing shifted from "housing as a social right" to "housing as a means to wealth", legitimizing speculative activity. As a consequence of this ideational shift, the Danish social democratic party diametrically reversed its electoral strategy just 2 weeks ahead of the 2007 parliamentary elections in order to rule out tax increases on property, but maintaining labor taxation. By doing so, the social democratic party alienated its organized labor constituents (who were arguing for the opposite) and, after an electoral success, helped further entrench the ideational shift in the Danish housing market.

Together, the "financialization beyond markets" literature makes two important points. First, financialization often emerges as a result of ongoing state activity that employs a full-fledged toolkit of economic actions that go far beyond regulation and taxation. Through their economic actions, states repeatedly take financial actors into account and orient their actions towards them. In the most extreme case, states become virtually indistinguishable from financial actors when they understand their actions as "signals" to shape price development on financial markets (Langenohl and Wetzel 2011). Thus, financialization is not just forged by the state and happens outside of it—rather, financialization profoundly alters *how* states act.

Second, financializing policymakers need to be understood as competent social actors who attempt to find creative ways to act in social situations where they feel compelled yet constrained to do so. These situations are, of course, highly diverse, ranging from raising inflation (Krippner 2011), constrained budget authority on a municipal level (Pacewicz 2012), to the uncertainty of electoral success (Mortensen and Seabrooke 2008). Thus, this literature points us to focus on the social dynamics inside and outside the state which lead policymakers to repeatedly believe that sponsoring financialization is a promising way to act.

But although this literature addresses the link between financialization and problem situations in policy fields, in many cases it does not view policymakers as positioned actors (exceptions are, for example, Pacewicz 2012, and Quinn 2010) in larger social structures. How to understand these structures, how they interact with problem situations, and what this interaction means for processes of financialization thus forms the main theoretical puzzle that this book attempts to address.

2.2 Social Impact Investing in the UK: Linking Financialization and Institutionalist Scholarship

Above, I have shown how financialization can be understood as a social process in which financial intermediaries enter existing social orders and redistribute monetary flows towards their intermediation activities. Highly debated in the academic literature, however, are the conditions under which these processes unfold: in essence, institutionalist scholars have argued that due to the constraining nature of institutionalized social structures, financial actors' capabilities to affect change are limited. By contrast, financialization scholars have shown how, very frequently, the state—rather than acting as such a constraint—has engaged in actively creating and shaping processes of financialization. These scholars have granted ideational processes a relative independence from institutional set-ups and have shown how new ideas regarding public policy issues such as housing have often led state actors to engage in financialization to address public problems.

My argument is that the case of social impact investing is a crucial one to discharge of this tension as it highlights both financial actors' creativity, as well as boundary conditions to their success. As I show in Chap. 5, SII *is* a case of financialization because it is the creation of a capital market within the welfare state. The rise of SII sees financial intermediaries gaining an increasingly central position in British social policy, while redistributing public subsidies, social service providers' revenues, and private donations towards their activities. At first sight, SII would therefore hardly be surprising for an institutionalist scholar: it may be interpreted as the continuation of a liberalization trajectory in a highly liberal market economy. However, taking a closer look in the empirical chapters of this work, I show how an institutionalist perspective would create large explanatory voids for the case of SII. For example, financial actors' social change attempts have in the beginning largely failed to take hold. They argued for the set-up of a social investment "wholesaler" to support their activities as early as in the year 2000. However, only after two parallel processes unfolded—the increasing dominance of HM Treasury inside social policy, and a boundary-expansion process of social organizations—were financial actors able to build cooperative ties with social organizations and the state in order to make their proposals come to life.

Thus, the insight for the debate between financialization and institutional scholarship on capitalism is twofold. In line with financialization scholarship, the case of SII shows how—in relative independence from the institutional set-up—financial actors regularly launch creative attempts to alter social orders. In contrast to the institutional model of a "liberal market economy" (Hall and Soskice 2001), the financing of social organizations was, before SII, dominated by lending while equity products only emerged after SII proponents mobilized significant amounts of subsidies. However, in line with institutionalist scholarship, the SII trajectory shows that there are structural constraints to their changemaking attempts. This is why the perspective I develop here attempts to understand trajectories of financialization by studying how financial actors are able to mobilize enough support *from nonfinancial actors* for their transformative attempts. This is why particular attention is needed to study the structural transformations within financial actors' proximate environment as structural conditions for financial actors' success. I argue in Chap. 3 that only Strategic Action Fields theory (Fligstein and McAdam 2012) offers such a view. But before transcending to the theoretical level, I will describe on an empirical level how SII forms a case in point to study such changes.

2.2.1 What Is Social Impact Investing?

Most generally, social impact investing is what those actors do who label themselves as social impact investors. Like any label, its use is contested and this is why, from an academic perspective, we need to add criteria that distinguish SII from other categories, fields, or practices. From my empirical experience with SII, I have observed one broad consensus as well as two main lines of contest and confusion. The vast majority of self-classified SII actors agree that SII are *repayable, private investments together with the intention to create "positive social impact" beyond financial returns*. Note that this is not an objective definition of what SII "is" but rather a common denominator of definitions from major SII actors inside and outside the UK and social services. For example, the 2010 JP Morgan study on SII, which received a very large global medial echo as it forecasted a $1 trillion size of the SII market by 2020, defined it as "investments intended to create positive impact beyond financial return" (JP Morgan 2010, p. 5). Likewise, in its report led by British venture capitalist Ronald Cohen, the G-8 understood SII as investments "that intentionally target specific social objectives along with a financial return and measure the achievement of both" (G-8 2014, p. 1).

As these two definitions show, the category SII is contested on a number of dimensions. First, terminology differs and is often used interchangeably. In the UK, the term "social investment" seems to be most widely used, while in the US the term "impact investing" is diffused through organizations such as the Global Impact Investing Network (GIIN), which was founded by the Rockefeller Foundation. I chose the term SII over social investment, in order to avoid confusion with social investment in the sense of Anthony Giddens' (1998) "social investment welfare state" which denotes *public* investment into the productive skills of a national population. I acknowledge that the confusion between both meanings of social investment might have been used strategically by for-profit investors (Kädtler 2011).[3]

Second, the question of profit extraction is a major line of conflict, on both the investor and investee levels, and translates into a number of sub-questions. On the investee level, prominent conflict lines are whether social organizations may or may not legitimately earn income through trading, whether or to what extent this income

[3]This might be particularly true for Michelle Giddens, the CEO of the oldest and largest British SII fund, Bridges Ventures, and daughter of Anthony Giddens.

may be distributed to owners or investors, and to what extent owners may earn a speculative return on sales of social organizations' equity. On the investor level, prominent questions are whether SII should denote only for-profit investments, or also include return-free investments or (some) grants. For example, some charitable foundations offer "venture philanthropy" grants in order to create profitable social start-up firms and these often self-classify as "social investors." By contrast, lending is a form of SII that often runs orthogonal to these questions since it allows redistribution even from non-income-earning charities.

Conflicts regarding SII run through the academic literature as well. Here, we find a chasm between critical sociological research and management scholarship regarding the social consequences of SII. The former has understood those as "harnessing social reproduction for profit" (Dowling and Harvie 2014), while for the latter SII "align[s] with the unique incentives and constraints of social enterprises" that form "sustainable hybrid organizations" around "institutional voids" (Battilana and Lee 2014; Mair and Marti 2009).

I chose to make use of the contestedness of SII as an important part of my empirical material, rather than attempting to give a seemingly objective definition. More precisely, I attempt to map SII from a relational perspective that focuses on the relations of investors to other, positioned actors. As we will see throughout the empirical chapters of this work, a relational view that opens up rigidly or functionally defined actor classes (such as those proposed by Hebb 2013; Nicholls 2010) to empirical analysis is particularly important to explain the emergence of SII. For example, SII actors' key strategic alliance with actors of the voluntary and community sector was strongly supported by the association representing VCS executives, ACEVO, which argued for organizational growth and public service delivery, while other VCS actors were more cautious. This is why my cartography of SII is based on two dimensions: positions and relations. To map the SII terrain, I thus analyzed with which other actors different groups of investors relate, and what these relations are like. From my perspective, these two questions allow for a view of SII that remains sensitive to its political-economic consequences while providing an explanation for its emergence that is grounded in wider social dynamics.

Regarding the first question, impact investors can be broadly distinguished into two groups (see Table 2.1). Both of these groups self-classify as SII and engage in financial intermediation as well as some form of "social impact assessment." These groups, however, differ in their relations to other actors. Empirically, we can clearly distinguish a set of impact investors that addresses firms in existing markets. Here, relations form between investors and actors that are situated in fields that have previously been organized through for-profit organizational templates and competition. Prominent examples here are consumer goods markets, such as fair-trade coffee, food or cosmetics, or agriculture. This type of SII is particularly prominent in the US and represents the main constituents of certification bodies such as B Corporation and its associated Global Impact Investing Rating System (for details, see Barman 2015, 2016). The second type of investors relate primarily to not-for-profit and public organizations. This is the dominant form of SII in the UK, and the type analyzed in this work.

Table 2.1 Ideal-typical, relational distinction between SII sub-types

	SII type 1	SII type 2
Investees	Firms in producing and service markets	Social and public service providers
Investee relations	Similar to "mainstream" investors	Venture-capital-type involvement in management
Main actors	Global investment banks and asset managers	Smaller funds and intermediaries
Main products	Debt, mezzanine capital and equity	Equity and equity-like; social impact bonds
Redistribution	Potentially less pronounced than in "mainstream" financial markets	Novel channels of extraction from not-for-profit and public organizations
Country of origin	United States	United Kingdom

Such a relational view provides an important insight into the political economy of SII. In the first case, it might be the case that SII *reduces* economic inequalities by imposing non-financial success metrics on firms that operate in thoroughly financialized markets. However, in the second case, wholly different political-economic consequences *necessarily* arise: for example, in the case of Social Impact Bonds, financial flows that have formerly been transferred directly from public to not-for-profit organizations are now channeled through financial intermediaries who may earn, from taxpayers' funds, financial returns of around the double of their investment sum.

The question regarding the kind of these relations is necessarily a hermeneutical one. From a perspective of financialization, the most interesting property of these relations is dominance and power differentials. However, to address this question we need to (a) clarify our conception of power, and (b) assess empirically the extent to which such power differentials prevail. In the following chapter, I attempt to provide the former on the basis of strategic action fields theory, while in Chap. 5, when describing the field structure of SII in the UK, I give more detailed empirical insight into the distribution of power between investors and other actors.

Given these empirical complexities, my assessment of SII will be restricted to those investors who relate to not-for-profit and public organizations. I show how SII can best be understood as investors' attempt to gain a central position in the field of social and public service delivery. By doing so, investors alter the rules of economic exchange that dominate the field in their favor and open up social organizations' revenues, private donations, and public funds as profit opportunities. I furthermore show the key role that the practice of social impact assessment plays here. By claiming the "creation of social impact" as *caused by* their financial investments, investors legitimate their entry into the field. At the same time, investors are the actors who define what does and does not count as "social impact"—and as I will show later, they do so strategically in order to gain materially. For example, investors have, in the case of Social Impact Bonds, argued against the introduction of children's school grades as payment-triggering "outcome metrics", while a few years later these very metrics have been advocated for (and later used by) investors as "surrogate outcomes"—thereby significantly reducing investors' risk from the SIB contract.

Thus, it is absolutely crucial to understand "social impact" as a contested set of rules that investors attempt to alter in their favor, and that, depending on the respective actors, may have profoundly different consequences on power relations. I argue later that, in the case of SII in the UK, this is a rather unilateral trajectory that increases the power position of investors, at the expense of government and social organizations. In the case of SII in consumer goods this might, however, be different. There, recent scholarship has shown how the process of impact metric construction has been informed by a variety of stakeholders that include both financial and non-financial actors (Barman 2015).

2.2.2 *Social Impact Investing and Social Policy Dynamics in the UK*

On an empirical level, my main argument is that to understand processes of financialization and their absence, we need to trace the emergence and development of cooperative ties between financial and nonfinancial actors. I argue that it is key to understand actors as both positioned vis-à-vis their proximate environment, as well as embedded in dynamic social situations. To understand how financial actors succeed in forging a cooperative tie thus means to understand the process how such a tie began to make sense for the respective nonfinancial actors. In the case of SII, these nonfinancial actors were a group of social organizations and social policymakers. In order to understand how the dynamic problem situations of these positioned actors affected the emergence of their ties with financial intermediaries, this segment will provide some important context information regarding the link between SII and dynamics in British social policy during the observation period. An overview of the relevant actor groups can be found in Table 2.2.

In the early 1990s, the Labour party was in a deep crisis. Although not overly popular, the Conservative party had won its fourth consecutive general election in April 1992. This crisis allowed the Labour party to challenge longstanding internal principles and eventually led to the rise of "modernizers" such as Tony Blair and Gordon Brown. Their program for government accepted a number of the political-economic and welfare reforms of the Thatcher/Major era and a commitment to macroeconomic growth, but, at least on a discursive level, placed a very strong emphasis on "social inclusion" and welfare reform (Lister 1998). Where the "old" Labour party built on close relationships with unions, and favored redistribution, particularly in the form of pensions, as the prime strategy against poverty, "new" Labour emphasized paid work and low unemployment (Connell 2010, Chaps. 2 and 3). The idea of labor market inclusion was indeed a central one, and marked one of New Labour's overarching social policy goals. To achieve this goal, Labour

Table 2.2 Key actor groups with positioning and organizational templates

Actor group	Positioning and organizational template
Community enterprise	For-profit businesses located in poor neighborhoods or owned by ethnical minorities
Community development financial institutions	Mostly for-profit financial intermediaries investing into community enterprise; mostly lenders, equity investment driven by later SII proponents
Voluntary and community sector	Often called "charities:" not-for-profit organizations engaged in social work and social services; under Labour increasingly contracted for public service delivery
Social enterprise	Challenger group between VCS and community enterprise, emerging out of co-operative movement from 1998; income-earning organizations with limitations on profit distribution
Social ventures	Organizational template developed by SII proponents in 2004; encompassing VCS, community enterprise, social enterprise, and for-profit firms that self-label a "social mission" ("profit-with-purpose" companies)
Social impact investors	For-profit investments into social ventures, often "active" investors affecting investee governance; emphasis on equity products and social impact bonds

attempted to create a "social investment welfare state" (Giddens 1998) that saw high levels of public investment into developing the skillset of the national workforce in order to achieve global competitiveness (Dobrowolsky and Lister 2008). To achieve this form of "social inclusion", the Labour government set up a "Social Exclusion Unit" at the Cabinet Office shortly after winning the 1997 general election. The Social Exclusion Unit comprised 18 "Policy Action Teams" (PATs) that were asked to develop strategies for social inclusion in different policy areas. The third one of these PATs was called "Enterprise and Social Exclusion"—it was located in the Treasury, and its 1999 report was, to my knowledge, the first time that concepts such as social enterprise and a precursor of SII were acknowledged as priorities for central government.

A second pillar of the New Labour program was to significantly increase the effectiveness of public service delivery (Powell 2000, 2008). For our endeavor it is unimportant whether or not Labour succeeded in achieving this goal, nor is it relevant to understand or question the meaning of effectiveness. Rather, the point is that public service reform was both a motivational aspiration as well as a justificatory basis for a host of policy initiatives during the Labour years. What makes the case of the UK somewhat unique is its—in comparison to other polities—rather "simple" (Schmidt 2008) nature. Particularly in England, where (in contrast to the other UK nations) no national parliament exists, the majority party has very far-reaching powers to fundamentally restructure the organization of government and public service. Indeed, political commentators have called this system "elected dictatorship" (Sturm 2009, p. 27) Thus, due to the structure of the Westminster polity, New Labour–as well as the following Coalition and Conservative governments–possessed, and used, the capacity to change public service delivery in very profound ways that not only included a swift change in organizational strategies, but also in terms of ownership and outsourcing.

New Labour's modernization agenda was built on a number of concepts that were used in different fields of public service delivery. The first concept was "government in partnership" and meant that nongovernmental advisors from the private and not-for-profit sectors were invited into the policy design process. Particularly when the affected areas enjoyed a "strong independent power base" (Larsen et al. 2006, p. 629) were external advisors frequently invited in order to ensure their constituents' support. In the case of SII, government in partnership enabled a transmission of ideas in a large number of instances throughout the whole Labour period. The second concept was the integration of voluntary and community sector (VCS) organizations into public service delivery. Already in 1998, the Labour government and key VCS associations signed a "Compact" that (informally) regulated the relations between the VCS and government. Subsequently, the integration of VCS organizations into service delivery became a sought-after means of public service modernization, both by Tony Blair and Gordon Brown (Kelly 2007; Smith 2010).

That being said, public service modernization was also highly contested within the Labour party. From what might in the beginning have appeared as a coherent "Third Way" soon became a contest between Brown's "British Way" and Blair's "Third Way" (Lee 2006). Particularly relevant for our endeavor is the contest between Brown's modernization model of "constrained discretion" and Blair's idea of "earned autonomy." Both of these models built on the idea that central government should prescribe quantitative "outcome metrics" to be achieved by the service delivering organization (Mulderrig 2011). However, where Blair argued that sufficiently performing organizations should be partially relieved of the close monitoring, Brown sought to maintain the control function while permanently granting service providers partial autonomy in selecting the means of delivery (Lee 2008).

These two centers of public service reform have developed gradually since the mid 1990s. In May 1994, Blair and Brown sat down in an Islington restaurant to discuss "Mr Brown's price for stepping aside in favour of Mr Blair in the party's 1994 leadership contest." Although denied by both politicians, the Guardian reported that they had agreed that Brown would be given authority to develop his "fairness agenda" comprising of "social justice, employment opportunities and skills" were Labour to win the 1997 election.[4] The key point is that after the election, Brown was located in HM Treasury, and not in, say, a ministry for social and public services. Such a ministry does not exist in the UK and the respective policy departments are dispersed across other government departments that are formally equal to HM Treasury. Thus, to convince other departments to follow his view on public services, Brown had to make use of those devices that were considered legitimate Treasury tools by policymakers in other departments. The most important

[4]Source: Tom Happold and Kevin Maguire. "Revealed: Brown and Blair's pact." The Guardian, June 6th 2003: https://www.theguardian.com/politics/2003/jun/06/labour.uk, accessed July 16th 2017

of those tools is to safeguard the public budget. During his tenure as Chancellor in 1997–2007, Brown thus not only expanded the Treasury influence over welfare reform and public service delivery, but did so on the legitimatory basis of the key tool he had available: "value for money" (Davies 2008; Deakin and Parry 2000; Larsen et al. 2006; Lee 2006, 2008; and see Chap. 7).

The point is that this has created a specific trajectory of welfare reform that has allowed the arguments of SII proponents gain ground in social policy. More concretely, from the Treasury perspective, public services were evaluated positively, if they achieved predefined outcomes for as little public funds as possible. Thus, if private providers were to "lever in" additional finance, then the "value for money" would be maintained. I show in great detail in Chap. 7 how the further entrenchment of this "Treasury view" into social policy preceded not only the relations between public and SII actors, but to a very large degree also the very ideas of the SII field itself. For example, I show how the idea of "impact measurement" followed the Labour ideas of "outcomes" and the assumed "added value" of the VCS vis-à-vis private providers in service delivery. Moreover, I show how the ruling parties' normative discourse anticipated impact investors' social problem descriptions.

Although the publicly sponsored creation of the SII market gained much more momentum under the two Cameron administrations (2010–2016), the Labour years were, so to say, the path-breaking, formative years of the SII market. It was during that time that key concepts were developed, central alliances forged, and counter-mobilization failed to appear. In addition, the Cameron administration accepted a number of Labour's progressive goals but attempted to present themselves as more capable managers (Beech and Lee 2015). Together with the Conservative focus on fiscal consolidation, this meant that SII proponents' arguments regarding the rapidity with which SII was depicted to "scale up" effective and innovative social services while "levering in" additional finance fell on an even more fertile soil. By contrast, service providers were deeply affected by the spending cuts and rapidly formed opposition to the Cameron government. Thus, only SII proponents were capable of maintaining ties with central government, which paid off in a substantive increase in subsidies for SII actors. Compared to the substantial, qualitative changes in social policy during Labour, the Conservative years brought, with reference to SII, merely quantitative changes. The only qualitative change was a reinterpretation of the meaning of community: under Cameron's Localism agenda, communities were partially institutionalized as owners and providers of public services. In the 2011 Localism Act, they were granted the rights to bid for and take over the delivery of a large set of public services to "community organizations" that could in principle distribute revenues to investors. Subsequently, investors discovered community delivery of public services as a business model and slightly adjusted their problem framing accordingly (see Chap. 6).

In summary, the development of social service delivery policy in England became increasingly oriented towards financial actors. While in the 1990s and early 2000s, the goal was to increase the number of charitable VCS organizations in public service delivery, by 2006, Cabinet Office formulated the growth of social enterprise as a core goal. In the following years, financial intermediaries were supported in order to grow social enterprise. In 2011, the strategy shifted from social enterprise towards SII. In doing so, the category of social organizations addressed by government discourse was expanded from social enterprises (which are limited in their profit distribution) to social ventures (which are not). This was the result of a change of relations between Cabinet Office and external constituents that saw increasingly close relations with SII actors and rapidly decreasing ties with VCS organizations. That said, at that point, the strategy was still mainly legitimated with reference to the growth of social ventures. With the updated strategy in 2016, the legitimatory basis had shifted yet again and depicted SII as a source of national pride, and references to social organizations were made only indirectly.

Although my formal observation period ended with the UK referendum to leave the European Union, the development since then partially supports my argument regarding the importance of meso-level processes in the social policy field for the development of SII. The resignation of David Cameron and George Osborne meant that the British core executive has partially lost the unity between No 10 and HM Treasury, since Theresa May, with her background as Home Secretary, focuses much more on immigration than on prudent economic growth and Treasury-led public service reform. Shortly after she became Prime Minister, the Office for Civil Society (OCS), which had been responsible for SII policy, was moved from Cabinet Office to a peripheral position in the Department for Culture, Media and Sports. In the 2017 general election, the OCS minister lost his parliamentary seat, and subsequently the OCS ministerial post had been disbanded and its functions merged with the minister for sports. Thus, the relation between impact investors and central government weakened with the decreasing Treasury view in social policy. As a consequence, investors received much less subsidies and it remains to be seen whether or not the loss of this significant income source will lead to changes in the size and structure of the SII market.

Together, this shows how the amplitude of SII in the UK makes a highly interesting case for the debate between financialization and institutionalist scholars. The development of SII did follow institutionalized trajectories, but in a different way than traditional institutional theories would predict: the legitimatory constraints placed on HM Treasury meant that the institutionalized structure of the British polity would significantly shape the development of social policy by allowing for the emergence of the Treasury view. That said, this is by no means a story of institutional complementarity or global competitive advantages, but rather of a power struggle between two centers in the British core executive, No 10 and HM Treasury. The fact that HM Treasury won this struggle provided fertile ground for the arguments of investors, but required them to shape their practices and frames in a way acceptable to policymakers. Thus, the state played both a direct and an indirect role in shaping the SII market. The emergence of products such as Social Impact Bonds and the "social investment bank" Big Society Capital did mean an increased authority for financial actors at the expense of the state since they were enabled to partially define what counts as positive outcomes. That being said, the events post 2016 showed that the state nevertheless remains able to withdraw its support for financialization—whether or not this will reduce financial actors authority in the social services field remains to be seen.

This section has shown how the meso-level dynamics at play in the emergence of SII mark an interesting case to discharge the tensions between the financialization and institutionalist literature. Next, I will proceed on a theoretical level, investigating current social theories for their explanatory potential both for the specific case and the financialization/institutionalist debate more generally. I will show how Strategic Action Fields theory (Fligstein and McAdam 2012) fulfills these demands. However, in discussing the theory in more detail, I will show how its current formulation lacks a mechanism to explain the emergence of new cooperative ties between actors located in different fields, which is so central for both the case at hand and the study of financialization more generally. As my empirical investigation will show, this mechanism is strongly related to actors' positionality and the dynamics of the situations they face.

Chapter 3
Financialization, Fields, and Change

The previous chapter has shown that financialization can often be understood as a *transformation of social relations* that engenders *institutional change with redistributive consequences*, building on *repeated government interventions*. However, contrasting the financialization literature with the institutionalist perspective has shown that institutions form important boundary conditions for the success of financial actors to affect such change. At the very least, financial actors need to convince government actors to perform financializing actions—however, their success in doing so will depend upon at least partially independent dynamics within governments. The contextualization of SII in the UK has pointed towards an interplay between government dynamics and financial market emergence. However, the conditions and forms of this interplay, as well as its consequences for financialization processes remain unclear. In this book, I attempt to show that particularly important for financialization are cooperative relations between financial intermediaries and government actors. Through an empirical study of the case of SII, I attempt to show that dynamic problem situations partaking actors find themselves confronted with form a key structural condition for the emergence of these relations.

In the previous chapter, I have pointed to the use of a meso-level perspective for addressing these questions. This is because only a meso-level view remains sensitive to both the creative actions of individual and organizational actors, as well as the structured social terrain in which they act. In this chapter, I aim to put this suspicion on a much more solid theoretical footing. In the first section, I will translate the empirical research on financialization into theoretical vocabulary in order to understand the demands those findings place on explanatory social theory. Then, I will argue that social field theories are exceptionally well equipped to withstand this explanatory stress test. Subsequently, I will compare the explanatory potential of prominent field theories for the empirical debate at hand. Based on this discussion, I will select Fligstein and McAdam's (2012) Strategic Action Field (SAF) theory as the theoretical avenue for this work. In the second section, I will scrutinize SAF theory's explanatory potential for financialization, and the question of the emergence of new ties across dynamic fields in particular. By doing so, I bring to light a conceptional

P. Golka, *Financialization as Welfare*,
https://doi.org/10.1007/978-3-030-06100-5_3

void in the theory: I argue that the theory currently lacks a mechanism to explain the emergence of *cooperative* ties as a result of skilled social action. In the following empirical chapters, I use the case of SII in the UK to develop, through abductive empirical research, a hypothesis for such a mechanism. In the last substantial chapter of this book, I qualify this hypothesis from the perspective of social theory.

3.1 Fields and Financialization

The previous chapter has shown how financialization in markets can often be understood as a social process in which financial actors enter a preexisting social order, such that extant actors begin to take them into account. By doing so, the rules governing social conduct change—often in favor of financial actors who gain profit opportunities. Here, the comparative capitalisms literature has argued for structural boundary conditions to the success of financial actors. The "state-sponsored" literature on financialization has shown that such financialization dynamics are not necessarily limited to markets, but may also occur in organizational realms of the welfare state. In both cases, however, financialization critically builds upon the state, as state actors begin to take financial actors into account in a very specific, repetitive, and often relatively stable manner. However, these literatures also point to the fact that all partaking actors show complex internal dynamics as well as transformations of and in their proximate environments. Moreover, the literatures show that often the emergence and change of interaction patterns is critically related to these dynamics.

This review and synthesis of the financialization literature will serve as a contrast to discuss the explanatory potential of different social theories in this section. As a first step, I argue that a theory for our case must be located on the mesolevel and capable of observing and explaining how actors interact. I argue that this is true for social field theories (Bourdieu 1998; Bourdieu and Wacquant 1992; DiMaggio and Powell 1983; Fligstein and McAdam 2012; Martin 2003). Then, I critically review the explanatory potential of one particularly prominent representative, new institutional field theory, before establishing SAF theory as a more viable alternative for the study of financialization.

3.1.1 The Use of Fields for the Study of Financialization

The problematization of the extant financialization literature has shown that processes of financialization commonly involve three empirical observations. First, a group of new—financial[1]—actors enters previously organized social space. In the

[1] I understand financial actors as those engaged in investment and speculation, in the sense of Knorr-Cetina (2009). Empirically, these are most frequently financial intermediaries.

"classic" case, these new actors are institutional investors—a group of actors not necessarily fully novel in this space, but having undergone such profound organizational change (including sheer size) from the 1960s to the 1980s that the actors as well as the relations to their environment can reasonably be considered qualitatively different to their precursors. Second, in parallel to the introduction of those new actors, extant actors in the target space begin to orient their actions towards these new actors. As a result, a new conduct emerges in the social space, which, in comparison to its old state, favors financial actors, usually at the expense of incumbent actors. Importantly, this does not mean that nonfinancial actors voluntarily change their way to act in this way as resource dependence relations may prevail. Third, this transformation builds on a continuous and far-reaching involvement of government and state actors. Usually, this involvement goes beyond mere regulative changes but furthermore involves some state organizations as economic actors. Together, this means that financialization often is a transformation of social relations that engenders institutional change with redistributive consequences, building on repeated government interventions.

Corresponding to these three dimensions of financialization, an explanatory theory requires three basic properties. Fundamentally, such a theory requires a conception of those "battlefields," or social arenas, that are populated by actors who take each other into account when developing their strategies. Positions in these arenas must be open for change: this means that there not only needs to be dynamic horizontal and vertical stratification, but more importantly, entrance to and exit from the arena must remain open at all times. Second, in these social spaces, actors are not only engaged in maintaining and challenging positions—critically, the rules themselves are open to change. One possibility thus is that both rules and positions form part of a competitive "game." Third, such a theory needs to account for the emergence and stabilization of coordination between state and finance actors: Governments somehow need to be understood as actors that are located within the arena. Beyond acting as a non-participating referee, in our case, government actors need to be conceptualized as competing participants as well. As the "state-sponsored" view on financialization has shown, this may include a competition between different state organizations, as well.

Social field theories accommodate these three demands and are therefore well placed to analyze and explain dynamics of financialization. Social field theories are not a uniform strand of social theorizing, but are rather an "umbrella term" for a number of social theories that use varying definitions of "fields" as their main unit of analysis (Kluttz and Fligstein 2016; Martin 2003). Most generally, fields are "mesolevel social orders" (Fligstein and McAdam 2012, p. 3) in which "a set of actors orient[s] their actions to one another" (Kluttz and Fligstein 2016, p. 185). Thus, "[f]ield theory implies that there is something at stake in such an order, that there are rules governing the order, that actors have positions and resources, and that actors have an understanding of the order that allows them to interpret the actions of others and frame a response" (Kluttz and Fligstein 2016, p. 185). The field metaphor, as it has been imported from physics, implies that actors differ in their positions, and that this positional difference has important implications for their actions: each position carries a distinct "vector of positional force" (Martin 2003, p. 5). Yet, field theories differ in what they assume this "force" is. For example, in Bourdieu's theory it is the concept of habitus, Beckert (2010) assumes networks, institutions, and cognitive frames as an "invisible set of forces" (Fourcade 2007, p. 1022, cit. by Beckert 2010) organizing action in fields, while Fligstein (2001a, p. 68) understands this force in terms of Podolny's (1993) status hierarchies. But despite these differences, field theories converge in emphasizing that dynamics in the proximate environment shape actions of individual (Bourdieu and Wacquant 1992) and organizational actors (DiMaggio and Powell 1983).

Thus, all field theories assume that actors create strategies, develop expectations, and interpret other actions in light of their position in a mesolevel social order. Field theories assume interests to be constituted through the rules of and positions in fields—rather than assuming "pre-social" interests such as in Marxism, or autonomous social systems. This does not, however, mean that field theories are agnostic to macro-level factors as actors need to confront institutional structures and may draw on normative standards as resources (Beckert 2011, p. 261). Field theories "propose only local action" but "insist that any case must be understood in terms of the global pattern" (Martin 2003, p. 15). By paying close attention to dynamic action patterns, particularly of and within the state, field theories may therefore provide a more nuanced understanding of financialization than macro theories.

In summary, field theories are well equipped to offer compelling insights to the study of financialization. They fundamentally converge in their emphasis on mesolevel dynamics. However, significant variance exists in regard to the second and third points outlined above. In the following segments, I therefore critically review the extent to which field theories incorporate the demands that emerged from a juxtaposition of different strands of financialization research. Due to limitations of space, I will only consider neo-institutional field theories and strategic action fields theory. Although Martin's (2003, 2011, Chap. 8) approach provides highly stimulating insights into the "structure" of field theory, it is not sufficiently elaborated to guide empirical research. By contrast, Bourdieu's field theory is extremely well elaborated and allows for a highly nuanced understanding of field dynamics. For example, in "The State Nobility," Bourdieu (1998) studies how corporations, government agencies, and elite universities together constitute a field—thus allowing for insights into dynamics of inter-organizational co-ordination. However, as his analytic perspective most frequently links individuals, (different forms of) capital, and the field, the organizational level is somewhat undertheorized. For example, Swartz (1997, pp. 211–217) points out how Bourdieu's analysis—in contrast to often-held criticism (e.g. by Kluttz and Fligstein (2016, p. 196))—is not overly statist, but does fail to understand conditions that shape field dynamics in response to a crisis. To account for field dynamics, Bourdieu investigates the links between habitus and field, but does neither acknowledge organizational influences in their own right, nor acknowledge how crises are always a question of interpretation (Blyth 2010, p. 180) and thus shaped by movement-like mobilization. As a result, Bourdieu's field theory is not equipped to answer the question how new organizational actors enter existing fields and thereby alter economic relations. It would be difficult to understand how impact investors entered the field of British social policy and appropriated public subsidies, organizational revenues and private donations without emphasizing movement-like dynamics and organizational relations. As I describe below, neo-institutional field theories incorporate either of these concerns, but only Fligstein and McAdam's perspective incorporates both.

3.1.2 Neo-Institutional Field Theories and Their Limitations

The literature that has become known as the "new sociological institutionalism" (NSI) assumes action to be based on legitimacy (besides material considerations such as efficiency (J. W. Meyer and Rowan 1977, p. 353)). It centrally built on Berger and Luckmann's (1966) perspective of social constructivism by acknowledging that social actions and objects such as interpretations, definitions or imperatives can over time acquire the status of social facts that become taken-for-granted and thereby profoundly shape action possibilities available to actors (Zucker 1977). To gain legitimacy, actors build upon these "institutionalized" elements (e.g. practices) of their environment (J. W. Meyer and Rowan 1977). Thus, neo-institutional theorists understand actors' (socially) proximate environment as a source for their restricted set of possible actions (DiMaggio and Powell 1983; Scott 1991). This environment is often understood as the "organizational field" (Scott 1995), showing how neo-institutional theories place utmost importance on the field level for their analysis of institutional dynamics. However, large disagreement exists regarding multiple key concepts of new institutionalism and fields in particular (Wooten and Hoffman 2017). I will focus my discussion on the "classic" NSI view of fields and describe how its perceived weaknesses have been addressed by some subsequent developments. Thereafter, I argue that most of these problems arise from the model of action assumed in the NSI.[2]

Building on the interorganizational field conception of Warren (1967) and Turk (1977), the earliest versions of NSI field theory understood fields as the organized social spaces that create legitimate ways to act for organizational actors, comprised of organizations in horizontal and vertical, as well as proximate and distant relations

[2]There are two important strands in the literature that I will ignore. First, issue fields (Hoffman 1999) which provide a more discursive and thus less functionalist definition of fields in comparison to DiMaggio and Powell (1983) and Scott (1987). This way, field dynamics can be understood as closely linked to membership dynamics. Nevertheless, issue field theory relies on a similarly problematic conception of agency as much of neo-institutional theory (see below). These problems are equally prominent in institutional logics theory (Reay and Hinings 2005; Thornton et al. 2012) albeit in a slightly different coloring. Assuming relatively homogenous field-level logics that are in coherence with the rationality criteria posed by the "society as an inter-institutional system" perspective and stabilized through individual-level cognitive scripts and schemas, the theory under-estimates the continuous creative capacities of human agency (Joas 1996) and resulting conflict in favor of a rather consensualist (albeit dynamic) view of institutions and fields (Fligstein and McAdam 2012, pp. 10–12).

(Scott 1991). For example, DiMaggio and Powell (1983) understood the organizational field as "those organizations that, in aggregate, constitute a recognized area of institutional life: key suppliers, resource and product consumers, regulatory agencies, and other organizations that produce similar services or products" (p. 148). Once a field is established, "powerful forces emerge" that lead organizations to become more similar to one another (p. 148). For example, these "isomorphic" pressures forged homogeneity of US art museums as a result of demands from field constituents such as the Carnegie foundation (DiMaggio 1991). In contrast to the often-held criticism that this literature focuses predominantly on organizational similarities (Greenwood and Hinings 1996), Scott (1991, p. 171) noted that organizational plurality may also be a result of field-level dynamics (J. W. Meyer and Scott 1991). Although most empirical studies have investigated dynamics of market fields, some studies have also applied the field methodology to investigate state dynamics. For example, Tolbert and Zucker (1983) have studied how municipal civil service reforms in the US increasingly became institutionalized as a goal in their own right. Although here, the state has been acknowledged as a field (or a set of fields), in the majority of empirical cases has the state only been studied as a referee that—without much further explanation—alters rules and thus forges organizational responses. Likewise, very often all kinds of public organizations have been lumped together as "the state" without acknowledging their complex dynamics (for exceptions, see Dobbin 2009; Edelman 1992).

Indeed, such an understanding of the state chimes well with the more general perspective that sees field dynamics as caused by exogenous shocks or "jolts" (A. D. Meyer 1982). Although such a conception of change makes sense given the NSI's classic model of institutions that provide actors with normative, coercive and cognitive imperatives, there are two problems with such an approach: first, it risks that empirical researchers post-hoc qualify all those external ruptures as "jolts" that have later been found to have caused institutional dynamics. Here, crises are seen as inherently a-social phenomena that they simply are not: Crises need to be interpreted as a "crisis of what" (Blyth 2010) and subsequently require significant organizational effort to construct and enact alternative rules and ways to act. As critical political economy scholars have repeatedly pointed out: despite severe crises, we may find a "strange non-death" of existing institutional configurations (Crouch 2011; Streeck 2013). Second, the emergence of "jolts" is difficult to reconcile with the theory's own perspective on agency. If action is constrained by rules that emerge from the field, then it cannot be social action that constructs a situation in which these rules are no longer binding (this has become known as the "paradox of embedded agency").

Concerns such as these have led to criticism that neo-institutional theory's "model of action decenters the role of actors in producing fields and creating the conditions of change" (Fligstein 2013, p. 48). Two main theoretical developments have emerged from this agency-related criticism: institutional entrepreneurship (Battilana et al. 2009; Maguire et al. 2004) and institutional work (Lawrence et al. 2011, 2009). I argue that both approaches fail to take the relational dimensions of fields seriously and are thus severely limited in their explanatory potential.[3] Scholars of institutional work are explicit about this, emphasizing that "[r]esearchers are encouraged to shift their gaze away from the 'organizational field' and large-scale social transformations, and attend more closely to the relationship between institutions and the actors who populate them" (Lawrence et al. 2011, p. 57). Scholarship on institutional entrepreneurship, by contrast, centrally builds on "field characteristics" (Battilana et al. 2009, p. 67) to explain the emergence of change-shaping institutional entrepreneurs.

The idea of "institutional entrepreneurship" was introduced by DiMaggio (1988), who built on an earlier formulation by Eisenstadt (1980). At its core, this notion assumes institutional entrepreneurs to cause institutional change. Its main empirical investigations have therefore sought to study the conditions for institutional entrepreneurs to emerge, as well as providing highly nuanced accounts of their actions, and attempts to link those actions to changes that "diverge from the dominant institutional template" (Battilana et al. 2009, p. 69). In short, it is assumed that field-level influences as well as actors' social positions are conditions for the emergence of institutional entrepreneurship, while the actions of institutional entrepreneurs are akin to social movement-like framing and mobilization (Battilana et al. 2009, pp. 73–87). As I argue below, I strongly agree that these factors are crucially important in field dynamics such as financialization. However, by studying how "levels of fragmentation and institutionalization" of the institutional entrepreneurs' proximate field environment affect what these *entrepreneurs* do (Battilana et al. 2009, p. 85), the theory not only misses the relational properties that are the very motivation for a field perspective. Even worse, by doing so, scholarship on institutional entrepreneurship theorizes institutional change as directly caused by the actions of institutional entrepreneurs—and hardly anything else. This concern has been raised by institutional work scholars, as well as political scientists such as Seabrooke (2010, pp. 85–86) who criticized the "legitimacy by proclamation" view prevalent in scholarship on institutional entrepreneurship that tends to ignore the myriad of actions required by large numbers of other actors in order to enact the dynamics institutional entrepreneurs strive for. Moreover, it seems very unlikely that all attempts at institutional entrepreneurship which follow the detailed recipes for such entrepreneurial action will result in successful institutional transformation. If we assume that actors are embedded in fields, then this will also be the case for those actors that institutional entrepreneurs seek to mobilize—and this is why there are *field-level conditions for the success of mobilization*. Ignoring these conditions means conflating the correlation between institutional change and a set of entrepreneurial practices with their causal relationship. This is even more the case as alternative visions are hardly ever crafted and transposed linearly but in highly

[3]There are more reasons why these theories are not suitable for our endeavor. One is that, being located in organizational theory, most scholarship uses these theories to explain organizational outcomes, e.g. as changes in "templates" (Battilana et al. 2009). However, my interest is more broadly located on the field level and includes positions, relations, and resources in addition to forms of organizing.

interactive and recursive processes (Fligstein and McAdam 2012; Knoll 2012). Together, neither theories of institutional entrepreneurship, nor of institutional work are capable of providing a theoretical avenue to understand processes of financialization in fields. As I will argue below, one possible solution is a pragmatist view on social action together with a more relational conception of fields.

As I have argued above, to understand field-level processes of financialization, we must understand how government actors—who themselves form and are embedded in fields with respective dynamics—repeatedly choose financializing actions. Otherwise we are left with a conception of the state as referee, subject to the game played by non-state institutional entrepreneurs. But assuming that the most powerful actor in virtually any field does not possess its own organizational goals, dynamics, and entrepreneurs would undermine the very foundation upon which much of neo-institutional theory is built. Any theory of field-level dynamics is therefore necessarily incomplete if it does not place utmost importance on how dynamics interact across fields.

3.1.3 Fligstein and McAdam's Alternative

Neil Fligstein's and Doug McAdam's (2011, 2012) theory of strategic action fields (SAFs) builds on many insights that have fueled the development of new institutional theorizing. Indeed, they point out how in "the early 1990s, rational choice institutionalists, sociological institutionalists, and historical institutionalists began to recognize that we were all engaged in a similar theoretical project" (2012, p. xii, see also Fligstein (2008)). Yet while the theory shares NSI's core insight on the causal role of mesolevel field dynamics for social action and the emphasis on social movement studies from institutional entrepreneurship, SAF theory differs from current forms of NSI in decisive ways. Two of those are critically important for our endeavor: an understanding of society as a web of *fields*, and an understanding of *situated* rather than institutionally embedded agency. Before explaining these, I will briefly summarize SAF theory as presented in the 2012 book (for a critique, see Sparsam (2014)).

The theory understands SAFs as "the fundamental units of collective action in society" since it holds that "[a]ll collective actors (e.g., organizations, clans, supply chains, social movements, and governmental systems) are themselves made up of strategic action fields" (Fligstein and McAdam 2012, p. 9). A SAF is defined as

> a constructed mesolevel social order in which actors (who can be individual or collective) are attuned to and interact with one another on the basis of shared (which is not to say consensual) understandings about the purposes of the field, relationships to others in the field (including who has power and why), and the rules governing legitimate action in the field (p. 9).

Fligstein and McAdam attempt to integrate the "unifying force of shared understandings" among actors in a "'taken-for-granted' everyday reality" that they attribute to new institutional theory, with a Bourdieusian perspective of "social power" as underlying the "structure and logic" of fields. As a result, they conceive of SAFs as "as socially constructed arenas within which actors with varying resource endowments vie for advantage" (p. 10). Thus, they share with recent NSI developments such as issue fields (Hoffman 1999) or field-configuring events (Hardy and Maguire 2010) the perspective that field membership is dynamic and the result of actors' constructivist processes, rather than due to functional criteria defined by the researcher: "The boundaries of strategic action fields are not fixed but shift depending on the definition of the situation and the issues at stake" (Fligstein and McAdam 2012, p. 10).

SAF theory, however, significantly differs from new institutional theory in its conception of institutions and institutional "logics" (Friedland and Alford 1991; Scott 2001; Thornton et al. 2012). This has two sides to it: a different conception of agency about which I will say more below, as well as a more relational understanding of institutions. Fligstein and McAdam (2012, p. 11) argue that "the use of the term 'institutional logic' tends to imply way too much consensus in the field about what is going on and why and way too little concern over actors' positions, the creation of rules in the field that favor the more powerful over the less powerful, and the general use of power in strategic action fields." This is why they propose an understanding of "institutional logics" based on four core properties (pp. 10–11). First, they import from Bourdieusian field theory the idea that actors generally understand what is at stake in the field—although they might disagree about what is legitimate. Second, they assume that actors in the field are aware of their own and other field members' positions that may for example be "friends" or "enemies", but furthermore imply an often inequal distribution of power. Third, in the field there is a shared understanding of its "rules." This "cultural understanding of what forms of action and organization are viewed as legitimate and meaningful" is different from the general idea of what the field is about. These three points are integrated by noting that—depending on their field *position*—actors possess an "interpretative frame" through which they make sense of what others do. Thus, powerful and powerless actors in the field may have an entirely different understanding of what is going on in the field. Here, Fligstein and McAdam (2012) accept Jens Beckert's (2010, 2011) criticism of new institutional theory. He argued that fields are organized around three interdependent but distinct "social forces"—cognitive frames, network structures, and institutional rules. Thus, rather than attempting to "endogenize" either cognitive frames or network structures into the definition of institutions (Beckert 2010, pp. 606–609), Fligstein and McAdam (2012) treat network positions, interpretative frames and institutional rules as distinct causal factors that *jointly* structure action in fields. As a result, they "see fields as only rarely organized around a truly consensual 'taken for granted' reality" (p. 11) and stress the "constant jockeying going on in fields as a result of their contentious nature" (p. 12).

The divergence of interpretative frames based on position can be seen clearly in impact investing: proponents describe their investments as a means to foster innovations and "scale social impact." Social service providers, by contrast, see a diverse set of funding based largely on non-repayable grants as such a means. Likewise, scholars in business school positions tend to see impact investing as a means to create “sustainable hybrid organizations” that might respond to “institutional voids” (Battilana and Dorado 2010; Battilana and Lee 2014; Mair and Marti 2009), while sociologists tend to perceive it as “harnessing social reproduction for profit” (Dowling and Harvie 2014).

Fligstein and McAdam analyze field members not in their functional roles as in early new institutionalism, but focus on their field position with regards to power: as challengers and incumbents. They stress that fields are a struggle not only over who wins (“who gets what” (Fligstein and McAdam 2011, p. 3)) but also over who writes the rules (Martin 2003). Thus, incumbents’ “interests and views tend to be heavily reflected” in the SAF rules, while field members’ “shared meanings tend to legitimate and support their privileged position.” Challengers, by contrast, “wield little influence over its operation” but usually “conform to the prevailing order, although they often do so grudgingly.” Nevertheless, they routinely “articulate an alternative vision of the field and their position in it” (Fligstein and McAdam 2012, p. 13). Often, “internal governance units” (IGUs) such as trade associations are part of the field, too. These facilitate the field’s “overall smooth functioning and reproduction”, but “are generally there *not* to serve as neutral arbiters of conflicts between incumbents and challengers but to reinforce the dominant perspective and guard the interests of the incumbents” (p. 14, emphasis in original).[4]

Critically, both challengers and incumbents constantly engage in strategic action. In contrast to definitions by Weber (1921/2002) or Habermas (1981), who conceive of strategic action as strictly goal-oriented action that includes the contingency of the social world in the development of action plans, SAF theory follows the conception of strategic action developed by Fligstein (2001a). There, Fligstein argues that the fundamental uncertainty of future prices leads economic actors to seek the production of stable social relations, instead of engaging in pointless attempts to maximize uncertain future profits (p. 71). Thus, Fligstein and McAdam define strategic action as “the attempt by social actors to create and sustain social worlds by securing the cooperation of others,” noting that this is “about control *in a given context*” (2012, p. 17, emphasis added). Since strategic action therefore arises in dynamic social

[4]I consider the conception of IGUs as one of the weaker parts of SAF theory, both theoretically and empirically. Theoretically, this somewhat functionalist construction partially contradicts the strict emphasis on social construction that prevails in the theory. If stable periods are achieved through mobilization and frame resonance, while at the same time all actors possess social skill, why would we then expect a norm-following organization such as IGUs constitutive of fields? Empirically, it has, for example in the case of intra-organizational equal opportunities officers, been shown how IGUs that were initially created by incumbent actors to maintain their rules in the face of growing criticism may develop an organizational interest in their own right that eventually alters the rules of the field contrary to incumbents’ interest (Dobbin 2009). Ultimately, upholding such a theoretically defined conception of IGUs would thus require us to ex ante define those as low skilled, interest-less, non-strategic actors, contradicting the theory’s assumption on the existential role of the social. For these reasons, as well as the fact that in the case of SII, trade associations can rather be considered as the very competing actors, I will disregard such a conception of IGUs for the remainder of this book.

situations where actors' understanding of the very situation differs in relation to their position, strategic action fundamentally becomes a problem of "getting outside of their own heads" and "tak[ing] the role of the other, and work[ing] to fashion shared worlds and identities" (p. 17). Fligstein and McAdam assume this type of strategic action to always prevail in fields as part of their anthropological reasoning on the *existential* function of the social, i.e. an existential *need* of humans to engage in meaning-projects that stabilize social worlds (pp. 34–45).

Since actors, independent of their field position, follow the need to act strategically—but because of their positions hold different views of legitimate rules—there is continuous contention in SAFs, even though both rather stable and tumultuous periods exist. Whether or not a field undergoes a period of tumultuous contention critically depends on internal and external factors. Externally, ruptures in exogenous but related fields can serve as a trigger for mobilization—especially if these are *internally* collectively attributed as threats or opportunities. In line with Blyth's (2010) insight that crises need to be collectively defined as a "crisis of what," Fligstein and McAdam hold that the process of contention is akin to social movement processes (pp. 19–23). Here, actors engage in the development and dissemination of interpretative frames that define the problem, propose a solution and introduce new collective ways to act. Due to the power differentials in fields, this change movement is only rarely successful as often the "material, cultural, political [advantages] enjoyed by incumbents may be enough to overcome crisis and restore order" (p. 22). In some cases, however, it might be the case that a novel "institutional settlement regarding field rules and cultural norms" emerges—often with support from state and other governance actors—that leads to a new period of relative stability in a field (p. 22).

As I noted above, there are two distinctive features of SAF theory that are particularly important for our endeavor. These are the conception of society as a web of fields, as well as a situated understanding of agency based on social skill. There are two implications of the society-as-fields assumption of particular importance for our case. First, in contrast to much of new institutional field theory, SAF theory understands the *interrelation of fields* as an important causal factor in the dynamics of virtually every field. Second, the state, too, is seen as subject to the same general field properties as are non-state fields—although here, a number of special points apply.

Fligstein and McAdam argue that since new institutional theory does not embed fields "in broader field environments", it has "no deeper structural accounts" for entrepreneurial action, yielding "a thinly veiled 'great man' theory of agency" (p. 28). To understand field dynamics, we need to understand how each field is "inextricably linked to events elsewhere in the dense latticework or system of interdependent fields that comprise modern society" (p. 58). This is because these relations, together with internal dynamics, "shape the developmental history" of any field (p. 59). Fields may be linked vertically ("dependent") or horizontally ("interdependent"), or are independent. These links are "shaped by a number of factors: resource dependence, mutual beneficial interactions, sharing of power, information flows, and legitimacy" (p. 59). Even in vertical links, e.g. the whole firm to one of its divisions, relations and authority will be contested. Citing Leifer's (1995) example of how the New York Yankees dominated the overall rules of the US baseball league, they note that actual dependence relations can exist either way, as well as being cooperative, in formally vertically related fields (p. 60). Likewise, horizontal links between fields may or may not invoke an inequal distribution of power, as much as cooperation or competition. Citing the example of Bourdieu's (1998) *State Nobility*, they argue that "to maintain their legitimacy, both the state and large corporations rely on the grandes écoles to certify the best students in the country. This produces a symbiotic and cooperative relationship between fields organized by large, incumbent organizations" (p. 61). Thus, SAFs may be linked directly or indirectly through an intermediary field with which both fields are tied. Field links may also differ in their number of ties, but for their stability/instability, dependence relations need to be taken into account as well (p. 62).

In SAF theory, the state, too, is conceived of as a web of fields, rather than as a monolithic entity (p. 69/70). State fields differ from non-state SAFs as state actors "have advanced the claim that they alone can define, or at least ratify, the rules for public strategic interaction in a given geographic territory and that these rules can be enforced by the use of physical violence" (p. 67). As the state claims rather than builds upon sovereignty, its "ability to exercise that authority is always open to contestation," making the state dependent upon support from "incumbents that control certain key non-state fields." This dynamic has consequences to the internal workings of the state, where it "will typically have some strategic action fields in formation, others that are stable, and still others that are in crisis" (p. 67). Hence, "within the state, there is constant conflict over which bureaucracy controls which set of issues" (p. 72).

Following from these two points, the authors suggest that it is "almost impossible to talk about action in a strategic action field without reference to its relationship to one or, indeed often, multiple state fields" (p. 71). This is because only state-led attempts to organize non-state fields create "the kind of predictability and security that allows non-state actors to create new fields" and thus creates reason for "investments in formal organization" (p. 71, see also Beckert (1996, 2003)). Indeed, these points are so central to their theory that they diagnose a "decided lack of a attention to how the opportunities and constraints that shape the prospects for strategic action within fields depend critically on the complex latticework of relations" between SAFs (p. 7). As state fields are dependent upon support from other fields, too, external crises may alter their shape. For example, if "enough challengers present demands to stop supporting incumbents so brazenly, they begin to challenge the legitimacy of state authority, resulting in a crisis of legitimacy for particular state strategic action fields" (p. 76). Hence, not only internal field dynamics are subject to strategic social action, but also the relations between all kinds of fields. This is why also "the *links* between all of those fields [...] need to be managed by actors with social skill" (p. 80, emphasis in original).

Social Skill is SAF theory's conception of (situated) agency. It was originally formulated by Fligstein (2001b) in order to find a "genuinely sociological" view of agency to supplement the NSI perspective on fields. In their 2012 book, Fligstein and

McAdam attempt to ground the idea of social skill on their concept of the "existential function of the social" that they define as the "meaningful worlds we fashion in concert with others that insulate us from the threat" of existential fears that arose with Homo Sapients social abilities (p. 42). As the question for anthropological justification exceeds the scope of this work, I will ignore the "existential function of the social"[5] and instead focus on the relation between social skill and field dynamics.

The authors define social skill as "the ability to induce cooperation by appealing to and helping to create shared meanings and collective identities." Building on Goffman (1959, 1973) and Mead (1934) they hold that this requires skilled actors to "empathetically relate to the *situations* of other people" and "provide those people with *reasons* to cooperate" (p. 46; emphasis added; see also Fligstein (2001b, p. 112)). Due to skilled actors' need to empathize with others, *framing* (Benford and Snow 2000; Goffman 1973; Snow and Benford 1988) is critically important: based on their perceptions of others, skilled actors "provide an interpretation of a given situation" and "frame courses of action that appeal to existing interests and identities." As a result, these "appeals elicit cooperation from members of their group and produce generally negative accounts of the identity of those with whom the group is competing" (Fligstein and McAdam 2012, p. 46). The authors assume the need for cooperation as so ubiquitous that social skill not only is "deployed routinely" but also "with a mix of motives" that may be more or less instrumental, thus making instrumental and altruistic action a "false distinction" (p. 47): "Skilled social actors produce meaning for others, because by doing so, they produce meaning for themselves" (p. 48).

As the social world is populated with situated actors in fields, socially skilled actors necessarily need to be somewhat flexible and account for social dynamics in their attempts to forge cooperation. Thus, "if one path is closed off, [skilled actors] will explore others" (p. 48). Here, skilled strategic actors differ decisively from utility-maximizing rational actors with fixed ends as they "keep their goals somewhat open-ended and are prepared to take what the system will give" (p. 48). This "pragmatic, open-ended approach to strategic action" (p. 51) does, however, not imply that they are altogether agnostic towards interests—rather, skilled strategic actors "focus on evolving collective ends" (p. 48).

Social skill is a "property of individuals" that virtually anybody possesses at least to some extent as the reproduction of fields builds on actors "skilled performances"

[5]I have two concerns with their perspective. First, assuming that we "seek out instrumental gain, social status, and power [...] because we want to prove to ourselves and others that we are worthy as people" (p. 46) fails to acknowledge that the construction of worth is socially contingent (Boltanski and Thévenot 2006; Stark 2011) and thus can hardly be assumed as a motivational force. As Beckert (2003) and Joas (1996) have shown, and as the authors themselves frequently point out, ends are constructed in social processes. It thus seems incorrect and contradictory to assume the cause of these different actions in their common motivational dimension. Second, noting that "by 'winning,' we confirm to ourselves and others that life is not meaningless" (p. 46) incorrectly assumes a motivational basis for winning. As my previous work has shown, faced with a situation where winning coincides with losing money, the "value of winning" is highly dependent upon an individual's hormonal testosterone levels (Van Den Bos et al. 2013).

(c.f. Giddens (1984); Fligstein 2001b, p. 106). However, "the *use of* social skill is heavily constrained by the individual's position within the field in question" (Fligstein and McAdam 2012, p. 48, emphasis added). Here, the authors synthesize the relational perspective described above with their concept of empathy: "successful deployment of social skill will depend on the actor recognizing her or his social position, being able to take the perspective of other actors (both those with whom they are trying to cooperate and those with whom they are competing), and finding a set of actions that 'make sense' given their position" (p. 48). Thus, affecting social change through skilled action depends on actors "structural position and opportunities" (p. 49).

Actors need to frame narratives that will mobilize others (p. 51). They will deploy various techniques such as bricolage, agenda setting, or brokerage (pp. 51–53, see also Fligstein 2001b) that have been extensively studied in literatures ranging from social movement research and institutional entrepreneurship, to pragmatist scholarship and network theory (Battilana et al. 2009; Kingdon 1995; Stark 2011; Vedres and Stark 2010). For example, agenda setting is related to skillful change in fields because "if a skilled actor can get others to accept what the terms of discussion are, much of the battle has been won" as by then "identity and interests of actors are framed" (Fligstein and McAdam, p. 51). However, all of this ought to happen on the go as fields and thus identities and interests are dynamic and therefore framing requires "to link broader frames to groups' existing conceptions of interest" (p. 51). But as identities and interests will even in a coalition never be fully homogeneous, skilled actors are furthermore required to shape a group identity that may accommodate "and help reorder" these differences, for example through a "resonant collective identity" (Ansell 2001).

The idea of social skill differs from institutional entrepreneurship in multiple decisive ways. First, it acknowledges that all social actors are skilled (as stressed by scholarship on institutional work) and thus routinely think beyond the shared meanings provided by institutions. Indeed, from a SAF perspective, the very meaning of an institution depends on an actor's position. Second, it emphasizes that institutional entrepreneurship depends on an actor's relation to others, making it a role sometimes available in the field (p. 17). Third, it holds that "all of the social skill in the world may fail to produce order where no one has enough claim on resources and there is no possibility to build common frames" (Fligstein 2001b, pp. 115–116).

Social skill and society-as-fields are crucial building blocks to understand processes of financialization. As shown above, financialization often builds on two ingredients: financial actors as new field members that shape nonfinancial actors' strategies towards them, and sustained interference from state actors that exceeds one-time deregulation and is upheld despite significant dynamics inside (and outside) the state. Thus, financialization requires at least to some extent the creation of cooperation between financial and nonfinancial actors: we therefore need to conceive of financial actors as socially skilled. However, as scholarship on capitalist variety has shown, financial actors have not been uniformly successful forging cooperation. Since it appears unreasonable to assume financial actors in the US to simply possess more skill than state and corporate actors, but not so in other countries, we need to clarify the role of field structures for the success, failure and shape of skilled actors' collaborative projects.

3.2 Strategic Action Fields and Financialization

The previous section has shown how our understanding of financialization processes benefits from the use of a field perspective. I have argued for two main advantages of SAF theory over NSI, which are, together, of crucial importance to explain financialization processes. SAF theory shifts our attention to the process through which skilled financial actors are able to alter action patterns of state and non-state actors that are themselves situated in dynamic fields.[6] Yet despite these indispensable advantages of SAF theory, I argue that to explain the full spectrum of financialization processes (which includes their absence), we need to sharpen the theory's explanatory tools and refocus its analytic lenses. To do so, I will revisit the financialization literature to carve out problems that are difficult to reconcile with the current state of SAF theory. I will demonstrate how the differential nature and impact of financialization in Western capitalisms as well as the fact that sometimes these dynamics lead to a reduction of state authority point to the same question: in which situations are skilled financial actors able to alter action patterns of state actors? In the second and third steps, I will show how this question translates into two problems for SAF theory: How is cooperation forged among equally skilled actors? And how are ties between fields shaped and maintained when those fields are highly dynamic?

3.2.1 Financialization Revisited

Above I have shown how financialization can be understood as a transformation in social relations that engenders redistributive institutional change, building on repeated government intervention. This can be seen in the US case, where an altered set-up of the mortgage finance field coincided with manifold and far-reaching state interventions, and where a transformation of state pensions has propelled further deregulation of the financial sector (Fligstein and McAdam 2012; Quinn 2010). Likewise, state actors have repeatedly turned to financial tools where their abilities have been constrained due to the institutionalized separation of power (Pacewicz

[6]Note that this does not imply that financializing state actions are *always* the result of financial actors' strategic efforts vis-à-vis the state. Sometimes these actions are intended to achieve different goals but have led to increased financialization in markets (e.g. Krippner 2011, or Fligstein 1990, Chap. 5). That said, it seems to be the case that in the past decades, in many cases, state actions appear to be directed towards and lobbied for by financial actors (e.g. Langenohl and Wetzel 2011). As I will show in the longitudinal chapter, the growth of impact investing in the UK serves as a case in point here.

2012; Quinn 2010). That said, scholarship has also shown less uniform progressions of financialization. In Germany, corporate managers did not fully embrace financial management techniques such as shareholder-value orientation (Lazonick and O'Sullivan 2000) or the "finance conception of control" (Fligstein 1990) even though elements of financialization discourse had been introduced to firms' communication (Fiss and Zajac 2004; Vitols 2002). Thus, if financialization is indeed the result of financial actors' social skill to alter action patterns of states and firms in their favor, then there must be boundary conditions for their success.

Do those findings mean that we need to refocus our analyses to a national level and investigate institutional complementarities (Aoki 2001) or path-dependence (Hall and Soskice 2001)? Hardly so: even proponents of institutionalist perspectives on capitalist diversity note that scholarship increasingly turns to "see institutions as less determinative of action, i.e., ascribing more autonomy and capacity of actors to alter (or avoid) institutions they no longer find amenable. While institutions may reduce uncertainty for actors, institutions do not fully circumscribe action" (Deeg and Jackson 2007, p. 160). Indeed, I have argued above that SAF theory's conceptualization of society-as-fields is a key strength precisely in this regard: as actors are situated in fields, *any* attempt to change intersubjective objects (such as rules) is dependent on the target actors' field environment. Of course, the actors' field environment is institutionally structured—however, depending on their position, actors will hold different views of these institutional rules. This means that SAF theory is highly reconcilable with a view that sees change trajectories as bound to existing institutional set-ups.

If anything, the financialization literature is an example of the manifold workings of social skill. State actors turn to financialization in order to "creatively work around" (Fischer In Preparation) institutional limitations in their authority, corporate managers sometimes do and other times do not follow institutional investors' demands, and financial actors have been tremendously successful in loosening regulation and, after the financial crisis of 2007–2009, avoiding qualitatively significant regulatory change. But this is precisely the point: social skill is abundant both in forging and resisting financialization and therefore cannot alone serve as an answer to when financialization does and does not prevail.

The problem of social change in situations of equal social skill is even more troubling for SAF theory when linking financialization and the state. As SAF theory poses, the interest of state actors is to set the rules in all (or at least as many as possible) SAFs in their geographical territory (Fligstein and McAdam 2012, p. 69f). But often, financialization is seen to reduce the state's authority, as for example in monetary policy. This is exemplified by the shift of formal monetary policy authority from the UK Treasury to the Bank of England during New Labour's first term, as well as in the creation of the European Central Bank according to ideas of monetarism. Likewise, impact investing is a case in point here: with the creation of Big Society Capital, the British central government has set up a financial organization with authority to define what counts as "social impact" (and thus as worthy to receive quasi-public funds) that sees only very limited government influence. Lastly, Langenohl and Wetzel (2011) have pointed out how in the European debt crisis of

2009–2013, state actions have become increasingly motivated by disseminating "signals" to "financial markets" in the hope to reduce interest levels charged on sovereign bonds of crisis-riddled European countries—rather than crafting regulatory tools or taxation.

Again, I argue that findings such as these are very well reconcilable with SAF theory—but that answers given thus far did not clearly establish a conceptual path. Understanding the state as a set of social arenas that is tied to a number of other fields and therefore highly dynamic provides the key avenue to understand these changes. From SAF perspective, we would argue that financializing state actions occur not in spite of state actors' social skill—but because of it. Indeed, to understand how state actors repeatedly and significantly engage in financialization we need to understand how internal and external field dynamics lead policymakers to cooperate with financial actors. The question why state actors engage in financialization, sometimes contrary to their seemingly "objective" interests, boils down to the question of how skilled financial actors are able to forge and maintain relations with dynamic state fields. Answering this question will require us to revisit the relation between fields and social skill.

3.2.2 *Social Skill, Cooperation, and Field Interdependence*

The question how skilled actors forge cooperation across interdependent fields is key to understanding processes of financialization.[7] As argued earlier, financialization often invokes a sustained transformation of nonfinancial actors' action patterns that allows financial actors to extract revenues, such as in the case of corporate governance (Lazonick and O'Sullivan 2000) or the housing field (Botzem and Dobusch 2017; Quinn 2010). In many cases, we can presuppose neither unilateral dependence of the nonfinancial field, nor disparities in social skill. For example, even though corporations are often formally owned by financial actors, their profit-extracting abilities are closely related to their portfolio companies' corporate performance. More so, financial actors in many European countries were only partially successful in imposing their "conception of control" on firms—despite owning growing percentages of corporate stock (van der Zwan 2014). This points to the fact that rather than being imposed through some kind of formal dependence, financialization unfolds as nonfinancial actors somehow encounter a "good enough reason" (Forst 2015b) to change their way to act. Even though the financialization literature is ripe

[7]Of course, changes in nonfinancial actors' action patterns are not based on cooperation alone: unilateral dependencies exist. My point here is twofold: first, I am only interested in situations where such unilateral dependencies do not (yet) exist, as is for example the case in field emergence or invasion by outside actors. Second, I argue that even where nonfinancial actors are critically dependent on financial actors' resources, they do not necessarily fully subjugate to financial actors' interests. Thus, there is room for nonfinancial actors' agency here, which needs to be understood in more detail.

with examples of such cases, the comparative capitalisms literature shows that in some situations, these reasons might just not be "good enough." Thus, financial actors ought to forge some kind of cooperation with nonfinancial actors who could principally act otherwise.

Why, then, do nonfinancial actors engage in cooperation with financial actors, when doing so often induces a change in the rules of the field that might be to their material disadvantage? One of the explanations offered by SAF theory is a discrepancy in partaking actors' social skill. As social skill is defined as the ability to induce cooperation, we might assume financial actors to possess more skill than nonfinancial actors and thus have higher chances in forging cooperation. We might conceive nonfinancial actors to be "tricked into" disadvantageous ties with financial actors. However, such an assumption may run danger of tautologizing by treating any case of financialization as an example of financial actors' superior social skill. Moreover, such an assumption partially contradicts core tenets of SAF theory: financialization alters action patterns of enormously powerful incumbent actors (such as governments and multinational corporations)—but since they are incumbents they must be highly skilled because it required social skill to achieve an incumbent position in the first place.

Fligstein and McAdam (p. 54) acknowledge that "whatever advantage skill might convey, it could be offset by the presence of equally skilled actors in the other group." They note that "this is frequently the case and we have no problem acknowledging that very often the social skill of challengers and incumbents is roughly equal." But how, then, is cooperation forged when there are neither unilateral dependence relations, nor known inequalities of social skill? Indeed, the problem of cooperation is central to financialization as financial actors penetrating a field not only need to forge alliances with extant members, but also a new settlement with proximate state fields (Fligstein 2013, p. 46). Thus, they need to accomplish two tasks: "fashion an alternative order attractive to a good many groups in the field" and "secure allied backing for the proposed new settlement" (Fligstein and McAdam 2012, p. 107).

Regarding the first case, SAF theory proposes that skilled actors act akin to movement organizers, in that they work "by convincing others to accept their own cultural conception (via an appeal that resonates with others' identities or meaning)" (Kluttz and Fligstein 2016, p. 195). To overcome the stabilizing forces of extant settlements (Fligstein and McAdam 2012, p. 107), skilled actors need to forge a "collective action frame" based on which disparate groups begin to act in concert (pp. 50–53). This requires skilled actors to "invent new cultural conceptions to help establish entirely 'new' institutions" (p. 109). As these new conceptions may "reorganize actors' identities and interests," and, by doing so, actors' position in the field, new and "unimaginable" coalitions may develop under these new collective identities (p. 110). Critically, however, skilled actors' ability to succeed in establishing such a movement along a new frame is intricately bound up with the extant state of the field. This is because "new cultural conceptions build on materials available to strategic actors that provide identities for collective actors that resonate with their *prior conceptions of themselves*" (p. 109, emphasis added).

Although the authors "equate the role of 'entrepreneur' with skilled strategic action" (p. 113), SAF theory breaks decisively with theories of institutional entrepreneurship as it sees change not only as a function of entrepreneurial activity, but also as conditioned by the situation of and in the field. Indeed, the authors go as far as arguing that:

> The position of entrepreneur is not a disposition or a quality of an individual, it is instead *a role that is available under certain conditions* of social fields. Entrepreneurs can act to bring together other groups in a political coalition in a social movement–like fashion by forging collective identities that allow the structuring of the field. They do so by recognizing what the system gives them.[8] (p. 181, emphasis added)

To forge cooperation, skilled actors, on the one hand, need to be sensitive to their counterparts' extant identities and open to some kind of opportunities whose emergence lies beyond their control, on the other. These opportunities emerge as even the most stable fields show some degree of dynamism, and they are exacerbated in crises (p. 112). To yield a possibility for change, however, these opportunities need to be utilized by skilled actors and translated into momentum through a process of collective attribution—but since mobilization is conceived of as a process of social construction, momentum may also be generated through the design of opportunities rather than their "objective" presence (pp. 106–107).

The problem of fostering inter-field alliances introduces a somewhat more competitive perspective to the issue of cooperation. This is particularly true in cases where actors aim to forge alliances with the state in order to establish a new settlement. This is because, "[a]s fields develop, savvy incumbents seek to ally themselves with leading state actors and vice versa; for their part, leading state actors—or those who aspire to such a role—see powerful incumbents in key strategic action fields as attractive allies" (p. 106). Thus, to forge ties with state actors, skilled actors face competition from incumbents whose ties to the state form a key basis for the state's own legitimacy. Here, the theory stresses the role of resources: "The ability to deploy money, connections to the government, connections to other important social actors, and ideas about how to organize and bring together other groups are distributed across socially skilled actors in groups. They will use whatever resources they have to exploit the system for gain" (p. 181, see also p. 54). Thus, resources can be thought of as a limiting factor in the role of social skill for forging ties with the state, and the authors warn us not to give skilled actors "too much credit and not seeing that what they were able to mobilize was as important as their skill in doing so" (p. 183).

The theory, however, has difficulties in explaining dynamics of non-state/state ties. On the one hand, it notes that "[i]f the state refuses to protect the extant settlement [...], the possibility for significant field transformation is high" (p. 100). On the other hand, the theory argues that "connections to government"

---

[8]This creates the contradiction that entrepreneurship is *and* is not an ability of the individual. This may be resolved by assuming entrepreneurship to be an individual ability conditioned by situations on the field level. I suspect that this is what the authors had in mind here.

will allow actors to establish a settlement. The point here is that only in the first case is the state assumed to be a dynamic entity with emergent interests, while in the second case the state is implicitly assumed to be an ahistorical and interest-less referee—thus contradicting core tenets of the theory. Thus, while resource inequalities certainly play a role in accounting for change, placing too much emphasis on resources as an explanatory factor for non-state/state ties underestimates the dynamism internal to the state that affects those ties. This is also the case in the other direction, as studies on the development of neo-liberalism have shown how a transformation in state fields has very profoundly altered resource distributions across virtually all economic fields, particularly in countries of the Global South (Harvey 2005).

In relation to the friction between the financialization and comparative capitalisms literatures, SAF theory might offer a useful "third way." In requiring skilled actors to (a) foster new frames based on partaking actors' extant identities, (b) exploit opportunities on the field and interfield levels, and (c) forge ties with other fields, the theory is principally capable of explaining *trajectories* of change without localizing their source in institutional arrangements themselves or in their internal "frictions." Emphasizing financial actors' skilled performances allows to perceive financialization as a potential change dynamic in all national capitalist arrangements. This reconciles scholarship on financialization with comparative capitalisms research. By acknowledging actors' need to foster consensus based on extant identities and across dynamic fields, SAF theory sees the stabilizing role of institutions not in determining action patterns, but in actors' abilities to foster novel, time-enduring *interaction* patterns.

That being said, in order to fulfill its potential as shared middle ground between theories of actors and of institutions by stressing their interaction in social situations, the three critical ingredients mentioned above need to be theorized more clearly. In particular, the theory needs to be clearer as to (a) how exactly other actors' identities come into play and therefore clarify the link between identities and positions, (b) what exactly constitutes opportunities and how they emerge, and (c) clarify how other field dynamics enable or threaten inter-field ties.

3.2.3 Settlements and Field Dynamics

As the literature review has shown, to understand trajectories of financialization we need to understand how intra-state dynamics shape financial actors' abilities to forge new settlements, particularly in fields beyond financial markets, such as corporate governance or social service provision. SAF theory is highly sensitive to the role of extra-field changes for intra-field dynamics (p. 173). As noted in the above section, SAF theory conceptualizes relations between state and non-state fields in two ways: first, the state as a (biased) referee, stabilizing non-state fields through support for key incumbents. The second notion stresses how the constant jockeying for position inside the state affects the stability in non-state fields.

Settlements are often dependent upon continuous, regulative involvement from the state. However, "the state may regulate in a large number of ways" (p. 174). Yet different forms of regulation (e.g. taxation, subsidies, regulatory bodies) directly translate into different rules in non-state fields and thus affect the balance of power in those fields. The question *how* the state regulates "is very much related to the politics of who is running the government, the composition of the membership in that agency, [and] the ideological commitment of those actors [...]" (p. 174). Thus, SAF theory assumes a direct and dynamic influence of intra-state dynamics on non-state fields in the case of regulatory settlements. The reverse is also true: as state fields depend on support from incumbents in key non-state fields, these non-state actors may also influence intra-state dynamics as they "precipitate efforts to replace their state allies, restructure the malfunctioning state strategic action field, or, in the case of a broader break-down in state order, join with others to bring about regime change" (p. 75).

Focusing on this "iterative stimulus–response 'dance'" (p. 173) of state and non-state actors, SAF theory is well equipped to study the interaction between institutional settlements and proximate field dynamics. To study *trajectories* of change, however, SAF theory allows us to enter the home stretch yet forces us to halt just short of the finish line. To explicate this point, let us recall that SAF theory's two core tenets are a situated conception of agency, and the idea of society-as-fields. Society is conceptualized as a dense "latticework" of interconnected fields that *all* show at least some degree of internal dynamics. This means that, as actors are situated in fields, they, too, will witness continuous dynamics in their social situatedness. Now as the task for socially skilled actors is to "empathetically understand situations" (p. 173), this introduces a sensitivity to proximate field dynamics into the conception of social skill: skilled social actors need to understand how others' situations change, and frame their own actions accordingly. Indeed, Fligstein and McAdam summarize the development of intra-field dynamics similarly:

> [I]f events in a proximate field are (1) *interpreted* by actors in a specific strategic action field as posing a significant threat to or opportunity for the realization of group interests and (2) that actor is able, through the appropriation or creation of an organizational vehicle, (3) to undertake innovative action, the result is likely to be a rupture in the existing settlement and the onset of a generalized crisis, or episode of contention, in the field. (p. 100, emphasis added)

This means that proximate field (i.e. state) dynamics are theorized as a necessary condition for skilled (i.e. financial) actors' efforts to mobilize and develop new strategic action frames and innovative collective action. This is an important addendum to the iterative "dance" noted above: state dynamics are not only critical to the stabilization and gradual transformation of rules in non-state fields but furthermore shape *opportunities* for skilled social actors. It is problematic, however, that currently, SAF theory does not go beyond the statement of necessity *that* state dynamics need to be interpreted as an opportunity. Key questions thus remain unanswered: Are strategic actors able to translate events in proximate fields into an opportunity for virtually *any* goal? Or do we need to assume a relationship between the *direction* of change in proximate fields and the nature of opportunities that result for skilled actors?

From my perspective, linking the direction of change in proximate fields with opportunities for skilled action is a direct logical consequence of the definition of social skill and the conception of situated agency. If we assume actor A seeking to cooperate with actor B whose proximate field environment has changed, then B may find A's argument no longer resonating with the rules and identities shared in her field environment. Thus, if A still seeks to cooperate, she must propose something different that reflects B's new reality. The role of B's *situated judgment* for A's ability to cooperate therefore represents the key theoretical puzzle we need to solve in order to understand our broader question regarding the emergence of new cross-field cooperative ties.

3.3 Understanding the Void: Cooperation, Opportunities, and Mechanisms

In the previous sections, I have contrasted two strands of the financialization literature with findings from the comparative capitalisms literature to show how, to explain this variety, we need a social field theory. I have argued that, here, SAF theory offers two conceptual advantages over other field theories: situated agency, and society-as-fields. Scrutinizing SAF theory's explanatory potential for financialization by emphasizing the centrality of horizontal cooperation, I have found that SAF theory is somewhat under-theorized to explain skilled actors' success or failure, particularly given ubiquitous field dynamics. Although we know that skilled actors will use whatever opportunity is available to them, we know hardly anything about the nature and structure of these opportunities. This is problematic as opportunities form the central tenet of the theory's conception of strategic action. This is why in the first segment, I will analyze how opportunities have been discussed in the works cited as theoretical inspirations by Fligstein and McAdam (2012). In the subsequent section I will show how this view on opportunities may be complemented by Neil Gross's (2009) conception of "pragmatist mechanisms" to yield a protostructure for the emergence of cooperation that we can carve out in detail by means of empirical research.

3.3.1 Opportunities and the Problem of Horizontal Cooperation

The issue of opportunities is a central one in social movement theory. Indeed, one of the authors of SAF theory, Doug McAdam, is well known for his contributions to the relation between movements and opportunities. Although SAF theory does not relate to opportunity theories in large detail, some references are made to particular opportunity theories. Concretely, the concept of "political opportunity" is mentioned (p. 112), and in discussing their own theoretization of "collective threat/opportunity attribution", the authors (p. 5, 20) refer to a number of related works from social movement theory (Goldstone 2004; McAdam 1982; McAdam et al. 2001; Tarrow 2011; Tilly 1978). I will briefly describe these and then attempt to relate them to social skill and horizontal cooperation.

The study of the relation between movements and opportunities dates back to Alexis de Tocqueville's (1856) famous observation that the French revolution gained momentum the more autocratic rulers were giving in to their demands (Kurzman 1996). One of the earliest systematic frameworks to study in detail *how* the structure of the polity affected the trajectories of contentious social movements was developed by Peter Eisinger (1973). He attributed the emergence (or lack of) of urban riots in some US cities in the 1960s to the "openness" of municipal government structures to citizen participation. Building on his work, Charles Tilly (1978) proposed a general model of social movements, which included opportunities as one of five main analytical variables. Opportunities were conceptualized as affecting movement actors' power as "[c]ontention for power always involves at least two parties. The behavior of the second party runs along a range from repression to facilitation" (p. 100). Despite its breadth, depth, and influence on the social movement literature,[9] Tilly's early conception of opportunities is difficult to apply to the problem of horizontal cooperation. As it stresses opponent actions to increase or decrease movement actors' "cost of participation," it is difficult to apply to the development of future cooperation—particularly in highly institutionalized contexts, such as the link between state and finance.

In his study of the US civil rights movement, McAdam (1982) largely built on key theoretical developments of Tilly (1978), as well as Rule and Tilly's (1975) idea of "political process." In contrast to these authors, however, McAdam (1982) stresses the social construction process of opportunities, and how these are bound to external events. He understood the changes in frames as the result of a collective process of attribution that saw the formerly oppressive rule "collectively defined as both unjust and *subject to change*" (McAdam 1982, p. 34, emphasis in original). This is because "[m]ediating between opportunity and action are people and the subjective meanings they attach to their situations" (p. 48). This conception of opportunities clearly resonates with SAF theory's situated agency model. Nevertheless, this "classical social movement agenda" (McAdam et al. 2001) remained essentially a structuralist literature that conceptualized opportunities as lists of "objective" social facts that would trigger emergence, shape trajectories, and determine success of social movements without granting strategic actors an independent

[9] Tilly's work was highly influential for the work of McAdam, particularly through his contributions to episodes of contention, the development of the challenger/incumbent model from Gamson (1975), as well as the introduction of Harrison White's network-theoretical concept of "catnets" (White 1970).

form of agency. Having been strongly challenged empirically (Goldstone 2004; Goodwin and Jasper 1999), the political opportunity approach is furthermore undertheorized in regards to the idea of society-as-fields. It does not acknowledge differential field-level impacts on groups of to-be-mobilized activists, but—in the case of the civil rights movement for good reasons—assumes their shared experience of oppression as a uniting force. For studying dynamic state-finance relations, however, we will need to take differential field-level impacts much more seriously, as we may expect different government departments with different identities and interests partaking in the negotiation process. In addition, large parts of this perspective focus on a contentious "mechanism" for social change—protest—rather than cooperative processes on the ideational level.

McAdam et al. (2001) developed a different angle of critique: Rather than tracing the development of single movement organizations through box-and-arrow hypotheses of "objective" facts, they emphasized the *dynamic interrelation* between challenger and incumbent (differentiated as state and member) actions. Here, the study of movements took a "relational turn" (p. xvii), as the authors emphasized that they had "come to think of interpersonal networks, interpersonal communication, and various forms of continuous negotiation—including the negotiation of identities—as figuring centrally in the dynamics of contention" (p. 22). As SAF theory builds on a number of concepts developed in this book, it is worthwhile to take a closer look.

The first key theoretical innovation lies in McAdam et al. (2001) conception of an "episode of contention", which has been taken over by SAF theory. In such an episode, challengers and incumbents are "simultaneously responding to change processes and to each others' actions as they seek to make sense of their situations and to fashion lines of action based on their interpretations of reality" (p. 46). In making sense of their dynamic environment, actors thus attribute threats and opportunities. In order to translate these perceived opportunities and threats into action, challengers need to create or appropriate an organizational vehicle. Critically, it is "a challenger's capacity to appropriate sufficient organization and numbers to provide a social/organizational base [. . .] which makes mobilization possible" (p. 47). Here, they have to "contend with established organizational leaders who do not share their interpretation of recent events as posing a significant threat to, or opportunity for, the realization of group interests" (p. 48). This mirrors the conception of social skill in SAF theory, where, in order to mobilize, skilled actors have to forge cooperation for their innovative frame. If successful, actors will "reimagine the legitimate purposes attached to established social sites and/or identities" (p. 48) and hence engage in innovative collective action that further increases uncertainty and thus provides new material for threat/opportunity attribution. Central to the model is thus the "formation of new actors and identities, and how they interact with others through the performances of contentious politics" (p. 61). Actors "undergo modifications of their boundaries and attributes as they interact" as identities are seen as a "connection" between actors' relations and their interactions (p. 56).

There are two important gaps in this conception of dynamics. First, as already implied by SAF theory's conception of "piecemeal" social change: contention does not necessarily mean opposition. Actors will often be successful in competing for power without openly opposing challengers or incumbents, but, for example, by forging strategic cooperation. Second, again, the relation between identities and opportunities remains undertheorized. In which situations may we expect attributed opportunities to actually allow forging new identities? Or can we conceive of cases where prevailing, or even novel, identities subsequently *decrease* the perceived opportunity?

Indeed, these two arguments may be related. If we take, for example, the case of sustainability and corporate practices, we can see how incumbent firms have gradually taken up sustainability discourse and practices and altered corporate governance without necessarily opposing the mobilizing efforts by challenger organizations such as activist groups (Hiß 2006). In many cases, corporations have been actively seeking cooperation with critical activist groups—yet by doing so, they have often been successful in changing the very idea of sustainability in their favor (Feist and Fuchs 2014; Hiß 2013). This means that, although challengers have engaged in threat attribution, in the appropriation of organizational vehicles, and have yielded innovative collective action—neither was there at all times open conflict and opposition, nor have challengers often been successful in reshaping corporate identities against material interests, while at the same time their own identities have partially been altered through the course of cooperation with corporations.

Departing from McAdam et al. (2001) conception, the introduction of social skill and society-as-fields in SAF theory has partially resolved these conceptual voids. In particular, SAF theory conceptualizes meso-level change as necessarily contentious, but only sometimes openly oppositional. Via ties with other fields, SAF theory allows for a conception of change that builds on identity shifts without requiring challengers to constantly engage in open conflict.

The point, however, is that although SAF theory embraces the relational view on opportunities and identities developed by McAdam et al. (2001), it still does not offer a compelling answer to the problem how extant identities relate to opportunities for successful social skill. I suspect that this arises from the hinge between Fligstein's and McAdam's components of SAF theory, the former stressing social skill and fields, the latter movements and mechanisms. A field-level mechanism to account for the success of social skill thus falls on the welding seam between the theory's two main components. In contrast to Martin (2011, p. 286 n.27, pp. 287–291), who argues that field theory is *per definitionem* irreconcilable with a notion of mechanism—but rather ought to base on an action theory that builds on American pragmatism—I argue that the notion of mechanism *per se* is not problematic if we link our understanding of mechanisms with the emphasis on positionality that is the hallmark of field theory. Indeed, the conception of social skill *is* a pragmatist action theory (Beckert 2010)—and as Neil Gross (2009) has argued, a conception of social mechanisms can indeed be developed on the basis of a pragmatist action theory.

That being said, I fully agree with Gross's concern of McAdam et al. (2001) conception of mechanisms, noting that they neglect or underestimate "the nexus of habituality, creativity and interpretation" (Gross 2009, p. 372). SAF theory addresses some of these concerns by incorporating social skill. Concretely, I see the creativity-critique as resolved as both Gross (2009) and Fligstein (2001b) relate to Joas' (1996) creativity of action. The same holds for the interpretative dimension as social skill boils down to "reading situations." This is why, in the following section, I provide a roadmap of key properties of such a mechanism were it to comply with SAF theory.

3.3.2 Pragmatist Mechanisms and the Emergence of Cooperation

Opening up SAF theory to alternative change mechanisms means to embrace a view that a repertoire of contention is "simply one type of habit that actors can enact jointly to solve problems" (Gross 2009, p. 371). Based on a pragmatist action theory, the quest for such a mechanism means describing a process through which some actors, when confronted with the problem of cooperation sometimes engage in the innovative action of forging new ties. This process can be conceived of as a "pragmatist mechanism" to account for the problem of cooperation. I argue that such a mechanism is imperative for SAF theory for two reasons: ontologically, building on both mechanisms and pragmatist action theory, this will be SAF theory's only way forward without expanding its foundational assumptions and thus running the risk of onboarding contradictions. Moreover, such a mechanism is an empirical necessity as cooperation is *the* defining problem for skilled social actors. This is why I will first introduce the concept of pragmatist mechanisms and then show how it can be used in accordance with SAF theory. This will provide the basis upon which I attempt to find such a mechanism to account for the emergence of cooperation across fields in the empirical chapters of this book.

To develop a definition of mechanisms, Gross (2009, pp. 359–362) attempts to find a common denominator between the theorizing offered by, amongst others, Hedström and Swedberg (1998); Stinchcombe (1998); Tilly (2001). From his perspective, the authors concord in understanding a mechanism as something social (a process or event) that *mediates* between cause and effect, unfolds in time, is at least somewhat general (i.e. reproduces under similar conditions), and that is located at a lower level than its explanandum (Gross 2009, pp. 362–363). In SAFs, contention is a good example of such a mechanism (indeed a bundle of mechanisms) as it is a lower-level causal social process that repeatedly occurs in similar situations across actors (e.g. in different countries) and thus helps explain more general field-level dynamics. Despite ontological and methodological differences between the aforementioned authors, Gross nevertheless develops a general definition of a social mechanism as

> a more or less general sequence or set of social events or processes analyzed at a lower order of complexity or aggregation by which—in certain circumstances—some cause X tends to bring about some effect Y in the realm of human social relations. This sequence or set may or may not be analytically reducible to the actions of individuals who enact it, may underwrite formal or substantive causal processes, and may be observed, unobserved, or in principle unobservable. (Gross 2009, p. 364)

The problem, according to Gross (and many others would agree) is that current formulations of social mechanisms—despite their analytic quality regarding "social causality as a philosophical concept"—are "less satisfactory when it comes to offering sociological theories of mechanisms," that is, theoretical accounts of "causal processes in the realm of the social" (Gross 2009, p. 364). According to his view, this is either because conceptions of mechanisms, such as Stinchcombe's, are simply not embedded in sociological theories and thus fail to "delimit the scope of possible mechanisms and provide no general account of their nature" (p. 364). Other conceptions of mechanisms, by contrast, build on rational choice theory (such as Hedström and Swedberg 1998), which Gross criticizes in order to point to the potential of pragmatist action theory for social mechanisms (pp. 365–368). Since critiques of rational choice theory, particularly from a pragmatist perspective, are plenty abound (Beckert 2003; Boltanski and Thévenot 2006; Diaz-Bone 2015) and indeed form the very basis for the conception of social skill (Fligstein 2001b, 2008), this justificatory step will be omitted here. Instead, I will unpack Gross' understanding of pragmatist mechanisms and show how it can be it can be linked with SAF theory.

Very briefly, Gross sees the main implication of the philosophical work of American pragmatists such as Dewey (1922) and James (1907/1975) for mechanisms in their action theory: "action, as a response to problem situations, involves an alternation between habit and creativity" (Gross 2009, p. 366). Here, habits are understood as learned from past experience and problem solving. Although they are mostly routinized, habits always imply at least some degree of individual agency, such as schema selection (Emirbayer and Mische 1998, pp. 975–983; Mead 1934, pp. 16–18). Creativity is understood as the human capacity to imagine and enact solutions or alternative futures (Beckert 2016; Joas 1996; Mische 2009). In this sense, Dewey's conception of creativity is closely related to Pierce's concept of abduction: as Tavory and Timmermans (2014) show, abduction is a creative act. But where Dewey is more focused on action, Pierce's conception of inquiry is somewhat more general.

For our endeavor, these differences are only of secondary importance. Yet it is key to understand that social skill is a pragmatist action theory in Gross's sense: although its emphasis lies on the creative dimension (innovatively solving the problem situation of forging cooperation), Fligstein's conception of what skilled actors actually do to achieve cooperation (e.g. framing) can be read as a list of habits. Only in its emphasis on empathy, i.e. actors' imagination of others' *present* situations, which was imported from symbolic interactionism, does the concept of social skill expand a pragmatist conception of agency in the narrow sense. But as empathy is not only innate but also socially learned,[10] we can think of it as a habit in the wider

[10]Although the ability to learn empathy appears to be bound by biological factors such as prenatal testosterone levels: individuals with higher prenatal testosterone levels appear to be less empathetic, more motivated by money, and more successful in competitive financial professions (Baron-Cohen 2002; Coates and Herbert 2008; Eisenegger et al. 2011).

sense. Importantly, habits are "enacted on the basis of culturally mediated interpretations of the situation one faces [. . .], not least interpretations of the intentions of interaction partners." This is because "[p]roblem situations present themselves to actors through the lenses of the cultural environments in which they are immersed" that "give meaning and help provide the content of the goals, orientations, identities, vocabularies of motive, and other understandings of the action situation that actors come to have" (Gross 2009, p. 367). From a pragmatist point of view, we may therefore see instrumental rationality as a habit whose signification as an appropriate way to act for a number of situations is fundamentally cultural, and hence subject to historical processes (MacKenzie 2016, for a similar idea). Despite such a cultural emphasis, pragmatist action theory does not counteract the idea of strategies but understands them as socially situated, hence implying dynamic ends in the course of action (Stark 2011)—Dewey's "ends-in-view" that are the basis for Fligstein and McAdam's conception of strategic action.

Neil Gross develops the idea of pragmatist mechanisms based on such a view of action. As social mechanisms linked to a sociological theory of action, pragmatist mechanisms allow a causal explanation of social processes (i.e. answer the question why a series of events happened, and under which conditions we would expect a similar chain to unfold again) without relying on methodological individualism, or "over-socialized" views of methodological collectivism or structural functionalism that are largely detached from individual agency. With his conception of social mechanisms and pragmatist action, comprised of problem situations, habits, and creativity, Gross has already pointed out the main ingredients of a pragmatist mechanism: they are "composed of chains or aggregations of actors confronting problem situations and mobilizing more or less habitual responses" (2009, p. 368). More formally, a pragmatist mechanism can be seen as "a structure or process S by which some input I leads to outcome O." To understand S, we would need to understand all involved individual or collective actors A_i ($i = 1, \ldots, n$) and, for each, how and why in problem situation P_i, when endowed with habits (that include resources) H_i, the response R_i will be the most likely one. This way, "S will then consist of all the relations A_{1-n} –P_{1-n} –H_{1-n} –R_{1-n} that, in aggregate or sequentially, bring about the I–O relationship" (p. 386).

Although rather abstract at first sight, pragmatist mechanisms can account for a number of processes from social movement scholarship and SAF theory. For example, brokerage (i.s.o. Fligstein and McAdam 2012) can be understood as a mechanism where a "subset of the actors involved faced problem situations that they sought to resolve by mobilizing habits of making social connections between disparate parties" (Gross 2009, p. 371). This means that neither networks, institutions nor cultural frames *per se* form a mechanism—rather, their structuring role is mediated through the mechanism. This way, a theory of pragmatist mechanisms takes up Jens Beckert's criticism about the causal and ontological problems of network, institutional and cultural theories attempting to "endogenize" each other (Beckert 2010, 2011). As I argue below, it furthermore agrees with his conception that these three "social forces" interact in fields. Yet, rather than arguing that mechanisms structure how "[i]nstitutions, networks, and cognitive frames form conditions and restraints *on each other* for their reproduction and change" (Beckert 2010, p. 612, emphasis added)—that is understanding mechanisms as some kind of causal intermediary between social structures—I follow Gross (2009) in conceptualizing mechanisms as sequences of situated actors forming responses. Thus, from my perspective, the three "social forces" interact (differently) *in* (each) mechanism—rather than *through* mechanisms.

How are SAFs related to mechanisms? Broadly speaking, fields as mesolevel arenas are simply another way of delimiting who acts and in what situation. For example, the field of banking would include a number of financial, nonfinancial and state actors A_i who are related in a particular way (e.g. through networks) and confront similar but not necessarily equal problem situations P_i (idiosyncratic combinations of institutional rules, network ties, and cultural frames, as well as different status positions). Through its action-theoretic assumptions, SAF theory has a particular view of what constitutes actors' habits H_i, and what responses R_i we might expect. That said, as SAF theory's social ontology is based on a pragmatist theory of action, the theory's conception of causality can be expressed in terms of pragmatist mechanisms—if key SAF vocabulary is linked to the A-P-H-R chain.

Let us take the "episode of contention" as an example. Fligstein and McAdam (2012) understand this as a "process" that consists of three "mechanisms": "attribution of threat/opportunity", "social appropriation", and "innovative collective action" (pp. 20–21). From a perspective of pragmatist mechanisms, these can be perceived either as three individual mechanisms or one aggregated contention mechanism. As individual mechanisms, we would understand attribution and appropriation as a 2×2 tableau of A-P-H-R chains. This is because, following the conception of Fligstein and McAdam, in those first two "steps", challengers and incumbents independently forge more or less creative responses to their specific problem situations (e.g. crises in adjacent fields). The innovative collective action mechanism is somewhat different as, here, challengers and incumbents base their actions on the perceptions of each other. For example, incumbents would face the problem situation of challengers' successful appropriation and would mobilize habits and resources for collective action (e.g. censorship, physical repressions, legislative change).

On an aggregated level, we could understand contention itself as a pragmatist mechanism, where challengers and incumbents face the problem situation of contested rules and engage in the habit of open conflict that yields a number of destabilizing changes. As with any causal explanation, the higher the level of analysis, the more lower-level complexity and dynamics are linearized. The point is that pragmatist mechanisms are fully coherent with the SAF perspective, yet allow for the de-contextualization of some of SAF theory's concepts and, by allowing for novel analytic models that remain grounded in SAF theory's set of ontological and causal assumptions, thereby help us to expand the theory's explanatory horizon. This is why searching for such a pragmatist mechanism to explain how and why skilled actors are successful in developing new cooperative ties represents the scavenger hunt that will take up the majority of the remainder of this work, and forms my theoretical contribution.

This book will proceed by briefly explicating my methodology and research methods (Chap. 4), before I describe in detail the SII field in the UK (Chap. 5) and the framing deployed by investors (Chap. 6). In Chap. 7, I piece these things together and provide a longitudinal study of the development of SII in the UK from 1997 until 2016, particularly in order to develop empirically a hypothesis of such a pragmatist mechanism. In Chap. 8, I discuss and qualify this hypothesis in regards to Gross' conception of pragmatist mechanisms, SAF theory, and the debate between financialization and institutionalist scholarship.

Chapter 4
Methodology and Research Methods

If you carefully consider the question of pragmatism you will see it is nothing else than the question of the logic of abduction
(Peirce 1934, p. 195, cit. by Timmermans and Tavory 2012, p. 182)

In this chapter, I will present my methodological approach as well as my research methods. To do so, I will first present my methodology on a rather abstract basis in order to show how following such an approach generates intersubjectively validatable research findings. In a second step, I will make transparent how this methodology informed my concrete research process and the perspectives and conclusions I derived throughout. In the third section, I will describe my research design and methods in order to justify the validity and generalizability of my findings.

4.1 Abductive Analysis

There are three reasons why I chose abductive analysis (Tavory and Timmermans 2014; Timmermans and Tavory 2012) as the underlying methodology for this study. First, abductive analysis is a methodology that builds on a pragmatist theory of action which is highly congruent (although not fully equal to) the action theory underlying Fligstein's model of social skill and Gross's conception of pragmatist mechanisms that I built on extensively to make my point. By using abductive analysis, I therefore do not need to make and justify assumptions why the people I observe act in a profoundly different way than I do when pursuing this research. Indeed, this is as much a necessary condition for the validity of my argument, as it is a normative view held by many sociologists. Assuming that people act in an iteration of habit and creativity that is tied to their social situations—but then arguing that my research emerged in a non-iterative (e.g. Popperian) way would have limited the

P. Golka, *Financialization as Welfare*,
https://doi.org/10.1007/978-3-030-06100-5_4

generalizability of my proposed action-related theory. Moreover, social and political philosophers have long argued for the "principle of rational justification" by which they understand a "recursive requirement that only those norms can claim general and reciprocal validity that can redeem this claim in a general and reciprocal, discursive manner" (Forst 2013, p. 3). From such a perspective, it would therefore not be good sociology (the norm in question) to make a claim on social action that I cannot redeem in application of my own actions. Indeed, arguments such as these have featured prominently in sociology: according to Diaz-Bone (2015), it was a similar argument on the position of sociology and sociologists vis-à-vis the ontological assumptions of social action and reflexivity that was key to the dissociation of Luc Boltanski from Pierre Bourdieu.

Second, throughout my work on this book, I carefully reflected upon my methodological approach. I found the most prominent approaches to be far removed both from what I did and what I felt was necessary to do. It would be plainly wrong to argue that I followed a "grounded theory" approach (Glaser and Strauss 1967; Strauss and Corbin 1990) because I frequently related back to established social theory in order to make sense of my findings and rephrase my research questions. As I iterated between empirical analysis, theory, and questions, I furthermore realized that it would have been insufficient to term my methodological approach a case study (Eisenhardt 1989; Yin 2009) or a qualitative content analysis (Mayring 2015). Although I did follow to a large extent these analytical procedures, neither of those methods was capable of capturing holistically how I engaged with my data. This is because they did not sufficiently theorize upon the role of theory in the process of inquiry. The same holds for modified versions of grounded theory such as the "Gioia methodology" (Gioia and Chittipeddi 1991; Gioia et al. 2013) that are increasingly prominent in organization theory: these methodologies nevertheless require an a-priori definition of research questions that I found myself unable to make. Confronted with this situation, I found that abductive analysis offered a way out, as it theorized my frequent iterations not only as justifiable but also as necessary for scientific inquiry.

Thus, in addition to finding abductive analysis to come close to what I had been doing for the first two or so years of working on this book, I found that it makes convincing epistemological arguments. Abductive analysis is grounded in Pierce's semiotic theory of inquiry (more on this below). From this perspective it necessarily follows that we cannot form an epistemological standpoint (let alone a practical one) that makes "a-theoretical" points, because theoretizations form the very basis of *any* act of meaning-making. Thus, if we accept such a perspective on social action—and above I gave reasons for why I did—then using grounded theory will be contradictory. Based on this perspective, Tavory and Timmermans (2014) argue that to build theory means to engage with social theories out there and carefully consider how our data creates puzzles for them. This is why from a perspective of abductive analysis it is not necessary to stick with a-priori defined research questions. Rather, we ought to be sensitive for situations—and indeed cultivate their emergence through a systematic approach—where our data leads us to beguiling theoretical puzzles. Only by iterating between data and theory can we understand for which theories our case will be interesting.

What is abductive analysis? Abductive analysis is a research methodology developed by Tavory and Timmermans aimed at theory production by cultivating abduction as a form of logical inference. Abduction refers to the "creative production of hypotheses based on surprising evidence" (Timmermans and Tavory 2012, p. 168). In contrast to both induction and deduction, abduction "starts with consequences and then constructs reasons" (p. 171). For example, I observed that impact investing proponents only gained large-scale access to the polity after they changed their position vis-à-vis not-for-profit social organizations *and* after the "Treasury view" began to take hold in social policy. Based on this observation I hypothesized that this was due to some form of "test" that linked policy field dynamics to policymakers' acceptance of impact investing proponents' cooperation offers.

As a research strategy, abductive analysis "rests on the cultivation of anomalous and surprising empirical findings against a background of multiple existing sociological theories and through systematic methodological analysis" (p. 169). In the example above, the concepts of field and cooperation are core tenets of SAF theory—and in the process of abduction, I came to realize that the empirical material I was confronted with represented a stimulating case for SAF theory. What makes abductive analysis unique is that it is a structured research process that integrates a view on theory, method, and empirical material in order to foster creative insights. As a research strategy, abductive analysis integrates abductive inference both with induction and deduction by following Pierce's theory of inquiry:

> In Peirce's view, then, abduction is an integral process of the scientific method. Once a hypothesis has been formed, deduction helps work out the hypothesis by providing a plausible generalization or causal chain. Induction constitutes the evaluation of the hypothesis because it provides the data that should conform to the deductively delineated premises. Abduction, Peirce noted, provides less certainty than induction, and both of those processes were less secure than deduction, but abduction had innovative potential. Induction was able to classify only by grouping particulars in a preformed general category, while abduction formulated the explanation, the category into which observations would fall. Abduction suggested explanations, which were then formalized into deductions, while induction confirmed them through empirical testing. (p. 171)

In order to integrate induction, deduction and abduction into a qualitative research process, three key questions need to be addressed: how to create generalizations through abduction? How to decide which generalizations to work out and evaluate through deduction and induction? And how to ensure the validity of the findings? To address these three questions, the authors developed a recursive research process model. Core to the model is the idea that "[t]heorizing in qualitative research amounts to a disciplined way to use observations and encase them in multiple ways, to present multiple vectors of meaning-making from various perspectives while checking them against the resistance of observations in the field" (Tavory and Timmermans 2014, p. 30). Thus, what abductive analysis amounts to is a process of "double-fitting" theory and data through sustained iteration. Theory is used to "see the phenomenon in sociologically interesting ways" whereas methods "are designed to compel us to revisit the same observation again and again, defamiliarize the known world, and apply alternative casings to our observations" (Timmermans and Tavory 2012, p. 176). In essence, abductive analysis thus addresses the first and third question through methods, while the second question is addressed through theory.

To perform abductive analysis, we need to find observations that we evaluate as surprising or unanticipated from the perspective of social theories. For example, the authors discuss Diane Vaughan's case study of the NASA decision to launch the Challenger space shuttle (Vaughan 1997, 2004). While she approached the empirical material with a view of organizational misconduct, she realized that the theoretical explanation did not fit the case. After re-analyzing the data, she developed an initial hypothesis of organizational mistake that appeared to fit a number of instances that were contradictory to the earlier theoretical perspective. From this novel theoretization, she deducted instances to serve as a hypothesis test and, after these passed the test, qualified her hypothesis from the view of established social theories. Thus, as she double-fitted data and theory, her research question changed (Timmermans and Tavory 2012, p. 174).

In abductive theory generation, the standardized research methods advanced by qualitative research programs such as grounded theory play two key roles. On the one hand, they allow the researcher to "revisit the phenomenon" and thus not only sensitize us for important anomalies by forcing us to see the empirical phenomenon from different angles, but also ensure that our theoretical generalizations are indeed supported by the empirical data (Timmermans and Tavory 2012, p. 176). This means that following standardized qualitative research methods opens up the possibility to productively use the variance that is internal to the empirical material for theory generation. This is why we need to make sure to include variation of data types, across situations, and over time in our data set (Tavory and Timmermans 2014, Chap. 5). On the other hand, standardized research methods help us to "defamiliarize" ourselves of taken-for-granted understandings and assumptions and thereby sensitize us for anomalies or surprises that we would otherwise "gloss over in our immediate experience" (Timmermans and Tavory 2012, p. 177).

The key to abductive analysis is to integrate these two functions of research methods in a context of existing social theories. To do so, the researcher should "case" the novel generalizations in the light of different theoretical perspectives. This way, a large majority of abductive generalizations can quickly be abandoned as they are easily explained by existing theories (p. 177). Those generalizations that cannot be abandoned are the ones that are worthwhile to pursue further by using induction and deduction to make sure they withstand the test of the empirical material, and if they do, through in-depth theoretical qualifications. If necessary, the empirical material can be recoded according to the hypothesis (p. 180).

Together, this means that abductive analysis as a methodology is fundamentally process-oriented. This is mirrored by Van de Ven and Poole (2005, p. 1378) who have argued that the process-focus is key to the family of methodologies building on American Pragmatism. As the guiding principle of the abductive research process is to "double-fit" theories and data, abductive analysis is not only open to reformulations of research questions, but also the use of multiple theories and research methods. This is why, in the following section, I will describe in detail how I engaged in a process of abductive analysis in this study. Before doing so, however, let us briefly turn to the third question posed above, the question of scientific validity and value.

In developing their methodology, Tavory and Timmermans (2014, p. 105) posit three criteria to evaluate the quality of empirical research: fit, plausibility, and relevance. Fit (or validity) is constructed by making sure that the abductively derived generalizations account for all three forms of variance included in the data set. However, they argue, that this alone is not a criterion of scientific value, because virtually any claim could be made to fit the empirical data by increasing its complexity. This is where plausibility comes in, i.e. the question whether other theories are better able to account for the findings than the abductively developed generalization. One way to achieve plausibility is to contrast predictions made by extant theories with the emergent theoretization (p. 114). If a theoretization is plausible, then the question becomes one of relevance, this means whether it will be useful for other academic questions or debates that are not related to the empirical phenomenon. While none of these three criteria is intrinsic to the theoretization itself but rather constructed by a "community of inquiry", the relevance question will be the most contested one as it is not bound up with analytical procedures that can be baked into the research process (p. 115).

4.2 Research Process

As described in the section above, abductive analysis is an open process methodology geared at stimulating theory creation. However, because of its openness it is important to make transparent the actual process the researcher underwent in order to ensure that the results did not emerge out of a strategic distortion of the research process. In what follows, I will describe the abductive process that formed the basis of this work. To substantiate my claim that this was my actual process of enquiry, time-stamped documents such as data analysis files, notes, explanatory sketches, and conference presentations are available upon request. Figure 4.1 gives a schematic overview of the research process and shows its key events.

Starting an abductive research project means being confronted with a chicken-egg problem. The researcher knows neither which empirical object to study nor how and why it is interesting—and answering either of these questions presupposes having an answer to the other question. I addressed this problem by using what Thomas (2011, p. 516) calls "local knowledge." Having been interested in social impact investing years before starting my PhD, and having worked in adjacent fields and in fundraising for social ventures with impact investors, I defined SII as my research object. Then I studied particularly relevant sociological theories until reaching two vantage points that I suspected to offer potentially interesting insights. I fixated a financialization perspective because I sensed that the very limited body of extant

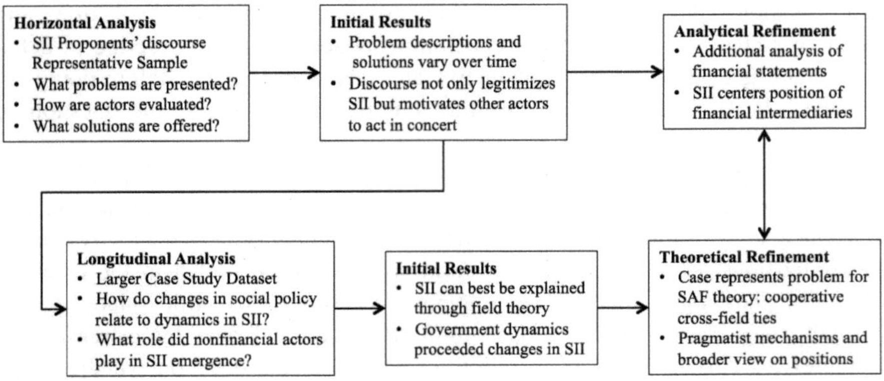

Fig. 4.1 Research process and key events

research on SII that used a similar perspective and had been published by then (Chiapello 2015; Dowling and Harvie 2014) only analyzed parts of the financialization process linked to SII. In addition, I embarked on an open longitudinal study with a broad interest in market emergence. Having established my two jacking points, I decided to first focus on SII in the UK because of the long history of SII in this country.

After having broadly fixed my perspective, I embarked on my first empirical analysis. From my prior work experience I recalled that SII presented a highly attractive proposition to a number of young graduates who shared a strong desire to "better" the state of the world. At the same time, I studied the works of French pragmatism (Boltanski and Thévenot 2006) and became interested in the understanding of social justice (or "order of worth") SII actors' propelled, and whether this narrative construction played a role in SII's popularity. I found this question interesting because, again, from my prior experience, I recalled multiple instances where impact investors' public discourse was starkly contrasted by their investment practices.[1] I decided to follow this hunch by asking whether SII proponents created a narrative that portrayed financialization as an inherently good and desirable thing. For this sake, I coded a representative selection of SII proponents' discourse with the analytical categories offered by orders of worth theory. By doing so, I followed abductive analysis, which argues that researchers should "code their empirical materials in light of their literature reading" (Tavory and Timmermans 2014, p. 125).

I wrote up the findings from this analysis into a "thick description" (Geertz 1973) of approximately 27,000 words. While writing, I began to collect additional data on a

[1]For example, an impact investor specializing in "sustainable" forestry demanded our German-Brazilian agroforestry company to purchase land off Brazilian smallholder farmers as a collateral for German asset owners. In multiple other cases, impact investors' due diligence process was almost exclusively focused on questions of return and risk, while internal rates of return far exceeding 10% p.a. were demanded. One impact investor directly asked us to reduce pay for Brazilian smallholder farmers in order to increase investors' profits.

number of the "best case examples" of social ventures or investment funds that were frequently mentioned and described as particularly successful or representative in SII proponents' discourse. In particular, I analyzed financial statements of some of these "best case" firms and transactions from a financialization perspective. After studying different field theories, I abducted that SII proponents' discourse could be seen not only as legitimatory, but also as a motivation for other actors to act in concert such that rules beneficial to investors start being reproduced. This created the puzzle whether this was in fact the case, and why nonfinancial actors engaged in such a mode to act. In parallel, I utilized the temporal variation baked into the analyzed data set (the reports ranged from 2000 to 2015) for abduction: I realized that SII proponents' description of social problems slightly shifted over time—thereby seemingly following the normative discourse of the respective ruling parties. Thus, from observing the consequences I abducted the causes: I hypothesized that SII proponents taking over government discourse was a key factor for why government engaged with them.

At this point, I began to develop a new data set to trace the longitudinal development of SII with an eye on my initial hypothesis. I introduced data, situational, and temporal variation by collecting reports from a variety of actors, parliament debates, government publications, academic political science commentary, interviews and other sources dating from almost two decades. I realized that ideas related to SII emerged in relation to New Labour's "social inclusion" agenda. Because my causal hypothesis built on a transformation in narratives, I followed abductive analysis (Tavory and Timmermans 2014, p. 98) in selecting the emergence of these ideas ("emplotment") with the 1997 general election as the starting point of my analysis. My first analytical step was to develop a timeline of key events both in SII, and in policy. Here, I built on how policymakers signified events by cross-referencing those in policy publications.

In parallel, I stumbled upon Jens Beckert's (2010, 2011) insight on how cognitive frames, institutions, and social networks jointly organize social action in fields. This was an important turning point for my theoretical approach, because it helped me make sense of the fact that neither new institutional field theory, nor orders of worth theory were able to fully account for the emergence of SII as I grasped it from my data. The notion that either of these theories often attempt to "endogenize" the other two "social forces" led me to code my data with a view on cognitive frames, institutional rules, and social networks. After coding the material, I began to analyze whether and how the key events I listed earlier were preceded by changes in any of those categories, and for which actors this was the case.

During this analysis, I realized that virtually all key events were somehow related to HM Treasury. Moreover, I realized that Treasury played an ever-increasing role in the transformation of British social and public services. From this observation, I abducted that the penetration of HM Treasury into social policy represented an opportunity for SII proponents to achieve a validation of their arguments regarding the position of financial intermediaries and government in the pursuit of social welfare.

Presenting my findings at the annual meeting of the Society for the Advancement of Socio-Economics in 2016, I was asked multiple times why there had not been any counter-mobilization to the growing support for SII actors. Expecting charitable social service providers to be potential opponents of the boundary-blurring process related to SII, I began to take their role and respective positions into account in much more detail. By doing so, I expanded my database accordingly.

In order to gain a better overview of what had become a complex set of entangled social processes, I began to write up the developments chronologically. At some point during this process, I realized that I could make sense of a whole lot of these findings from a perspective of SAF theory not just because of its relational view on institutional rules and cognitive frames, but also because it allowed to link intra-field dynamics with cross-field ties. Reading through SAF theory in great detail, I realized that precisely the question regarding the emergence of cross-field cooperation was not sufficiently worked out in the theory, and that my empirical analysis on cross-field links and intra-field dynamics could prove highly insightful in this regard. At the same time, I realized that SAF theory was highly suitable to discharge of the tensions between the institutionalist literature on capitalist variety and financialization. As a result, I fixated SAF theory and the problem of cooperation as the theoretical basis for this study and began to rework my analyses from this perspective. Such an approach to research question building and theory construction is known in the literature as "problematization" (Alvesson and Sandberg 2011).

Particularly important in this regard was to shift my analysis of SII proponents' narrative to a perspective of field-level strategic action frames (Snow and Benford 1988). This allowed me to disentangle the diagnostic, prognostic and motivational components of their frame and put those into context with developments both in social policy and the field of social organizations. Based on this analysis, I hypothesized that the emergence of cross-field cooperation was preceded by a change in either of those fields such that a strategic action frame motivating such a cooperative tie became acceptable to actors within that field. This abductive moment was critically informed by my realization that very similar processes occurred in very different situations. To achieve cooperation in other government departments for its view on social policy, Treasury referred to its role in safeguarding the public budget that rendered its demands acceptable to other policy departments. On the other hand, SII proponents' claims regarding public service delivery became acceptable to policymakers only after SII actors began to position themselves as supporters of the voluntary and community sector—the introduction of VCS organizations to public service delivery being a long-held Treasury goal.

After abducting this initial hypothesis on the emergence of cooperation, I tested it by studying other cases of emergent cooperation in the case of SII and found support for my claim. For example, VCS actors began to cooperate with SII actors only after the emergence of social enterprise had rendered income generation and partial profit distribution legitimate for social organizations. Motivated by the successful abductive analysis, I qualified my hypothesis on a theoretical level by linking the notion of pragmatist tests with SAF theory's society-as-fields ontology and its view of skilled but positioned social actors. Thus, my model on resonance spaces emerged by studying consequences and hypothesizing their cause. Rather than posing a limitation to the validity of my analysis, this is indeed a core feature of abductive analysis. My findings are substantiated by testing them on the grounds of situational and temporal variance, as well as (limited) data source variance. That said, additional ethnographic studies on the hypothesized mechanism remain an important task for future research.

4.3 Research Design

The first section of this chapter has described abductive analysis as both a methodology and an open research process aimed at fostering creative insights to develop theory. In the previous section, I described how I applied these tools to navigate my idiosyncratic empirical and theoretical environment. In this section, I will describe the standardized methods I applied throughout the iterative process described above. Although abductive analysis is an open research strategy, it nevertheless builds on the use of elaborated research methods to foster insights and to establish their validity. For my endeavor, I found a single case study method to be particularly well-suited. This is why I begin the following section by showing how I constructed a single case design according to the case method, and why such an empirical approach made sense given my research questions. In the second section, I describe in more detail my approach to data selection. In the third section, I describe how I analyzed these data in order to produce reliable results.

4.3.1 Single Case Study Design

There is a large variety of qualitative case study approaches known in the social sciences (Eisenhardt 1989; Ragin and Becker 1992; Snow and Trom 2002; Yin 2009). Reviewing prominent case study approaches of the social movement literature, Snow and Trom (2002) define a case study as:

> (a) investigation and analysis of an instance or variant of some bounded social phenomenon that (b) seek to generate a richly detailed and 'thick' elaboration of the phenomenon studied through (c) the use and triangulation of multiple methods or procedures that include but are not limited to qualitative techniques. (p. 147)

By contrast, Thomas (2011) reviews case studies from a much broader field of social sciences and defines them as:

> Case studies are analyses of persons, events, decisions, periods, projects, policies, institutions, or other systems that are studied holistically by one or more methods. The case that is the subject of the inquiry will be an instance of a class of phenomena that provides an analytical frame—an object—within which the study is conducted and which the case illuminates and explicates. (p. 513)

Key to all definitions of case studies is that they are bounded empirical phenomena that represent "a case of" something. Thus, I will first describe how I progressed towards these two criteria. By making transparent how my research question featured into the construction of the case, it will become evident why such a research design made sense for addressing my research questions.

As noted earlier, I began my analysis of SII based on "local knowledge" (Thomas 2011) of the case. Based on this knowledge, I attempted to understand SII as a case of financialization. This is why the first step of my analysis was to ask how and to what extent SII in the UK could be seen as related to financialization. Working through the financialization literature and my empirical material, I realized that SII could be seen on the one hand as a "revelatory" (Yin 2009, p. 42) case for financialization, because I found processes related to financialization (such as redistribution towards financial intermediaries) that occurred in a social context (the welfare state) where they had, to my knowledge, not yet been studied before. On the other hand, I found that the case of SII was "critical" (p. 41) for the institutionalist view on capitalism as I did not find support for a number of its predictions (such as its agency model or theory of path dependence). Later during the analysis, I abducted that SII could be seen as a "typical" (p. 41) case of field emergence and transformation in the sense of SAF theory as its predictions were able to explain most of the social processes at play here. Such a theoretical layering of the empirical case is qualified by Snow and Trom (2002, p. 152) as theoretical "triangulation" that helps, together with other forms of triangulation about which I will say more below, to gain understanding of the social processes at play in the case. From a perspective of abductive analysis, this represents the theoretical "casing" of the material to foster an abductive insight. Through this process, I was able to fixate my interpretation of SII as a *case of field-level financialization.*

Building on this interpretation, I began to delimit (and collect) my empirical material for the longitudinal analysis. Snow and Anderson (1991, p. 162) liken such an approach to an "exploratory geological expedition" where "more focused probes [occur] after the contours of the landscape have been mapped" and hold that "consequentially, new or unanticipated events, relations or processes, as well as data sources, frequently surface with the turn of the corner." As case studies always focus on something that is internally linked or structured, such as a "system of action" (Snow and Trom 2002, p. 149), cases are always spatially and temporally limited. To trace the contours of a case, then, means to unravel this internal structure. For my case, I found that the link between financial intermediaries and government was particularly important, this is why I decided to focus on the government that seemed to play the most important role: the British central government. Building on this insight, I was able to delimit my case to the UK only. Moreover, I built on my finding that SII was revelatory due to its relation to the welfare state: It might well be that impact investors who aim at altering firms in established producing markets exist as well—but for my case only those were relevant that take part in the welfare-related system of action. To delimit my case temporally, I traced backwards the emergence of those narratives that SII actors frequently related to (i.e. the "emplotment") and found that they came to the fore around the 1997 change of government, with a few significant events occurring some years earlier.

Guiding my case selection from the study's focus on field-level financialization, I constructed what Yin (2009, pp. 42–45) would call an "embedded single case." Although my case study featured only one level of analysis—the field level—it was necessary to study all units that make up the field level. Only this way, I was able to make use of actors' positions—as well as preceding intra- and inter-organizational dynamics—for explaining the emergence of relations between different types of social actors. As shown in Chap. 2, the relevant units of analysis were the three fields of community enterprise and finance, social enterprise, and the VCS, as well as their links to and the dynamics within the respective government departments Treasury, Department of Trade and Industry, and Home Office. During the course of the observation period, these units of analysis were partially reshaped to form SII, social ventures, and the Office of the Third Sector. Yin (2009, p. 45) notes that shifts such as these are a key reason to establish different units of analysis through an embedded case design. That said, he also argues (p. 45) that it is equally important to translate the findings back to the aggregated level—to do so, I attempted to show the significance of these lower-level events for the transformation of the social welfare field more generally.

Single case study designs are often criticized in the literature for not yielding theoretical insights that are generalizable beyond the particular social context. Following such an argument, Siggelkow (2007, p. 20) argues that such designs should only be used if the case is as interesting as the proverbial "talking pig." I argue that a variety of scholarly communities may signify the case of SII as such a curiosity. Scholars of hybrid organizing (Battilana and Lee 2014) might be surprised by the fact that the hybridization present in SII first and foremost serves investors' financial interests. Welfare state theorists (Esping-Andersen 1990) might be intrigued by how social impact bonds commodify what was established as a means of decommodification in the first place. And economic historians could be excited (or worried) to see structures similar to nineteenth century poor houses famously described by Polanyi (1944) on the rise again in England. Yet more importantly, the methodology of abductive analysis strongly contradicts such criticism. Due to the theoretical layering and casing of the empirical material, single case designs allow for a conversation between theories that is well suited to refine their explanatory potential. Utilizing the case's inherent variation and "double-fitting" theory and data, adding a second case would unnecessarily complicate such an epistemological approach—at least at an early stage. Lastly, there is a problematic assumption on causality hidden in such a critique. As pragmatist scholars have repeatedly pointed out, social actions cannot be explained independently from their social context, as the context (by way of, for example, yielding culturally mediated problem situations) *is* the structuring mechanism (Gross 2009; J. L. Martin 2011).

4.3.2 Material

To (a) address how SII represents a case of financialization and (b) analyze its emergence and development, I constructed two distinct yet overlapping corpuses of empirical material. To address the first question, I had to understand whether and how what SII actors do could be interpreted as a case of financialization. As this required me to gain an understanding of what SII actors do, I had to find material that would provide me with reliable and representative information of SII actions. Here, I found reports published by SII actors to be representative of the views and actions of SII organizations individually, as they are the "result of internal negotiations designed to portray a particular point of view" that is "developed through group processes, and formatted for public consumption" (Reay and Hinings 2005, p. 361). Given their length, they are a particularly rich data source that not only describes but also justifies to the public the actions of SII actors. During the process of data analysis, I realized that these reports go even further by providing a very detailed description of SII actors' field-level strategic action frame.

In order to yield a representative sample of reports, I consulted the "knowledge databases" of five SII actors and associations that I recalled from my previous job to be often cited as central and important actors. These were:

1. GIIN Library: http://www.thegiin.org/cgi-bin/iowa/resources/research/index.html
2. Big Society Capital Library: http://www.bigsocietycapital.com/social-investment-research-library
3. Social Finance Library: http://www.socialfinance.org.uk/news-views/publications/
4. Social Investment Taskforce: http://www.socialinvestmenttaskforce.org/
5. Social Impact Investment Taskforce (G-8): http://www.socialimpactinvestment.org/

I catalogued all 313 reports that were published online at the point when I began my analysis in July 2015. I followed a three-step selection algorithm to yield a representative sample of reports. In the first round, I excluded 189 reports because they either focused on different or too specific topics, or on different countries. I excluded another 53 reports based on the title, keywords, and, if necessary, abstracts because their topics were too distant from my research question. Based on the full material of the remaining 71 reports, I selected 28 of those into a core sample that underwent full coding, and a supplementary corpus of 43 reports that I consulted when encountering ambiguities during the analysis. In constructing the core sample, I followed a logic of representativeness and therefore included reports from a large variety of actors, including investment banks, non-investing intermediaries, and charitable foundations. Moreover, I aimed at including a large set of social issues, such as SII in education, employment, or drug treatment. After compiling a set of 28 reports totaling 1134 pages, I found both theoretical saturation and manageability of the material to be reached. A list of all 313 reports as well as the core sample, including justifications for data set inclusion for each of its reports, can be found in Appendix D.

Many scholars agree that case studies fundamentally build upon a "consideration of the array of relevant actors and voices" (Snow and Trom 2002, p. 154) that allows to view the empirical phenomenon from a variety of perspectives. This is why, for the second sample that I used to study the entrenchment and development of SII, I attempted to gather a large and varied dataset from field-level actors as well as other relevant data sources. Qualitative researchers emphasize that for interpretative social science, the context of data generation is as relevant as its content (Mayring 2015). To make sense of this context, I followed the society-as-fields ontology offered by SAF theory and understood the material by acknowledging actors' positions and relations (Fligstein and McAdam 2012, p. 191).

Starting from the representative sample noted above, I systematically collected material from all actors mentioned in these reports, particularly various central government departments, as well as VCS and social enterprise actors. Moreover, I conducted eight semi-structured expert interviews (Merriam 2009) with field-level representatives (see Appendix C) that I acquired through targeted snowball sampling. As these interviews included policymakers, civil servants, SII proponents, and VCS actors, all relevant actor groups were represented in the interview sample. I used information obtained from the interviews to collect additional data. In the process, I developed a timeline of key events from these data as well as published academic work on SII and related fields, and ensured a sufficient data coverage on all of these events. Eventually, the sample comprised over 200 documents that I analyzed using MaxQDA computer software. These documents included reports, government White and Green papers that describe government strategy, legislation, parliamentary debates, formal guidance, public budget statements, press releases, speeches, and party manifestos. A full list of these documents can be found in Appendix D. In addition, I used the Internet Archive's Wayback Machine to analyze the development of field-level actors' public discourse by tracing longitudinally changes in their online public self-descriptions. To make sure I included the voice of all relevant field-level actors, I browsed through all Third Sector magazine articles that were published online a few months before and after a number of key events. For practical reasons, the last two data sources were not included in the MaxQDA file. Together, this data collection procedure ensured the creation of a holistic data set through which I was able to trace the development of SII in relation to developments both within the social services and social policy fields throughout the observation period from 1997 until 2016. Ensuring the inclusion of all relevant actors' voices means that my dataset was representative of the developments on the chosen level of analysis.

4.3.3 Data Analysis

Scholars of abductive analysis share with both case study scholars and grounded theory advocates the view that a rigorous and systematic approach to data analysis is a necessary, albeit not sufficient, step to ensure the scientific validity of qualitative research. They furthermore agree that the choice of analytical procedure has to be linked with the respective research questions. Moreover, they argue that the procedures need to be sufficiently open in order to allow for surprising findings to emerge (Gioia et al. 2013; Snow and Trom 2002; Timmermans and Tavory 2012).

The emergence of such a surprising insight can be seen during my first analysis. I used a set of theoretically derived codes to analyze the first data set with the use of computer software MaxQDA. More precisely, I used the analytical grammar offered by orders of worth theory (Boltanski and Thévenot 2006) to analyze how SII proponents evaluate other actors in the field. I used the theory's classification of "high worth" and "low worth" for objects that SII actors evaluated positively or negatively, as well as "cause of low worth" and "investment formula/strategy for high worth" to understand what SII actors attribute as reasons for the "low worth" of actors and what actions they propose for a transformation to a "higher worth." I crossed this vector of codes with actor and action types, such as government, financial intermediaries, social organizations, individuals or communities, to yield a category matrix (see Table 4.1). Full-coding the complete material, I yielded a total of 452 such text samples of an average length of 1–3 sentences. In addition, I coded 177 text samples that attempted to legitimize the practice of SII, 39 samples that defined SII, as well as a number of in-vivo codes.

I used these findings to develop a "thick description" of SII proponents' discourse, and at that point I realized that their depictions strikingly mirrored a field-level strategic action frame as known from the study of social movements (Snow and Benford 1988). Based on this abductive insight, I studied the codes for a second time and used them as a basis for the frame analysis presented in Chap. 6. As I realized that SII proponents' frame changed over time, and particularly following changes in government, this abductive insight formed the basis for my second analysis.

Table 4.1 Main coding scheme analysis 1

	High worth	Low worth	Cause of low worth	Change formula
Actors				
Investors				
Government				
Social organizations				
Communities				
Individuals				
Actions				
Investments				
Social policies				
Social interventions				

For the longitudinal analysis, I coded the material along six main avenues as well as a number of issue-related codes (fox example Social Impact Bonds) that yielded a total of 1328 coded segments. First, I marked all instances that were either evaluated in the material as important events or that I interpreted as important, yielding 112 coded segments. Second, I mapped how each partaking actor framed relevant events, issues, and other field-level actors. This yielded a total of 614 coded segments across 17 categories. Third, I coded how partaking actors defined and legitimated field-level boundaries, yielding 97 coded segments. Here, the boundaries of highly contested categories such as "social enterprise" or "third sector" were particularly important. Fourth, I coded the related category of conflict yielding 57 segments. Here, my emphasis was more on grasping which actors were in conflict with what other actors, and over what issues. Fifth, I studied how institutionalized rules that were relevant to the field changed over the course of the observation period, yielding 76 segments. A key focus here was on formal rules for public organizations in the field of social service delivery. Lastly, I coded all segments (95 in total) regarding social networks. A large number of these codes were lists of work group or commission members that I used to trace network dynamics in relevant policy advisory fields. The remaining 277 segments were coded with specific issues (e.g. SIBs, Big Society Capital, referrals to the 2008 financial crisis) or deductive testing (e.g. the government "leverage" strategy I abducted from the material, see Chap. 7).

In a second step, I translated these findings into text. To do so, I proceeded chronologically, starting in 1997. I built on the timeline of events that I developed from the codes and systematically traced whether and how these events were preceded by changes in any of the five main analytical avenues described above. I paid particular attention to how changes in network structures and institutional rules preceded changes in cognitive frames. While writing down my findings, I observed a particular pattern that eventually formed the basis for my resonance space hypothesis. As my hypothesis developed and my theoretical perspective using SAF theory became more firmly established, I studied the codes and my longitudinal description for a second time in order to rewrite my findings into what forms Chap. 7 of this work.

In between writing Chaps. 6 and 7, I revisited more systematically the political economy dimension of the events and social processes covered in both empirical samples. Building on insights from the financialization literature, I began to study different forms of financial redistribution towards SII intermediaries, which are presented in Chap. 5. Using the second sample, I developed an overview of all direct and indirect central government subsidies for SII. Collecting financial statements from "best case" examples mentioned in the first sample, I traced how investors extract revenues from social organizations that investors themselves label as particularly representative for social impact investing. Moreover, I gathered data on pay in such "best case" examples in order to study labor-related redistribution processes. Lastly, I worked through my codes regarding charitable foundations and the role of grants in order to trace the redistribution of private donations towards SII actors.

Chapter 5
The Financialization of Welfare

In the previous chapters, I have shown how financialization can be understood as a transformation of social relations that engenders institutional change with redistributive consequences, often building on repeated government interventions. I have argued that to analyze financialization processes this way it is particularly fruitful to build on SAF theory. From a SAF perspective, financialization can be seen as a process through which financial actors become incumbents in a given field while the institutionalized rules change in their favor—including material redistribution. Here, changes in financial actors' relations to other actors are of critical importance. This is on the one hand because social positions are relational properties: incumbents are only incumbents inasmuch their position is reproduced in specific social relations. On the other hand, the empirical financialization literature has shown that the relation between financial actors and governments is a particularly significant one. Often, financialization is associated with the emergence of cooperative ties between state and financial actors: rather than tightly regulating or highly taxing financial intermediation, in these ties government actively supports the creation of financial markets, actors, and products.

My theoretical contribution is to find a mechanism for the emergence of such cooperative ties through abductive analysis of the case of SII in the UK. This puzzle will be addressed in Chaps. 7 and 8. However, to get there, we first need to understand whether and how SII in the UK is a case of financialization. This is why, in this chapter, I will first describe the field of SII in the UK and introduce the partaking actors with an ideal-typical analysis of their respective roles in the field. But since financialization is a change dynamic between an "input" stage as well as an outcome, I will furthermore provide brief descriptions of the social services field pre- and post-SII in order to show what has been financialized here. The last two sections of this chapter shed light on the two most significant political-economic transformations in this financialization process: redistribution of material resources, and the authority to define and evaluate what counts as "positive social impact." Together, I name these changes the *financialization of welfare*.

P. Golka, *Financialization as Welfare*,
https://doi.org/10.1007/978-3-030-06100-5_5

5.1 The Field of Social Impact Investing in the UK

In this section, I will give a highly concentrated overview of SII in the UK in order to provide a roadmap for the following chapters. As discussed in Chap. 2, I argue that we can analytically distinguish two types of SII. In the first type, investors attempt to change the operation of firms in established markets, such as material goods production, by introducing some kind of social or environmental metrics. The second type is different since its main locus of change lies within the welfare state. This type of SII therefore shows a much higher degree to which relations between financial and state actors are affected and transformed. Moreover, as financial actors are those who earn incomes through financial intermediation, SII, where it affects the welfare state, requires some form of income or profit extraction and redistribution from welfare state organizations that include government, public organizations, and social service providers. Although impact investors of the first type exist in the UK, too, I am only concerned with the latter type because understanding their success in forming cooperative ties with government actors forms a large part of the puzzle I attempt to solve.

As has been argued in Chap. 3, strategic action fields theory departs from current formulations of new institutional theory in particular by emphasizing actors' *positions* in fields as well as the emergence of relations between them. This view is of critical importance to understand the emergence and development of social impact investing in the UK. As can be seen in Fig. 5.1, the emergence of SII is related to dynamics on two principal analytical levels. The first one revolves around the contest

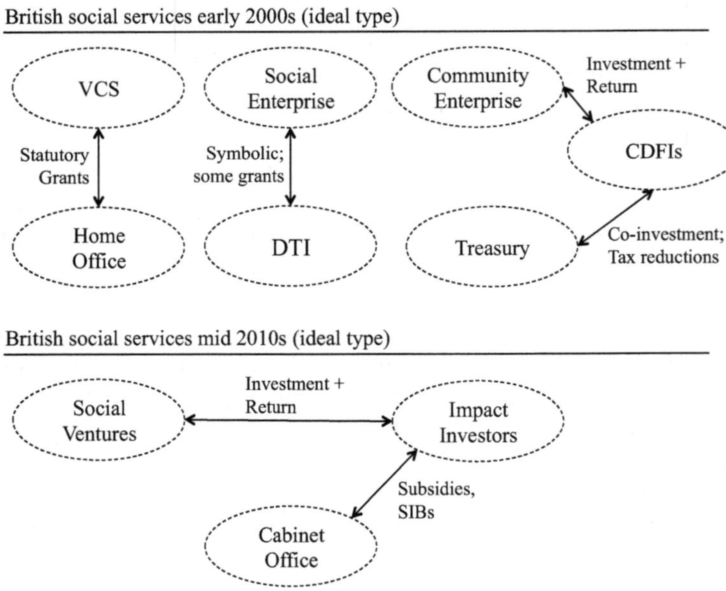

Fig. 5.1 Field-level transformations in British SII and social services

of which types of organizations are to be considered as "social" ones. Here, in the early New Labour years the categories of "social enterprise" and "community enterprise" emerged in addition to the traditional incumbent, the voluntary and community sector. These were linked to the respective government departments Department of Trade and Industry, Treasury, and Home Office. Within government, there was a second line of contention around the issue of how to organize for public service delivery that eventually led to the development of a new government department, the Office of the Third Sector at Cabinet Office. From this perspective, the emergence of SII in the UK was the development of financial intermediaries that built on cooperative relations, on the one hand, with an expanded category of social organizations ("social ventures") and on the other hand with a government department that increasingly accepted this new, expanded organizational category.

The emergence of SII was closely tied to New Labour's agenda of "modernizing" British public services. As I will describe in Chap. 7, one of its key goals was to introduce not-for profit organizations, the so-called "voluntary and community sector" (VCS) into public service delivery. At least since winning the 1997 election, policymakers argued that VCS organizations would—in contrast to both public and private, for-profit organizations—create an "added value" in the delivery of services such as education or social care, particularly on a local level. Traditionally, the VCS was related to Home Office, which financed VCS organizations through statutory grants. The introduction of VCS into public services, was, however, driven mostly out of Treasury and Cabinet Office. The growth of a second group of social organizations was related to the Treasury, too: community enterprise. These were for-profit businesses that were either located in impoverished neighborhoods ("disadvantaged areas") or owned by people of ethnical minority origin. So-called "Community Development Financial Institutions" (CDFIs) specialized in lending to these organizations, which frequently reported problems in accessing capital from "mainstream" banks.

Against this backdrop, a group of challengers from the cooperative tradition attempted to develop a third organizational template, which they called "social enterprise" (SE). As I will show in Chap. 7, the very beginning of social enterprise was framed against both VCS and community enterprise—but in contrast to the cooperative movement that built on a one-person-one-vote principle, social enterprise included for-profit organizational forms such as companies limited by guarantee, too. This early plurality of organizational templates addressed by social enterprise proponents led to a settlement that defined social enterprises as organizations that "principally reinvestment" their profits. In a legal form that was designed in the mid-2000s to cater for social enterprise, this "principal reinvestment" meant a maximum profit extraction of 35%. Like the VCS, social enterprise claimed the creation of an "added value" for the delivery of public services.

Social impact investing emerged out of community enterprise. The first British impact investor, Bridges Ventures, was created in the early 2000s as Bridges Community Ventures and invested as a venture-capital-like equity investor into community enterprises. By 2004, they began to measure their "social impact" in order to validate claims regarding the creation of "added value" similar to VCS and social enterprise. While initially, impact investors positioned themselves *against* VCS and SE, around 2006 they began to form alliances with those actors, arguing that—independent of profit distribution—the broader category of "social ventures" (that includes "profit-with-purpose businesses") would create such an "added value" or "social impact." The extent to which VCS and SE accepted this expanded category, and why they partially failed to maintain the boundaries to for-profit social ventures will be discussed in more detail in Chap. 7. Important for now is to understand that the SII field essentially means a venture-capital type relation between financial intermediaries and "social ventures", and, to the extent these enter public service delivery, also the state. Thus, for public service delivery, SII transforms the formerly direct relations between government and VCS into indirect ones that are mediated by financial actors that are often called Social Investment Finance Intermediaries (SIFIs) or impact investors.

SIFIs are financial intermediaries that raise funds from other intermediaries, organizations, or wealthy individuals and invest into social ventures. Example SIFI organizations are Bridges Ventures and Social Finance. The "social investment bank" Big Society Capital is through the 2008 Dormant Accounts Act legally required to invest its funds only into such SIFIs. Hence, in the UK, SIFIs form part of a settlement with government that institutionalizes the rules of the SII field. As I show in the section below, these rules materially benefit SIFIs in multiple regards. This is because SIFIs can build on multiple types of relations with government and social organizations. Most important for our endeavor are so-called Social Impact Bonds (SIBs) and equity investments. In addition, SIFIs may operate as lenders or, rarely, as donors to social organizations.

SIBs are contracts between government authorities and SIFIs for the achievement of specific "social outcomes" (Dowling 2016). These outcomes can range from improving school grades of children from poor families to avoiding in-patient treatment for drug-addicted individuals. In a SIB contract, a SIFI agrees to finance (either through own funds or by raising capital from investors) the delivery of social services aimed at achieving the predefined outcomes. If an external evaluator finds that the outcomes have been met, then the government authority repays the SIFI its invested capital plus a variable return on investment that is defined in the contract. As of 2016, there have been 33 SIBs commissioned in the UK.

Although the Cameron administration planned to commission SIBs of a total volume of £1 billion, after the repercussions of the "Brexit" referendum, the central government department responsible for SIBs has largely been disbanded. This government department has to date paid approximately £200 million in central government subsidies for SIBs. The impact of these changes on SIB commissioning remains to be seen. That being said, the financialization perspective I develop here is particularly well-suited to understand dynamics such as these. This is because its focus on positioned actors sensitizes us for the contests between actors on central and local government levels, and how these relate to ties with a forming SIB interest group. This interest group is comprised of charitable foundations that have invested their capital endowments into SIBs, as well as performance evaluators, and SII intermediaries.

Apart from SIBs, SIFIs relate to social organizations by attempting to "scale impactful innovations." As I will argue in Chap. 6, the narrative of scaling social impact is a key legitimatory account advanced by SIFIs, and plays a critical role in fostering acceptance for their field-level strategic action frame. From a field perspective, this translates into two main activities performed by SIFIs: financial investments and the definition and governance of "social impact." Financial investments may take the form of equity or debt (or combined) investments. In addition, SIFIs and other SII proponents such as some foundations create "incubator" programs for social ventures. These incubators often follow the model of "venture philanthropy" where non-refundable grants are used to finance the start-up costs of a social venture that aims to access for-profit financial capital at a later stage (Mair and Hehenberger 2014; McGoey 2012, 2015). As the goal of these incubator programs is to create "scalable" for-profit social ventures, impact investors often act as co-sponsors in these programs. Thus, they have a say not only in the admission process but also influence the social ventures' strategy development during the whole duration of the incubator program and, possibly, the subsequent investment-financed growth stage. Investors' influence on social ventures' strategies enjoys a relatively high legitimacy in the field, as exemplified by the case of fitness company The Gym, where investor Bridges Ventures communicated its pride in having incubated the firm from its foundation throughout to its initial public offering (see below).

The definition and governance of "social impact" plays a key role in allowing investors' profit extraction. From a SAF perspective, "social impact" is a contested set of rules that serves as an action orientation for social ventures, but as it is often defined by investors, it grants those relatively large degrees of freedom. In the section below, I will show how the meaning of social impact differs according to investors' material interests. As I found through analyzing a representative sample of reports from a group of somewhat heterogeneous organizations that all advocate SII, a number of non-investing organizations have taken over, theorize, and communicate very similar understandings of social impact that are in accordance with investors' material interests. Thus, investors form the incumbents of a field that is organized around rules that have acquired a somewhat taken-for-granted status although they remain contested.

5.2 Social Impact: Definitions and Governance

This chapter aims to establish the point that SII is a case of financialization. As social impact investing means that investors describe their own practice as geared towards the creation of "positive social impact" it might be tempting to interpret SII as a "reduction" of financialization. We might argue that since SII introduces nonfinancial criteria into decision-making processes, we may observe a "hybridization" of the institutional logics of "finance" and "social impact." As pointed out in Chap. 2, multiple scholars, particularly from business schools, have understood SII this way (Battilana and Lee 2014). From my perspective, this argument is somewhat flawed as it neglects the relationality of any institutional logic. Viewing SII through SAF theory we understand the institutionalized rules of impact and investment as inextricably linked with actors' position in the wider field. Thus, my perspective points to the fact that the institutionalization of "social impact" has different consequences for different groups of actors. While "social impact" might mean a "reduction" of financialization for firms operating in established markets, I argue that this is clearly not the case for the organizations of the British welfare state that are the focus of this work.

In this section, I will explicate this argument by comparing what it means for different actor groups to be evaluated by impact investors as acting towards "social impact." Contrasting the different meanings of social impact as they relate to different actors, I aim to show how social impact is a set of rules that grants investors by far the largest degrees of freedom to act of any actor in the SII field. The following segment will then show how these different meanings are translated into profit opportunities for investors. Epistemologically, this segment therefore represents an important step in the abductive analysis: using the different meanings of social impact as empirical variation, I developed the theoretization of field-level financialization as a means to account for the empirical variance (Tavory and Timmermans 2014).

Social impact is a discursive construction that forms a central component of SII-proponents' field-level strategic action frame. In this chapter, I focus on those dimensions of social impact that make actors in the SII field prescriptions to act and interact. This view on social impact as an action orientation will be complemented with a mobilization perspective on the impact frame in the following chapter. Although social impact is very frequently used by SII proponents as a distinguishing signifier, its meaning is rarely explicated, differs across addressees, and is sometimes internally contradictory. Holding the concept together is a vague reference to consequentialism, in that SII proponents negatively evaluate organizations that are "output" oriented and positively evaluate those that are "impact" oriented. However, its relevance for action may be more or less institutionalized across situations. While investors may choose to either prioritize "impact first" or "finance first" to qualify as impact-oriented, for social sector organizations participating in a social impact bond, impact measures are highly institutionalized in the form of a binding contract.

For investors, the meaning of impact orientation is both the most abstract, as well as the least rigid. Impact investors have developed a plethora of impact measurement devices and no shared definition of social impact exists in the field. For example, JP Morgan defines impact orientation in this way:

> For many impact investors, the impact thesis is usually driven by the value set of an individual or organization and can reference a theory of change with respect to poverty alleviation or environmental sustainability for example. The impact thesis may be integrated into the mission statement of the business, or it may be a separate, complementary statement in the organizational charter. (12_JPMorgan, p. 73)

Although in recent years some organizations have pushed for standardization, such as, for example, in the case in GIIRS ratings (Barman 2015), the rigidity remains weak as these rating systems make, through quantification, impact ratings commensurable over very large sets of social and environmental indicators. For example, in the case of GIIRS ratings, investors may receive a high impact rating by considering multiple environmental factors in their decision-making process while neglecting labor or workplace criteria (Golka 2015). Beyond that, SII proponents grant investors relatively large degrees of freedom in terms of the actual weight of anticipated social impact in investment decisions. For example, New Philanthropy Capital notes that:

> [I]nvestors have different perspectives on the importance of social impact: for the mainstream bank lenders, there are few if any demands as to how impact is generated or measured. For social investors, the creation of social benefit as a primary purpose of the organisation is a 'filter' through which potential investees must pass. Beyond that, the creation and/ or measurement of social impact is rarely a deal-breaker. (12_ClearlySo, p. 175)

Thus, while some investors might "filter" investment proposals by demanding that investee organizations commit themselves to the "creation" of social impact, the meaning of social impact and its measurement principles are only of secondary importance as long as financial criteria are matched. The contradiction between, on the one hand, distinguishing impact investments as an asset class by referring to the distinctness of impact orientation, while on the other hand neither coherently defining nor enforcing it is commonly resolved by referring to impact investors as a "spectrum" or "continuum" of all those financial organizations that "fall between" philanthropic donors and "mainstream" financial investors. Frequently, a categorization between "impact first" and "finance first" investors, which has been developed by the management consulting firm Monitor in 2009, is being adopted. This categorization breaks down the "impact continuum" into two actor classes with distinct action orientations (e.g. 13_Bridges_10, p. 5).

Impact orientation for "finance first" investors means that, although their primary investment decision criteria are based on financial return and risk estimations, they apply an "impact floor" minimum threshold (10_CAF, p. 8). In practice, this might mean that thematic funds are set up for industries or assets that investors deem impactful, such as, for example, microfinance, real estate, or community enterprise. For example, Bridges Ventures set up a "Sustainable Growth Funds" in 2002 that sought to create impact by investing into "deprived areas." In its 10 years Report, Bridges describes one particularly successful investment of this funds as follows:

> In 2004, Bridges backed The Hoxton Hotel – a start-up concept hotel to be built on a piece of land being used as a temporary car park in a deprived part of Shoreditch in Hackney (an area in the most deprived 3% of England). Seeing the potential for a flagship hotel to stimulate economic dynamism in the area, Bridges played a lead role in financing its construction and ongoing success. By May 2012, we sold The Hoxton Hotel for a return of £13.3m to Bridges Ventures' Sustainable Growth Fund I, representing a highly attractive return for our

> investors. The hotel played an important part in the regeneration of Shoreditch and Hackney, with 76% of The Hoxton Hotel staff living in underserved areas (to whom nearly 70% of the total wage bill accrued) and an 85% supplier-spend in the local area.[1] (13_Bridges_10, pp. 17–18)

In other cases, the impact "generated" from an investment was, for example, the number of first-time gym users for a gym franchise (13_Bridges_10, p. 13), i.e. the marketing success of the investee firm. In sum, impact orientation for "finance first" investors defines an action orientation that is centered around the generation of financial return, but is only applicable to cases where investors are able to create some kind of impact narrative.

For "impact first" investors, impact orientation means the self-assessed willingness to sacrifice financial returns for the sake of social impact. For example, Bridges Ventures describes those investors as "willing to back sustainable, profitable business models that cannot generate market-rate returns either because of the enterprise's structure or the disadvantaged consumers it targets (or both)" (13_Bridges_10, p. 35). For example, the "impact first" investor Impact Ventures UK has invested into, and in 2016 exited from, the construction company K-10 that will be described in more detail below. These investors usually commit themselves to the application of some form of impact measurement device. However, the extent to which impact measurement results and expectations influence decision-making varies on the conceptual level and remains unknown on the empirical level. Equally, the ability to define what counts and does not count as social impact lies with the investors, and no sanctioning mechanisms exist.

For government, impact orientation means to accept the proponents' frame regarding a SII capital market and to act as its "market builder", "market participant" and "market steward" in order to maximize the production of social impact (14_G8NAB). Here, impact is a far more restrictive and highly institutionalized action orientation. Concretely, it means to (a) commission more social services via SIBs, (b) deregulate the social and public services field, as well as the fiduciary requirements for foundations to allow them to invest their endowment capital into SII funds, and (c) subsidize impact investors directly or indirectly.

In public service commissioning, "outcomes" are a template in procurement contracts that take the form of "payment by results," including SIBs. In these contracts, organizations are not paid for the delivery of specific services, but rather for the "outcomes" these services achieve. In SIBs, the definition of these outcomes is negotiated for each contract between the public commissioner and the interested SII intermediaries (Interview D). For example, in the case of the first Social Impact Bond at Peterborough prison, the contractually binding outcome metric was a

[1]From a critical perspective, one might add that the process described here follows a pattern of gentrification, in which low asset prices in some geographic areas are used as an opportunity for real estate speculation resulting in a highly unequal distribution of the accrued profits. Inequality can also be observed in pay, where the salary for those living in poor neighborhoods was 92% of the company's average salary, while those living outside of poor areas were receiving 125%. Thus, whether this type of impact investment may result in a reduction of poverty may be questioned.

reduction in criminal reoffending of those former prisoners who participated in the social interventions financed by the SIB of at least 7.5% overall (or 10% for each of the three cohorts) as compared to a matched control group of other ex-prisoners (Social Finance 2011). Importantly, once formally defined in a contract, outcomes become legally binding for government, social service providers, and investors. For example, one report has argued that for the commissioning of Social Impact Bonds, school grades are only an "output metric" and therefore should not be used as a means to trigger investors' success payments; the impact metric rather being pupils' success in finding a job after graduation (Social Finance 2012). A few years later, however, SIBs were commissioned based on school grades, arguing that they serve as a "surrogate outcome" that not only provides a good-enough estimate of their job market success, but also reduces the waiting period for investors and hence improves a SIB investment's return/risk structure (Social Finance 2014). This is no exception: In the case of the Manchester City Council SIB, one outcome metric is the number of weeks children participate in a psychotherapy intervention offered by the SIB,[2] which would have been classified as an "output" metric in other cases.

Second, in its role as "market steward" (14_G8NAB) impact orientation means for government to create legal forms for social ventures that allow both the binding definition of an organizational mission statement, as well as the distribution of profits to investors. Additionally to loosening regulation on profit distribution, impact orientation for government also means to grant social organizations greater flexibility in generating profits. Third, in order to maximize impact production in a respective country, government ought to subsidize impact investment through various forms. Tax credits should be put into place in order to "incentivize" investors to invest in impact, as should co-investments into private funds either directly or through legislating the creation of a "social investment wholesale bank." Furthermore, "social outcome funds" should be established to subsidize SIB outcome payments in order to motivate local governments to commission SIBs. Lastly, grants should be given to social sector organizations to increase their "investment readiness" (see below).

Taken together, proponents argue that for government to maximize its creation of social impact, it should support the creation of an SII capital market by subsidizing capital market actors and adjusting regulations in their favor. Thus, impact as an action orientation for government restricts its capacities to act regarding regulation and taxation as the act of governance is redefined in the new cooperative tie between state and financial actors.

For social sector organizations, impact orientation depends on the type of finance they receive. As contracted party in a SIB, social organizations ought to "produce" whatever is defined in the SIB contract as the outcome metric. As part of the contract, they will work closely with investors who expect them to "innovate" and continuously improve their interventions in an "agile" way. This means that "performance

[2]Source: Cabinet Office SIB Knowledge Box: https://data.gov.uk/sib_knowledge_box/manchester-city-council-children-care-sib,last updated September 26th 2017, accessed January 18th 2017.

management" systems are in place that track the achievement of outcomes and put pressure on the service providers to meet the contractually defined results (14_UKNAB_The, pp. 99–101). Within these organizations, the authority of management teams ought to be large such that the organization develops "strategic leadership" and "performance leadership" (14_UKNAB_Building, p. 139) In short, organizations are demanded to understand outcomes as their "bottom line" and import organizational templates, structures, and practices that investors perceive to be "best practice" in for-profit business.[3]

Similar demands are placed on social service providers that take on other forms of impact investments. Particularly those organizations taking on equity investments are demanded rapid growth rates in order to allow for a profitable "exit" (see section below). Yet, as organizational growth is equated with a greater reach of the products or interventions that are deemed impactful ("scale"), growth pressure is placed on all types of organizations if they are to consider themselves as having an impact. At the same time, any type of organization that can locate itself on the "impact spectrum" of social ventures may perceive itself as impact-oriented. Since SII proponents often equate finance-driven organizational growth with social impact (e.g. 10_JPMorgan, p. 68) this means that, to be impactful, social ventures must be capable of repaying a for-profit impact investment. Thus, for social service providers taking on an investment, impact orientation means a for-profit organizational growth strategy (see Chap. 6).

For foundations and grant funders, impact orientation means spending their funds as subsidies to for-profit organizations. Here, the underlying rationale is to make these organizations "investment ready" in order to allow them to rapidly and significantly "scale" their activities by taking on an impact investment. This may be achieved by taking over the "first loss piece" of financial investments, providing loan guarantees, or by setting up social venture "incubator" programs. As the amount of funds available from impact investors is theorized to far exceed the funds from foundations, this is theorized as allowing charitable foundations to "leverage" their funds and multiply the social return they generate from their philanthropic budget (see Chap. 6).

To summarize, social impact in the SII field is a set of rules that organizes a field-level action cascade, which, on the one hand, coordinates interaction patterns of a diverse group of actors. On the other hand, these rules grant investors a central position in the field as well as much higher degrees of freedom than other actors. As such, they serve investors' material interests of profit redistribution that will be described in the following section. Establishing impact orientation this way requires a transformation of action patterns of government and social service providers as they are to develop new cooperative ties with financial actors in which these frames

[3]What these outcomes are is dependent upon the specific contract. In most cases, outcomes are some form of disciplinary intervention for groups of individuals who require expensive public services. This is because the main legitimation for SIBs is the hope for future public budget reductions that gained resonance in policy with the increasing dominance of the "Treasury view" (see Chaps. 6 and 7).

are reproduced. Analytically, accepting impact orientation as argued for by SII-proponents would restrict the government's ability to regulate and tax SII actors but legitimate increased contracts with and subsidies to financial actors. For social service providers, impact orientation means forming SIB contracts with investors and forging organizational growth through for-profit investments. Together, this means that the financialization perspective developed here allows us to uncover the field-level relationality engrained in the concept of social impact. The following section will show how impact investors capitalize on this relationality by redistributing monetary flows towards themselves.

5.3 Social Impact Investing and Redistribution

As discussed in Chap. 3, financialization is a process that materially benefits financial at the expense of many nonfinancial actors. There are multiple forms of redistribution associated with financialization. In SII, too, different forms of redistribution towards financial actors exist (See Fig. 5.2). Probably most striking is the case of Social Impact Bonds where financial investors claim ownership of and financial rewards for the behavioral change of individuals. As we will see below, this comes at particularly high costs for government and public organizations, and leaves relatively little material benefit to social workers and service providers, and none to those individuals who change their behavior. This section will systematically review the channels of redistribution that are established through SII. In the first segment, I describe different forms of redistribution through investors' financial intermediation. The second segment will provide an overview and quantitative analysis of government subsidies. Thereafter, I show potential avenues of investors' profits from the reorganization of private organizations' action patterns. Finally, I provide a glimpse into how investors benefit from a reduction of labor costs. Together, these segments show how the financialization of welfare advocated by SII proponents profoundly counteracts the idea of decommodification that was the rationale for the creation of the British welfare state (Esping-Andersen 1990; Polanyi 1944).

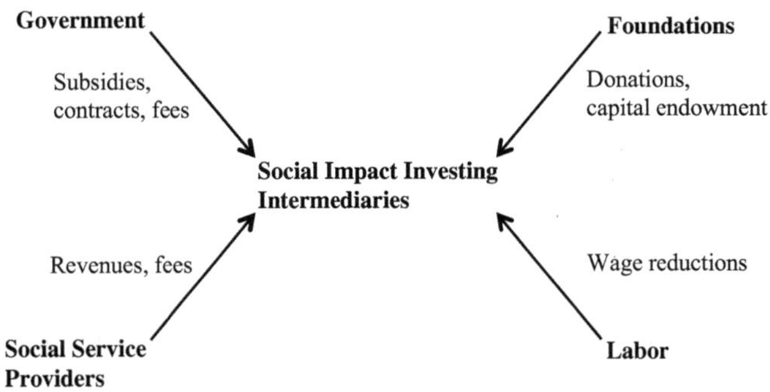

Fig. 5.2 Redistribution towards SII intermediaries

5.3.1 Financial Intermediation

The very idea of for-profit investment means that more capital is returned to the investor than initially deployed. Investors seek to "generate" financial returns with various forms of financial products that include, but are not limited to, debt and equity investments. Where investors are, like most impact investors in the UK, intermediaries, capital is returned to the asset owner after the respective financial vehicle is closed or the debt is paid back. Here, I will neglect investors' onward payments and instead describe the return-seeking activities of financial intermediary organizations as these are key to understand the establishment of financial circuits. Three principal income sources for intermediaries are frequently distinguished in the literatures on financial intermediation and financialization: fee payments, interest payments, and returns from speculation (Milberg 2008; Van der Zwan 2014). In SII, all three forms of income generation are widespread, varying across financial products and between financial intermediaries. Here, I will describe the key SII financial products, SIBs, equity, and debt investments, in more detail and point out how resources are redistributed to investors in each of the products.

Social Impact Bonds redistribute funds from public budgets to private investors. SIBs are a contract between government departments, social service providers, a SIB intermediary firm, and investors (see Fig. 5.3). For example, in the case of the Essex SIB, eight investors from the UK, Belgium, and Germany invested into a special purpose vehicle (Children's Support Services Ltd.) that contracted the intermediary firm Social Finance to manage the SIB, and the social service provider Action for Children to provide a psychotherapeutic intervention for children who were identified as being likely to be transferred into foster care homes in the future. Based on the

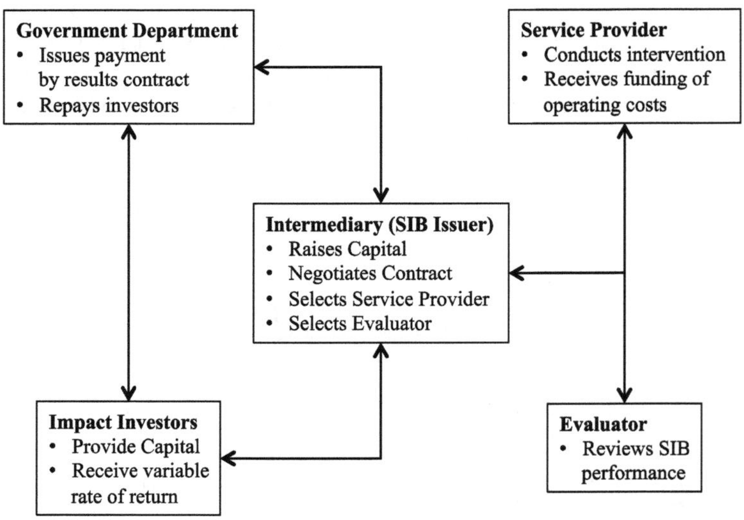

Fig. 5.3 Social Impact Bonds structure and relations

number of days that the children receiving the intervention did *not* spend in a foster home in the 30 months after the intervention, the investors received a variable "outcome payment" from the Essex County Council. In total, investors have provided an investment of £3.1 million. For this investment, they may be reimbursed with variable outcomes payments of up to £7 million, depending on the extent to which the "beneficiary" children change their behavior to avoid causing public expenses (14_SF_Prevention).

It is important to note that these public expenses take the form of "fictional expectations" (Beckert 2016), as they are statistical projections of the time these children would likely spend in foster homes, multiplied with the "unit cost" of annual foster home care. This way, the Essex SIB is thought to "create" gross public savings of £17.3 million of which the £7 million outcome payments are deducted to yield projected savings of £10.3 million. Whether or not these "savings" *actually* accrue, e.g. through closing down public foster care facilities, is, however, not related to the SIB outcome payments.[4] Unambiguous, however, is the redistribution of up to £7 million of public funds to investors in return for their £3.1 million investment—if the children change their behavior accordingly.

In addition to the outcome payment, several other direct payments are made by government departments in order to ensure the operation of the SIB. In the case of the Essex SIB, the Departments of Health, of Work and Pensions, and the Department for Education made additional payments for setting up the SIB as well as for "evaluations." Individuals familiar with the commissioning process of the Essex SIB told me in an email conversation that the partaking investors and intermediaries were keen not to disclose the non-outcome payments they received for SIB operation. Even as the non-outcome payments are not directly related to financial intermediation, they show how public welfare budgets are redistributed towards the work of establishing a financial circuit.

A second type of SII financial products are equity investments that aim at generating a return on investment from profitable onward sales of the investee company. These products are akin to the venture capital practice of growing entrepreneurial start-up firms and have been promoted particularly strongly by British venture capitalist Sir Ronald Cohen. Equity impact investors earn revenues by purchasing shares of profit-distributing firms, using the liquidity from the investment to grow the company, and hoping to sell the shares with a profit to other investors, to the company itself, or by floating the shares on the stock market with an initial public offering (IPO). The income strategy of SII equity funds thus does not primarily focus on appropriating investee revenues, but rather on achieving a high share price in the onward sale of the firm. This may, however, include interventions into the organizational structure that favor investors' material interests as the firm's profitability may be used as an argument to support a higher share price. In many

[4]Source: Cabinet Office SIB Knowledge Box: https://data.gov.uk/sib_knowledge_box/essex-county-council-children-risk-going-care, last updated September 26th 2017, accessed September 12th 2017.

cases, impact investors set up "incubator" programs that provide a stipend to founders of social ventures in exchange for an equity stake in the to-be-founded company.

A case example is the fitness company The Gym that has been "incubated" by Bridges Ventures. The social impact ascribed to the company is to provide health services to "underserved" (i.e. poor) customers (13_Bridges_10, p. 115). To do so, the company is offering an "affordable" subscription model for fitness centers that are predominantly located in geographic areas with low median incomes ("highly accessible"). To maintain low membership fees and corporate profitability, Bridges Ventures has used "investment in a robust IT platform" to "significantly cut operational spend" and notes that "The Gym does not have any membership or administration staff and its website generates all its reporting." (15_Bridges_10, p. 116). Thus, the company gains revenues by transforming low-income individuals into customers, and seeks to increase profits by reducing labor costs. This is furthermore highlighted by the statement that The Gym "is providing employment to around 200 full-time employees and contracts with more than 550 self-employed personal trainers"[5] –the shift from salaried employees to self-employment contracts being a common strategy to minimize labor expenses, such as employer contributions to social security. Having financed the growth of the company from 2007 to 2013, Bridges Ventures sold a significant part of its shares to Phoenix Equity Partners in 2013 but retaining an equity ownership of 25%. In 2015, The Gym has been listed at the London Stock Exchange, yielding a stock market valuation of £250 million, or approximately six times the cumulative investment committed by Bridges Ventures. Bridges Ventures furthermore indicated to retain a "significant minority stake" into The Gym, thereby receiving dividends from the company's profits.[6]

The investment into The Gym is one of many of the Sustainable Growth Funds investment vehicle of Bridges Ventures. To date, this vehicle is comprised of three funds, of which the latest has a volume of £125 million. The target companies of the fund are described as the following:

> We typically invest £2m–£20m in businesses pursuing organic growth, buy and build and multi-site roll out strategies across any of our impact themes. In particular:
>
> - Growth businesses, typically with revenues of £5m to £50m, run by strong management teams and looking for investment to fund further growth, change of ownership (MBOs/MBIs) or an acquisition strategy
> - Earlier stage businesses targeting a large addressable market that have already achieved sales traction, requiring investment to scale[7]

[5]Source: Bridges Ventures press release, 2015: http://www.bridgesfundmanagement.com/the-gym-completes-250m-london-listing-further-proof-that-commercial-growth-and-social-impact-can-go-hand-in-hand/, November 9th 2015, accessed February 7th 2017.

[6]*ibid.*

[7]Source: Bridges Ventures website: http://www.bridgesfundmanagement.com/for-investors/bridges-sustainable-growth-funds/, accessed February 7th 2017.

Here, social impact is used as an "investment theme" by which potential investee ventures are selected—but the primary decision-making criteria remain based on profit and risk. This way, Bridges Ventures has successfully sold 10 companies, yielding profits of 1.6 to 22 times the investment sum (i.e. a return of 60% to 2,100%).[8] How exactly the investment returns are distributed is a matter of confidentiality. However, given the organizational structure as a partnership and the venture capital socialization of its founder Sir Ronald Cohen, it is likely to assume that Bridges Ventures is structured similarly to venture capital funds. This would mean that Bridges Ventures will receive a management fee ("carried interest", an annual fee of usually around 2% of the assets under management) as well as a fixed percentage of profits beyond a certain hurdle ("hurdle rate", usually around 20% of profits if these exceed an annual 5–8% return on equity). This income is used to cover salaries and expenses, while all remaining profits are split among the partners of the fund vehicle (Bridges Ventures currently employs a total of 16 partners across all of its funds[9]). The remainder of the profits is transferred to the asset owners, in the case of Bridges a large and highly diverse set of British and international investors that ranges from wealthy individuals to large pension funds.

Besides SIBs and equity investments, debt is a third financial product in impact investing. In SII, debt is used in a vast variety of ways that are impossible to describe in full detail here. For example, SII debt investments include: loans to financial intermediaries or funds-of-funds structures, corporate bonds, "leverage" in equity-based transactions, mortgages to social organizations that are limited in their profit distribution such as social enterprises and charities, consumer credit, and microfinance (see e.g. JP Morgan 2014). Historically, debt was the first financial product in SII, while equity and SIB products emerged much later. As I have argued above, SII emerged out of specialized lending to community enterprises. Here, a group of community finance challengers around venture capitalist Sir Ronald Cohen began to argue for a need to create equity products for social ventures, too. While this story will take up much of Chap. 7, here I will only note that one of equity proponents' key justifications was that "[i]t is not practical to saddle very early stage organisations with debt, which can also change the incentives around how they innovate, nor for small charities that are in precarious financial positions already, where debt at this stage can bring undue risk of collapse" (14_UKNAB_The, p. 149).

The argument that SII equity products are required in order to relieve social organizations from the pressures of debt is, however, starkly contrasted by the empirical reality. Returning to the case example of The Gym cited above, it seems more appropriate to conclude that equity investors are indeed "saddling" early stage organizations with debt. In the year before its IPO, The Gym was earning a revenue of £45 million that yielded a loss of £8.8 million. At the same time, The Gym held

[8]*Ibid.*

[9]Source: Bridges Ventures website: http://www.bridgesfundmanagement.com/us/our-team/, accessed February 7th 2017.

debt of around £70 million while Bridges Ventures had cumulatively invested around £42 million into the company yielding a debt-to-equity ratio of at least 160%.[10] Such high levels of debt aid the material wealth of equity investors since the debt capital can be used to grow the company (and hence increase potential stock-market valuation) without reducing the owners' equity stake. However, given relatively low incomes during the growth phase, debt levels such as these would pose a serious threat to organizational survival. One way to relieve a company of its debt while still allowing equity investors to benefit from a high leverage ratio is to aim for a rapid IPO. This way, proceeds from the IPO may be used to repay corporate debt. Indeed, this has been the case at The Gym, where £54 million of its £90 million IPO proceeds have been used to repay its pre-IPO debt (15_TheGym_Financial, p. 27).

Taken together, the diversity of financial products in SII paints a picture similar to the low degree of standardization in impact assessment metrics and the lack of their enforcement described above. In SII, financial actors have considerable degrees of freedom in how to earn returns on their investment, e.g. from a redistribution of tax revenues, an appropriation of corporate revenues and individual incomes, or the realization of speculative gains. Thus, regarding the redistribution of economic resources towards financial actors and the activities of financial intermediation, impact investing does not seem to be in any way less redistributive than "mainstream" investment. This is mirrored by the fact that in a recent survey conducted by JP Morgan, 77% of impact investors indicated to pursue either "competitive, market rate returns" or financial returns slightly below "market rate" (14_JPMorgan_Spotlight, p. 5).

The strong similarities between impact investors and "conventional" financial actors in how they earn revenues is furthermore underlined by the fact that both actor types earn not only from the provision of capital, but furthermore by charging fees for other services. For example, fees are charged in the process of a "community takeover" of public assets and public services following the 2012 Localism Act. In this regard, SII firms may offer share issuing or underwriting services to social enterprises (14_BSC_Communities). That said, fees from these activities appear to be marginal to date: for example, in 2015, Big Society Capital has received a total of £30,000 in fees while having spent £127 million on investment (15_BSC_Financial, p. 15).

However, investors may also earn fees from activities related to the three main financial products described above. In the case of SIBs, these are management fees for the SIB contract. In the case of investment funds these are fees for capital management (including the carry und hurdle fees described above). For example, in 2015, Big Society Capital has paid £2.7 million in management fees to SII

[10]Exact figures of the Bridges Ventures equity investment are not available. However, as the company has, as cited above, indicated that the £250 million stock market valuation represents six times the cumulative investment, it seems reasonable to assume £42 million as an upper limit of the equity investment. It seems equally reasonable to assume that The Gym has repaid parts of its debt prior to 2014, which is why £70 million are a lower limit of the firm's indebtedness.

intermediaries (15_BSC_Financial, p. 15). In equity investments, impact investors may also impose board members on the investee firms and charge fees for doing so. For example, Bridges Ventures has received an annual fee of £30,000 for the appointment of one non-executive director at The Gym (15_TheGym_Financial, pp. 51–52).

Although most impact investors are private firms, a number of exceptions exists. Globally, public and multilateral development banks form the most important exception. Indeed, according to a JP Morgan survey, 42% of all global SII assets are held by public development banks (JP Morgan 2014). In the UK, two important exceptions exist apart from development banks. The first are public and quasi-public funds such as futurebuilders, Adventure Capital, Social Investment Business, Big Lottery Fund or the Investment and Contract Readiness Fund that provide grants and/or loans to social organizations. The second exception is the "social investment wholesale bank" Big Society Capital. Although SII proponents sometimes classify these organizations as SII funds (see e.g. 07_CUA), I will discuss these separately in the segment dealing with public subsidies. This is because these organizations use public or publicly mandated funds to enhance the return/risk ratio for private impact investments.

Taken together, this segment has shown that impact investors deploy various strategies to earn income from investment and other related activities. In SII, financial redistribution is performed through very similar, if not equal ways to "conventional" financial markets. But what then distinguishes SII from mainstream financial intermediation? Proponents would argue that it is the "mobilization" of large amounts of capital to the "solution of entrenched social problems"—whether or not this is the case, this glimpse into redistributive practices of impact investors has shown that in SII, only those "solutions" will receive financial resources that are able to provide investors with their expected financial returns. This point cannot be overstressed: as we will see throughout this work, impact investors repeatedly make substantial and specific prescriptions for actors including governments, social organizations and philanthropic donors. For investors and asset owners, however, virtually no prescriptions are made (except a commitment to some form of impact measurement), particularly not regarding return expectations.[11] As I will argue throughout this book, *this* is precisely what distinguishes SII from "mainstream" investment: the creation of a field in which a variety of actors begins to act as to enable, support, and maintain investors' return expectations.

---

[11]Note that in the case of investments into the French "social and solidarity economy", investment returns are legally capped at 2% p.a. (Chiapello and Godefroy 2017), but this is not the case in the UK.

5.3.2 *Capital Mobilization and Public Subsidies*

SII proponents frequently argue that SII has the potential to solve "entrenched social problems" by "mobilizing" vast pools of private capital for social issues. This claim is, however, starkly contrasted by the empirical reality. In 2014, UK SIFIs invested a total of £168.4 million.[12] By contrast, the British central government alone has spent over £1.3 billion[13] in direct and indirect subsidies for SII between 2000 and 2016—subsidies from the devolved administrations and city councils are not included, nor are salaries of involved public servants and management fees paid to fund managers administering parts of these subsidies. My analysis has identified three main types of public subsidies for SII. The first type, direct support for various types of impact investors, totals to date around £560 million. Second, central government has subsidized Social Impact Bonds to date with at least £200 million. Third, various types of social businesses have received "capacity building" and "investment readiness" support of around £587 million. A full list of all subsidies that I found in the analyzed materials can be found in Appendix B, and an overview of dynamics in these subsidies in Fig. 5.4.

SII has received public support through direct and indirect subsidies aimed at investments and financial intermediaries. The creation of Big Society Capital (BSC)

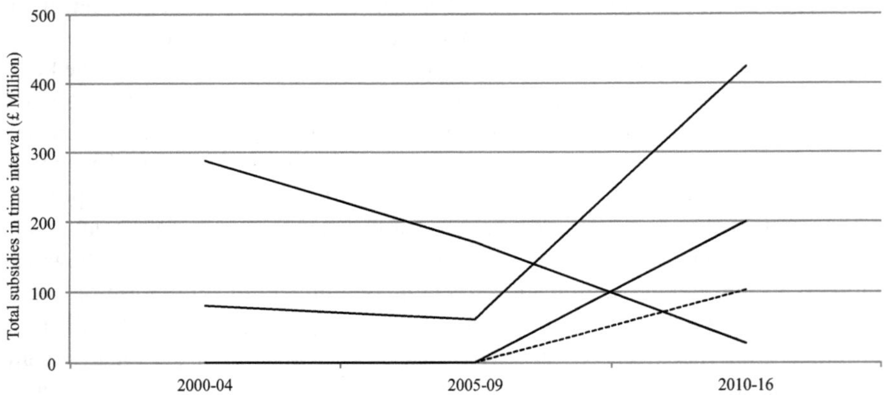

Fig. 5.4 Accumulated central government subsidies to SII actors (direct and indirect)

---

[12]Source: Cabinet Office, SIFI Report, July 2016, p. 11: https://www.gov.uk/government/uploads/system/uploads/attachment_data/file/535068/rr923-growing-the-social-investment-market-update-on-sifi-social-investment.pdf, accessed February 8th 2017.

[13]Not adjusted for inflation.

represents by far the largest single subsidy for financial intermediaries. Although the approximately £400 million[14] transferred to BSC as share capital through the Unclaimed Assets mechanism are not technically publicly owned but "unclaimed" funds on private bank accounts that have not been used for at least 15 years, they may be counted as public subsidies because they have been transferred via legislation and governmental decision-making. BSC is a private organization that is legally required to invest exclusively into SII intermediaries, while only one of its eight directors is a government representative. BSC is majority-owned by the Big Society Trust (60% of the shares and 80% of the voting rights), while a minority ownership with reduced voting rights has been granted to four banks (Barclays, Lloyds Banking Group, HSBC, Royal Bank of Scotland) in exchange for an additional investment of £50 million each (15_BSC_Financial, pp. 2–3). While the Big Society Trust is obliged to reinvest dividends into BSC, up to 40% of BSC's profits may be distributed to the shareholding banks. BSC is not obliged to pay interest, fees, or distribute dividends on the capital received through the Unclaimed Assets mechanism. But as all of this "free" capital is directly invested into SII intermediaries, BSC directly supports impact investors' financial return generation. Since inception, BSC incurs financial losses (around £7 million in 2015 alone, 15_BSC_Financial, p. 12) that are covered through the unclaimed assets capital. If, however, BSC's organizational survival were solely dependent on its financial return generation (and its fundraising dependent on other investors' risk and return estimation of an investment into BSC), higher risk premiums charged from impact investors would have been very likely. Thus, BSC has similar effects on SII as have other public subsidies.

There are three other types of public subsidies that directly affect impact investors' financial returns: tax reliefs, co-investments, and direct financial support. For impact investments, two tax reliefs have been made available to investors: Community Investment Tax Relief (CITR), and Social Investment Tax Relief (SITR). The former allows investors to annually deduct, for 5 years, 5% of the total investment sum from their income tax payables—if the investments are made into intermediaries classified as Community Development Financial Intermediaries by HM Treasury. CITR is available to both individuals and companies.[15] As CITR is based on the overall investment sum, it allows investors a guaranteed annual rate of return of 5% over 5 years—if their income tax receipt exceeds this sum. The Social Investment Tax Relief allows individual and corporate investors a 30% reduction of income tax, as well as an exemption from capital gains tax for impact investments.[16] In both

[14]As of December 31st 2015, £357 million of the pledged £400 million had been transferred to BSC as share capital (15_BSC_Financial, p. 14).

[15]Source: Cabinet Office, Guidance: Community Investment Tax Relief (CITR), 2014: https://www.gov.uk/government/publications/community-investment-tax-relief-citr/community-investment-tax-relief-citr, last updated April 16th 2018, accessed February 10th 2017.

[16]Source: Cabinet Office, Guidance: Social investment tax relief, 2014: https://www.gov.uk/government/publications/social-investment-tax-relief-factsheet/social-investment-tax-relief, last updated November 23rd 2016, accessed February 10th 2017.

cases, however, the overall level of subsidies per investor is limited due to EU State Aid rules.

Over the full observation period, central government has frequently co-invested into private impact investment funds, or provided guarantees or subsidized loans to other SII intermediaries. In total, approximately £140 million have been made available with these two forms of direct support for financial intermediaries. In the case of direct contributions to SII intermediaries, such as for example the £42 million Phoenix support program from Community Development Financial Intermediaries, the relationship between government support and investors' return is direct: particularly in the case of grants, public subsidies may be used to cover expenses and thereby increase the residual earnings available to stockholders. In the case of co-investments, a direct relationship holds only for subsidized investments. This is, however, frequently the case: for example, in the £20 million co-investment into Bridges Ventures' community development fund, government provided subordinated debt (i.e. taking over a greater share of the financial risk) that was furthermore capped in terms of profit distribution (03_SITF, p. 6).

The second type of redistribution from tax funds to impact investors are central government funds for the set-up, operation and financial reimbursement of Social Impact Bonds. Thus far, approximately £200 million have been committed to these kinds of funds. This is, however, only an imperfect measure of the direct redistribution from state to finance for two reasons. First, some of these funds are used to cover operational expenses of social service provision and are therefore not distributed towards financial actors. Second, however, the overall volume of all 32 SIBs currently commissioned in the UK is higher, as local councils often provide the majority of SIB funding. But despite the limitation regarding the overall volume, the redistributive process from state to finance in SIBs is unambiguous. In the segment above, I have already described the case of the Essex SIB, where investors may receive up to £7 million in return for a £3.1 million SIB investment. An even higher level of redistribution can be seen in the SIBs commissioned via the DWP Innovation Fund. This fund pays investors up to £28.4 million in outcomes payments in return for a "mobilization" of £10 million in private investments for a duration of 3 years.[17] The exact level of redistribution from state to finance in SIBs is difficult to calculate due to the lack of available data. However, we may estimate that of the £28.4 million, not more than the original investment sum will be paid for social service provision, as the investment sum is to fully cover service provision and operational cost. Therefore, a financial return of up to £8.4 million may be paid to investors, in addition to a repayment of capital and operational expenses. While public expenditure on SIBs is real, savings to public budgets are often fictional, as such savings would require a reduction in public service delivery that is often grounded in other decision-making processes. Taken together, SIBs directly

[17] Source: Cabinet Office, Guidance: Social Impact Bonds, 2016: https://data.gov.uk/sib_knowledge_box/department-work-and-pensions-innovation-fund, last updated September 26th 2017, accessed February 10th 2017.

translate public funds into financial assets and are therefore the clearest example of how the redistribution of public funds to impact investors enables and sustains their creation of a financial return.

The last type of subsidies for SII is the most indirect one: grants made to social enterprises and social ventures for "capacity building." Over the observation period, at least £587 million have been spent—in most cases as non-repayable grants—by central government departments in this regard. While some of these funds, such as futurebuilders (which was the only program offering a substantial percentage of funds in loans), focused mostly on "capacity development" for social enterprises aiming to bid for large public service delivery contracts, in many other cases funds aimed specifically at increasing social ventures' "investment readiness." A clear trend in the objectives of these types of funds emerged: earlier funds, such as the £100 million endowment to set up the social enterprise support organization UnLtd. aimed at establishing the concept of "social enterprise" in the social services and poor geographic areas. Later funds, particularly after the 2010 change of government, have more clearly focused on "preparing" social organizations to take on an impact investment. This was often accompanied by a shift from targeting social enterprises with restricted profit distribution to social ventures with fewer limits on profit distribution. In both cases, capacity development grants support investors' financial return generation—if the grant-receiving social enterprise/venture subsequently raises a financial investment. If this is the case, then grant income may directly increase the residual profits distributable to investors, as well as indirectly reduce the investment default risk. This is particularly the case for "investment readiness" grants that are designed to establish organizational strategies and management practices mirroring investors' interests.

Apart from the three types of monetary subsidies, other government actions have supported impact investors' creation of financial returns. For example, in 2004, the creation of the Community Interest Company (CIC) as a legal form has allowed investors to extract up to 35% of social organizations' annual profits. While initially, other limits on profit extraction had been in place, such as a limit on dividends per share and interest payments, these have, following consultations between the CIC Regulator and impact investors, been either completely abolished or significantly weakened.[18] Investors may furthermore benefit from the 2012 Localism Act. With the "Right to Bid" and the "Right to Challenge", this act has given community organizations (including some forms of profit-distributing companies) far-reaching opportunities that may be exploited by impact investors. With the "Right to Bid", community organizations may bid to "take over" (i.e. privatize) public assets. Here, investors may earn financial returns, for example, by lending to these organizations. With the "Right to Challenge", private actors may challenge the provision of virtually any public service to enter compulsive competitive tendering. If a private

[18]Source: Department of Business, Innovation, and Skills, Consultation outcome: Consultation on the dividend and interest caps, 2013: https://www.gov.uk/government/consultations/consultation-on-the-dividend-and-interest-caps, last updated December 10th 2013, accessed February 10th 2017.

organization wins the tender (e.g. by reducing labor costs compared to public servants), the respective public service has to be delivered by the private organization. Here, investors may earn financial returns from the tax revenues appropriated by the social organization in return for service delivery. For example, Big Society Capital has invested £1 million into "DERiC" which aims at earning a profit by "using community-owned social capital (volunteers)" in the delivery of public services (15_BSC_Comm, p. 14).

As this segment has shown, impact investors have significantly benefitted from various forms of public subsidies far exceeding £1 billion in the period between 2000 and 2016. The overall level of public subsidies for SII provides strong evidence for the claim that SII entails the creation of a financialized field in which various actors orient their actions towards each other in a form that allows investors the redistribution of financial resources towards themselves and asset owners.[19]

5.3.3 Private Subsidies

From the perspective of SII, positive social impact is a direct result of the size of the "impact delivery organization" which is expected to finance its growth through the use of impact investments. In proponents' discourse, other forms of organizing either do not exist, or are described as "barriers" to the growth of SII. In this context, non-repayable grants are a particularly important object of contest: redefining the legitimate role of grants to serving the financial interests of impact investors is a central pillar of SII proponents' strategic framing that will be discussed in great detail in the next chapter. For now, it is sufficient to note that grants as a form of continuous organizational income either do not exist in SII proponents' discourse, or are valued negatively as "grant dependence" thought to be reducing entrepreneurial growth of an organization. Likewise, grant-financed organizations are perceived as a threat to investment-financed social ventures as "grant-funded enterprises are able to under-price competing social enterprises attempting to operate sustainably" (15_BSC_Education, p. 100). Moreover, grants are a threat to investors' business model as they are "cheaper" for the social organization and hence represent competition to investments:

> Grant funding is plainly more attractive to the investee than repayable finance, and the very best enterprises will be exactly the ones that are most able to access grant funding. [. . .] [It] is not surprising that many of the best social enterprises are finding sufficient access to grant funding to meet their growth plans. There is a danger that social investors suffer from a selection bias problem, unable to invest in the best enterprises. (13_Young, p. 281)

[19]This is not unknown to actors in the field. A former civil servant noted: "What is that SOCIAL investment, if it's dominated by the hand of government? [. . .] [P]ouring hundreds of millions of pounds into this market, that's government-backed money, but then giving it a label of Social Investment, [. . .] that's kind of lying really, that's not really social investment, that's public investment"(E: 39:46).

The fact that the availability of grants is a serious threat to impact investors' organizational survival has led investors to oppose the role of grants in forms that are harmful to their businesses. To an increasing extent, they have been successful in convincing policymakers of their perspective. For example, a senior civil servant noted on the creation of BSC that "this social investment bank shouldn't invest directly in social enterprises, it should work at the wholesale level, because there were existing organizations that were investing and it should strengthen them rather than effectively displacing them" (D: 16:00). Thus, policymakers shared SII proponents' view regarding public grants as a challenge to SII intermediaries.

But while investors are capable of affecting the availability of public grants to the extent that they form a cooperative tie with government actors, this is somewhat more difficult to achieve with private grants and donations, as a vast number of private donors exist. In the case of private donations, investors have therefore distinguished between legitimate and illegitimate donations, where the former aid their material interests.[20] Two forms of grants are considered legitimate by SII proponents. First are grants that aim at increasing the "investment readiness" of social ventures. These grants can be used to "buy support from specialist experts and advisors" that provide the investee with financial tools, skills and knowledge on how to "scale up" the organization using for-profit impact investments (14_BLF, p. 90).

> Grants to support the development of business plans and capacity building are necessary in order to ensure that organisations have the confidence and professional capability to access and support repayable finance. (07_CUA, p. 161)

Grants may furthermore be used to finance the earliest stages in the investees' organizational "life-cycle", such as concept and business plan development. In these early stages, organizational incomes are low while failure rates are high. This is why SII proponents argue for charitable donations to be made in these very early stages (see 09_Monitor).

The second form of grants advocated for by SII proponents are contractually linked to a for-profit impact investment. In these cases, grants may for example be used to pay for expenses that are not directly linked with income generation: "There is a strong case to be made for grant support from foundations and/or government to help organisations build up the capacity to measure their impact" (14_G8NAB, p. 30). But grants may also be linked more directly to an investments' return/risk profile: legitimate forms of grants can be used as credit default guarantees in debt investments, as "catalytic first loss capital" purchasing higher risk tranches from impact funds, or as other means to "de-risk the profile for investors" (15_BSC_Communities, p. 11).

> Philanthropy can also use grants to provide risk reduction insurance for financing terms, such as flexibility on the repayment dates of loans, that can help impact delivery organisations attract impact investment or, indeed, mainstream commercial funding. The Gates

[20] I do not make any claims regarding SII proponents' motivation: the argument is solely *that* non-repayable grants pose a threat to impact investors' organizational survival. Inasmuch this direct competition between grants and investment is mitigated, this threat is reduced.

> Foundation has made several interesting moves in this area, such as providing mortgage guarantees to charter schools buying their buildings. (14_G8NAB, p. 23)

Despite granting legitimacy to these two forms of non-repayable grants, SII proponents are clear that grants may only play a role subordinate to for-profit investments. Furthermore, they remain skeptical of non-repayable funds in general and appear to be afraid of a potential loss of capitalist work ethic in grant-receiving organizations:

> Funding of investment readiness through grants should be provided with great caution, with appropriate funding mix, in collaboration with investors, to ensure commitment maximises entrepreneurial potential of the grantee (12_ClearlySo, p. 21)

These two forms of grants are provided particularly by new philanthropic organizations that have emerged during the observation period. In the UK, these include Impetus-Private Equity Foundation, which has been created in 2013 as a merger of Impetus Trust (founded in 2002) and Private Equity Foundation (founded in 2006), as well as Venturesome, a subsidiary of Charities Aid Foundation, founded in 2002. Globally, foundations set up with endowments of Silicon Valley and technology entrepreneurs, such as Omidyar Network or the Bill and Melinda Gates Foundation apply a similar approach, as are numerous corporate foundations such as Shell Foundation, or BMW Foundation. Some of these actors offer "incubator" programs that select "scalable" social ventures, provide them with early stage grant funding and, later, for-profit impact investments. Additionally, some established British foundations such as the Young Foundation and the Esmée Fairbarn Foundation are increasingly deploying grants for these forms. Moreover, these foundations increasingly invest parts of their endowment into SII.

Taken together, this segment has shown that the creation of the SII field comes with a redefinition of the role of grants and donations such that they are deployed in a way to enable, sustain and increase impact investors' pursuit of a financial return. The redistributive consequences of this new role structure are similar to the transformations in public action described above. However, due to a lack of publicly available data, I was unable to estimate the magnitude of these effects.

5.3.4 Labor and Redistribution

As discussed in Chap. 3, financialization processes are often associated with a redistribution from labor to financial actors and financial capital. In the case of SII, two forms of labor-related redistribution are particularly salient: surplus appropriation via small financial elites (Godechot 2015), and redistribution from non-financial work to financial actors (Lin and Tomaskovic-Devey 2013) that takes various direct and indirect forms.

In addition to the case of surplus appropriation by financial intermediaries that has been described above, SII aims at establishing financialized corporate management practices that have been found to be particularly beneficial to corporate executives

(Fligstein 1990). The case of The Gym, which has already been described in previous segments, serves as a case in point here. According to its financial report, the CEO showed a 26.8% benefits increase in the year of the firm's IPO, while other staff gained an average of 3.9% (15_TheGym_Financial, p. 53). The CEO compensation at The Gym is comprised of a fixed salary, a short-term, and a long-term bonus. According to the financial report, the CEO's salary grew by 11%, while no short-term bonus change was indicated. This means that the largest change in CEO payment in the year of the IPO has come from equity-based, long-term bonus payments in relation to the IPO. In fact, these payments are described in the remuneration committee statement as the "long-term incentives" of a pre-IPO "Private equity-backed pay practice" that represent the "[p]otentially most valuable element of the [pay] package. Large 'one-off' equity-based awards granted, linked to a successful exit event" (p. 43). This practice has expanded to the firm's senior management team, thereby taking up a significant percentage of the firm's IPO proceeds.

The redistribution from labor to capital in impact investing is often entangled with the concept of social impact. Here, employment, but not necessarily sufficient salaries, are described as a form of social impact. This is particularly true for "beneficiary" populations such as prisoners or long-term unemployed individuals: here, SII proponents often negatively value the provision of social services, such as professional training, as an "output" measure that not necessarily translates into a positive "social impact." Against this backdrop, SII proponents argue that an individual's "distance travelled" along the "pathway towards employment" represents a more adequate measure of the value, or impact, that social services create. Therefore, they argue, placing beneficiaries into positions of unpaid labor—or "sustained volunteering"—will be a more appropriate means towards creating large-scale social impact:

> The best measure for employment readiness is sustained part time or voluntary work rather than the completion of training courses (which is an output rather than an outcome). This metric would pay for achievement of sustained part time or voluntary work. [. . .] [I]t is appropriate to incentivise the journey towards employment in order to drive education, training, interview preparation and voluntary work so that service users (and service providers) focus on the end goal of finding sustained employment. (12_SF_Enabling, p. 30)

One important institutional transformation that has allowed for a larger-scale redistribution from labor to capital via SII in the case of public services has been the Localism Act. As it allowed for community organizations to force a competitive tender on social service provision, services run by unpaid "volunteers" may have good chances to winning the tendered contracts. That impact investors seize this opportunity is exemplified by Big Society capital, which has invested "£1.05 million to Developing and Empowering Resources in Communities CIC (DERiC) which provides finance for community-owned social enterprises that will use community-generated social capital (volunteers) to improve local services" (15_BSC_Communities, p. 14). As in some Social Impact Bonds placement of "beneficiaries" into "sustained volunteering" positions serves as a contractualized outcome that triggers financial payments to investors,[21] an ecology of organizations benefitting from labor-to-capital redistribution in social welfare may emerge.

A similar two-stage redistributive process can be observed with apprenticeships, which count for SII proponents as a second "pathway towards employment." Like in the case of volunteering, here, impact investors profit from low labor expenses as apprentices often receive lower salaries than other full-time employees. The for-profit firm K10 is a telling example in this regard. K10 offers up to 400 apprenticeships in London's construction industry, especially for unemployed people. K10 has won the 2011 "Big Venture Challenge" run by the National Lottery by showcasing the delivery of "social impact at scale." The growth of K10 has been financed by impact investors: The £36 million for-profit fund "Impact Ventures UK", a Luxemburg-based funds vehicle with investments from BSC, Deutsche Bank, Liechtenstein bank LGT, and others,[22] has given a £600,000 loan to K10 in February 2014. In September 2016, K10 has raised another £500,000 from a consortium of impact investors, and will use parts of these funds to repay the Impact Ventures loan and grow the organization.[23] Thus, Impact Ventures and its asset owners have been able to generate a return on their investment into K10. Parts of this return have been created through the onward investment—another part, however, will have most likely been made by redistributing K10's income. As a provider of construction industry apprentices, K10 bills its contractors, but salaries to its income-generating apprentice workforce are between £145 and £170 per week.[24] By comparison, the Living Wage Foundation defines the London living wage at £9.40 per hour,[25] or £376 for a 40-hour week. Thus, at least parts of the impact investors' returns are generated by exploiting K10's suppression of labor expenses. Impact investors may furthermore earn financial revenues from placing beneficiaries into such apprenticeships via Social Impact Bonds. For example, some of the DWP Innovation Funds SIBs pay financial rewards to investors if they succeed to place unemployed individuals into apprenticeship programs.[26]

More generally, Social Impact Bonds elicit labor-related redistribution in two regards. First, in order to create actual savings to the public budget, the hypothetical

[21]For example, the Greater London Authority SIB aimed at reducing numbers of homelessness. Here, outcome payments to investors are made if, among other criteria, a homeless person participating in the SIB program has sustained a "volunteering" position. The other criteria include, for example, the homeless person leaving the UK, in case of alien citizenship. Source: Cabinet Office, Guidance: Social Impact Bonds, 2012: https://data.gov.uk/sib_knowledge_box/greater-london-authority-homelessness, last updated: September 26th 2017, accessed February 16th 2017.

[22]Source: Impact Ventures UK, http://www.impactventuresuk.com/wp-content/uploads/2015/03/IVUK-final-close_FINAL_27-Feb-2015-3.pdf, accessed February 17th 2017.

[23]*ibid.*

[24]Source: K 10, https://www.k-10.co.uk/apprentices, accessed June 1st 2016.

[25]Source: Living Wage Foundation, www.livingwage.org.uk/calculation, accessed June 1st 2016.

[26]Source: Cabinet Office, Guidance: Social Impact Bounds, https://data.gov.uk/sib_knowledge_box/department-work-and-pensions-innovation-fund, last updated September 26th 2017, accessed February 17th 2017.

savings that SIBs produce would need to be "cashed-in".[27] Since SIBs usually affect the public delivery of social services that are often very labor-intensive, these savings, such as the closure of foster care homes will reduce public labor expenses. Second, although SIBs pay for labor-intensive social interventions, the success payments are recuperated by financial actors. In a report by management consulting firm McKinsey explicating the principle of SIBs, social service providers would receive a $0.4 million "success fee" if the SIB hit its target outcomes, while investors would receive a $3.7 million financial return, in addition to the $15.9 million repayment of operating costs (12_McKinsey, p. 50).

To conclude, there are various forms of labor-related redistribution elicited by SII. For scholars of political economy, the concept of relabeling unpaid work as a solution to poverty, as is the case in the SIB concepts of "sustained volunteering" and "employability" might sound familiar. In both, its redistributive consequences and its legitimatory accounts, this concept strikingly resembles the Elizabethan and Speenhamland "Poor Laws" described by Karl Polanyi (1944, Ch. 7).

[27]Indeed, SIB providers such as Social Finance have developed tool-kits to ensure the actual "cashability" of the SIB's hypothetical savings (14_SF_Prevention).

Chapter 6
Financialization as Welfare

> *This new approach is built on a number of shared beliefs: that, in some cases, investment can be more effective than donations in helping the poor; that social motivations harnessed to financial ones can sometimes do good more effectively; and that in many situations there is no inevitable trade-off between financial and social return.*
> *(14_G8NAB_Invisible, p. 4)*

In the previous chapter, I have applied the method of abductive analysis to make the point that social impact investing in the UK can be understood as a process of financialization. Earlier, I have argued that we may fruitfully understand financialization as a field-level social process that transforms social relations between actors, such that financial intermediaries gain a central position in the field and benefit materially from these changes. Applying strategic action fields theory (Fligstein and McAdam 2012), I have argued that the emergence and trajectories of financialization processes can be better understood as successful attempts to mobilize a heterogeneous group of actors to interact according to a novel frame, rather than as the outcome of macro-institutional configurations. However, I have argued that albeit SAF theory is well equipped to explain processes of openly oppositional mobilization, this is much less the case for the emergence of cooperative cross-field ties. But for financialization processes, these cooperative ties are of primary concern—particularly with regards to the interaction between state and financial fields.

The next chapter addresses the question regarding the formation of cooperative ties by showing how policymakers came to accept propositions made by financial actors inasmuch these were interpreted as solutions to problem situations policymakers found themselves confronted with. This chapter, however, serves as the central link between the previous argument that SII can be understood as a financialization process and the question regarding the emergence of cooperative ties. To do so, I will describe in great detail the field-level strategic action frame that SII proponents use to mobilize support from nonfinancial actors, such as state and social organizations, thereby eliciting the field-level financialization process. As

P. Golka, *Financialization as Welfare*,
https://doi.org/10.1007/978-3-030-06100-5_6

I will show, SII proponents' frame attempts to establish field-level financialization as a superior means to achieve social welfare. This is why I term it the *financialization as welfare* frame. With this frame in mind, the following chapter may turn to the framing and network dynamics, as well as critical turning points in order to develop through abduction a hypothesis for a causal mechanism regarding the emergence of cooperative cross-field ties.

As discussed in the theory chapter, I will build on Snow and Benford's (1988) conception of strategic action frames in order to conceptualize SII proponents' strategic action frame. Although a plethora of frame conceptions exists (Cornelissen and Werner 2014), I chose this conception not only because it has been extensively applied and scrutinized in social movement research, but also because it is used as the framing concept in SAF theory (Fligstein and McAdam 2012, p. 32). Moreover, as I will show in Chap. 8, this conception of strategic action frames chimes well with the pragmatist view on strategic action that forms the ontological basis of SAF theory and hence the to-be-developed explanatory mechanism.

The first section describes SII proponents' diagnostic framing which makes frequent reference to "entrenched social problems." As I will argue in the following chapter, these social problems grant credibility to the frame as they are imported from the ruling parties' normative discourse. The second section will describe in detail the innovative set of causes SII proponents ascribe to these problems. These theoretizations establish a link between the diagnostic and prognostic components of the frame. As these, too, often build on policy discourse, they form an integral part in the mobilization process (see Chap. 7). The third section describes SII proponents' motivational framing that serves as a call to arms for a diverse group of state and social organizations as well as charitable foundations to act according to the field-level frame. Although I spent considerable time searching for it, I have not found much evidence for a counter-movement. This is why this chapter will only describe the framing advanced by proponents while the following chapter attempts to give an explanation for this rather unilateral change trajectory.

6.1 Entrenched Social Problems

Virtually all documents in the representative sample of SII proponents' discourse analyzed attempted to legitimize the field-level frame as a superior means to solve "entrenched social problems" (e.g. 13_Schwab, p. 6). Often, SII proponents argue that these problems are "too large and too complex to be solved by government and the social sector alone" (14_G8NAB_Invisible, p. 5). Indeed, even nonfinancial actors supportive of SII seem to have accepted this claim. For example, then Prime Minister David Cameron said in a speech about SII:

> We've got a great idea here that can transform our societies, by using the power of finance to tackle the most difficult social problems. Problems that have frustrated government after government, country after country, generation after generation.[1]

In the following two segments, I will provide a constructivist perspective that understands these "social problems" as valuations (Lamont 2012) made by positioned strategic actors (Fligstein and McAdam 2012). To understand what SII proponents count and do not count as social problems, I have analyzed empirically how social problems are created in SII proponents' discourse. I found that three sets of problem descriptions are identifiable and distinguishable across financial products. These will be presented in the first segment. The second segment will shed some light on how structural and labor-related issues are omitted in these problem definitions.

6.1.1 What Counts as a Social Problem

The depth of theorizing on "social problems" varies considerably across the reports studied. Those reports that aim at legitimizing SII for a global audience, such as the G-8 report, tend to only briefly mention a set of situations valuated problematically. On the other hand, those reports aiming to advertise Social Impact Bonds to policymakers, and hence aim at creating cooperative ties with social policymakers tend to go into greater detail. There are three distinguishable social problem descriptions observable in SII proponents' discourse, one addressing individuals, and two addressing communities (see Table 6.1). The individual-centered discourse strongly

Table 6.1 SII proponents' social problem discourses, emergence and links to policy fields, and related financial products

Object	Social problem	Evaluative basis	Emergence and policy link	Financial products
Individuals	"Disadvantage"	Present or future public expenses	Since 90s: New Labour social inclusion	Social Impact Bonds
Communities (1)	Poverty	Public expenses, economic growth	Since 90s: social inclusion at treasury/PAT-3	Community lending and venture capital
Communities (2)	Disempowerment	"locally owned" public services	Since 2010s: Conservative Localism agenda	Investment banking-like, debt, equity

[1]Source: Speech by David Cameron at the launch of the G-8 Social Impact Investment Task Force on June 6th 2013, gov.uk/government/speeches/prime-ministers-speech-at-the-social-impact-investment-conference/ accessed September 12th 2017.

resembles the idea of "inclusive economic growth" propagated by the New Labour government (Lister 1998) and prominent ideas such as the "social investment welfare state" (Giddens 1998). The earlier one of the two community discourses emerged in the early 2000s and aimed at including poor neighborhoods into economic growth, thereby following the "community development" strategy propagated by HM Treasury. The later community discourse aimed at including communities into public service delivery, in accordance with the Big Society idea developed by the Cameron governments.

The individual-level social problem discourse is constructed by grouping individuals as "disadvantaged", such as "disabled people; the elderly; the financially excluded; people with addiction issues or mental health needs; homeless people; and ex-offenders" (14_BSC_Employment, p. 2). In most cases, these disadvantaged people are not so much evaluated negatively due to the consequences these conditions have on their own lives, for example by reducing their own quality of life. Rather, they are evaluated from a work-centered ethic that understands those people as excluded from labor markets, and theorizes negative consequences from this kind of exclusion:

> Unemployment carries significant costs for individuals, society and the government. Firstly, unemployed individuals often lose the skills they have previously acquired. They lose the opportunity to develop their social networks and often fail to develop or maintain a link between effort and reward. Being unable to find a job for more than twelve months can also have a significant impact on a person's confidence, well-being, employability and finances, and worsens social exclusion as existing social networks degrade (14_BSC_Employment, p. 2)

From this perspective, introducing individuals into the labor market serves as the prime means to solve social problems ranging from unequal education outcomes to crime and drug addiction. This perspective on welfare strongly resembles the concept of "social inclusion" and its related operationalization of "welfare-to-work" and "social investment welfare" that were propagated by New Labour (Lister 1998) and in large parts maintained by the Cameron administration (Seldon and Finn 2015). As a solution, SII proponents very frequently propose behavioral interventions that focus solely on labor market inclusion: "[...] education, training and employment programmes funded through a SIB mean that service users can move towards a productive new life that is free from benefits and contributes positively to society" (12_SF_Enabling, p. 5).

In the reports analyzed, these problem descriptions and valuations are used particularly frequently when SII proponents attempt to legitimize Social Impact Bonds. This finding is well in line with predictions from the framing perspective on social movements: here, scholars have argued that in order to mobilize actors towards a common goal, one necessary step is to build on a shared problem diagnosis (Benford and Snow 2000). In SIBs, the primary goal for SII intermediaries is to establish a contract with government commissioners, thus taking over the normative problem discourse advanced by government increases their success chances. Likewise, as SII proponents attempt to motivate SIB commissioning by creating an imaginary of reduced public expenses, evaluating individuals from the costs they cause to the public purse can be seen as a strategic move aimed at enhancing commissioning success.

This argument is furthermore supported by historical variation (Tavory and Timmermans 2014) within SII proponents' discourse. As I will argue in Chap. 7, introducing not-for-profit VCS organizations into public service delivery became an increasingly important public policy objective in the mid and late 2000s. As SIBs are essentially service delivery contracts with VCS organizations (although mediated by SII intermediaries and paying variable rates of returns to investors), we would expect the individual-level discourse to take the form of advocating for VCS innovations only after these developments in the policy field. Indeed, earlier individual-level SII discourse did share the normative perspective on inclusive economic growth, but rather than seeing ties with the VCS as a solution, argued for the creation of for-profit community enterprises to counteract the "culture of philanthropy, paternalism and dependence" (00_SITF) argued to be prevalent in the VCS. Moreover, government was called upon to alter the provision of benefits rather than public services:

> Public policy obstacles to entrepreneurship exist. For example, the benefits system must encourage rather than discourage claimants wishing to take the first steps out of poverty into self-employment or micro-enterprise (00_SITF, p. 14).

Indeed, these examples showcase the dynamics of SII proponents' normative problem discourse. Emerging out of the financing of for-profit community enterprises, the first diagnostic framing advanced by SII proponents was focused on poor neighborhoods ("communities"[2]). Thus, the problem SII proponents address here is poverty in geographic areas. As I will argue in Chap. 7, the creation of economic growth and a reduction of public expenditure are primary concerns at HM Treasury, particularly at that time. Thus, to mobilize policymakers' support for community development finance, early SII proponents diagnosed that poor neighborhoods had become "no-go areas for investment" (00_SITF, p. 4). The lack of private investment is described as a key factor in maintaining poverty within these communities:

> Under-invested communities suffer from a spiral of multiple disadvantage. Industries that were previously major employers have collapsed, leading to loss of employment, incomes, wealth and purchasing power. In such circumstances, it is often the case that private sector investment dries up and that even those financial resources available within a community are spent outside it. Confidence collapses and, with it, the climate for enterprise. In some poor communities, research has shown that as much as 75% of the cash in circulation may come from central and local Government. The result can be an intransigent form of welfare dependence, where the state confines its contribution to providing a minimum level of income and social services, but ignores wealth creation (00_SITF, p. 10).

---

[2]Indeed, the term community as a reference to poor geographic neighborhoods, particularly those with high levels of immigrated or ethnical minority inhabitants, was introduced with New Labour's discourse on social inclusion (Worley 2005).

Further resonating with the Treasury's view, SII proponents have argued that community development represented an area of ineffective public spending, as it did not help "mobilize" private investments into these areas:

> Public expenditure programmes have done little to increase the incomes or personal assets of the people living in these areas. Public funding has too often "compensated people for being poor" rather than helping them find ways of creating wealth. Public money comes in, through welfare, housing, public services and regeneration projects, but it leaks straight out of the area rather than fostering local markets and enterprise (00_SITF, p. 10).

Thus, they argued, a "new approach to addressing the needs of under-invested communities would help to rebuild their economic base" for example by "rising property values" and finance from CDFIs (00_SITF, p. 11). I will discuss SII proponents' prognostic and motivational frame in more detail below.

The third problem frame refers to communities in a more general sense that is not restricted to poor neighborhoods. Here, communities are represented as "disempowered" in that they have not been able to participate *as actors* in the provision of public services.

> Communities across the UK have faced a decline in government spending both nationally and locally, resulting in weakened socio-economic outcomes, as well as a general lack of empowerment to affect change. In the past, several initiatives have attempted to improve the state of communities however many of these were not community-led, nor were the solutions owned by local people. In recent years, local authorities across the country have been looking to dispose of assets, owing to changes in policy as well as the economic climate. (15_BSC_Comm, p. 3)

This problem framing has emerged subsequent to the Conservative Big Society idea that on the one hand built on a significant reduction in public expenditure overall, while on the other hand giving private "community organizations" ample opportunities to privatize the delivery of public services. This way, SII proponents circumvent a negative evaluation of Conservative austerity measures, but rather see the creation of new community organizations as an opportunity to create "local solutions to local problems." These "local solutions" are theorized to positively affect particularly those communities hit by spending cuts. This may be achieved by

> starting-up enterprises with the community's interests at heart, as well as acquiring and developing important local assets which hope to deliver sustainable revenue streams alongside social change. Examples of these range from community shops and pubs, to solar and wind projects, libraries, housing and industrial buildings. (15_BSC_Comm, p. 3)

In this context, SII is presented as a means to "empower" communities in order to allow them to operate public services via private community organizations, rather than public delivery.

> There are many challenges facing communities that want to deliver projects of this nature including a lack of time and appropriate skills within the community, lack of available finance, difficulty in developing a financially viable business model, challenges around governance, low representation of minority groups and precarious relations with local councils. (15_BSC_Comm, p. 3)

Together, this supports my hypothesis that SII proponents' discourse forms a relational, field-level frame: depending on the addressed actor, problem descriptions are changed. As we will see later, this communicative change is strategic in the sense that it is geared at forging cooperation.

6.1.2 What Does Not Count as a Social Problem

In this chapter, I advance the claim that the emergence of SII can be understood as proponents' attempt to create a financialized field by mobilizing nonfinancial actors according to their field-level strategic action frame. In the previous segment, I have shown how three descriptions of social problems can be distinguished and linked to problem discourses within social policy fields. In this segment, I aim to show that although the problematizations SII proponents advance are widely shared, they are nevertheless strategic in the sense that references that could harm the development of SII, and investors' material interests in particular, are omitted from their problem framing.

As political economy scholars of financialization have pointed out, the increasing centrality of financial intermediaries in economic fields was accompanied with increased wealth and income inequalities, as well as a reduction in structural bargaining power of labor over finance (Konings 2009; Tomaskovic-Devey and Lin 2011). Thus, I theorized that if SII does indeed represent a case of financialization, then the problem descriptions offered by its proponents would not link increased financialization, the demise of organized labor, the bifurcation of work, or other structural factors from which financial intermediaries materially benefit to the description of social problems.

To investigate this hypothesis, I performed lexical analyses for 19 structural terms in the representative sample of SII proponents' discourse. Lexical searches yielded one match for "living wage", but in a different context. The keywords, "living salary" "fair wage", "fair salary", "in-work poor", "working poor", "in-work poverty" and "casualisation", "precarisation" did not yield any matches. Two matches were found for "precarious", yet again in a different context.

Of the seven matches for "wage" only one case related pay to social impact: "The hotel played an important part in the regeneration of Shoreditch and Hackney, with 76% of The Hoxton Hotel staff living in underserved areas (to whom nearly 70% of the total wage bill accrued) and an 85% supplier-spend in the local area" (13_Bridges_10, p. 18). Here, wages paid to staff living in underserved areas were indeed presented as having a social impact—however, as noted in Chap. 5, the salary paid to those living in underserved areas was 92% of the company's average salary, while those living outside those areas received 125%. Hence, while wages per se were linked to social impact, this was not the case for income inequalities.

Lexical search for the radical "salar*" found a total of two matches, whereas only one was in the relevant context. This case was a positive description of a behavioral intervention targeted at 16 to 24 year-old school drop-outs: "[t]he salary matches what they would otherwise have received as jobseekers allowance, while being employed encourages them to have genuinely meaningful employment over the course of the programme" (13_Young, p. 28). In accordance with the individual-level problem discourse described above, SII proponents described the act of working as beneficial in its own right, while the structural dimension of pay did not form part of their normative evaluation. Of the 103 matches for "pay", none was referring to its meaning as wage or salary. The single match for "pay gap" was the following:

> Studies have also shown that an extended period of being NEET [Not in Employment, Education or Training, PG] post-education has a profound effect on life-time earnings and career prospects. A young person who is NEET for just 6-months will, by their forties, lose up to £50,000 in lifetime earnings compared with their non-graduate peers. This issue brings a significant cost to society. Research by York University estimates an average lifetime public finance cost of £56,301 for a young person who is NEET aged 16 to 1816. The resulting estimated aggregate public finance costs of 16–18 year old NEETs range from £12 billion to £32 billion. (15_BSC Education, p. 5)

Although here, inequalities arising from unemployment were evaluated negatively, the main point in this paragraph was focused on the public finance costs arising from this fact. Moreover, in the remainder of the report, this case was used as a legitimation for employment-related SIBs. The radical "inequal" was found in 13 instances, out of which two related to mentioning growing economic inequalities and 10 related to inequalities in education or health services. In one case, SII was seen as a potential driver for economic inequality: "Community asset projects could increase social inequality if owned and controlled by a group of non-representative individuals within a community" (15_BSC_Comm, p. 10). Of the 21 matches for the word "union", none referred to trade unions. Likewise, none of the 15 matches for "labour" showed any relation to structural variables. Furthermore, "bargaining" did not show any matches.

Lastly, the radical "pension*" showed 84 matches in the analyzed reports. Most of these cases referred to pension funds as potential SII investors. Two exceptions were noteworthy: in some cases, the privatization of pensions was seen as an opportunity to develop new SII financial products:

> Government policy is also increasing the emphasis on individual responsibility, particularly with regard to pensions and universal credit. This increases the risk that those with low financial capability will become further financially excluded, but also poses a significant market opportunity for services tackling financial exclusion. (14_BSC_Financial_incl, p. 6)

In other cases, pension liabilities for public servants were described as risks for the creation of community organizations aimed at privatizing public service delivery under the 2011 Localism Act (so-called "TUPE liabilities", e.g. 15_BSC_Comm, p. 9).

Together, this section has shown that SII proponents' social problem descriptions can best be conceptualized as attempts to movement organization by positioned strategic actors. On the one hand, problem descriptions of the ruling parties' normative discourse were taken over. On the other hand, problem descriptions that would reduce investors' abilities to extract and redistribute revenues from nonfinancial actors were strikingly absent in SII proponents' discourse.

6.2 Theorizing Causes: The Impact and Investment Narratives

In the previous section, I have argued that SII proponents offer three forms of social problem descriptions that strongly resemble problem descriptions within social policy fields. But while a shared problem diagnosis is a necessary first step, mobilization furthermore requires an agreement over prognostic and motivational components of strategic action frames (Snow and Benford 1988). In this section, I will show how SII proponents develop a causal account that links the two principal features of impact investing—impact orientation and private investments—to solutions for the problem descriptions described above.

6.2.1 The Under-Investment Narrative

The importance of the under-investment narrative for the success of SII proponents' attempts to mobilize nonfinancial actors can hardly be overstated. First of all, there is the rather obvious reason that what investors do is investing and hence inasmuch nonfinancial actors believe that there is a problem of under-investment, investors will inevitably be perceived as providers of solutions. For the specific case of SII, a second point was still more important. This was a crucial shift in *what* was described as under-invested. As I will show below, until around 2005, SII proponents argued that for-profit community enterprise was under-invested, while entrepreneurial behavior was *inhibited* by practices in the voluntary and community sector. Around 2006, however, they began to argue that *the VCS was under-invested*, and subsequently an alliance between key SII and VCS representatives began to develop. As I will argue in Chap. 7, this alliance fueled the development of SII and coined its current form. In particular, the emergence of the impact narrative described in the following section would have been difficult to imagine without this crucial turning point.

As described in the section above, early SII proponents described poor communities as "no-go areas for investment" and thus viewed them as "under-invested" rather than poor in the first place. They argued that in order to thrive, these communities would require the creation of a tailored capital market that aimed to grow for-profit organizations owned by locally residing individuals.

> For a community to thrive, it needs individuals seeking to create wealth for themselves and their families and investors seeking a financial as well as a social return. Poor communities do not have enough of either, which is why they are better described as under-invested communities. This is not to say that there are no entrepreneurs within these communities,

rather that their efforts and potential are undermined by lack of capital, skills or business mentoring. (00_SITF, p. 10)

SII proponents attributed two causes to this lack of community enterprise that they saw as a social problem: the lack of private capital, as well as practices within the VCS were seen to inhibit the emergence of innovative community entrepreneurs.

> Entrepreneurial behaviour in the voluntary sector tends to be fettered by its traditions, laws and established practices. Social and community entrepreneurs recognise that they need to take well-judged risks, develop commercial competencies, attract business and management skills and increase management capacity. Risk averse trustees and a culture of "begging and benevolence" are raised as just two factors which work against the voluntary sector promoting and practising entrepreneurship (00_SITF, p. 14).

With regards to the lack of private capital, they argued that due to the "disadvantagedness" of the communities, private investments within those would not be sufficiently profitable in order to mobilize the large amounts of private capital needed: "At present, [Community Development Financial Institutions] are unable to offer the rates of return needed to attract large-scale private sector investment and managerial talent" (00_SITF, p. 13). As I will argue in more detail later, what they proposed as solutions were government subsidies for investors to increase the profitability—which they later received—as well as the creation of a community investment bank—which they failed to create resonance for at that point. One of the key steps, I argue, was SII proponents' move around 2006 to give up opposition to the VCS but rather shift the locus of under-investment to VCS organizations and forge cooperative ties with them.

This shift in SII proponents' perspective regarding the VCS can most clearly be observed by comparing the first and second reports of the Commission on Unclaimed Assets, which was key to mobilizing widespread support for the idea of a "social investment wholesale bank." While in the first report, the Commission argued that VCS addressed only the "symptoms of poverty", noting that the necessity "to be poor and remain poor in order to qualify to receive" its interventions "creates a system of perverse incentives and rewards" (2006_CUA) A year later, they argued that the VCS' "role in combatting disadvantage and building a more cohesive society has never been more important. Its ability to respond to need and pioneer new approaches [...] is almost universally acknowledged" (2007_CUA). Since then, SII proponents began to argue that the VCS, rather than poor communities, was "under-invested."

> The third sector is fragmented, under-capitalised and, in aggregate, unable to invest in sustainable growth and development. Funding is chronically insecure and often focused on current projects rather than investment in organisational capacity or infrastructure. (07_CUA, p. 1)

But rather than arguing for more VCS *funding* in the form of non-repayable statutory grants or service delivery contracts, SII proponents compared VCS organizations with businesses and argued that they lacked "access to *finance*", and given the strong involvement of key SII actors (Ronald Cohen, Bridges Ventures) in venture capital, they particularly emphasized VCS organizations' "access" to equity capital.

> For-profit start-ups have traditionally received funding from venture capitalists and others that allows them the flexibility to finance their growth. By contrast, the vast majority of grants to social sector organisations are allocated entirely to a specific project. This constrains social sector organisations from investing in their organisation's operational capacity—whether through hiring the right executive talent, or creating back-office infrastructure that improves efficiency (14_G8NAB, p. 10)

The reason for this lack of finance was, however, not seen in investors' high return expectations (as for example the Bank of England argued in a 2003 report, see Chap. 7) but in organizational properties of the VCS. On the one hand, they argued that the VCS lacked "investment readiness" which they described as part of its structural and cultural properties:

> A large part of the third sector is not geared up to use any form of repayable funding—many organisations are too small, or their asset levels are too low to attract capital. No less important than addressing funding gaps, it is critical that professional and knowledge gaps are also addressed. Third sector intermediaries and organisations both require access to professional financial training and advice. Grants to support the development of business plans and capacity building are necessary in order to ensure that organisations have the confidence and professional capability to access and support repayable finance (07_CUA, p. 11).

> Business discipline: Social investment can also help organisations increase their effectiveness through requiring them to improve their financial and business processes, and to be very clear on their priorities and objectives. (14_BLF, p. 9)

On the other hand, SII proponents argued that regulation in the social sector inhibited the flow of private capital into the VCS. For example, they opposed regulation that links an organization's charitable status with its inability to earn income or distribute profits, describing it as "regulations that reflect old thinking about the social sector organisation/for-profit divide", and theorizing that these "prevent money from flowing into mission driven entrepreneurial organisations" (14_G8NAB, p. 13).

Together, SII proponents describe the lack of for-profit financial investments as a key reason for the sustained presence of social problems. Although they acknowledge that investors' unmet return expectations are among the key reasons for the lack of investments, they do not problematize these expectations, but rather demand transformative changes from social organizations and governments. Thus, the nucleus of SII proponents' motivational framing (that aims at mobilizing social organizations and government to act in order to allow the creation of a financialized field) is already laid out in investors' theoretizations regarding the origins of social problems.

6.2.2 *The Impact Narrative*

In the previous segment, I explained how SII proponents attribute the reproduction of social problems to a lack of private investments, particularly into poor neighborhoods and social service providers. There is, however, a second theoretization SII proponents routinely deploy in order to increase acceptance of their field-level strategic action frame. This narrative ascribes the reproduction of social problems to a prevailing "output" focus of field-level organizations that should, from the perspective of SII proponents, be replaced with an "outcome" or "impact" focus. From a social movement perspective, the impact frame serves at least three important functions. First, by positioning impact investors as those following the proposed solution, they gain an in-group identity and a strategic position vis-à-vis "output-oriented" opponents. Second, as I will argue in Chap. 7, a number of the arguments made in the impact frame have been developed and shared by VCS and some government actors and thereby allowed investors to develop cooperative ties. Third, as pointed out in Chap. 5, the notion of impact allows a host of actors, particularly profit-distributing social ventures, to position themselves as in-group members and hence oriented towards social welfare. Thus, while the under-investment narrative alone would only legitimize private investments into community enterprises and social service delivery organizations, the impact narrative broadens the boundaries of social organizations. This way, SII proponents may classify a much larger set of for-profit investments as having social impact, and thereby legitimize private investments as increasing "the scale of this impact by growing the ventures and serving more of our target population" (12_NESTA, p. 6).

In Chap. 7, I describe how the impact narrative only emerged after the "Treasury view" began to dominate policy discourse on public service delivery by the mid-2000s. Earlier, SII proponents had described their activities as "financial transactions intended both to achieve social objectives and deliver financial returns to investors" (00_SITF, p. 31). Only after interpreting the concept of "outcomes" developed in social policy discourse and governance as a business opportunity in the mid-2000s, did they introduce the following frame.

The impact narrative is central to SII proponents' shift towards embracing VCS organizations and introducing the broader category of "social ventures" into the field of welfare. While earlier, SII proponents opposed VCS practices, in the impact narrative they evaluate the VCS contribution to social welfare positively, but diagnose a lack of organizational effectiveness. They attribute two causes to this problematization: under-investment, which I have described above, and a lack of impact orientation. For example, the UK "National Advisory Board" that was part of the G-8 SII group established under David Cameron and led by Ronald Cohen narrated impact as follows:

> There is no doubting the high ambitions and great intentions of E-type organisations[3] on behalf of the people they serve. The problems they are tackling are complex and entrenched. However, the lack of understanding and acquisition of outcome-producing capabilities is a

[3]These organizations are defined as "the Embedded Model" that essentially denotes the social venture category that includes charitable and profit-distributing organizations (14_UKNAB_Building, p. 5).

> key cause of E organisations not-being as effective as they should be in achieving long-term outcomes. The external environment—funders of all stripes and commissioners—has significantly contributed to this lack of capacity.
>
> Grant-makers, including philanthropic foundations and government departments, have been keen to incentivise, and reward, efforts that result in growth in activities (for example, increasing the number of people you serve), but less so efforts that result in growth in outcomes (for example, increasing the rate of success at securing long-term outcomes). Alignment with a funder's or department's own priorities is also frequently rewarded with funding, even if it is likely to pull an organisation off-mission, which reduces its chances of creating impact. (14_UKNAB_Building, p. 14)

What exactly SII proponents mean by "outcome-producing capabilities" or "impact orientation" is only of secondary importance here: in the previous chapter, I have shown how impact orientation is a set of rules that allows investors to gain and maintain a central position. What I am interested in here is how the impact orientation concept is used strategically by SII proponents in order to create a field-level strategic action frame. The important insight here is that, on a discursive level, *investors side with service providers* by arguing that the funding environment, and not service providers themselves, have caused an ascribed lack of organizational effectiveness. Although large parts of SII proponents' discourse are devoted to showing investee organizations how to change their organizational strategies towards maximizing social impact, from a strategic action fields perspective it is much more important to understand how cross-field ties were formed through strategic framing. I argue that for this reason, significant parts of SII proponents' discourse are devoted to problematizing government forms of engagement with the VCS as a source for lacking organizational effectiveness in social services. How investors formed alliances with government despite opposing their funding practices will be shown in Chap. 7.

Theorizing the causes of the lack of service providers' impact orientation, SII proponents frequently argue that social services funded from public budgets and commissioned by the public sector do not address the "root causes" of social problems. This argument takes two forms. In the first case, the commissioning of social services is described as following the internal "logic" of its own system, rather than being based on the "needs" of beneficiaries.

> Current procurement models are not well designed for programmes that address complex human needs. Commissioned services tend to procure for services that follow well-established patterns and that do not allow for flexibility or adaptation. This leads to rigid programmes that are not suited or tailored to those they are trying to support. (14_UKNAB_The, p. 30)

SII proponents argue that "[t]raditionally procured services can be perceived as 'one-size fits all', dehumanised, process oriented services defined to fit the needs of the system and not the users" (14_UKNAB_Recommendations, p. 1). These forms of procurement are described to limit the creativity of social service providers in finding ways to "tailor" social service delivery to the "needs" of the beneficiaries—a key strategy SII proponents understand as impact oriented. This is ascribed to the extant forms of procurement, which are said to either focus on "inputs" (i.e. costs to the public budget) or "outputs" and therefore restrain service providers' creativity in maximizing "outcomes" in relation to the social problems described above:

> Nevertheless, an input- or output-focused approach can undermine the delivery of effective public services. Public sector commissioners are encouraged to focus on defining the methods of service delivery rather than the impact of those services on clients' lives. Specifying service delivery in this way can leave little flexibility for service providers to tailor their services to local needs and develop locally-appropriate solutions.
>
> A focus on inputs and outputs can also create the wrong incentives for service providers, driving them to find more cost-effective ways of achieving the agreed outputs without enough thought for the desired outcomes. For instance, training providers may have an incentive to put young people through a Health and Safety certification because they are paid on that basis. To reduce costs, providers may supply the minimum training necessary for young people to pass. The provider is unlikely to provide additional career support as they are not financially rewarded for helping young people to find employment. Consequently, inputs- and outputs-based commissioning can fail to deliver the desired policy goal: in this case reduced youth unemployment. (10_SF_Towards, p. 14)

One of the consequences SII proponents attribute to output-based commissioning is the exclusion of smaller, social sector service providers from access to government contracts. This is because smaller service providers are theorized to not be able to compete on a cost-efficiency basis with large, private sector providers. However, SII proponents ascribe the integration of these small providers into service delivery as desirable as they attribute to them an "added value" in service delivery. As we will see in Chap. 7, the very same argument has been advanced both by the Association of the Chief Executives of Voluntary Organizations (ACEVO), as well as "modernizers" in public service delivery around Gordon Brown in the Treasury.

> [C]ontracts tend to be won on the basis of the proposed cost of delivering outputs rather than the cost-effectiveness of delivering outcomes. This system favours larger, often private sector, providers who compete by providing lower cost services, often to the easiest to work with individuals. Social sector organisations, that may try to negotiate a broader, more flexible set of services for their service users, often lose out. They may be further disadvantaged by contracts that pay for services in arrears, and hence require significant access to up front funding to cover the costs of operations before payment. This is a shame as social sector organisations are often established to deliver to the needs of a specific target population. As a consequence their interests are often well-aligned with those of their service users [...]. (10_SF_Towards, p. 15)

The second issue SII proponents diagnose as a cause for the lack of impact oriented government funding runs much deeper into the organizing principles of government: here, SII proponents argue that due to the structure of government, individual departments lack the *financial incentives* to commission outcome-oriented services. This argument takes two forms. As I have described above, the social problems and causes SII proponents describe on an individual level are often forms of deviant social behavior that are evaluated normatively on the basis of public expenses and demanded to be solved by innovative behavioral interventions. Thus, in the case of, say, drug addiction, public expenses might arise in the form of medical provision to the Department of Health (DoH), and in the form of policing to the

Department of Justice (DoJ). Now SII proponents argue that the reason why no innovative intervention targeted at reducing drug addiction is funded to date is the "siloed" nature of government funds. For example, DoH might finance medical interventions that reduce drug-related medical expenses, but does, according to SII proponents, not have a reason to fund interventions that reduce criminal offending as it would not materially benefit from these savings.[4]

> [M]any SSOs [Social Sector Organizations, PG] are working with beneficiary groups with multiple needs. Accordingly, effective interventions may require a holistic approach. However, many of the potential funding streams for SSOs are siloed (as commissioners themselves work in silos), which creates a hurdle to delivering effective interventions. (14_BSC_Employment, p. 8)

> The effectiveness of outcomes based commissioning lies in the ability to align the incentives of multiple stakeholders around the same objective/s. While this seems an obviously positive proposition, to date the silo-ed nature of public services and ineffective contracting approaches have often prevented this from happening. (15_SF_Technical, p. 33)

The lack of financial incentives within government bureaucracies is furthermore theorized by SII proponents to cause a lack of preventative social services. These services are often evaluated as "outcome-oriented" as they are about "building a fence at the top of the cliff rather than running an ambulance to the bottom" and hence

> - Address the root causes of a problem rather than its symptoms
> - Reduce the size of the problem and its negative consequences by intervening earlier
> - Act at a time when it is easier to address the problem due to behaviours that are less entrenched
> - Aim to improve outcomes to a greater extent than acute or crisis services
> - Reduce spending over the long term by reducing demand (14_SF_Creating, p. 8)

It is important to keep in mind that most Social Impact Bonds qualify as such preventative services, hence the topic of prevention is a central one in SII proponents' framing. As stated above, SII proponents see the cause of the lack of preventative services in a lack of financial incentives within government bureaucracy:

> A central issue here is that the department that invests in early intervention often does not see the financial benefits of a programme's success. For instance, Local Authorities do not currently have a financial incentive to prevent offending. If given a custodial sentence, the costs of offenders are borne by the National Offender Management Service rather than the Local Authority. The Local Authority could even stand to make savings from reductions to local services (e.g. police, social services, etc.) if an offender goes to prison. It therefore has little financial incentive to improve outcomes. (10_SF_Towards, p. 12)

What differentiates the case of prevention from the argument of the silo-ed nature of government funds is that there is a time component to preventative services. As preventative services require government spending before expenses

[4]Again, in Chap. 7 I will show how combating this "silo-ed" funding was not only a core priority of Treasury-based modernizers, but also one of the two key issues in which other government departments saw a high legitimacy of Treasury-led interventions.

(e.g. for policing) accrue, SII proponents argue that preventative services create a financial risk that public commissioners are for good reasons not willing to take.

> [T]he financial gains from investment in prevention may not be realised for several years. In the meantime the public sector has to find funding, on top of its existing budgets, to pay for the preventative programmes. If the preventative interventions fail, the public sector will find itself paying for two sets of costs—the up front costs of the interventions and the ongoing costs of failing to prevent the social problem. This risk deters investment in prevention. It is therefore unsurprising that government tends to underspend on preventative interventions, particularly when funding is tight. (10_SF_Towards, p. 12)

As I will argue later, here, SII proponents create a situation of brokerage, where, in addition to siding with service providers, they can present themselves (through SIB contracts) as allies to government commissioners and relieve them of the burden of financial risk taking.

6.3 Financialization as Welfare

In the previous section I have described how SII proponents ascribe the reproduction of social problems to a lack of for-profit financial investments, as well as organizations and government contracts aimed at maximizing social impact. From a framing perspective, this paves the way for a field-level strategic action frame to be presented as a solution to social problems as well as a means to foster cooperative ties between investors and nonfinancial actors. In this section, I will describe in detail how SII proponents translate their problem diagnosis into a field-level frame that theorizes solutions and motivates field-level action.

As social movement research has demonstrated extensively (McAdam 1982; McAdam et al. 2001), a key task in mobilization is to convince others that solutions to problems exist not only in theory, but also that reality is changeable by participating in the movement. In SII, this role is filled by a "social innovation" discourse which celebrates innovative individuals ("social entrepreneurs") and organizational forms ("social ventures") as positive role-models that have been able not only to "create" positive social impact, but also to challenge and redefine the prevailing rules of social welfare. Due to its importance in mobilization, I describe the social innovation frame in the following segment. Thereafter, I describe investors' prognostic framing regarding the role of impact investments for the solution of social problems. In the concluding segment, I show how all of these narrations piece together to motivate participation in SII proponents' field-level strategic action frame.

6.3.1 *Celebrating Disruption: The Social Innovation Discourse*

SII proponents frequently relate to innovation in their strategic action frame. The radical "innovat*" matched a total 340 times in the documents analyzed, while the adjective "new" matched 459 times. For writing this section, I compared all of these 799 quotes and developed categories through abductive analysis. I realized that the plurality of meanings SII proponents associate with innovation was best accounted for by its function for field-level mobilization. I found that SII proponents relate to innovation in three distinct ways: as a possibility, as a necessity, and as an organizational template (see Table 6.2). Empirically, these meanings are frequently enmeshed.

Showing that innovative action in regards to social problems is possible, and hence that social reality is changeable by participating in movements, is a core task of mobilization. In SII discourse, this can be seen most clearly in the structure of the reports. In virtually all documents analyzed, boxed descriptions of "best case examples" are presented throughout the text. For example, in 20 pages of content, the 2007 Commission on Unclaimed Assets report alone showed seven case examples such as this one:

> **Enabling through investment: Broadreach House.** Broadreach House was set up 23 years ago to provide treatment, support and residential care for people who were dependent on alcohol and drugs. Its vision and belief is that people have the power to change their lives, if they get the right psychological, educational and social help. [. . .] (07_CUA, p. 7, emphasis in original)

Most of these case descriptions follow a similar structure: the creation of an innovative organizational vehicle to combat a social problem is presented with a positive normative evaluation. In the vast majority of cases, however, these organizations are of a particular type: revenue-earning and distributing companies that utilize for-profit impact investments. Often, the case narration includes a personal story that shows how the founders were people "like you and me" to facilitate identification with the movement. In other cases, shared biographical characteristics of innovative movement actors and an assumed readership are pointed out in order to

Table 6.2 Three forms of social innovation discourse

Innovation as. . .	Discourse	Function
Possibility	Shared biography between social innovators and assumed readership	Facilitate mobilization
Necessity	Institutional transformation necessary for innovation addressing social problems to emerge	Theorize prevailing institutional order as "barriers" to legitimize its change
Organizational template	For-profit impact-firms are such a necessary form of innovation	Motivate a particular form of institutional change

foster mobilization. For example, addressing the World Economic Forum, its two founders wrote:

> My husband Klaus Schwab and I started the Schwab Foundation for Social Entrepreneurship over a decade ago because, although the World Economic Forum had engaged leaders from traditional civil society organizations for many years, we sensed that a distinct, more entrepreneurial approach to alleviating problems associated with poverty was beginning to take hold. We saw a new generation of social entrepreneurs, often well educated, some with promising private-sector careers, who were experimenting with business models, innovating new distribution and replication methods, and holding themselves accountable for results. (13_WEF, p. 3)

Apart from showing the possibility of change through social innovation, SII proponents consistently argued that reducing social problems necessitates innovation. These statements confer a sense of incitement and urgency to field-level actors, particularly government, to pursue social innovation: "To make an impact it is not enough to throw money at old approaches; we must adapt and innovate [...]" (13_Young, p. 25). Often, these statements take an appellative form, such as: "If we get this right, we can unleash the world's next wave of entrepreneurial innovation, following on the great tech wave of recent decades" (14_G8NAB, p. 16), or "we need to unleash a whole new wave of social entrepreneurs" (13_WEF_Breaking, p. 5).

Often baked into the necessity-dimension of SII proponents' discourse on social innovation is a claim that prevailing rules and structures inhibit the development, or act as "barriers" to innovation. Ever since SII proponents sought to cooperate with the VCS, the locus of these arguments has shifted from the VCS to public procurement ("commissioning rarely allows innovative services to develop" 07_CUA, p. 7) as well as formal and informal rules that inhibit impact investors' profit extraction:

> [T]here are cultural barriers against private providers, especially businesses, in the provision of social services (14_G8NAB, p. 15);

> [...] regulations that reflect old thinking about the social sector organisation/for-profit divide and which prevent money from flowing into mission driven entrepreneurial organisations (14_G8NAB, p. 13).

Such an interpretation of the status quo already hints to the fact that, for SII proponents, only a highly specific organizational template counts as a social innovation. From their perspective, a social innovation is a profitable social venture that uses financial investments to grow its activities:

> There has been a rapid rise globally in the number of impact entrepreneurs who want to find innovative ways to solve society's problems, and they are increasingly deploying the methods of business and private capital if that helps them to do so. They include people in the social sector who can now tap the markets for finance in addition to seeking grants from donors, and philanthropists who are willing to fund businesses rather than social sector organisations if that offers a greater likelihood of achieving the social impact they desire (14_G8NAB, p. 1).

As I will describe in more detail below, SII proponents present SII as a tool that is uniquely positioned to foster social innovation:

> Impact investing does not relieve governments of their responsibilities. But it can help to fulfil them more effectively. By financing innovative approaches, impact investing also has the potential to help deliver services more efficiently and, in some cases, tackle the underlying causes of growing demand for social services instead of just trying to cope with their consequences (14_G8NAB, p. 1).

How exactly SII proponents create the discursive link between SII, innovation, and the effective solution of social problems will be described in the following segments.

6.3.2 Prognostic Framing: Impact Investing and the Solution of Social Problems

Up to this point we have been primarily concerned with SII proponents' interpretation of the past and present. I have shown how SII proponents' diagnostic framing builds on a highly specific set of social problems that are attributed to an equally specific set of causes. Moreover, I have argued that in spelling out the possibility and necessity of social innovation, SII proponents create an imaginary that social change regarding the problematizations disseminated in the diagnostic frame is possible for individuals and organizations alike.

In this section, I will show how the specificities that have been baked into SII proponents' diagnosis come to the fore in their prognostic framing. In their prognostic framing, SII proponents relate the creation and growth of a SII capital market to the solution of social problems. To do so, they ascribe a specific role and position to impact investors, and create an imaginary of consequences (Beckert 2016) to follow from the growth of SII. As their prognostic frame theorizes how SII intermediaries' central position would positively affect social problems, it forms the foundation for the motivational field frame that, if followed, orchestrates these field-level positions. The motivational frame will be described in the final segment of this chapter.

SII proponents' prognostic framing builds on the two entangled narratives that form the basis of the diagnostic framing: impact and investment. They argue that investors are in a unique position to ensure that investee organizations focus on the creation of social impact. The theoretical accounts differ for SIBs and other SII financial products and imply contradictory statements' regarding investors' motivations and interests. Proponents argue that in SIBs, investors have an interest in maximizing outcomes because this would directly translate into higher financial returns to them. At the same time, better outcome achievement is theorized as higher savings for government. Together, SIBs are therefore presented as "aligning incentives" between partaking actors and hence representing "a source of rational, non-erratic funding, to facilitate growth and sustainability" (14_UKNAB_Building, p. 4) of social organizations.

> SIBs fund preventative and early intervention programmes which tackle the underlying causes of specific social problems. Incentives are aligned across public sector commissioners, external investors and service providers, all of whom are acting to achieve improved social outcomes as defined in a contract. The main objectives of the SIB are to:
>
> - Increase the pool of capital available to fund early interventions;
> - Encourage a broad diversity of service providers and collaboration between providers;
> - Create more market discipline and offer predictable revenue streams for service providers to enable those that are effective to thrive; and
> - Align public sector funding more directly with improved social outcomes (11_SF, p. 2).

In contrast to SIBs, where impact investors are assumed to act as profit maximizers, in other financial products (such as equity investments) they are ascribed a voluntary commitment to the creation of social impact. Here, investors are demanded to extend their decision-making criteria to "risk, return, and impact" (14_G8NAB), because, by doing so, they would demand their investee firms to rigorously produce social impact:

> If investors fully understood and demanded strong social outcomes, and valued those as strongly as they value financial returns, front line providers would need to pay more attention to producing reliable social outcomes. (14_UKNAB_Building, p. 19)

This is mirrored by David Hutchison, then CEO of intermediary Social Finance, who argued that the most important effect of SII is the creation of close ties to social organizations that force these organizations to focus on the production of outcomes:

> [T]he real change comes from the partnerships forged by social investment models, the rigour that the social investors bring to performance manage the social interventions and the flexibility and long term nature of the funding. By giving organisations sight of long-term funding for their interventions, social investors can bear the risk involved in new innovations and allow the social organisations to concentrate on delivery and the development of their models with an eye to sustained and evidenced impact. (13_UKSIF, p. 9).

Once these social outcomes are "reliably produced", then, SII proponents argue, investors' interest in SII further increases, making more capital available to social organizations, and hence further strengthening the link between impact and investment. Particularly if social impact could be made comparable in the sense of a "social return on investment", more capital would be available and hence more impact created:

> Where it is possible to estimate likely social returns and compare the performance of the organisations that deliver them, measurement will help to attract significant capital from a spectrum of investors that seek different combinations of financial and social returns. A degree of global standard setting in measurement will boost the flow of trade and capital. (14_G8NAB, p. 28)

This description hints to the "spectrum" of impact investors ranging from "finance first" to "impact first" investors that has been described in Chap. 5. This way, impact investors establish themselves as a distinct category of financial investors primarily interested in the creation of social impact, while making the question of financial returns independent from the pursuit of social impact. According to SII proponents, impact investors' actions create social impact—whether or not they are willing to sacrifice financial returns.

The link between investments and impact is established by SII proponents through one key theoretization: *scale*. Indeed, the argument that investments "scale" the creation of social impact is so central to proponents' frame that it has been noted a total of 250 times in the 28 reports studied. The argument that impact investments "scale" social impact has been made with regards to all three problem discourses. However, it is most salient in relation to equity investments into social ventures, where investors finance "a growing number of impact entrepreneurs who pursue social innovation by starting for-profit companies" (14_G8NAB, p. 8). The idea of "scale" originates in the venture capital industry, and its close connections to SII become visible here[5]:

> Impact investing can help entrepreneurs take their good ideas to scale, much as the emergence of a large venture capital industry in several countries over the past four decades has led to a huge increase in the number of entrepreneurial start-ups growing into big, successful companies. (14_G8NAB, p. 9)

By scale, impact investors mean the growth of an organization's "impactful" activities by engaging in finance-led growth. Critically, SII proponents do not differentiate between profit-distributing businesses and not-for-profit VCS organizations, but understand "scale" as a property of the expanded "social venture" category (e.g. 12_NPC). For example, fitness company The Gym discussed in Chap. 5 "scaled" its impact as it sold more membership contracts to poor individuals since a lack of "access" to "affordable" fitness programs was identified as a social problem. As argued in Chap. 5, very frequently, "scaling" social impact is equivalent to increasing organizational revenues for products that investors theme "impactful." In these cases, reducing organizational expenses is relabeled as making a product more "affordable", while increasing its turnover means expanding its scale. Impact investors indicate that through their close ties with social ventures, they "help" organizations to develop strategies such as these. They argue that scaling social impact requires:

> a laser focus on what makes a product most valuable to consumers, and a trimming of what does not. For example, through our investment in The Gym Group, we have learned to focus on figuring out how much we can bring cost down while maintaining high quality and profitability. While its locations are highly accessible and have best-in-class equipment, our investment in a robust IT platform means it has significantly cut operational spend (13_Bridges_10, p. 14)

Indeed, SII proponents very transparently ascribe positive social consequences to organizational profit orientation. Hence, the "finance first" group of investors may readily identify with SII without significantly altering financial decision-making practices:

[5]The first British impact investor, Bridges Ventures, started by advancing venture capital principles in community enterprise, where previously lending dominated (see Chap. 7).

> Key to the success of impact investments is the fact that they are investments expected to generate a financial return. This aim should co-exist with the intent toward positive impact, though one or the other may be the primary focus for a given investor. In fact, the pairing of these two motivations by investors will hopefully encourage businesses to develop in financially sustainable ways, thus facilitating the growth of the impact delivered by those businesses. (10_JPMorgan_Emerging, p. 15)

There are two ways in which SII proponents' prognostic framing is geared towards legitimizing the amalgamation of profit and impact motives. First, they argue that by turning the "production of social impact" into a profitable proposition, vast pools of capital would immediately be available and hence very rapidly relief the world of social problems: if "we succeed in developing a thriving global market in impact investment, then vast quantities of capital will be mobilised to invest in the rapidly expanding global efforts of impact-driven organisations" (14_G8NAB, p. 39). In a study that spurred a large global media echo, investment bank JP Morgan predicted that the creation of an SII market place would "channel large-scale private capital for social benefit", reaching a market volume of $1 trillion by 2020 (10_JPMorgan, p. 5).

This imaginary of rapid relief through the creation of profitable impact investments is enhanced by pointing towards a lack of charitable donations:

> Recognizing that charitable donations will never reach the scale needed to address the world's problems, and that business principles and practices can unleash creativity and scale in delivering basic services and addressing environmental challenges, impact investment introduces a new type of capital merging the motivations of traditional investments and donations. (10_JPMorgan, p. 13)

After the 2008 financial crisis and the following bank bailouts strained public funds and, particularly in the UK, elicited a rise in fiscal austerity, the argument regarding the magnitude of "impactful" capital was expanded to public funds as well.

> All of the countries on the Taskforce also face growing pressure, in a context of fiscal restraint, to allocate government spending more efficiently and effectively to social needs. Impact investing does not relieve governments of their responsibilities. But it can help to fulfil them more effectively. [...] As the global impact investment market grows, governments will not only have access to vast new pools of capital but also the ability to share in the entrepreneurship and innovation expertise of business and the social sector. (14_G8NAB, p. 1)

As SII proponents do not differentiate between for- and not-for-profit organizations but rather create the novel category of impact-producing organizations or social ventures, SII positions itself as a partner for both government and charitable foundations in maximizing impact production of their limited capital resources. In this context, SII proponents frequently relate to a recycling metaphor, arguing that for-profit finance can be "recycled" as investors may invest it again, thereby creating multiples of impact for a fixed sum of capital (the political economic consequences of establishing such financial circuits are ignored in SII proponents' narrations). For example, Big Lottery Fund described the "advantages" of SII as follows:

> It recycles the money we have: there is simply less money available, and there is bigger demand for the grants that are still available from government, donations or charitable trusts. Because social investment returns to the investor, it can be used again to support more charities and social enterprises; and help ensure grants go to where they are needed most.
>
> It attracts new money: social investment can also help to address the decreasing resources available by attracting money from new sources: from individuals, mainstream finance, or the private sector. This can help add to the existing money that is available. (14_BLF, p. 4)

The second way how the introduction of for-profit templates into social welfare is legitimized in SII proponents' prognostic framing is through narratives of opportunities and flexibility. A large SII capital market, proponents argue, would grant social organizations more flexibility in finding forms of capital that are "tailored" to their "needs." In their descriptions, social organizations "had to make their essential, and often considerable, contribution to society without access to the full range of financing options available to regular businesses" (14_G8NAB, p. 2). Here, impact investors position themselves as those providers that close this financial "gap" and hence increase social organizations' effectiveness:

> For-profit start-ups have traditionally received funding from venture capitalists and others that allows them the flexibility to finance their growth. By contrast, the vast majority of grants to social sector organisations are allocated entirely to a specific project. This constrains social sector organisations from investing in their organisation's operational capacity—whether through hiring the right executive talent, or creating back-office infrastructure that improves efficiency (14_G8NAB, p. 10)
>
> [T]he Bridges Social Entrepreneurs Fund aims to address the funding gap often faced by fast growing social enterprises looking to scale. The Fund brings together social investors wanting to support social impact with social enterprises seeking to grow. (13_Bridges_Spotlight, p. 5)

The advantages of an impact investment over non-repayable forms of finance have been described by the quasi-public Big Lottery Fund in a guide to social organizations as the following:

> Flexibility: Investors are likely to be more flexible than grant funders about what you do. If you find your business plan isn't working, an investor is likely to be happy if you change your business model to one that's more likely to succeed. Active involvement and support: Investors are more likely to want to get actively involved to support your organisation. This can be useful, especially for start-ups.
>
> Less restricted: Social investment tends to be less restricted to particular projects and outcomes than conventional grant funding, giving your organisation freedom to use it most effectively; it can also mean less distraction chasing grants. Business discipline: Social investment can also help organisations increase their effectiveness through requiring them to improve their financial and business processes, and to be very clear on their priorities and objectives. (14_Big_Lottery_Fund, p. 8)

Lastly, SII proponents argue that a large SII capital market would make it more easy for "community organizations" to take over the delivery of social or public services. Even for organizations that aim at creating "local solutions to local problems" rather than a large scale, SII proponents argue for the importance of impact investments: particularly in the early phases, impact investors could support the creation of new community organizations by providing up-front capital, organize share issues, or offer other financial products:

> Servicing high levels of debt puts strain on cashflows at critical stages. Social investors could act as initial (co)-owners and developers of assets with a view to transferring to communities once developed and viable. This asset transfer could be funded through community share issues or a social mortgage. (15_BSC_Communities, p. 12)

SII proponents argue that impact investors' unique position within capital markets would allow for these investments:

> Bransholme Community Childcare grew to four nurseries within five years and received financial support from Key Fund to acquire a new site after being rejected by banks and other traditional sources of finance. (15_BSC_Communities, p. 12)

Together, SII proponents' prognostic framing links the two diagnostic narrations regarding impact orientation and under-investment in order to position impact investors as part of the solution of social problems. Through their narration of organizational scale, SII proponents legitimize the introduction of the for-profit category into social welfare. By emphasizing how SII could co-operate with extant field-level actors to increase the respective organizations' effectiveness in addressing social problems, SII proponents depict the creation of a capital market as part of the intrinsic interests of partaking field-level actors. In the following segment, I describe how this prognostic analysis is translated into a field-level motivational recipe that orchestrates partaking actors' strategies in order to enable the creation of an SII capital market.

6.3.3 Motivational Framing and the Impact Investing Field Frame

Social impact investors' motivational framing pieces together their diagnostic and prognostic frames by creating instructions to act that take the form of concrete next steps for partaking actors in their respective field-level positions. As I have argued throughout, these field-level instructions are shaped in a particular way as to grant SII actors a central position within that field. To benefit from material redistribution from charitable foundations, government, and social organizations, impact investors need to establish a frame that allows these diverse groups to identify with the proposed diagnosis, prognosis, and motivation from their respective positions. In Chaps. 7 and 8, I will shed more light empirically and theoretically on to how and to what extent investors' frame became a "good enough reason" (Forst 2015b) for the addressed actors to alter their strategies. The nuanced sets of justifications, which provided idiosyncratic reasons for all partaking actors to identify with SII, have been described in the previous sections. Yet to understand how justification translates into action, we furthermore need to understand the missing link: the motivational component of SII proponents' discourse (Vaisey 2009). This will be provided here.

From their earliest report in 2000 until the most recent reports analyzed, SII proponents' motivational frame was located at the field level. At all times, SII proponents argued for the establishment of a financialized field with financial intermediaries in central governance positions.

> Our recommendations are critical to the success of impact investment. They define what is needed from all actors in our society: government, business, the social sector and foundations, institutional and private investors, and most importantly impact entrepreneurs. The role of each of these groups is addressed in this report. Impact investment is emerging as a new unifying force among them in dealing with social issues, driving innovation and prevention to improve lives. It harnesses the forces of entrepreneurship, innovation and capital and the power of markets to do good. One might with justification say that it brings the invisible heart of markets to guide their invisible hand (14_G8NAB, p. i)

Ever since, motivating government to regulate, tax, and subsidize in accordance to the interests of financial intermediaries has formed a fundamental building block of SII proponents' motivational frame. For example, in 2000 they argued:

> Perhaps the best example in the UK of how the creation of an enabling framework has acted as a driver for success and wealth creation is the UK venture capital industry. There, the establishment over 20 years ago of a "system" by introducing stock markets for small companies, legal vehicles for venture capital funds, lower tax rates and Government support of entrepreneurs stimulated a process which has led to today's thriving venture capital industry. (00_SITF, p. 15)

By 2014, their arguments regarding the respective roles of finance and government remained remarkably similar:

> Over the past 40 years, governments have played an important role in supporting business entrepreneurship and technological innovation. They have done so by adjusting regulation, providing tax incentives, and using grants of various kinds; [...] and by favouring the establishment of an effective venture capital sector and specialised stock exchanges capable of providing risk in helping to build valuable, innovative companies. To empower ambitious impact-driven organisations and entrepreneurs to achieve real impact on social issues, governments now need to play a similar role in supporting impact investment. [...] Governments need innovation in delivering social services and they need to attract the risk capital to finance it. (14_G8NAB, pp. 39–40)

In both cases, SII proponents argued that the creation of a SII financial market was first and foremost in the government's own interest. Although other parts of SII proponents' frame changed, their instructions to act for government remained remarkably similar throughout the observation period. In essence, SII proponents argued for what I term the *leveraging state*. From their perspective, government should use public funds not to pay for social welfare directly. Rather, government should use its funds to subsidize private financial investments into social welfare, as well as alter regulation to support financial intermediaries. This way, they argue, government could "lever in" vast sums of additional private capital into the "production of social impact." Subsidizing the creation of a SII capital market would provide government with "a way to leverage and maximize limited resources and to deliver public services as efficiently as possible" (13_WEF, p. 7).

> The key policy levers that governments can use to facilitate impact investment include regulatory change, fiscal incentives, supplying catalytic capital and building market infrastructure. Use of these policy levers will free up large pools of capital to address pressing social needs. (14_G8, p. 26)

There are various forms of such "leveraging" government actions that SII proponents motivate. These actions are related to the shape of the respective SII financial products. For example, regarding debt and equity investments that "scale" social ventures, government is motivated to subsidize financial intermediaries directly through co-investments into private funds, guarantees, or tax reductions for investors, as well as the creation of a "social investment bank" that provides capital to SII intermediaries.

> As a first step, the Task Force proposes that the Government should make available £100 million over the next few years to match £100 million from the private sector, for example by scaling up the Phoenix Fund. (00_SITF, p. 19)

> To expand the pool of investors willing to invest in the sector, there is a need for Government incentives to bring returns closer to market rates. The clearest way to do this is through tax credits. (00_SITF, p. 15)

> The Big Society Bank should operate as a wholesale funder providing capital and liquidity to retail intermediaries. Previous government retail funds were criticised for distorting rather than leveraging private capital, and have proven short-lived. (10_CAF, p. 12)

In addition to these direct subsidies to SII intermediaries, indirect subsidies at the investee level are also advocated for. Here, government subsidies play the role of reducing investors' risk, for example by financing the early and risky start-up phases, or sponsoring training programs aimed at making social organizations "investment ready" (more on this below):

> To scale the innovations of social enterprise, government can help businesses build capacity, attract capital and increase demand for their products. Again, a variety of policy tools are available to prepare enterprises for growth, from technical assistance to direct investment; the appropriate policy solution should be grounded in an understanding of the needs of entrepreneurs and their current obstacles to scale (13_WEF_Breaking, p. 9).

But also for other financial products, SII proponents motivate concrete government actions. This is particularly true for Social Impact Bonds. SIBs relate to somewhat different public budgets (service provision contracts) and include government actors at the Local Authority level. This is why the SIB motivational frame is highly nuanced with respect to these different inner-governmental positions. But more generally, SII proponents motivate government to accept a field-level role in partnership with financial actors. Consistent with their diagnostic and prognostic framing, they argue that government should alter its commissioning practices such as to include financial intermediaries into the process of public service delivery:

> There is an urgent need for a revolution in government purchasing, with paying for the successful delivery of specific outcomes at its core. A decisive move to focus on purchasing outcomes (whether by governments or other entities) is the clearest way of stimulating a flow of revenue to impact-driven organisations that rewards them more directly for the social value they create. This can have a profound effect on the way impact is delivered, as well as

> ensuring that innovation and effectiveness are incentivised. We believe there is a huge opportunity to create better outcomes for society, and investible opportunities, by expanding the role that governments and philanthropic foundations play as buyers of specific outcomes from impact-driven organisations. (14_G8NAB, p. 14)

Charitable foundations are ascribed a "leveraging" role that is highly similar to government. More concretely, foundations are asked to use both their endowments as well as their grant-making programs in order to grow the SII capital markets.

> After governments, foundations and the charitable trusts of wealthy individual philanthropists have the opportunity to be the most active force in the development of the impact investment market. This will require the courage to challenge cultural norms in the philanthropic sector, including how endowments are invested, and the willingness to embrace the risk involved in backing innovative new ideas that can improve society. (14_G8NAB, p. 40)

As I will show in Chap. 7, after a key person of the SII movement became head of the Charity Commission, charitable foundations became legally allowed to invest their endowments into SII. Regarding grantmaking, I have argued in Chap. 5 how SII proponents motivate foundations to avoid the creation of "grant dependence" but instead "incubate" social ventures until they take on a repayable investment.

> One promising development has been the emergence of 'venture philanthropy' firms that seek to apply many of the 'hands-on' capacity—building techniques of venture capital to social sector organisation start-ups—including providing general operating support, mentoring, help with recruitment, strategic thinking and embedding a revenue model from the start. (14_G8NAB, p. 10)

Social organizations are motivated to develop a business model that is capable of creating "scalable" social impact and financial returns. This requires a "culture or mind-set change from a traditional charitable model to a business model" that is described as difficult and time- and resource consuming: "even award winners and visionaries need a huge amount of tailored support" to master this transformation (12_ClearlySo, p. 22). Key to this transformation process is for social organizations to acquire "investment readiness." The concept of "investment readiness" only emerged around 2010 as a counter-mobilization by SII proponents against the critique that the significant public resources granted to SII intermediaries could not be used efficiently by social organizations (see Chap. 7). Since then, it formed a central part of SII proponents' motivational frame, matching 135 times in the analyzed post-2010 reports. Although this is an activity to be performed by social organizations, SII proponents' mobilization hinges upon emphasizing the difficulties of the process and the need for external support in order to achieve this goal. This way, it is easier for social organizations to identify with the goal of investment readiness: not only because the blame for the lack thereof is shifted to the external environment, but also because accepting this goal is tied with access to additional resources for these organizations and an evaluation as an innovative challenger.

> **Becoming investment ready is a time-consuming and resource-intensive process.** It is important to recognise that the few organisations that have been successful in securing investment often owe their investment readiness to capacity development paid for by grants and pro bono supporters. [...] Developing these three critical attributes—the impact narrative, sales strategy and an adaptable revenue model—can be a catch-22 situation. They

require financial resources that SSOs are unable to meet organically, but without which they cannot access growth capital. This is why the relationship between grant funders and providers of risk capital is so important (13_Young, p. 39, emphasis in original).

At the fringes of SII proponents' motivational framing are some notions aimed at asset owners. However, while proponents' motivational frame towards social organizations and governments is equally well elaborated as it is crafted in a rather imperative tone, asset owners tend to be addressed conciliatorily. SII proponents often hold that asset owners intrinsically want to increase social well-being with their financial investments, but are to date held back due to the small size of the SII market.

There is great potential to unlock new capital as banks offer impact investing products to their clients on their mainstream wealth management platforms. A report by Bank of America shows that half of their high-net worth clients want to reflect their societal values in their portfolios, and the proportion is higher the lower the age group. (14_G8NAB_Invisible, p. 25)

But even when addressing asset owners, SII proponents emphasize the central role played by financial intermediaries. This way, asset owners are motivated to invest their funds with impact investors, rather than "mainstream" financial intermediaries:

Fund intermediaries can also relieve some of the burden of managing the investments post-commitment, which can often require a high level of engagement due to the early nature of many impact businesses. Some investors may even prefer to utilize a double-layer of intermediation, through a fund-of-funds structure, to either bring a more diversified exposure across sectors and regions or to allow for a limited partner role that would allow a more passive approach. (12_JPMorgan_Portfolio, p. 30)

In summary, SII proponents' motivational frame addresses all field-level actors and motivates them, based on detailed diagnostic and prognostic elaborations, to interact in accordance to SII proponents' field-level strategic action frame. To the extent these actors do so, impact investors acquire a central position in the field and benefit materially. Enacting SII proponents' frame would thus forge the financialization of welfare.

Chapter 7
Field Emergence and Stabilization

At the time when Labour won the 1997 general election, financialization and welfare were two separate things. Although a host of public services had been privatized to for-profit corporations under the previous Conservative governments, there was a group of not-for-profit organizations, the voluntary and community sector, which enjoyed close ties to social policy, particularly via Home Office. In considerable distance of the VCS operated a tiny group of challengers that was swept into policy in the heyday of Labour's idea of "inclusive economic growth", building on close ties with the Chancellor of the Exchequer at HM Treasury. These challengers propagated finance-led growth of organizations located in poor neighborhoods as a prime means to achieve public welfare. Most simply, what we know as SII today is the success of this challenger group to partially alter the frames and rules in the social policy field such as to allow for a central position of financial intermediaries within that field.

What makes this case exciting on a theoretical level is that this process did not occur via an episode of contention as strategic action fields theory would predict, but nevertheless built on substantial mobilization efforts (Fligstein and McAdam 2012). Although I spent considerable time looking for it, I simply did not find a vocal opposition to the financialization propagated by SII proponents. Rather, I found VCS incumbents being supportive, at times very outspokenly, of field-level financialization, even calling for government support. This created a puzzle for SAF theory that I addressed by studying the situational and temporal variance baked into the development of SII through abductive analysis (Timmermans and Tavory 2012).

One of the things I found striking about SII is how, without apparent or imminent sanctions, SII proponents could claim that their for-profit investees were some kind of "social" organization. Indeed, what I recall from working in the field (although in Germany) prior to beginning to work on this book, and what I found ubiquitously in my data was a confusion, ambiguity, and contest around what counts as "social organizations." This is where the story of "social enterprise" comes in. For a timeline of key events in SII development, see Table 7.1.

P. Golka, *Financialization as Welfare*,
https://doi.org/10.1007/978-3-030-06100-5_7

Table 7.1 Timeline of key events in the development of SII in the UK

Year	Event
1997	Labour wins UK general election: start of observation period
1998	Formation of Social Enterprise London
1999	Policy Action Team 3 Report
2000	Social Investment Taskforce
2001	Labour wins UK general election
2002	Social enterprise field settlement through Department of Trade and Industry strategy
2002	Treasury Cross-Cutting Review on social organizations in public service delivery
2002	Creation of Bridges Community Ventures
2004	Creation of Futurebuilders England
2004	Bridges Community Ventures develops "social ventures" frame
2005	Labour wins UK general election
2006	Creation of Office of the Third Sector in Cabinet Office and renewed social enterprise strategy
2006	Creation of the Commission on Unclaimed Assets
2007	Gordon Brown becomes Prime Minister, initiates Council on Social Action, and restructures Office of the Third Sector
2007	Creation of Social Finance Ltd.
2008	Dormant Bank and Building Society Accounts Act
2008–2010	First subsidies for equity financial products and first Social Impact Bond
2010	Conservatives win UK general election and form coalition government
2011	Office for Civil Society publishes Social Investment strategy
2011	Localism Act
2011–2016	Multiple central government subsidies for social impact investing, including "outcomes" funds for social impact bonds and "investment readiness" funds
2012	Creation of Big Society Capital
2015	Conservatives win UK general election
2016	United Kingdom European Union membership referendum and subsequent government reshuffle: end of observation period

Today, social enterprise in the UK is, at least in terms of economic institutions, a rather settled field. Its internal governance unit Social Enterprise UK requires social enterprises to "principally reinvest" their surpluses into the organization. Yet my argument is that, viewed longitudinally, the emergence of social enterprise (SE) played a fundamentally important role for the development of SII. While previously only not-for-profit organizations had been labeled as "social", it was social enterprise that, for the first time, blurred these boundaries on a large scale. SE proponents argued that neither income generation nor legal form per se hindered an organization from being "social"—rather, what mattered from their perspective was an organization's achievement of a "social mission." Although very quickly a settlement emerged that did limit profit distribution, the emergence of SE nevertheless increased ambiguity regarding the boundaries of what counts and does not count as "social." Moreover, as SEs were, not only on a legal level, businesses, the emergence of social enterprise brought *finance*, in the sense of loans or growth capital, into the discussion that had previously centered around *funding*, i.e. non-repayable grants or donations.

This development alone, I argue, would not have led to the creation of SII. As I showed in Chap. 5, SII has mobilized approximately £1.3 billion in public subsidies in its 15-or-so years of existence. Although I do not have data on SII intermediaries' turnover, from the low levels of their overall investment (at best a few hundred million pounds per year), I suspect that these public funds were vital life-support for the SII field. Thus, for SII to blossom, it was not enough to enter the field of social organizations with financial products. Rather, government needed to be convinced to hand out substantial amounts of public funds to impact investors.

Here, New Labour policy ideas played a fundamental role as they opened up problems situations that SII proponents' field-level frame (Chap. 6) claimed to solve. To achieve its overarching goal of prudent yet "inclusive" economic growth, New Labour fundamentally reshaped the field of public services. In essence, public services were redefined as the "value for money" achievement of specific "outcomes" defined by central government. However, this change was not a straightforward, a-social transformation. Rather, it was the result of a power struggle between HM Treasury and other government departments, which the Treasury eventually won. The point is that to win this struggle, Treasury, too, had to rely on the strategies of field-level mobilization described by SAF theory: they had to forge cooperation with other, formally equal government departments. Yet they were constrained by what others perceived as the legitimate authority of HM Treasury. The result was a restructuration of British public services through Treasury tools that were by no means neutral (Chiapello 2015)—but instead implicated a particular valuation, a view on what makes *good* public services. This, in turn, generated an opportunity for all social organizations that could claim the creation of "added value" to enter service delivery.

As SII proponents were very closely linked to HM Treasury (senior civil servants noted in interviews that they would very frequently, at times daily, talk to the leading SII proponent, Ronald Cohen for more than a decade), they sensed an opportunity in these developments. This led to a significant change in their strategy: they began forging cooperation with their former opponents, the VCS, while at the same time taking up government discourse on "added value" and "social outcomes" into what they later termed "social impact." The point is that both of these cooperative ties were only possible *after* events in proximate fields: the process of boundary blurring regarding which organizations count as "social" as well as the increasing dominance of the Treasury view in social policy.

Such a strategy is known in the sociological literature as brokerage (Vedres and Stark 2010) and is cited as a key change mechanism in SAF theory (see Chap. 3). However, this perspective on change does not recognize *intra-field dynamics in a causal role* for the emergence of such cross-field ties. My point is that SII actors were only able to create and exploit such a brokerage situation because dynamics in *proximate field environments* rendered their arguments for cross-field ties acceptable in the eyes of government and social organizations. However, to make use of this opportunity, SII proponents had to adjust their frame as well as their organizational practices.

Gaining an understanding of the development of SII through SAF theory, I had an abductive moment as I realized that the trajectory of the "Treasury view" in the public services field was shaped by the same underlying mechanism as the field of SII. In this chapter, I use the term *resonance space* as a placeholder for my initial hypothesis, demarking a *situation where the emergence of a new cross-field tie was preceded by a change in either of those fields, such that a strategic action frame motivating such a cooperative tie became acceptable to actors within that field.* In the following chapter, I will further elaborate this initial hypothesis and qualify it on a theoretical level.

In this chapter, I use this theoretical perspective to analyze the development of SII in the UK from 1997 until 2016. The sections proceed chronologically and are structured according to the qualitative significance of the covered events for the development of SII. The first section describes Labour's first term in office: here, social enterprise emerged in between VCS and community enterprise. The second section focuses on Labour's second term in office. In this period, Labour's increased focus on public services led to the entrenchment of the "Treasury view" in social policy, while social enterprise became a policy field in its own right. The third section disentangles two key developments that occurred during a very short time around 2006: SII proponents' frame shift vis-à-vis the VCS, as well as the merger of the three formally distinct policy fields into one government department. The fourth section shows how these dynamics catalyzed in between 2007–2010: with Gordon Brown becoming Prime Minister, SII proponents' ties with government expanded from Treasury to No 10. Building on unprecedented influence with government as well as support from the VCS, key SII innovations were developed and accepted by field-level actors during that time. The fifth section describes the development of SII since 2010. Although quantitatively, this period saw an explosion of SII, this was merely a "scale up" of the innovations developed and agreed upon earlier. That said, two qualitatively important events occurred during this period: the Coalition government embraced SII as part of its wider ideological "Big Society" program, and emerging resistance to SII was addressed by government by further entrenching the financialization frame.

7.1 1997–2002: Policy Innovation and Disparate Fields

This section focuses on New Labour's first term in office. In the first segment, I will describe how New Labour changed, or attempted to change, the social policy field. To do so, the introductory sub-segment will briefly describe key elements of New Labour's policy style more generally. The following two sub-segments will describe in more detail the relation of two key government departments, Treasury and Home Office, to social policy, and the respective sub-fields of community enterprise and VCS. In the second segment, I show how this organizational set-up related to the earliest developments of SII. In its first sub-segment, I zoom into the development of SII's precursor, community investment. In the second sub-segment, I describe the birth of social enterprise as a new, boundary-blurring category between not-for-profit VCS and for-profit community enterprise.

7.1.1 Setting the Stage: British Social Policy Around the Millennium

After a sustained series of election losses, the Labour party was in a state of crisis that opened up to debate even some of its most fundamental policy pillars. By the mid-1990s, a group of reformers around Tony Blair and Gordon Brown had won the party-internal contest for direction and began to develop the strategy for "New Labour." Until the mid-1990s, Conservatives had often been successful in framing themselves as competent managers of the British economy, while painting an imaginary of Labour as a threat to economic growth, not least due to its adherence to Keynesian deficit spending. However, after the UK withdrew from the European Exchange Rate Mechanism following "Black Wednesday" in September 1992, the Major administration's reputation for economic policy plummeted (Newman 2001; Seldon 2007). Against the backdrop of decreased public confidence in Conservative capabilities in economic policy, New Labour began aggressively campaigning its agenda of fiscally prudent and "inclusive" economic growth. By doing so, Labour ruled out income tax increases and argued that it would finance key policy interventions by increasing the efficiency of public organizations and public services (97_Labour_Manif).

The idea of "social inclusion" meant that a Labour government would seek to establish social justice not by attempting to reduce inequalities of income and wealth via redistributive taxation. Rather, New Labour would invest public resources into social and public services such as to increase the "employability" of poor individuals (Lister 1998). This is the core idea of the "social investment welfare state" as propagated by New Labour advisers such as Anthony Giddens (Dobrowolsky and Lister 2008). The hope was that by establishing such an "equality of opportunity" (Giddens 1998), poverty would be reduced as the distribution of life chances through paid work would become more evenly distributed. As such a view sees social justice as a question of individual opportunities and not structural factors (e.g. income distribution), British overall public welfare would be increased if those social organizations working towards increasing employability and inclusion would become more effective. Thus, this paradigm shift introduced a growth logic to social welfare: not only were social services justified inasmuch they contributed to economic growth, but the public good itself would be increased to the extent that the "productivity" of social organizations would grow. This was a necessary component for the acceptance of the "scale" argument later propelled by SII proponents. Of more immediate importance, however, was the fact that New Labour altered the key constituents of the social welfare field: unions played a much smaller, but social organizations a much larger role.

In addition to these policy ideas, New Labour introduced particular policy styles, of which three were particularly important for our case. "Government in partnership" denoted the practice of introducing non-government individuals and organizations into the design and implementation of policy (Larsen et al. 2006). For example, New Labour formed a uniquely large number of "commissions" staffed with individuals from both inside and outside government. Perhaps the most prominent of these were the 18 Policy Action Teams (PATs) of the Social Exclusion Unit that were charged to design and implement policy on social inclusion. But partnership also meant that nongovernmental organizations, particularly of the voluntary and community sector, were introduced into the delivery of public services. Second, "joined-up government" denoted the practice of restructuring public services and policy fields in order to create "joined-up solutions to joined-up problems." One example would be to link policy development on the medical and criminological consequences of drug abuse. To achieve its goals, Labour introduced the style of "outcomes management" that obliged subordinate public actors to ensure the delivery of quantitative outcome metrics defined by central government and HM Treasury in particular (Mulderrig 2011).

In the following two sub-segments, I will show how these developments shaped the emergence of SII. First, I will describe the influence of HM Treasury for social policy and show how it grew throughout the Labour government. Second, I will describe the "status quo" of VCS policy as organized at Home Office, to show just how profound are the transformations described in the remainder of this chapter.

HM Treasury and Social Policy

The rising influence of HM Treasury over contents and processes of social policy was a distinct development of New Labour, closely associated to the institutional entrepreneurship of Gordon Brown. Serving as Chancellor from 1997 until becoming Prime Minister in 2007, Brown very significantly impacted the set-up and operation of HM Treasury. In part, he had the ability to do so because of the so-called Granita agreement with Tony Blair of 1994 that guaranteed him wide authority over domestic social policy in return for not standing in the upcoming Labour leadership election.[1] Thus, this development was driven out of dynamics in the field of Labour party-internal politics and translated into the policy field. For example, a senior civil servant working at HM Treasury since the 1980s notes[2]:

> Question: Can you tell me more about what the Treasury influence over social policy was, how it was implemented and whether it was something special under Brown or similar under the Thatcher and Major governments?

---

[1]Source: Tom Happold and Kevin Maguire, Revealed: Brown and Blair's pact, The Guardian, June 6th 2003: https://www.theguardian.com/politics/2003/jun/06/labour.uk, accessed July 16th 2017.

[2]Similar observations have been noted in four other interviews, as well as in Lee (2008, pp. 72, 93, 105ff.), and others.

Answer: Yes it was peculiar to Gordon Brown. When he became Chancellor under Blair, they had an arrangement between them, which was very much that Gordon would have quite a lot of influence over domestic policy. And so on becoming chancellor, they [. . .] wanted to make sure that the Treasury expanded its role, so it wasn't just a finance ministry but it became an economics ministry. He really wanted to develop that. So in all aspects of policy, education, health, ahm, one to name, he grew the number of policy makers. So before that, say under Major or Thatcher, if you were a Treasury official, you tended to be a finance person who wanted to try and control the budget, very much so, control the finances, that was your job, really. It was to stop other departments spending money. Whereas under Gordon Brown you had two functions. One was to oversee the budget, not necessarily to stop them spending money, but get them to spend money on the things he wanted them to spend money on. (B: 00:57-02:03)

The relations between HM Treasury and other government departments are both hierarchical as well as somewhat equal. As no formal hierarchies between cabinet ministers and government departments exist, Treasury officials needed to at least partially create resonance with policymakers from other departments to affect change. That being said, HM Treasury does have (within limits) the formal authority over the government budget—and all other government departments are unilaterally dependent on the Treasury in this regard. Thus, to affect change in other government departments, the Treasury may change the rules of how departments access public funds. Yet this nevertheless remains a delicate task as subjugated policymakers ought to be at least partially convinced of the legitimacy of these changes. This is even more the case the easier policymakers may access control mechanisms, which is why Treasury influence is much weaker in the UK nations other than England (Lee 2008).

There were two principal avenues through which Treasury expanded its authority over social policy: value for money, and cross-departmental issues. In particular the first one proved to be both highly effective as well as crucially important for the increasing acceptance of the financialization as welfare frame in social policy. The legitimacy for Treasury's commitment to value for money arose out of a combination of its traditional, generally accepted role in safeguarding the public budget, as well as the Labour party's 1997 commitments to prudent economic growth. Due to the "simple polity" structure in the UK, these high-level commitments are under intense public and parliamentary scrutiny. This is why, around that time, a resonance space for the Treasury's value for money agenda existed in most other government departments.

In one of his first moves as Chancellor, Brown transferred the responsibility for large parts of monetary policy from the Treasury to the Bank of England (Deakin and Parry 2000) and thereby increasing resources available at the Treasury for its to-be-developed policy function as an indirect consequence. The policy function was gradually developed by expanding the prescriptions regarding "value" with the available resources, while expanding the use of prescriptions regarding "for money" via the Treasury's formal role in public budgeting. Already in 1997, Treasury introduced biennial "Comprehensive Spending Reviews" that required spending departments to justify their spending with regards to government commitments from zero up—rather than as adjustments to previous years, as had been the case before (Deakin and Parry 2000, p. 199). These Comprehensive Spending Reviews, as well as the Budget and Pre-Budget Report granted Treasury ample yet constrained opportunities to affect rules and frames in adjacent social policy fields. A senior civil servant notes:

> [T]he way he [Gordon Brown, PG] ran things was very, ahm, very organized. So, in the Treasury there are 2 or 3 set pieces. So every year a budget, usually in March, unless it's an emergency, every year you have an Autumn statement, or a Pre-Budget-Report, which is usually around November. So twice a year, you get the chance to make decisions, spend money, do ... change things, do stuff, announce things. That's the way he ran it. And then, every couple of years you'd to have a Spending Review, which is a much bigger thing. So the Budget is mainly about Tax, but he used to though in other bits and pieces as well. So twice a year every year, you have two times where you could issue announcements or where you could decide to spend money on new things. And then you have Spending Reviews every 2 or 3 years where you really change the whole, kind of, shape of things. And what he would do is, he would commission studies that would be published on Budget Day or on Spending Review Day, or on Autumn Statement Day, or PBR day [...]. (B: 03:14-04:10)

Through these devices, together with Treasury guidance such as the Green Book, Departmental Investment Strategies as well as numerous guidance regarding procurement, the Treasury was able to influence how other government departments spent their money. In addition, Treasury gained an increasingly central network position across government departments, particularly in relation to public services:

> Brown further entrenched his control over domestic policy by sitting on eighteen of the thirty-two principal ministerial committees of the Cabinet, including all those concerned with reform of the public services. Brown, rather than Blair, chaired the Cabinet committee on Public Services and Public Expenditure [...] (Lee 2008, p. 105)

The Treasury used its increased power particularly for its Value for money agenda. Crucially, several of the binding Treasury guidelines for maintaining Value for money prescribed specific understandings of *what counts as public value*, and therefore defined for what to spend money, rather than merely defining processes of how to spend money. Although these changes in content remained contested, HM Treasury was able to draw on a second resonance space by combining its established role as the safeguard of public finances with the political discourse on *outcomes* and public service reform. This is exemplified by Tony Blair's statement in the foreword to the very first Spending Review in 1998:

> We have stuck rigidly to tough spending plans since the Election and we will keep to our two touch fiscal rules for the entire Parliament. This Government will spend only what it can afford, and will spend wisely to achieve specific outcomes. (98_Treasury_CSR, p. 5)

These policy outcomes acquired a legally binding character with the introduction of Public Service Agreements (PSAs) that contractually tied departmental spending to their achievement. Over the years, PSAs were modified and extended, until they were abolished by the incoming Coalition government in 2010. Nevertheless, they were cornerstone in New Labour's broader public service reform agenda that understood public value as the cost-effective achievement of measured outcomes (Mulderrig 2011). The policy styles of "value for money" and "outcomes management" are fundamental building blocks for the Treasury view on social policy.

Importantly, this change in the underlying principles, categories and devices of social policy changed what were acceptable arguments and policies in that field. What previously might have violated institutionalized rules of how to organize for social policy might not have done so anymore. Subsequent changes were enabled as the justificatory basis shifted. For example, we may conceive of actors that under the old rules would not have been evaluated as factually part of social welfare, while under the new rules their introduction might have become factually possible although normatively inappropriate. In fact, I argue that these changes to the organization of British social policy have created such a resonance space for SII proponents. Where before, their field frame might have been dismissed by policymakers on formal grounds, I will show throughout this chapter, how this evaluative basis has changed to a gradually diluting normative basis.

This resonance space for the financialization frame built on at least three issues. First, the principal indicator of public value became not public ownership, but the achievement of outcomes. This way, outsourcing and the creation of public-private-partnerships became a legitimate strategy to enhance social welfare, if predefined outcomes were achieved.

> While there are limits in what the markets can deliver in some public services, there are some cases where private sector suppliers and market mechanisms can deliver the best diverse outcomes for public services. For example, the expertise of private sector contractors to deliver cost-effective high-quality investment in the infrastructure supporting a range of public services can be, and has been, used to good effect [...]. This use of the private sector to deliver public services is termed 'Public Private Partnership' (2004_Treasury_Microecon, p. 340)

From the Treasury's perspective, a particular advantage of contracting out public services to private providers is the transfer of financial risks off the public balance sheet:

> [T]here was a lot of interest in the idea of transferring risk, particularly, transferring the financial risk. I mean that was a big part of the driver behind the Private Finance Initiative, the idea that, you know, private companies would invest, there would be a fixed return to them, irrespective of how much it actually cost them. So they would bare the financial risk. Now, ahm, I think one could debate how successful these transfers really were. And I think that there is probably quite a strong argument that in reality not much of the risk was actually transferred [...]. BUT the wish to transfer risk was quite a big driver for policy in that time. (A: 15:12-16:15)

The drive to transfer financial risks to private contractors was one of the main reasons behind the increased usage of the Private Finance Initiative (PFI) under New Labour: in theory, PFIs require private service providers to deliver a predefined outcome for a fixed price. But also beyond contracts and PFIs, the idea of risk transfer was one of the core pillars of value for money. For example, Treasury guidance describes as one of the main drivers of value for money:

> A rigorously executed transfer of risks to the parties which are responsible for them, ensuring that the allocation of risks can be enforced and that the costs associated with these risk are actually borne by the parties in the manner originally allocated and agreed. (2006_Treasury_Value, p. 11)

The third consequence of the value for money and outcomes management perspectives relates to deregulation. With the increased focus on outcomes, rules governing the *process* of public service delivery increasingly lost their legitimacy.

> PSAs are most successful where [...] they focus on outcomes rather than process, thus empowering providers to develop their own approach to service delivery [...]. (2004_Treasury_Microecon, p. 369)

As we will see later, proponents of Social Impact Bonds would centrally build their argumentation on these three ideas. But while those became acceptable from a viewpoint of formal rules, their normative appropriateness was established through a shift in New Labour's political discourse that was tied to Treasury's increasing influence.

One of the central tenets of New Labour's social policy has been the shift from redistribution to "social inclusion" (Lister 1998). Although social inclusion had been broadly defined before the election, it was translated into policy only subsequently. To do so, Tony Blair established a "Social Exclusion Unit" in Cabinet Office in December 1997, which established 18 "Policy Action Teams" (PATs) that sought to translate the new concept of social exclusion into policy. The PATs were structured according to "government in partnership" and "joined-up government." Thus, not only did external representatives hold formal positions in the PATs, but their policy staff was selected across government departments. Yet despite reporting directly to the Prime Minister, the PATs allowed Treasury to expand its policy function and significantly influence policy development. As Deakin and Parry (2000) note, the Treasury sat in ten of the eighteen teams, while chairing two. Moreover, the Social Exclusion Unit was led by a former Treasury civil servant who, despite moving to Cabinet Office, "emphasized that the Treasury still paid her (and fed her in its canteen)" (p. 210). The Treasury influence in the PATs builds on the second resonance space for Treasury influence mentioned above—the perception of legitimate involvement in cross-departmental policy issues.

But even besides its influence regarding network structures in the PATs, the Treasury furthermore drove its own political agenda that was closely associated to Gordon Brown's perspective on welfare to work. As such, the Treasury led *contentual* policy development in the "PAT 3—Enterprise and Social Exclusion" which was formally supported by a Treasury minister and chaired by the head of the Treasury's Enterprise Team (99_PAT3, p. 144). The PAT 3 played an important role for the resonance of the financialization frame in social policy, as it linked financialization (to my knowledge) for the first time with social issues while furthermore establishing social enterprise as a policy object, and linking it to social welfare. The PAT 3 embodied numerous ideas regarding social welfare that make up the Treasury view on welfare, although the Treasury view is anything but limited to PAT 3.

The Treasury view on welfare linked New Labour's (and particularly Brown's) ideas of social policy and public services with the long-held Treasury view on economic policy: "In Brown's definition, the Treasury was to be 'not just a Ministry of Finance but also a Ministry working with other departments to deliver long-term economic and social renewal'" (Lee 2008, p. 72). Thus, with increasing Treasury influence, social and economic policy became increasingly merged under the umbrella of "economic and social renewal."

The Treasury view on economic policy resembles liberal ideas on economic growth, enterprise creation, and international competitiveness, and it strongly emphasizes financial markets as a means to achieve these goals. Traditionally, Treasury maintained close ties with City banks and organizations but its influence on policy was limited by a strong, Keynesian Department of Trade and Industry (Davis and Walsh 2015). However, starting with the Thatcher administration, this balance tilted to unilaterally favor Treasury ideas on finance-led macroeconomic policy particularly by replacing officials in the DTI with Treasury staff. The dominance of the Treasury over the DTI, as well as the support for finance and financialization in economic policy had continued if not increased under Gordon Brown's chancellorship (Walsh 2013).

For our endeavor, two dimensions of the Treasury view on economic policy are important: an emphasis on *enterprise creation and economic growth as a public welfare end* in its own right, as well as *financial markets as a superior means* to achieve that. These two perspectives were introduced to *social* policy with the PAT 3 report on community enterprise and the subsequent 2000 Social Investment Taskforce. What was argued for here was government support for financial intermediaries investing in firms located in poor neighborhoods. A civil servant at HM Treasury describes the rationale behind these support activities, including the Treasury's 2002 co-investment into a Bridges Community Ventures fund, as follows:

> So I guess the purpose of the original Bridges fund, the social purpose of it was ahm, investing in areas that were deprived. And actually, that was quite a Treasury view, too. You know, you want economic activity, who cares what happens to the profits, you know, we want the economic activity. And that in itself has a public good, a social benefit. (G: 28:59-29:33)

Taken together, the Treasury had a particular view on social policy that made the arguments of finance proponents more acceptable, both on a formal as well as a normative level. Besides its own normative program, the Treasury view was furthermore shaped as it had only constrained ability to wield legitimate authority over formally equal government departments and therefore necessitated a legitimation via its traditional role in cross-departmental issues and value for money. To develop and implement policy, Treasury altered network structures and used its authority over the budget to introduce new institutional rules for other government departments.

Home Office

Around 1997, policy regarding the voluntary and community sector was located at Home Office. Following its "government in partnership" principle, the incoming Labour administration quickly established a "Compact" to define the future partnership between central government and the VCS. The idea for the Compact was based on the 1996 Deakin Review and developed by Labour in Opposition. At its core, it was a reaction to contemporary fears that increasing numbers of contracts between government and the VCS, which were during the Conservative government tendered within the same competitive framework for both the VCS and for-profit firms, might impair the sectors' independence vis-à-vis government (Kendall 2000; Lewis 2005).

As a consequence, the 1998 Compact explicitly granted the VCS the right to influence policymaking and advocate its own interests (1998_Compact, §9.1). Later during the New Labour years, this would become important as it allowed ACEVO to demand a larger role for the VCS in public service provision. In addition to granting the VCS specific rights, the Compact also settled the VCS' boundaries. Critically, here the sector was defined in the title as the "Voluntary and Community Sector" and later defined as "the nation's 'third sector'", comprised of "[v]oluntary and community groups, as independent, not-for-profit organisations [that] bring distinctive value to society and fulfill a role that is distinct from both the state and the market" (1998_Compact, §5). Thus, this early definition understood the third sector as not-for-profit, and linked this quality with some "distinctive value" the sector brings to wider society. Being not-for-profit, voluntary and community groups

> enable individuals to contribute to public life and the development of their communities by providing the opportunity for voluntary action. [...] Voluntary and community organisations make a major and literally incalculable contribution to the development of society and to the social, cultural, economic and political life of the nation. They act as pathfinders for the involvement of users in the design and delivery of services and often act as advocates for those who otherwise have no voice. [...] They help to alleviate poverty, improve the quality of life and involve the socially excluded. (1998_Compact, §§5, 6)

Critically, here, the public benefit of the VCS is argued to arise as a consequence of its not-for-profit and voluntary nature that complements both government and for-profit firms. As we will see later, these clear boundaries have later been increasingly blurred, and the creation of public benefit has been attributed to "social ventures" largely independent of their voluntary or not-for-profit nature.

In the early days of New Labour, government funded the VCS based on "the value of long-term, multi-year funding, where appropriate, to assist longer term planning and stability" (1998_Compact, §9.3). This was institutionalized through Home Office's "Active Communities Unit" that has been set up during Labour's first year in office. Its "Main Grants Programme" funded

> national, generalist voluntary organisations which aim to increase the effectiveness of the UK voluntary sector by providing services and support to other voluntary organisations, and/or to the voluntary sector as a whole. (This support may be for continuing activity or for specific projects.) [...] National voluntary organisations promoting voluntary activity—including self-help and community development in the statutory or voluntary sectors. (1999_ACU p. 3)

Thus, in the early days of New Labour, the VCS was funded through statutory grants merely *for being engaged in* voluntary work. Outcomes achievement, public service delivery, and social enterprise have, during this time, played no role in the relationship between government and social organizations. This changed during the later Labour years. As Macmillan (2010, p. 3) notes, overall funding to the sector been "increasing from £8.4 billion in 2000–2001 to £12 billion in 2006–2007", but only "£4.2 billion of the statutory funding in 2006–2007 was received as grants, down from £4.6 billion in 2000–2001, whilst contract funding increased over the same period from £3.8 billion to £7.8 billion." This rise of service delivery contracts was an important institutional transformation in social policy that preceded the emergence of Social Impact Bonds, which are a special type of service delivery contract.

7.1.2 Precursors of Social Impact Investing

As I have argued above, SII developed from the community enterprise finance field. There, key SII proponents around Ronald Cohen had argued for a financialization as welfare frame—but did not succeed in garnering more than marginal support. This only changed after the concept of social enterprise was born, introduced into social policy, and partially recuperated by SII proponents. To provide evidence for this claim, the following sub-segment will describe the emergence of social enterprise in England. Thereafter, I will shed light onto the link between the community enterprise finance field and the creation of the financialization as welfare frame. In both of these cases, HM Treasury played an important and facilitating role.

The Emergence of Social Enterprise in England

In contrast to theories of institutional entrepreneurship that often depict the emergence of social enterprises as a creative attempt to bridge institutional "voids" (Mair and Marti 2006, 2009), I argue that the emergence of social enterprise in England was driven by strategic actors. My argument is that SE took the shape that we know today in large parts because its pioneers were required to build resonance with policymakers in order to develop a cooperative tie that would materialize into subsidies and favorable regulation. Yet to do so, they had to shift their frames according to those prevalent in the proximate policy field.

Social enterprise in England developed from the merger of two London-based co-operative development agencies into Social Enterprise London (SEL) in 1998 (Teasdale 2011). According to Teasdale (2011, p. 11), SEL's memorandum of association described its organizational goals as:

> 'to promote co-operative solutions for economic and community development' and 'to promote social enterprises, in particular co-operatives and common ownerships, social firms, and other organisations and businesses which put into practice the principles of participative democracy, equal opportunities and social justice.'

This early SE definition is linked to the co-operative model that features one-person-one-vote governance and allows profit distribution only to its members rather than corporate shareholders. Very quickly, however, SEL developed networks with other associations that positioned their member organizations as those responding to some kind of market failure—particularly within poor neighborhoods—and included development trusts as well as social housing initiatives

(Teasdale 2011, pp. 11–12). This initial expansion led to a situation where such different organizational templates were included into SE that forging an internal identity of the field would inevitably require decreasing the salience of these formal boundaries as a signifier for the field.

In parallel to the creation of SEL, HM Treasury ran an extensive consultation to develop the Policy Action Team 3 report. The remit of PAT 3 had been to "draw up an action plan with targets to encourage more successful business start-ups in poor neighbourhoods" (1999_PAT3, p. 143), thus seeing business growth as a means to achieve social welfare. To develop policy proposals in this regard, the PAT was staffed according to New Labour's "partnership" principle: in addition to cross-departmental officials and representatives from the for-profit and community investment sectors as full members of the PAT, a large number of organizations in various fields related to community development had taken part in a consultation process in between December 1998 and May 1999 (1999_PAT3, p. 148). Here, newly formed SEL had been able to raise policymakers' awareness to the concept of SE.

From the perspective of SEL, inclusion of the SE concept in the report was favorable, as PAT 3 explicitly stated enterprise creation and growth as a policy objective. Hence it promised a significant boost of resources for the new category. However, to enter PAT 3, SE would need, on the one hand, to show its potential to achieve the PAT 3 policy objectives of "neighborhood renewal" and "social inclusion", while on the other hand position itself as a category distinct from ethnic and minority-, as well as community enterprises that were the main target of the report (see below). This tension had been addressed in the report by giving a conflicting, inherently contradictory definition of SE as both business and not-for profit.

The business definition of SE is a blend of the traditional co-operative model with other organizations that operate in the field of "social regeneration and help" but are *not* confined to the democratic ownership structures of co-operatives. They include "large insurance mutuals and retail co-operatives" as well as "social firms (e.g. for production by people with disabilities), or social housing." SEs "are in most ways like any other private sector business" (1999_PAT3, p. 105). By contrast, the not-for-profit definition understands social enterprises as

> those organisations who are independent of the state and provide services, goods, and trade for a social purpose and are non-profit distributing. The sector is funded, and achieves viability, through a mix of trade, income generation and grants. The sector needs to make profits (or at least avoid losses) to be viable, but profits are not sought for distribution to shareholders. (1999_PAT3, p. 105)

The not-for-profit perspective highlights that as SEs do not distribute profits, they "can be effective at developing services which may be unattractive or inappropriate for the private sector." Moreover, as they do not distribute profits to shareholders, SEs

> can be also be valuable in engaging local people in economic activities in ways that public agencies have found difficult. The social economy does not simply provide substitutes for real jobs and services where there has been market failure. It also helps develop a stronger sense of community. (1999_PAT3, p. 105)

Thus, to create resonance with Treasury and hence gain resources for the new category, SE proponents imported from PAT 3's formal remit an engagement with neighborhood renewal as the defining characteristic of social enterprise, and abandoned SEL's earlier requirement of ownership structures. This way, SE could distinguish itself from the co-operative movement. Yet as social enterprises were described as trading companies, SE furthermore set itself apart from the VCS. However, creating resonance with Treasury furthermore required SE to position itself vis-à-vis the extant category of for-profit community enterprise. To do so they added a (partially contradictory) not-for-profit dimension to the SE definition. This way, social enterprise entered the terrain of the voluntary sector—which would open up an identity struggle for the field in the years to come. At the same time, SE was linked to a government department, HM Treasury, that favored finance-led organizational growth. Although a Social Enterprise Unit was later established at the Department of Trade and Industry, key civil servants as well as its minister, Patricia Hewitt, moved from the Treasury.

Community Investment and The Roots of the Financialization as Welfare Frame

The Policy Action Team 3 was a key event in the financialization of welfare for another reason besides the emergence of social enterprise. As I have argued above, Treasury had for a long time favored a finance view on economic and industrial policy. With PAT 3, however, this frame expanded into social welfare, yielding a field-level strategic action frame that is remarkably similar to SII proponents' financialization as welfare frame described in Chap. 6. The key frame innovation PAT 3 proposed was to strengthen specialized financial intermediaries, Community Development Finance Institutions (CDFIs), in order to achieve social policy goals. This recommendation built on the fact that key CDFI proponents were members of the PAT.

In the PAT 3 report, the diagnostic framing described low enterprise creation in poor neighborhoods as a social problem that was theorized as due to "'market failures' in access to finance, which mean that not enough capital is available for projects with high returns to society" and "a weak culture of support for enterprise, across the whole range of local and national institutions" (1999_PAT3, pp. 1–2). Mirroring the entrenchment of financial economics at Treasury, although blaming commercial banks for the lack of finance, their actions were described as rational from a perspective of Agency Theory. But rather than proposing regulation, PAT 3 opted for a growth of CDFIs as a solution to the financing problem (p. 71). This is particularly noteworthy as the mandatory lending provisions for commercial banks of the US Community Reinvestment Act of 1977 are cited as a positive example to grow community lending but are not listed as a possible solution (p. 69).

The prognostic framing shares with SII proponents a view that specialized financial intermediaries are in a unique position to support the growth of community enterprises, while arguing that their absence proves problematic for poor neighborhoods:

> the coverage of such intermediary organisations, which can help bridge the gap between business needs in deprived areas and commercial requirements of bank lending, is at present

patchy. These community finance initiatives tend to be thinly capitalised. (1999_PAT3, p. 65)

The motivational frame saw the required actions to grow CDFIs first and foremost with government. To achieve organizational growth of these financial intermediaries, they should be "able to exploit public and charitable funding in order to lever in commercial lending, thus scaling up their operations significantly" (p. 70). As described in Chap. 6, "scale" and "leverage" are key theoretizations by which SII proponents attempt to justify public support for financial intermediation as in the government's own interest. The same rationale was already noted in the PAT 3 report:

> While funds in the public and charitable sector are scarce, initiatives should draw on the private sector. The issue is therefore how to make community development a bankable proposition, and how commercial institutions can be persuaded to invest. (1999_PAT3, p. 66)

More concretely, all policies proposed as part of the PAT 3 motivational frame favor the material interests of CDFIs. For example, the report proposes the establishment of a "loan guarantee scheme" to repay lenders in the case of the investee's bankruptcy. In support of this option, the Small Firms Loan Guarantee Scheme set up under Thatcher is cited as a positive example, noting its high "value for money" (p. 78). Other proposed interventions are deregulation in order to allow CDFIs securitization of their loan portfolios, as well as tax reductions for community investments (p. 79).

The strategic action frame proposed in the PAT 3 resembled the financialization as welfare frame not only in its positive view on financial intermediaries, but also in its opposition to non-repayable grants as well as not-for-profit voluntary and community organizations. For example, the report argues that "the public and voluntary sectors are too stuck in a culture of grants" (p. 4) and proposes that this can be changed by increasing the focus on lending. Here, the political-economic consequences of debt are ignored, while its organizational consequences are valued positively:

> Loans have major incentive benefits compared to grants, as they can create a greater discipline to use resources productively. So lending is in general preferable to grant-giving, even if it is not on fully commercial terms. Support for loans can also be a more efficient use of limited public money, as it can be spread more widely. These facts are not sufficiently recognised in public policy. (1999_PAT3, p. 10)

In 2000, shortly after the PAT 3 publication, a Social Investment Task Force has been set up by Gordon Brown in order to develop the PAT 3 proposals further. Although the frame advanced by the task force largely mirrored PAT 3, it placed a much larger emphasis on equity and venture capital investments. One of the reasons has been the influence of Ronald Cohen who chaired the task force. At that time, Ronald Cohen was the head of a venture capital fund and had been described as the "father of venture capital" in the UK. He did, to the best of my knowledge, not have experience in community lending. It is unclear what exactly led Brown to invite

Cohen. It might have been the Treasury's favorable view on venture capital, but one of the reasons has certainly also been Cohen's role as a key donor to the Labour party.[3]

The introduction of venture capitalist Cohen was a path-breaking event for the emergence of SII. While previously, the financialization as welfare frame was dominated by discourse on lending as well as community lenders, now the policy discourse increasingly shifted to equity financial products. The problem description, however, stayed the same: community finance did not suffice the return expectations of financial intermediaries and was thus argued to require public subsidies (rather than a reduction in financial return expectations):

> Many enterprises in under-invested communities find it difficult to access finance because their financial returns are insufficiently attractive for lenders and equity providers. There is a need, therefore, for strong incentives to be provided in order for significant finance to flow to CDFIs and enable them to guide and finance the growth of businesses as well as social and community enterprises. After considering many alternatives, the Task Force proposes a tax credit which would provide lenders to, and equity investors in, CDFIs with a guaranteed minimum rate of return.[4] (2000_SIT, p. 4)

The shift to equity became evident in the task force recommendation that "the successful principles of venture capital, namely long term equity investment, business support to the entrepreneur and rapid growth of the company backed, should be applied to community investment through the creation of Community Development Venture Funds." These funds should be supported by direct co-investment from public sources. In 2002, Cohen founded Bridges Community Ventures as the first of such venture funds and received a £20 million co-investment from HM Treasury into its first investment vehicle. Moreover, the task force argued that these venture funds should be supported by specialist intermediaries on the "wholesale" level. But despite arguing that such a community investment bank "need to emerge in the next 3 years" and demanding government support for its creation (pp. 24–25), these proposals were *not* taken up by HM Treasury. Although some 10 years later, Cohen succeeded in convincing government to set up such a "wholesale" support particularly for equity investors, at that point in time, his proposals did not create sufficient resonance.

As we will see later, a key point in achieving frame resonance was that equity proponents later began to embrace challengers within the VCS, particularly those representing its chief executives. This process started with the 2000 Social Investment Taskforce. Its formal remit was "to unleash new sources of private and institutional investment" and "to explore innovative roles that the voluntary sector,

---

[3]A former politician mentioned to me in a private conversation an alleged deal between the two that saw Brown to guarantee keeping taxes on venture capital and private equity on the low levels inherited from the Conservative period, in return for Cohen committing the venture capital and private equity industries to more "social" investment activities.

[4]This tax credit was based on the investor's personal income tax, and not on the capital gains tax on potential profits. Investors were able to reduce their income tax by a total of 25% of the investment sum, while furthermore receiving the investment's profits.

businesses and Government could play as partners in this area" (2000_SIT, p. 3). Moreover, the task force recruited Geraldine Peacock, who had previously been the chair of the VCS' chief-executives' association ACEVO and a long-time supporter of entrepreneurial activity and earned income in the VCS. Her view on VCS incumbents largely resonated with that of finance proponents: In an interview with Third Sector magazine in 2002, she noted that "[t]here is still a perception that charities should go around with begging bowls" and that trustees, donors and foundations "don't like you to be too business-like, which is mad."[5] In an opinion piece, she argued that charities have become dependent on grants as a single source of income, creating a "culture of dependency that sits uncomfortably in the competitive contemporary world." Moreover, she saw "a breed of not-for-profit financial services companies (Community Development Finance Institutions)" as a means to "break" this "dependency culture."[6] Note how her view on these financial intermediaries as not-for-profit organizations starkly contrasted the view of the task force that centered on investors' profits.

The social investment task force joined VCS challengers in their combative strategy of open opposition. They noted that poor communities are "heavily dependent upon philanthropy and public money" which can "discourage or crowd out private sector investment" and therefore sustain a "culture of philanthropy, paternalism and dependence" rather than "one of empowerment, entrepreneurship and initiative" (p. 4). They argued that inertia in the VCS are main reasons for this situation:

> Entrepreneurial behaviour in the voluntary sector tends to be fettered by its traditions, laws and established practices. [...] Risk averse trustees and a culture of "begging and benevolence" are raised as just two factors which work against the voluntary sector promoting and practising entrepreneurship. (00_SIT, p. 14)

As a solution, they demanded a "major cultural shift from the public, charitable, voluntary and community sectors towards a more entrepreneurial approach" in addition to "finance through a range of appropriate CDFIs" (p. 10), as well as "innovative relationships between CDFIs [...] and private companies and the voluntary and community sector [...] which explore new ways to link money and talent" (p. 25).

Taken together, the 2000 social investment task force mirrored the Treasury's view on finance-led organizational growth as a public policy goal as well as its field-level motivational frame. In contrast to PAT 3, the task force argued for a much greater role for equity products and sought to expand its prescriptions into the VCS.

---

[5]Source: Lexie Goddard, Social Enterprise: Compassionate Profit, Third Sector, March 22nd 2002, http://www.thirdsector.co.uk/social-enterprise-compassionate-profit-charity-pays-its-own-way-sounds-unlikely-social-enterprise-charitable-activity-become-self-sustaining-lexie/article/614062, accessed March 28th 2017.

[6]Source: Geraldine Peacock, Opinion: Thinkpiece—Time to break the old culture of dependency, March 20th 2002, http://www.thirdsector.co.uk/opinion-thinkpiece-time-break-old-culture-dependency/article/619834, accessed March 28th 2017.

However, although equity proponents were successful in mobilizing some government subsidies in Labour's second parliamentary term, their big successes only came about a decade later. As I will argue next, this hinged upon two important developments: the rise of social enterprise and the subsequent boundary- and opposition-blurring in the VCS, and the introduction of the Treasury view into social policy and public services.

7.2 2001–2005: Contesting Social Enterprise Policy and Public Service Delivery

During Labour's second term in office, three processes started that began to dilute the financialization as welfare with the VCS and public service delivery. The development of SE was an important hinge between all three of those, which is why I will devote the first segment to describe this key phase in its development. Early during Labour's second term, a settlement of the SE field emerged that allowed both SII proponents and VCS challengers to interpenetrate in the novel field. The SII side of this process will be described in more detail in the second segment. The third segment will describe key developments within public policy that began to link these three issues: Labour's increased focus on public service reform. Here, two models of public service reform competed for authority within central government: Blair's "earned autonomy" and Brown's "constrained discretion." To advance Brown's model, HM Treasury sought to expand control over other government departments. By doing so, its normative view on finance, too, began to take hold in other policy fields as well.

7.2.1 Social Enterprise: Settling the Rules, Expanding the Scope

After Labour won the 2001 general election, a Social Enterprise Unit was established at the Department of Trade and Industry. In 2002, the unit published "Social Enterprise: a Strategy for Success" that established multiple important definitions, theoretizations, and action imperatives that took the form of a field settlement. Besides settling the institutional rules of the SE field, the 2002 strategy also served as a strategic action frame of (positioned) DTI-Treasury actors within government and state fields to reorganize policy according to their interests. Key to both dimensions was that the 2002 report established the first formal (albeit not legal) definition of SE, which read:

> A social enterprise is a business with primarily social objectives whose surpluses are principally reinvested for that purpose in the business or in the community, rather than being driven by the need to maximise profit for shareholders and owners. [...] By using

> business solutions to achieve public good, the Government believes that social enterprises have a distinct and valuable role to play in helping create a strong, sustainable and socially inclusive economy. [...] They include local community enterprises, social firms, mutual organisations such as co-operatives, and large-scale organisations operating nationally or internationally. There is no single legal model for social enterprise. They include companies limited by guarantee, industrial and provident societies, and companies limited by shares; some organisations are unincorporated and others are registered charities (2002_DTI_Social Enterprise Strategy, p. 7)

This definition is noteworthy in several regards. First and foremost, it holds that profits ought to be "principally"—but not fully—reinvested. Thus, under the DTI definition, some profits may be extracted—even by shareholders—and redistributed towards a not further defined "community." Moreover, the definition heavily emphasized the business (and not the voluntary) nature of SE. Thirdly, the definition did not limit SE to particular legal forms, and included companies limited by shares as well as organizations with co-operative ownership. This business-oriented, rather permissive SE definition was mainly due to the members of the SE Unit and the "working groups" contributing to the report. The head of the unit, Patricia Hewitt, was the former head of PAT 3, two of the eight groups were chaired by PAT members (Andrew Robinson of NatWest bank, and Ed Mayo of New Economics Foundation), and numerous members came from co-operatives and the New Economics Foundation. Not a single member came from the VCS (2002_DTI, pp. 79–81). Thus SE was a challenger group that, by accessing public resources, penetrated the field of social welfare.

Within government and state fields, the SE strategy helped to further entrench the Treasury view into social policy. This was because SE proponents within the DTI argued for the increased use of social enterprises for the delivery of public services. For example, Patricia Hewitt noted that:

> if we are to encourage a greater spirit of enterprise in our public services, then there is no reason why all the partners in this process should come from the mainstream private sector. There are very real opportunities, I believe, to promote social enterprise as a key component in the process of modernising and reforming our public services (2002_DTI, p. 6)

Thus the DTI strategy, for the first time, linked SE with Labour's 2001 election pledge to modernize public service delivery. By drawing on the not-for-profit component of the SE definition described above, the strategy argues that SEs, with their "combination of enterprise, social purpose and customer focus" are "an effective method of delivering improved public services" (p. 24). To organize growth of SE as well as to introduce it into public service delivery, the DTI strategy identified eight SE growth "barriers" of which three are particularly important for our case:

- poor understanding of the particular abilities and value of social enterprise;
- little hard evidence to demonstrate the impact and added value of social enterprise;
- difficulty accessing and making use of what is perceived to be limited appropriate finance and funding available; (p. 8)

Remember that a key question in this work is how policymakers came to accept the argument that for-profit finance "creates social impact." The DTI settlement sheds light into this process. The key juncture here was a circular argument: SE was assumed to possess some kind of "added value" that justified its role in public service delivery. Yet, it was diagnosed a lack of "understanding" and "hard evidence" of what this "value" was. Based on this, a motivational frame was developed to "establish the value of social enterprise" (p. 8). These attempts to measure and formalize the "added value" and "impact" of SE coincided with an increased reformulation of public service as the delivery of outcomes by all kinds of, and not just publicly owned, organizations. In parallel, finance proponents began to argue that their investments would grow SEs, and hence "scale" their impact. Thus, the DTI settlement significantly reduced the chasm between policymakers focusing on outcomes and SII proponents. By advocating social enterprises' inherent impact, DTI increased frame resonance between SE and SII advocates, and social policymakers.

Besides this, DTI's decision to establish the social impact of SE had important consequences for the network structure of the SE field. The DTI set up an Impact Working Group that would be "working through the existing New Economics Foundation/Development Trusts Association Research Group" in order to "devise methods of evaluating the social and economic impact of social enterprises that would be rigorous and robust enough to convince lenders and policymakers" (2002_DTI, p. 80). This research group was chaired by Ed Mayo who had previously studied with the New Economics Foundation how the social impact *of the VCS* could be measured in order to allow VCS organizations more access to government funding (2003_ACEVO). A year later, he was a guest author in an ACEVO publication and developed ideas very similar to SIBs. The DTI strategy therefore not only settled the rules of the field and propelled the frame inside other government departments, but also established a network structure that led to the introduction of VCS actors into the SE field.

In summary, the DTI settlement established SE as partially for-profit, growth-oriented businesses that create some kind of "social impact." Within state fields, DTI sought, with support from both No 10 and Treasury, to establish SE as a vehicle for public service delivery. Although subsequently, VCS actors would enter the field, at that point, SE was defined in contrast to the VCS as growth-oriented businesses "making the transition from a grant dependent voluntary sector or community organisation to one which is independent" (p. 21). The role of grants was to be confined to "initial pump priming" (p. 66) on social enterprises' road to financial "sustainability." In the words of a civil servant at the Social Enterprise Unit:

> it was very important to the sector, you know, Jonathan [Bland, the founder of Social Enterprise London, PG] and his peers, that social ENTERPRISE was seen as.. that was SUCH a big issue in the early days.. was seen as a part of business, and not NOT seen as part of the voluntary sector. (G: 09:30)

There were two direct consequences of the settlement: first, the government grant-funded the set-up of the Social Enterprise Coalition (later re-named Social

Enterprise UK), an umbrella organization that would act "as a voice of social enterprise" and advocate its benefits vis-à-vis policymakers.[7] Second, the government designed a bespoke legal form for SEs following the settlement. In contrast to co-operative forms, the Community Interest Company (CIC) does not limit individual influence on firm governance and allows the distribution of 35% of the firm's profits, but requires the firm to work for "community benefit" as well as "lock in" its assets with a "social mission."[8]

7.2.2 Early Dynamics in Social Investment and Social Enterprise Finance

The DTI settlement defined SEs as organizations that "principally reinvest" their surpluses without specifying legal forms. Thus, the settlement created both opportunities and constraints for financial actors to enter the emerging SE field. The largest opportunity was lending, as profit extraction via debt instruments was possible under the settlement. After all, community lenders represented a significant proportion of the DTI's "finance and funding" work group members. The 2002 strategy argued that "if social enterprises are to move towards greater financial independence, they will need improved access to the loans and other forms of finance" (p. 68), but also:

> Initiatives which seek to provide equity/venture capital do not exclude social enterprises. In practice, because of the high rates of return required, it is anticipated that only a small number of social enterprises will attract finance of this type. (2002_DTI, p. 67)

Thus, for-profit equity investors seeking "commercial" rates of return on their investment played only a minor role in the SE field at that stage. However, equity proponents were not fully excluded from the field but were part of the "finance and funding" work group linked to the DTI strategy. Moreover, they used their direct relation to HM Treasury to advocate for such "commercial" equity finance as a means to solve problems of social welfare. In 2002, Treasury followed the recommendations of the Social Investment Taskforce and gave a £20 million co-investment for the £40 million fund that marked the creation of Bridges Community Ventures. As noted earlier, equity proponents' view resonated strongly with the Treasury view that focused on economic activity and was rather indifferent regarding profit distribution. By contrast, proponents of the emerging SE field argued for a limitation in profit distribution. In this situation, equity proponents on the one hand maintained ties with Treasury, while on the other hand developed a strategy of boundary blurring that built on taking up the "social impact" discourse

[7]Source: Social Enterprise Coalition website, archived October 2nd 2006, accessed March 31st 2017: https://web.archive.org/web/20061002133410/http://www.socialenterprise.org.uk/page.aspx?SP=1346

[8]Source: Office of the CIC Regulator, Setting up a Social Enterprise: https://www.gov.uk/set-up-a-social-enterprise, accessed November 9th 2017.

developed in the SE field but linked it with equity financial products that featured significant profit distribution.

In the early days, Bridges Community Ventures described itself as a "community development venture funds" and followed the Treasury's view on investment in poor neighborhoods. The company did *not* present itself as an investor into SEs.[9] However, in 2004, Bridges Community Ventures raised a grant from the government's Phoenix Fund and developed a report on "equity-like capital for social ventures." The lead author of this report was the CEO of Bridges Community Ventures, Michelle Giddens, the daughter of Anthony Giddens, and she was also a member of the DTI strategy's Finance and Funding workgroup. The purpose of Bridges' report was to show how "[e]stablishing a social venture fund would support social ventures by using innovative equity-like financing instruments to avoid the problems that some social enterprises face when issuing pure equity" (04_Bridges p. 5). Here, numerous boundary blurring concepts cornerstone to later SII have been developed.

Most importantly, the report talked about "social *ventures*" as including SEs *as well as* "socially driven businesses—revenue generating and profit distributing with a social mission" (p. 9). Thus, both, companies with and without limits on profit distribution were grouped as those having a "social and/or environmental purpose." Of these "social ventures", the fund would invest into "high potential social ventures [. . .] planning significant growth and are highly scalable with the potential to deliver some financial return as well as high social return" (p. 9). To legitimize the expanded category, the goal for the fund would be to "maximize social value within financial constraints" (p. 35). For this reason, they argued, the "social venture fund would need to work hard to remain at the cutting edge in terms of evaluating and measuring social impact" (p. 34). To do so, the fund should use the Social Return on Investment concept developed by the New Economics Foundation (p. 50). Financially, the fund would seek a return on each investment of 5–30% p.a. (p. 26). In order to extract the necessary levels of funds from distribution-limited SEs, the fund would use "equity-like" instruments.[10] Although Bridges set up a funds targeting SEs only in 2009, this report nevertheless shows how SII proponents, from the start, used the emergence of SE as an opportunity to blur boundaries regarding profit extraction and target a much wider group of organizations than community enterprise.

The argument that SE growth abilities are significantly limited by their reduced "access to finance" was shared by equity proponents, CDFIs and SE associations. Following a recommendation of the DTI strategy's finance workgroup, the Bank of England was asked by the DTI to "review the provision of debt and equity finance to social enterprises" (2003_BoE, p. 5). Its findings were, however, in stark contrast to the claims made by finance proponents: The Bank of England found that although

---

[9]See for example a 2003 snapshot of the company's website, accessed April 3rd 2017: https://web.archive.org/web/20030213000433/http://www.bridgesventures.com/

[10]These are loans with royalties, i.e. loans charged with a contractually agreed distribution of the investee's income in addition to interest rates (p. 43). As these royalties target an organization's income, not profits, they would still fall under the SE definition.

28% of surveyed SEs had been rejected by lenders, 60% of those have been successful in raising finance elsewhere (16 out of 27 organizations; 2003_BoE, pp. 24–25). Moreover, the study found that only 32% of all surveyed SEs cited "access to finance" as a problem inhibiting their growth. Lastly, the study found "little evidence of demand for, or supply of, conventional venture capital or business angel finance to the social enterprise sector" and argued that this was "not as a result of a market failure but is instead due to the specific characteristics of the social enterprise sector, in particular *the difficulty of providing a commercial financial return*, ownership issues and the lack of an exit strategy" (p. 1, emphasis added). But they also argued that there was demand for "patient finance" in which "investors are willing to accept lower [. . .] financial returns in exchange for social outputs" (p. 1).

However, the findings of the Bank of England did not reduce the importance of "access to finance" in the DTI workgroup. To the contrary, in 2003 the DTI finance workgroup was restructured and saw the entrance of representatives from commercial banks and increased influence by equity proponents (2003_DTI, pp. 77–79). The following 2003 Progress Report on the DTI strategy argued that "there is a requirement for an 'equity equivalent' product to address the lack of finance available for start-up and growth social enterprises" (2003_DTI, p. 48). In addition, in noted that:

> Patient capital is not a 'stand alone' type of finance. It includes a range of types of funding and is on a spectrum of finance—from unconditional grants at one end to full commercial finance at the other. Social and community enterprises need to be confident in their knowledge of the full range of financial options that may be open to them and how best (and when) to tap into each. (2003_DTI, p. 50)

Thus, where just a few years before, increasing access to finance for SEs meant increasing the supply of grants, contracts, or loans, the policy goal was now to "make available" the "full spectrum" of financial products for SEs. This means that the DTI strategy began to resonate with the key boundary-blurring frame innovation developed by equity proponents.

In 2004, former Social Investment Taskforce member Geraldine Peacock became director of the Charity Commission and stated her objectives as follows:

> I would like to move the voluntary sector towards a more sustainable funding environment where it is making full use of all the available financial instruments. This would, I believe, mean that those organisations which can take loans and investments will be doing so, leaving grant money to be accessed by those who need it most. (05_SITF, p. 11)

This statement is noteworthy not only because it includes the "full spectrum" argument advanced by equity proponents, but also because the VCS—rather than community enterprise or SE—was presented as its addressee. Although it would take until around 2007 for such a viewpoint to resonate with key VCS actors, in the years following 2003, a group of new actors emerged. Actors such as Impetus-Private Equity Foundation, Venturesome, Big Issue Invest, or New Philanthropy Capital all shared equity proponents' frame and advocated for investments into "high growth, high impact" organizations while being less clear on limitations to profit distribution. Importantly, all of these actors were related to or owned by charitable foundations. A key accelerator here was the link between the Social Investment Taskforce and

Charity Commission. In its 2000 report, the Taskforce had argued for a deregulation of charity law to allow charitable foundations to invest their capital endowment into for-profit investments that followed their charitable objectives. With its "Investment of Charitable Funds: Basic Principles (CC14)" guidance of 2004, the Charity Commission accepted these recommendations (04_CharityCommission).

7.2.3 Treasury Appropriating Social Policy: Towards Hybridization and Resonance

Besides the growing proximity between equity proponents and social enterprise, the years of Labour's second term in office saw two other key developments. The first one was increased boundary-blurring between SE and the voluntary and community sector. Second, this blurred field began to play an increasing role for the delivery of public services. Based on this policy approach, a positioned group of VCS actors, its organized executive management, began to argue for finance-led organizational growth as a means to enable VCS public service delivery. But remember that, like any field, public service reform was highly contested, too. Here, Treasury was a positioned, strategic actor that argued for its "value for money" view in social policy. As the Treasury view began to link the hybrid VCS-SE field with public service delivery, a number of policy structures were formed that were a few years later used by proponents of Social Impact Bonds.

HM Treasury entered the realm of social policy with the 2002 Spending Review, which featured an additional Cross-Cutting Review on "The Role of the Voluntary and Community Sector in Service Delivery" (2002_Treasury_CCR). This review established the VCS as a central delivery vehicle for public services based on its assumed "added value." But critically, in the review, "the 'voluntary and community sector' has *not* [emphasis in original] been tightly defined. It is intended to be wider in scope than 'general charities' and the 'voluntary sector', inclusive of [. . .] social enterprise". As part of the review, Treasury granted Home Office an additional £188 million over 3 years and set up a "one-off investment fund to help voluntary and community organisations in their public service work" named futurebuilders with an additional £125 million (2002_Treasury, p. 7). Thus, as part of its strategic attempts within state fields, HM Treasury attempted introduce the expanded VCS-SE category into public service delivery by granting it significant additional resources.

Within the VCS, this had two consequences. First, VCS incumbents saw the rise of SE as a threat, as these challengers, who explicitly understood themselves as businesses and not charities, had convinced DTI and Treasury to set up bespoke support for SEs with the Small Business Service, Business Links, and Regional Development Agencies (e.g. 2002_Treasury, p. 24). Thus, VCS actors attempted to reclaim the category. Earlier, VCS actors had argued for social *entrepreneurship* (in contrast to social *enterprise*) as a distinctive practice and value of VCS organizations (1997_Leadbeater, 2003_ACEVO). Based on this argument, the VCS began to argue that "the widest understanding of social enterprise as an activity as well as a type of organisation is taken on board, both within the sector and across government" (2004_NCVO, p. 38). VCS incumbents attempted to include VCS organizations into social enterprise, and did so by joining the Social Enterprise Coalition.[11] But they also worked towards excluding for-profit and co-operative SEs from their own VCS definition (2007_NCVO, p. 7). But while, vis-à-vis government, they succeeded in widening the SE category, they did not succeed in maintaining the strict VCS boundary.

The second consequence of Treasury's penetration of social policy for the VCS was the creation of debt financial products to allow social organizations bid for public service delivery contracts. To establish legitimacy with the VCS for an increased role in public service delivery, the Treasury accepted two of the VCS' long-held demands: "full-cost recovery" and "irrecoverable VAT". Particularly a group of VCS chief executives organized at ACEVO had been vocal that statutory grants to VCS organizations did not resemble their organizations' full cost. In line with their material interests from representing the management of voluntary organizations, they argued that grants did not allow VCOs to cover their "overhead" costs, such as management expenditure. The Treasury accepted this argument and subsequently worked to introduce full-cost recovery into spending departments.

> So, before the Cross-Cutting Review, third sector organisations would get money to run a service. [. . .] But they wouldn't get full cost, they would only get like a grant, say.. so let's say "ok we'll give you half a million pounds and you do this and this." But that half million did not cover the organization's running costs, you know, their office, staff. So in the Cross-Cutting Review, all the complains were about that. [. . .] So we were trying to convince funders so that that the central government departments, local authorities and other public organizations that when you are funding third sector organizations you have to take into account their overheads, their running costs. (B: 37:47)

This coincided with VCS demands that it was disproportionately affected by value-added tax in comparison to the private sector and therefore demanded VAT reductions from the Treasury. However, being unilaterally dependent from EU regulation in this regard, the Treasury did not follow these demands:

> [The VCS, PG] wanted to say, 'when you're a third sector organization, you don't have to do the VAT thing.' There is no way, there is no way in the world that any government is going to go down that road. Not gonna happen, I don't think any EU country would do that. I mean, the [EU, PG] Commission would just laugh at you. [. . .] I think we did go to the Commission and talked about it. And in fact, as I recall, [. . .] the answer to the problem was: 'Spend money on social housing instead. Because we're not gonna change any VAT law. So you can forget that.' (B: 35:46)

Based on this idea, the Treasury decided to partially follow the VCS's demands by spending additional funds on the sector. This was combined with ACEVO demands regarding "full-cost recovery" and strengthening the management

[11]Source: Social Enterprise UK, Coalition members, website snapshot archived February 6th 2007, accessed April 5th 2017: https://web.archive.org/web/20070206012052/http://www.socialenterprise.org.uk/Page.aspx?SP=1637

"capacity" of VCS organizations to yield the £125 million fund called futurebuilders to "help develop an investment culture in the sector with less dependency on short-term grants and more emphasis on earning income."[12] To do so, social organizations—both VCS and SEs—were eligible to apply for publicly financed debt if they sought to deliver public services in the future. The repayment of the loan was then tied to the organization winning a public service delivery contract (05_Futurebuilders_eligibility, p. 1). This was strongly supported by ACEVO who argued that loans and public service delivery "were very natural bedfellows" and supporting the latter meant expanding the former (H: 23:05). They argued that having to continuously apply for grants to cover operational expenses diverted resources that, with an up-front payment in the form of a loan, could have been used more productively (e.g. Ed Mayo in 2003_ACEVO). Second, they argued such investments into the "organizational capacity" and financial management skills were necessary if VCS organizations interested in public service delivery were to avoid that the Treasury would "wipe the floor with them" during contract negotiation (B: 39:15). The Treasury, on the other hand, saw the importance of growing VCS "organizational capacity" as a means to ensure value for money during contract delivery. Based on this frame resonance, a public investment fund was set up that gave loans to VCS organizations. Adding further confusion to the field, this practice was termed "social investment"—even though it had hardly anything to do with the private equity investments the Social Investment Taskforce was arguing for.

As argued above, Labour's second term saw an increased focus of the core executive to "modernize" public service delivery. However, Gordon Brown's vision of "constrained discretion" was competing with Tony Blair's idea of "earned autonomy," thereby causing "the most bitter of the battles over domestic policy" between these two parts of the British core executive (Lee 2008, p. 106). For our endeavor, it is unimportant how exactly the competition played out, but eventually Brown succeeded in imposing his vision of "constrained discretion." This meant that modernizing public service delivery would be understood and increasingly institutionalized as spending departments' delivery of Public Service Agreements and other policy outcomes. The execution of this modernization agenda was principally driven through the Treasury, and the Spending Review in particular (Lee 2008, pp. 106–110).

To forge resonance with other government departments for "constrained discretion," the Treasury used the resonance space "value for money." This had two important consequences. First, the Treasury aimed to raise "public service productivity", understood as the delivery of outcomes:

> At the heart of the Government's approach to improving public services' productivity is the proposition that the performance of public services should be judged on the basis of the outcomes achieved by these services. For example, the performance of the health service

[12]Source: futurebuilders England online self-description, archived August 3rd 2004, accessed April 5th 2017: http://web.archive.org/web/20040803054927/http://www.futurebuilders-england.org.uk/aboutus/vision.asp

should be assessed in terms of the results achieved in improving the nations' health, not in terms of the numbers of hospital staff or operating theatres. (2004_Treasury_Micro, p. 346)

Crucially, this change in the evaluative basis for public service delivery meant that a private provision of public services was—from the perspective of HM Treasury—formally legitimate if and only if it would result in superior outcomes.

This outcomes-focused approach means that choices between different methods of delivering public services should be based solely on an assessment of which option is most likely to deliver improved outcomes (for example, better health for the nation), and not be tied to a particular set of inputs (for example, the number of nurses), type of output (number of operations or amount of medication prescribed) or mode of provision (public or private). (2004_Treasury_Micro, p. 346)

Thus, a service could have been delivered by private providers, or even investors, if the Treasury was convinced that this yielded superior value for money. Other evaluative criteria, such as public ownership, lost their decision-making relevance as a result.

Public services have traditionally been defined as those services that are directly provided by the public sector. However, this traditional conception of a public service confuses one particular method of delivering public services with their essential characteristics. (2004_Treasury_Micro, p. 341)

Second, with value for money being increasingly understood as the *future* delivery of outcomes, there was an inherent *risk* that public services would be financed without yielding outcomes. From the Treasury's perspective, one way to reduce such "delivery risk" was to *transfer the risk* to private providers. The principal avenue through which the Treasury sought to transfer risk was the Private Finance Initiative.

Whereas with the public procurement of the past private companies built and then walked away, PFI requires the companies involved to compete to deliver a clear level of service, locked-in over the long term and at a fixed price, and with substantial levels of private capital at risk to performance. This link between payment and performance helps ensure that public investment is used efficiently and effectively. (2004_Treasury, p. 372)

Later, proponents of Social Impact Bonds found a resonance space in the idea of delivery risk transfer, while outsourcing contracts structurally similar to SIBs had already extensively been piloted with PFIs. Importantly, the Treasury saw such a rationale particularly important in "health and social care, crime and social cohesion, in education and for children and young people" (p. 32). These are precisely those fields deemed as particularly fruitful for the SIB-like "Voluntary Finance Initiative" proposed around that time by Ed Mayo, as well as, later, by SIB proponents.

The more the Treasury view penetrated public service delivery, the more the value for money creation of outcomes became a key social policy device. This created a resonance space for SII proponents' arguments beyond SIBs, too. To be contracted by government, now potential service providers had to show that they created "added value" for the public purse—rather than be of any specific type of organizational structure (2002_Treasury, pp. 15–17). But on the other hand, they could also convince policymakers by referring to the "for money" side of the argument by raising additional private funds. This is why in the 2002 report, SEs were—in contrast to not-for-profit VCS organizations—seen as particularly important for delivering value for money public services: they could "lever in additional finance" (2002_Treasury, p. 23).

Together, this means that in between 2001 and 2005, the fields of community enterprise and finance, social enterprise, the VCS, and public service delivery were beginning to move towards each other. But only in 2006 was a critical juncture reached.

7.3 2006: Critical Juncture

In 2005, Labour won its third subsequent general election. But where its promise of a "fresh start" led to a landslide victory in 1997, after being in government for 8 years, its electoral result significantly weakened. Although there certainly were a number of reasons for this, such as Blair's highly unpopular decision to participate in the Iraq war, Labour was looking for ways to show that it had not lost its capacity to innovate. As such, its 2005 manifesto saw a doubling in the use of the term "innovation" and has introduced innovation as a key policy goal into the field of social and public services. At the same time, 2006 formed the peak of the global financial services boom that saw unprecedented income levels being distributed across London City banks. How favorably financial innovations were viewed back then is epitomized by the decision to award Muhammad Yunus, founder of Grameen Bank and one of the most prominent advocates of microfinance (Mader 2015), the Nobel Peace Prize.

Around that time, the British core executive became equally enchanted by the perspective to use financial instruments in order to foster social innovation. Not least driven by the hope to shine in his gloriole, Gordon Brown and his team at HM Treasury invited Yunus to consult the British government on how to further develop these kinds of social innovations. Although nothing substantial emerged out of this meeting, it nevertheless shows the candor and interest policymakers in general, and Gordon Brown in particular, had for these ideas (Interview A). Note that in December 2005, David Cameron had taken over the lead of the Conservative party and since then feverishly argued for social enterprise and social innovation, and the government's role in expanding these fields. Not only to remain ahead of the Conservatives in the terrain that Labour-related actors had created just a decade earlier, Labour considerably stepped up its support for these issues. As SE and social innovation was supported by both Brown and Blair, the three distinct policy fields at Treasury, Home Office, and DTI were merged into a central one at Cabinet Office. With the parallel creation of the Commission on Unclaimed Assets (CUA) by Ronald Cohen, which included VCS and SE proponents, the time around 2006 saw a critical juncture of what formerly had been relatively independent fields. I will begin to explicate these changes by focusing on the CUA. Thereafter, I will describe the developments in the policy field.

7.3.1 Unclaimed Assets and the Birth of Social Impact Investing

It is unclear how exactly Treasury first realized the existence of "unclaimed assets" in "dormant" bank accounts—i.e. funds that have not been accessed by their formal owners in a given number of years. But around 2004, the Permanent Secretary to the Treasury personally added the topic as a Treasury priority. At that point, there was a prevailing view in the Treasury that, as these funds did not belong to the banks, they should be used in the public interest rather than by banks to cover their liabilities (B: 54:25-58:13). Subsequently, Labour pledged in its 2005 election manifesto to

> establish a common definition and a comprehensive record of unclaimed assets. We will then expect banks, over the course of the Parliament, to either reunite those assets with their owners or to channel them back into the community (2005_Labour_Manif, p. 11)

After Labour won the election, banks began working with Treasury officials on a definition as well as a recovery mechanism for these funds (B: 57:30). The important political question thus became what exactly it meant to "channel" the funds "back into the community." In the 2005 Pre-Budget Report, Brown announced that all unclaimed assets would be invested to "improve youth and community facilities."[13] Subsequently, "financial inclusion" was added as a second priority (2007_OTS_Treasury). These two priorities were not very popular and were later abandoned.

In opposition to the Labour-internal discussions about how to spend unclaimed assets, Ronald Cohen set up the Commission on Unclaimed Assets (CUA) in 2005. The CUA argued for the creation of a "Social Investment Wholesale Bank" from the unclaimed assets. Besides Ronald Cohen, the commission included a former investment banker of Lehman Brothers, a board member of NatWest bank, representatives from charitable organizations—as well as Ed Mayo, who had earlier propelled arguments for increased finance to and service delivery via the VCS, and for SE impact measurement (2006_CUA, p. i). Moreover, the commission included in consulting roles numerous members of the 2000 Social Investment Taskforce, such as Michelle Giddens and Geraldine Peacock, as well as leading VCS and SE representatives such as Stuart Etherington of NCVO, Stephen Bubb of ACEVO, Jonathan Bland of the Social Enterprise Coalition, and Peter Wheeler, a former partner at Goldman Sachs, co-founder of New Philanthropy Capital, and CEO of futurebuilders.

The importance of the CUA for the establishment of the SII field can hardly be overstated. For the first time, finance proponents (led by the sub-group of equity proponents), VCS, and SE actors created a network that propelled a shared goal: the use of parts of unclaimed assets to establish a social investment bank to invest into financial intermediaries. This had four important implications: first, the finance

[13]Source: Full text of Gordon Brown's Pre-Budget Report Speech delivered to the House of Commons, The Guardian, December 5th 2005, https://www.theguardian.com/money/2005/dec/05/publicfinances.budget2006, accessed April 6th 2017.

frame was expanded and adjusted in the process of creating resonance with the strategies of VCS and SE proponents. Second, with an acceptance of the frame came an increasing acceptance of the role structure that saw *financial intermediaries* as creators of social impact and placed them into a central field position. Third, the frame legitimized the material creation of the social investment bank, that is, the allocation of significant cash-flows to be distributed according to the SII field frame. Fourth, the applicable situations of the finance field frame were expanded from community enterprise to the broad "social ventures" category proposed by Bridges Ventures—and this was accepted by VCS and SE actors.

Given its significance for the development of SII, I will describe the process of resonance building in more detail (see Table 7.2). The CUA launched an open consultation on its early social investment bank proposal in between its 2006 and 2007 reports. As a result, the CUA changed its strategic action frame from being centered on enterprise creation in poor communities to support for "third sector" organizations. In the 2006 report, the CUA held that public and third sector organizations

> provide services that meet expressed needs and alleviate the symptoms of poverty. But often these interventions do not address the underlying characteristic shared by poor neighbourhoods or poor people: the lack of wealth. Indeed, for many beneficiaries of the services that these agencies deliver, it is still necessary to be poor and remain poor in order to qualify to receive them. This creates a system of perverse incentives and rewards. (06_CUA, p. 5)

Its prognostic framing held that:

> What distinguishes the most effective third sector organisations is that they pursue the opposite approach, building on resources and creating opportunities. This works on two different levels: they build the assets of their own organisation and they also build the assets of those they seek to serve. (06_CUA, p. 5)

However, already in its early frame, the CUA began to take up the arguments of full-cost recovery propelled by ACEVO in the years before:

> Many funders do not cover core costs, restrict grants to specific projects rather than building up the capacity of community organisations and only provide support for short periods of time, typically three years or less. This means that organisations suffer from overstretched and low paid management, scant reserves and a lack of funds for new product development or organisational growth (06_CUA, p. 6)

Table 7.2 Shift in SII proponents' strategic frame during resonance building with VCS

	2006 CUA report	2007 CUA report
Problem	Public and third sector programs do not resolve poverty	Third sector is under-capitalized and unable to grow
Cause	They do not focus on wealth creation	Lacks access to financial markets
Prognosis	Successful organizations build assets, but need finance to grow. Therefore support intermediaries	Support existing intermediaries, but maintain grant-funding, too
Motivation	Use unclaimed assets for social investment bank	Use parts of unclaimed assets for social investment bank

Furthermore, the CUA acknowledged the opportunities for the VCS arising from government's change from grants to contracts and argued for the need of financial investment, including equity investments, to make use of these opportunities.

> Government has worked with the third sector to improve the latter's ability to negotiate robust contracts for the provision of public services. [...] If the third sector is to take advantage of these opportunities to grow, innovate, and take on significant responsibilities for further service delivery it will require a more varied and sophisticated funding approach. (06_CUA, p. 6)

After the consultation, the CUA's 2007 strategic action frame subtly but critically altered the prognostic and diagnostic framing, while maintaining the motivational component of the finance field frame. The new diagnostic framing established "under-investment" of the VCS, SE, and social ventures as problematic. Rather than describing, like in the 2006 report, the VCS as addressing only the "symptoms" of the real problem while focusing on an enterprising challenger group as the solution, the 2007 report established *all* social ventures as part of the solution:

> The role of the "third sector" in combatting disadvantage and building a more cohesive society has never been more important. Its ability to respond to need and pioneer new approaches—beyond the reach of both the public and private sectors—is almost universally acknowledged. (2007_CUA, p. 1)

Likewise, the 2007 report acknowledged that

> third sector organisations vary tremendously in the range of their activities and in the level of their trading income. The Commission observes that this diversity merits a variety of capital flows with levels of subsidy varying according to the nature of the receiving organisation. (2007_CUA, p. 11)

Thus, sustaining variance in the "third sector" now became part of the solution. This also meant that the CUA conceded that "grants will always play an important role for many organisations at key points in their development" (2007_CUA, p. 11). Moreover, investment as a means for all types of "third sector" organizations to access government contracts was stated as an explicit goal of the social investment bank (2007_CUA, p. 15). As a solution to this "under-investment", the CUA argued for a "wholesale" financial intermediary:

> There is a demand for an institution that is capable of using tax credits and other incentives provided by the Government in order to attract capital and then distribute it through financial intermediaries in the third sector. The "Social Investment Bank" would act as the dynamic gatherer and mobiliser of such capital for the sector (06_CUA, pp. 6–7)

In particular, the CUA drew on the "leverage" and "recycling" metaphors described above to establish that *financial capital* rather than social organizations are a creator of social impact. For example, they argued that a social investment bank "will enable far greater total investment through recycling capital and improving access to private finance", and thereby "multiply the impact of unclaimed assets through gearing and by attracting additional capital to the sector" (07_CUA, p. 2). But while similar frames had already been disseminated by the Social Investment Taskforce 7 years earlier, now the key difference was that the CUA explicitly began to address VCS and SE organizations as well as for-profit companies. Critically, with the 2007 CUA report, VCS and SE proponents, for the first time, began to accept the field-level role of financial intermediaries as well as its justification.

Why did VCS representatives not object (or succeed with objecting) this boundary expansion? One explanation might be the changes in between the 2006 and the 2007 reports. The 2007 report was much more explicit in incorporating ACEVO's full cost recovery campaign as a problem for the third sector, directly citing two of ACEVO's reports (p. 8). Moreover, the emphasis on the "varied funding environment" and an acknowledgment that only parts of the unclaimed assets should be used to set up the social investment bank might have secured NCVO support. In fact, Stuart Etherington said at the launch of the 2007 report

> While social investment is increasingly important, there is a need to remember that different funding tools are needed by different organisations for different activities. In particular, the funds from dormant accounts should be used to support a small grants programme and programme-specific initiatives, as well as providing equity finance through the social investment bank.[14]

Another explanation might be the ambiguity of the term "social investment", which by then denoted for-profit finance, as well as public organizations such as futurebuilders and the Adventure Capital Fund. It might have been the case that VCS representatives like Stephen Bubb, then also chairman of the Adventure Capital Fund, simply assumed that for-profit finance proponents such as Ronald Cohen meant non-profit-distributing finance when they talked about social investment.

> I think Stephen's [Bubb, PG] and Ronny's [Cohen, PG] agendas kind of overlapped, and Stephen saw Ronny as a powerful political figure. Ronny was talking about capital for social good, Stephen thought "well that's what I mean, I'm talking about money for social good so this is the same thing, so yes, I agree, let's have a Social Investment Bank, I agree with this Ronny Cohen agenda, Social Investment... we want Social Investment!" I don't think at that point Stephen had any idea about what he meant by Social Investment, but you then ended up with this lobby group outside government that was a combination of representatives of social sector organizations like Stephen, and people like Ronny who perhaps came from a financial services background [...] but didn't come to it with a connection to the social sector [...]. (E: 11:30)

This hypothesis is also supported by my interview with a leading VCS representative:

> A: I can tell that BSC can only invest in non-profit organizations, it can't invest in...
> Q: But I think it can invest in, for example, CICs, and they have 35%...
> A: Yeah yeah, but that's the third sector, but that's technically still non-profit. [...]
> Q: Ahm, ok, but I mean with the social impact bond, for example, that could be, as far as I understand...
> A: Still third sector. The constitution of Big Society Capital is that they can only invest in the third sector, not for profit. (H: 0:26:44)

[14]Source: Commission on Unclaimed Assets Recommends New Social Lender, Report Release, Charity Times, March 14th 2007, http://www.charitytimes.com/pages/ct_news/March_07_news/140307_unclaimed_assets.htm, accessed April 7th 2017.

In summary, by March 2007, finance proponents around Ronald Cohen had created resonance for their SII frame with leading VCS and SE representatives. The result was on the one hand a boundary blurring between VCS, SE, and for-profit sectors that would later become part of a new settlement under the Coalition government. On the other hand, a strategic action frame that prescribed a specific role structure centered around finance-led growth had been at least partially accepted by a large group of non-government actors. Critically, by achieving resonance for the financialization frame with VCS and SE actors, the very identity of the finance project changed. From focusing on community enterprise and entrepreneurial wealth creation and depicting large parts of the VCS as problematic, the idea was now to encourage finance-led growth of all organizations that considered themselves as "social."

Note that this frame resonance only occurred after a number of changes on the structural level. While finance proponents had already in the 2000 taskforce argued for a "wholesale" financial intermediary, at that point, their ideas were not followed up upon. However, as the boundaries of which organizations count as "social" were increasingly blurred due to the consequentialist "added value" view propelled by SE advocates and Treasury, income generation and partial profit distribution became legitimate organizational practices for social organizations. Thus, to build alliances with VCS actors, finance proponents only had to make them accept a little broader version of what had already become a "spectrum" of organizations. They did so by linking their for-profit finance frame with the futurebuilders discourse on publicly financed, low-interest loans to remove fundraising pressure of VCS organizations aiming at public service delivery that emerged out of ACEVO's full-cost recovery campaign.

Through this new alliance, SII proponents were enabled to furthermore penetrate the field of public service delivery. Yet this required them to create resonance with policymakers, too. However, at that point, the policy field was not yet ready to introduce the broad category of "social ventures" into service delivery. Although with the increasing dominance of "constrained discretion" this became formally possible, a number of other obstacles persisted still. These will be discussed below.

7.3.2 *The Office of the Third Sector: Hybridizing Social Enterprise Policy*

The formation of the VCS-SE-finance alliance in the CUA coincided with an important transformation of the polity. In May 2006, the DTI Social Enterprise Unit was merged with the Home Office Active Communities Unit as well as some Treasury civil servants to form the Office of the Third Sector (OTS), located at Cabinet Office. This had two important consequences: being located in a core executive department and chaired by a minister with OTS as their sole responsibility, third sector policy now gained in status vis-à-vis other policy fields. Now policymakers could "open doors and get in other departments in a way that is hard when you're in another department" while having "more direct access to No 10 and see Ministers" (D: 33:15).

But even more important for our endeavor is that third sector policymaking was now integrated into *one* unit that encompassed SE *and* VCS policy. As part of its new strategy, the OTS would on the one hand seek to increase "access to finance" for both VCS and SE organizations, while on the other hand attempt to increase their role in public service delivery. The result of which was a new settlement that merged both the VCS and SE fields, while maintaining the more permissive institutional rules that previously made up the distinct SE field.

The creation of the OTS has been strongly advocated for by ACEVO, and Stephen Bubb in particular. He argued that at Home Office, VCS policy was "always bottom of the pile"[15] and demanded a more central position for VCS policy in the core executive. The shared perspective on the role of the VCS in public service delivery across Labour's two core executive centers—Number 10 and the Treasury—thus created a resonance space for ACEVO's arguments. Stephen Bubb, who "knew Blair" then organized a meeting with him, and was, after the OTS was set up, appointed to work on the "Third Sector Service Delivery Plan" (H: 0:17:14), which, in line with his long-held strategy to reclaim the SE category, included both VCS and SE.

But while the creation of the OTS marked a victory for the VCS contract proponents, incumbents of the SE field were concerned that the merger of the DTI unit with the—much larger—Home Office unit would threaten the DTI settlement that established social enterprise as a category distinct from the VCS. SE advocates "felt they have spent since 1997 arguing that they were businesses, and suddenly they were going backwards, that they were being re-merged with the voluntary sector" (G: 59:30). Thus, DTI staff had to "reassure them that that wouldn't happen" and that "actually it was in their interest because, you know, they get much more voice, and, ahm there would be more money around" (G: 1:00:10).

Another explanation for why the three departments had been merged, however, is not linked to Blair, but to the rising influence of HM Treasury. Remember that since the 2002 cross-cutting-review, the Treasury sought to increase the role of both SEs and VCS organizations in public service delivery. Yet the division of "third sector" policy into DTI and Home Office reduced the Treasury's control over the policy field. Treasury had to set up two teams, one to "shadow" each department, while the different organizational culture at DTI and Home Office added more complexity. (B: 5:40). Moreover, Tony Blair frequently changed personnel in DTI and Home Office, which made it increasingly difficult for the Treasury to achieve its goals.

> [A]t the beginning of Tony Blair's government and Gordon Browns position as a chancellor, there were people in the home office who were very, very sympathetic to the charity sector,

[15] Source: Statement by Stephen Bubb in Jamie Carpenter, Cabinet Office to oversee policy on third sector, Placemaking Resource, May 12th 2006: http://www.placemakingresource.com/article/558703/cabinet-office-oversee-policy-third-sector, accessed April 8th 2017.

> and I think there were also people in the DTI who were very sympathetic to social enterprise. So while that was the case, the Treasury could get what it wanted. When ministers changed, and different people were appointed to different departments. Because Tony Blair did change his ministers, he didn't change Gordon Brown for 11 years, but he did change other ministers frequently, always, always change of personalities. So, when ministers changed in those departments, Gordon Brown often got very frustrated that the minister he had been dealing with who was fairly in agreement with his own views suddenly got minister somewhere else. And then he had to deal with somebody else who didn't really care. And then the subject slid right down to the bottom of the agenda. And he found that EXTREMELY annoying. It didn't matter how much he beefed up his staff in the Treasury, he was always bashing at, hit against a great wall, really, if he didn't have the right person on the other side. It worked, I mean, it worked really, really well for quite a number of years we have arrived [with] people in power, the right people in the right jobs, as far as he was concerned. But there came a time when it just got to be too frustrating and that's really where the idea of the OTS came from [. . .]. (B: 7:20)

It therefore seems likely that the creation of OTS was at least in part driven by the Treasury's wish to increase control over "third sector" public service delivery. This was particularly the case when Brown became Prime Minister in 2007, and I will come back to this point in the next section.

The 2006 OTS "Social enterprise action plan: Scaling new heights" was an important milestone in the development of SII. In the report, OTS claimed that "Britain's social enterprise sector is one of the most successful and vibrant in the world" and asserted that it is "championed by government." Moreover, the document noted that SEs, which now always included the VCS, "tackle some of society's most entrenched social and environmental challenges" (OTS_2006, p. 3). In comparison with the 2002 strategy, the 2006 strategy continued to presuppose the positive contribution of social enterprise, but now sought to legitimize the role *of government* as a "champion" of an industry that achieves success in global comparison.

This is particularly important in relation to public service delivery. In the 2006 strategy, SEs were not only understood as value for money contractors for public service delivery, but also as "offering a market-based, business solution to a social problem" (p. 50). Thus, "they may bring additional benefits to public services that are not accounted for in the price of the contract." Thus, the arguments that had initially been made for not-for profit VCS organizations had now been fully supplanted to the broader organizational category. Moreover, the OTS began to argue that these SEs should be reimbursed for this additional public value they were thought to create (p. 53). Although the OTS's initial proposal to do so, so-called "social clauses" did not become very successful, this point shows how policymakers increasingly found themselves in problem situations that, some 2 years later, finance proponents argued were being solved by Social Impact Bonds.

The idea that SEs create "social impact" has already been mentioned multiple times in the 2002 DTI strategy. But the government strategy to "scale" social enterprises and "maximise" their social impact (e.g. pp. 5, 30, 55) emerged only with the 2006 strategy. In the 2002 cross-cutting review, SEs have been described—along with VCS organizations—to create additional public benefit for highly specific reasons that could—in situations where these reasons hold—increase the efficacy of public service delivery. In 2006, however, SEs have been established as organizations that create public welfare in their own right. Thus, reducing "barriers" and affecting organizational growth of SE would—beyond public service delivery—create social impact. A full chapter in the 2006 strategy was devoted to "access to finance" for SEs (pp. 42–48) and took over finance proponents' frame by describing, for the first time in government discourse, finance-led organizational growth as a means to scale social impact.

Moreover, the 2006 strategy followed SII proponents' arguments that "increased use of *commercial* finance correlates to a reduced dependency on grants, which may allow the entrepreneur more freedom" [emphasis added]. Likewise, the strategy took over the distinction between legitimate and illegitimate grants developed by SII proponents (see Chap. 6) in arguing that they should only be used "in the start-up or early expansion phases of a social enterprise" (p. 44). Government furthermore accepted SII proponents' frame regarding equity:

> While the supply of debt finance, particularly secured debt finance, appears to be increasing, social enterprises still report difficulties in accessing more high-risk investment. This lack of equity is often perceived to be a barrier to high-growth social enterprises [. . .]. (2006_OTS, p. 45)

In contrast to the 2002 strategy and the 2003 Bank of England report, the OTS focus on finance-led growth made the lack of equity financial products a problem of public welfare. But as the OTS maintained the 2002 definition that saw social enterprises as limited in their profit distribution, the strategy was seeking equity investors accepting *reduced* financial returns compared to "commercial" equity investment:

> However, there are investors in the market, ranging from trusts and foundations to ethical investors, that are prepared to take a blend of financial and social return, and may be willing to invest in an organisation in a way that does not take a share in the ownership of the enterprise. (2006_OTS, p. 47)

To address this issue, the OTS "commissioned two projects to investigate methods to encourage private investment in social enterprise" where the reduced financial return was seen as crucial. Otherwise, they argued, it would be "unlikely that many social enterprises will benefit from these interventions, because of the level of return required and because many social enterprises do not issue shares that funds can buy." In order to attract such investors, OTS held that "[c]o-investment by the public sector may act as an incentive for the private sector to invest in this market" (p. 47).

In summary, the 2006 OTS strategy merged policy on SE and VCS fields and expanded the concept of and normative view on finance-led growth to the broader category. By theorizing that these organizations intrinsically create social impact, the OTS strategy argued that finance-led growth of these organizations would, inside and outside public service delivery, maximize overall social impact. Thus, the 2006 strategy conflated two formerly separate ideas, SEs additional impact vis-à-vis private sector firms as developed in the DTI, and the Treasury idea of social organizations' value for money in the delivery of policy outcomes. This allowed SII proponents to establish growth-oriented equity finance as a means to "scale" the impact of a broad set of organizations. However, as the OTS upheld the DTI definition of "principal" profit reinvestment, for-profit SII proponents' influence remained limited. However, this dramatically changed when Gordon Brown became Prime Minister in 2007.

7.4 2007–2010: Piloting Social Impact Investing

Although by 2006 the OTS's and finance proponents' strategic action frames largely resonated, social policymakers did not yet identify the creation of a capital market within the welfare state with the maximization of the country's overall welfare. Two chasms remained: a situation of discursive dissonance regarding profit extraction, and a disconnect that separated social networks of SII and public service delivery. Key to bridging both of these chasms was that Gordon Brown became Prime Minister. This is why the first segment will describe his Prime Ministerial influence in more detail, while the following two sections will focus on the how the two chasms were bridged. As a result of these two processes, the first Social Impact Bond was born. One surprising insight that emerges out of this perspective is that it allows us to see the emergence of SII as the mere continuation of a process of resonance that had begun much earlier, rather than placing an important explanatory role on the 2008 financial crisis and the subsequent austerity politics (Dowling and Harvie 2014).

7.4.1 Gordon Brown as Prime Minister

With Gordon Brown becoming Prime Minister on June 27th 2007, three major social processes unfolded that rapidly impacted the remaining dissonance and disconnect in the dynamic fields. First, Brown's policy advisory networks convoluted as he formed the Prime Minister's Council on Social Action (CoSA) shortly after taking office. Here, both SII and VCS/SE public service delivery proponents were working together, asked to achieve shared goals. This culminated in the creation of Social Finance Ltd.—a SII intermediary key in advancing (and materially benefitting from) both the social investment bank proposal and Social Impact Bonds—which was led by key Social Investment Taskforce, CUA, and CoSA personnel. In addition, network structures of civil servants changed as former Treasury staff followed Brown into Cabinet Office and No 10 roles. Second, frame resonance increased: with social innovation becoming a policy end in itself, a key building block of SII proponents' prognostic framing entered the social policy field. Third, in one of his final actions as Chancellor, Brown devised another cross-cutting review on public service delivery that allocated £500 million to the OTS. This meant a dramatic increase in resources for the "hybrid" OTS focusing on SE, VCS, and public service that was increasingly exposed to the Treasury view, thereby allowing finance proponents further access to the field.

Less than 1 month after assuming office as Prime Minister, Gordon Brown gave a speech at the launch of his book "Britain's everyday heroes" in which he outlined several of his social policy priorities. His goal was to forge "a new partnership of individuals, independent community organisations and a government working together to empower and help all those working for social change" (2007_Brown). To do so, he stressed the need of social innovation, which became not only his policy goal, but furthermore the justification for allowing his convoluted networks of advisors to shape policy development:

> This Government's social change agenda must go beyond the traditional to embrace the new and diverse ways in which individuals, organisations, communities and business engage in social change. And so it requires a whole new approach from government: new kinds of support and a new style of inclusive leadership. To bring social innovators together to generate ideas on how the whole of government can support the efforts of all those striving for change, in all their diverse ways, I am creating a new Council on Social Action, led by David Robinson, which will advise the Government on new initiatives to celebrate, connect and inspire those working for social good. (2007_Brown)

The CoSA included both SII and service delivery proponents, as well as promoters of preventative action and "public value." Finance proponents were, for example, represented by Peter Wheeler, a former investment banker and founder of New Philanthrophy Capital, who, together with CoSA chair David Robinson, held a non-executive board position at Social Finance at least since 2008.[16] They were joined by Rob Owen, also a former investment banker, who, as a CEO of St. Giles Trust advocated for preventative services under the Trust's motto of "breaking the cycle of reoffending",[17] and whose Trust became a delivery partner in the first-ever Social Impact Bond at Peterborough prison. Julia Unwin, CEO of the Joseph Rowntree Foundation, one of the UK's largest donors, had with her pioneering 1999 ACEVO publication "Who pays for core cost?" (1999_ACEVO) laid important intellectual groundwork for full-cost recovery and VCS public service delivery contracts.[18] Moreover, the CoSA included Geoff Mulgan, who had in 2002 as the head of Blair's strategy unit co-authored a report on "creating public value" as a "framework for public service reform" (2002_CO, p. i), but who had been "disappointed that no ministers or senior officials showed much interest in this agenda" (Ball and Exley 2010, p. 157) and subsequently chaired the National Endowment for Science, Technology and the Arts (NESTA) and the Young Foundation, and worked with Oxford Business School on how to "accelerate social innovation", including through the use of for-profit financial actors such as Bridges Community Ventures (Mulgan et al. 2007).

---

[16]Source: Social Finance website, archived October 10th 2005, http://web.archive.org/web/20081005234949/http://www.socialfinance.org.uk/about/people.php, accessed April 11th 2017.

[17]Source: St. Giles Trust website, Our history, http://site.stgilestrust.org.uk/who-we-are/our-history, accessed April 11th 2017.

[18]Source: David Brindle, Pressure on government to reward charity commitment, The Guardian, March 21st 2001: https://www.theguardian.com/society/2001/mar/21/charities.charityfinance, accessed April 11th 2017.

The CoSA therefore brought together challengers from a variety of fields, asked by the Prime Minister to not only create "social innovation" but also "explore alternative forms of financing social action, with a particular focus on cross-sector collaboration to fund prevention and early intervention" (08_COSA_05_Commentary, p. 4). This situation allowed finance proponents to create resonance in public service delivery by merging their ideas on finance-led growth with contract-, public value-, and prevention proponents. This resulted in the first SIB, about which I will say more below.

In parallel, the CoSA network, which was more focused on public services, convoluted with equity investment proponents, and key actors of the CUA in particular. Remember that the CUA itself represented an alliance between equity proponents, SE-, and VCS advocates. In 2007, Ronald Cohen co-founded Social Finance Ltd. that described its organizational goal as:

> Social Finance's ambition is to transform the ability of the third sector to respond to society's changing needs by enabling greater access to a variety of investment instruments. We are building a pioneering organisation to develop financial products that marry the needs of investors and the sector [...].[19]

Besides Ronald Cohen (Bridges Community Ventures, Social Investment Taskforce, and CUA) and the two CoSA members described above, Social Finance's board and senior management included: Toby Eccles (CUA), Matthew Pike (CUA), Geraldine Peacock (CUA, SIT, Charity Commission), Bernard Horn (CUA, NatWest), as well as, for example, David Blood (Goldman Sachs) and Victoria Hornby (Sainsbury family trust and two former DTI working groups).[20] With Social Finance, an organization had been created that sought to create financial products and advocate the "public benefit" of financialization in relation to the broad "social ventures" category and public services. Moreover, its founders continued to hold key advisory positions to then Prime Minister Brown.

In addition to the dynamics of Brown's policy advisory networks, also the network structures at the OTS changed under the new Prime Minister. On June 4th 2007, four new teams were set up at the OTS.[21] In particular, the former "social enterprise team" was changed into a "social enterprise and investment team" and a civil servant of the former DTI social enterprise unit had been appointed as its deputy director. With the changed focus of the team to include "social investment" as a policy objective, a policy manager position has been created, aiming to make senior policymakers "care" about SII (E: 16:30).

---

[19] Source: Social Finance self-description, Office of the Third Sector appoints four Deputy Directors to spearhead new team structure, May 21st 2007, archived December 12th 2008, http://web.archive.org/web/20081211013418/http://www.socialfinance.org.uk/about/index.php?page_ID=1, accessed April 12th 2017.

[20] Source: Social Finance self-description, archived October 05th 2008, http://web.archive.org/web/20081005234949/http://www.socialfinance.org.uk/about/people.php, accessed April 12th 2017.

[21] Source: Cabinet Office Press Release, Office of the Third Sector appoints four Deputy Directors to spearhead new team structure, May 21st 2007, archived October 05th 2008, http://webarchive.nationalarchives.gov.uk/20081027190237/http://cabinetoffice.gov.uk/third_sector/news/news_stories/070521_appoint.aspx, accessed April 11th 2017.

In addition to reshaping the focus of the social enterprise team, a "public sector partnership team" was created and staffed with the former "Head of Charity and Third Sector Finance Unit" at Treasury. But also in the OTS more generally, the set-up of civil servants was restructured in order to increase co-operation and "synergies" (G: 1:01:30) between the former Home Office and DTI units. This was because, before the reshuffle, the OTS workgroups had, according to a civil servant, largely co-existed in accordance to the former, tripartite field structure (G: 1:02:25). In summary, the change of civil service networks at OTS reflected an increasing influence of the Treasury view on the field of third sector policy: the question of finance-led growth was made a policy topic and received a full-time position, while the work on third sector public service delivery was led by a former Treasury employee.

Lastly, the Brown years marked an unprecedented increase in subsidies to "third sector" organizations, and, increasingly, financial intermediaries. With the 2007 cross-cutting review, £500 million had been allocated to "third sector policy", mostly for OTS and its subsidiary funding bodies such as Capacitybuilders, or Community Assets Fund (2007_Treasury_OTS). The timing of this transfer of funds is particularly noteworthy: Gordon Brown was, as Chancellor, responsible for developing the cross-cutting review with the 2007 Spending Review—but upon becoming Prime Minister, he would become the review's main beneficiary as OTS was located closer to Prime Ministerial control at Cabinet Office. Thus, Brown became able to impose his "Treasury view" on social policy both via Prime Ministerial authority and by directly affecting public spending. In the words of a Treasury civil servant: "it was very well planned campaigning [laughs] to get [OTS] where he wanted it to be" (B: 8:47).

Another effect of Brown becoming Prime Minister was that Blair's potentially different view on social policy decreased in salience. This situation facilitated SII proponents' attempts to build resonance, as described by an OTS civil servant:

> Because Blair left, and Brown was then the person that Ronny Cohen was.. Brown and Ronny Cohen always had a relationship, but because it was.. because Brown was in the Cabinet Office/No.-10-bit of a world, and Ronny was able to say to him "this stuff is important," Brown could then get to [Ed, PG] Balls in the Treasury and say "this stuff is important!" [. . .] Had it still been Blair not Brown.. I don't think Ronny would have gotten to Blair [. . .]. (E: 1:02:15)

The result of this development can be found in the 2007 cross-cutting review. For the first time, government pledged to grow the "social investment market"—that is, to use OTS-allocated public funds to create a private capital market in between the third sector and public services. Critically, here, the loose CUA definition—and not the much narrower SE definition—had been followed: social investment was described as an "investment made for a social purpose in organisations that are committed to delivering benefits for society and the environment" (2007_OTS_Treasury, p. 81)—without restrictions regarding profit extraction.

> The Government is strongly attracted to boosting social investment and is keen to find ways to develop this as part of wider third sector policy over the 2007 CSR years. The Government will commit resources to boost social investment. (2007_Treasury_OTS, p. 82)

As we will see later, this "boosterist" (Wiggan 2017) approach to SII was particularly strong in the Coalition government discourse. But this example shows that—more than being a distinctive style of Conservative policymaking—it is an argument advanced by finance proponents around Ronald Cohen, which had created resonance in social policy already under Labour and due to the field-level processes described in earlier sections.

7.4.2 Creating Resonance for the Financialization of Welfare

In Chap. 5, I have described today's SII field structure and termed the extent to which it penetrated social and public services the financialization of welfare. Key to the financialization of welfare are SII intermediaries that take a central governance position in the field. However, it was only in 2007 that the first "real" SII intermediary, Social Finance, emerged.[22] Here, I will describe how, after shifting strategic action frames vis-à-vis the VCS with the 2007 CUA, SII proponents' were now able to create resonance for their field-level frame with social policymakers.

With the 2007 restructuring of the OTS, the Treasury view took hold of what were previously three distinct policy fields. As argued above, one key feature of the Treasury view was that it allowed policymakers to validate claims made by SII proponents, if those were able to convince policymakers that they would "lever in" resources to the creation of outcomes. After winning support from VCS and SE actors, this was precisely what the social investment bank proposal did, because the Treasury had already earlier seen the growth of VCS and SE organizations as a value for money intervention. Thus, with the Treasury asserting that a social investment bank "would be saving the Treasury money" (B: 59:15), frame resonance between policymakers and SII proponents had been achieved. On July 24th 2007 Gordon Brown announced:

> And it is now my priority to examine how a new Social Investment Bank and other new approaches to social investment might help to ensure that voluntary sector and community groups can access more secure and sustainable funding. (2007_Brown, p. 51)

In addition to the resonance with extant political discourse and the new institutional reality of social policymaking in the OTS, using some of the Unclaimed Assets to set up a social investment bank would furthermore allow Gordon Brown to gain political capital. Not only were some of his key external advisors advancing the idea, but also Ronald Cohen was at this time one of the largest donors of the Labour party.

> I think we all thought that Ronny Cohen was leading on Gordon Brown with this threat of not funding the Labour party, and saying, you know, 'you've got to get behind this stuff.' (E: 18:30)

[22] Although before, Bridges Community Ventures had propagated a similar frame, their frame began to expand to the wider field of social ventures only a few years later.

The decision to support the social investment bank was not a budget allocation decision, but legislation that needed *parliamentary* approval, while a section in the Dormant Accounts Act would define legal uses of Unclaimed Assets in England. Critically, the Conservative opposition was highly supportive of the idea as it saw the social investment bank as an alternative to two Labour party "pet projects:"

> [W]e must express some sympathy for Sir Ronald Cohen and the Commission on Unclaimed Assets. It must have thought that when Sir Ronald [...] suggested that money from unclaimed assets should go to a social investment bank, the recommendation would have been accepted. However, that was until the then Economic Secretary—now Secretary of State for Children, Schools and Families [...] pulled rank and put two of his own pet projects in the list of priorities. He added youth services, in a nod to his future job, and financial inclusion, which was one of his priorities as Economic Secretary. That means that it is not clear whether sufficient funds will be available from this exercise to provide the sort of contribution to a social investment bank that the commission thought was necessary. (Mark Hoban, MP, Oct 6th 2008[23])

The Dormant Bank and Building Societies Account Act was enacted on November 26th 2008. Thus, in England (for the other UK nations, the act devolves the decision-making authority), dormant account funds "must be" made for youth services, financial inclusion or "to a social investment wholesaler" which "means a body that exists to assist or enable other bodies to give financial or other support to third sector organisations." These were defined as organizations "that exist wholly or mainly to provide benefits for society or the environment" (s. 18(1)(*c*), 18(2)).

This means that, not only has a "social investment wholesaler" been legally defined as an organization to finance exclusively financial (or other "support-giving") intermediaries. But the definition of "third sector" organizations also followed the propositions made by the CUA such that no formal limits to profit distribution had been established. Under the Dormant Accounts act, profit-distributing firms could qualify as "third sector" organizations[24] as long as they would "wholly or mainly" provide "benefits for society or the environment." Although the social investment bank was only set up in 2012, by 2008, the legal basis of a for-profit field had been set.

Although the legal avenue had been created with the legislation, it still remained a political decision at the executive's discretion to decide how the Unclaimed Assets should be allocated across the three possible causes. Following the enactment of the legislation, the social investment bank nevertheless remained third priority and multiple government publications stated that unclaimed assets would only be used for its creation "resources permitting" (e.g. 2009_OTS_Consultation). This changed

---

[23]Source: Hansard Records of House of Commons Debate, October 6th 2008, https://www.publications.parliament.uk/pa/cm200708/cmhansrd/cm081006/debtext/81006-0008.htm, accessed November 10th 2017.

[24]This loose definition of the "third sector" was already present in the Bill as introduced to the House of Lords on November 8th 2007 and, according to Hansard records, this topic was neither mentioned in parliamentary debate, nor were any amendments made in that regard.

only 2 months before the general election when the March 2010 Budget announced that:

> To support the creation of a [social investment bank] the Government will provide up to £75 million of Dormant Accounts money as a minority stake in a private sector social investment fund of funds. [. . .] The Government will work actively with potential co-investors and will look to appoint a fund manager following an open competition, selecting on the basis of their ability to leverage in private capital for social investment. (2010_Treasury, p. 101)

Thus, by 2010, the proposal had moved higher in the government's priorities, while at the same time understanding the social investment bank as mainly based on private capital. This points to the fact that during the Brown premiership, the government's frame on social policy had increasingly moved towards private capital. This can be seen particularly clearly in regard to another chasm that previously existed between SII proponents and policymakers' frame—the role of equity capital.

As described above, in the early 2000s, the consensus was that there was neither demand nor need for equity financial products for social organizations, given issues regarding ownership transfer and high financial returns sought by equity investors. For example, in 2003 the Bank of England reported that there would only be demand for "patient capital" equity-like investments, if required financial returns would be considerably lower. At the same time, the Treasury *did* follow equity proponents' arguments, but only for the narrow field of for-profit community investment. But since then, SII proponents began to shift their strategic action frame and embrace the much broader category of "social ventures." In the years between 2007 and 2010, policymakers increasingly began to follow this frame dilution.

In its 2006 strategy, the Office of the Third Sector pointed out that the lack of equity-type financial products was "often perceived to be a barrier to high-growth social enterprises" (p. 45). Even though research commissioned by the OTS did not find evidence for the existence of such an "equity gap" (2007_OTS_Access), OTS nevertheless followed SII proponents herein. But in contrast to equity proponents, OTS saw the nature of equity products as irreconcilable with the definition of social enterprise (of "principal" profit-reinvestment) and therefore argued for the development of equity products with reduced profit extraction. In the 2006 OTS strategy, it was announced that £10 million would be made available to "assess demand" for such low-profit equity investments.

Following the 2007 reorganization of the OTS it was decided to spend these £10 million for the creation of a "social enterprise risk capital funds." In contrast to the previous goals, the OTS now built on the 2004 Bridges Community Ventures document described above as a model for such an equity fund. Based on this argument, the to-be-created fund should "lever in" for-profit risk capital and "demonstrate that there are a meaningful number of investors interested in making a *profit-maximising investment* [emphasis added] in the area of social enterprise" (2007_OTS_Consult, p. 7). However, as this would be difficult to reconcile with the SE definition of the current settlement, the OTS noted in the consultation document for the fund that this was "*one* [emphasis added] definition of a social enterprise" and asked: "What level of demand does the market anticipate from social enterprises fitting the above definition?" (2007_OTS_Consultation, p. 15). Thus, for the first time, the government was considering to challenge the 2002 social enterprise settlement in order to create a market for equity financial products.

Both challengers and incumbents of the DTI settlement replied to the consultation, some proposing to widen the SE category, while others proposing the opposite (2008_OTS_Consultation_response, p.21). Critically, government decided *not* to change the SE definition (p. 22). Even though the "Social Enterprise Risk Capital Fund" was formally tendered in late 2008, the fund has never been launched. Although the exact reasons are unclear, it seems likely that the requirement for the fund's investees to "principally" reinvest their surpluses limited too severely investors' ability to earn an income from respective financial intermediation.

Despite the failure of the Risk Capital Fund, the OTS became, after its 2007 reshuffle, increasingly supportive towards for-profit SII, and equity investments in particular. For example, in 2009 it launched, together with NESTA, a "Social Enterprise Access to Investment" program that—justified via the alleged "equity gap"—paid "Investment Readiness Providers" a premium of 3–5% of the total investment sum, if their clients were able to raise an equity investment following the participation in an investment readiness program.[25] Moreover, OTS invested £5 million into a "Social Entrepreneurs Fund" set up and managed by Bridges Ventures in order to "improve access to risk capital for new and growing social enterprises that deliver a high social impact."[26] In addition, OTS set up "social investment pilots" to "increase private sector finance in social enterprises" and "increase the range of finance available for social enterprises" (2008_OTS_pilots, p. 5). Moreover, OTS began to define "social investment" as a policy field in its own right but accepted finance proponents' view on social investment as including profit-maximizing investors. Mirroring the boundary-expansion of SII, OTS listed Bridges Community Ventures as a "social investor"—alongside public agencies such as futurebuilders. The goal became to increase the size of the social investment capital market: "The Government needs to tackle barriers that might prevent investors from investing in social enterprises, or social enterprises from seeking appropriate finance."[27]

In summary, the Brown premiership saw policymakers increasingly accepting the arguments made by SII proponents. With the restructuring of the OTS, the Treasury view that favored finance-led organizational growth began to take hold in the policy

---

[25]Source: Cabinet Office Press Release, Social Enterprise Access to Investment (SEATI) programme, last updated September 7th 2009, http://webarchive.nationalarchives.gov.uk/20130128101412/http://www.cabinetoffice.gov.uk/third_sector/seati.aspx, accessed April 19th 2017.

[26]Source: Cabinet Office Press Release, Angela Smith, Minister for the Third Sector, announces new investment and support for social investment, September 15th 2009, http://webarchive.nationalarchives.gov.uk/20130128101412/http://www.cabinetoffice.gov.uk/third_sector/news/news_stories/090915_socialinvestmentannouncement.aspx, accessed April 19th 2017.

[27]Source: Cabinet Office Press Release, Social Investment, last updated 18th September 2009, http://webarchive.nationalarchives.gov.uk/20100407183222/http://www.cabinetoffice.gov.uk/third_sector/funding_finance_support/social_investment.aspx, accessed April 19th 2017.

field that focused on a much wider group of social organizations than the original case of community enterprise. Policymakers were confronted with an unusual alliance between equity proponents and VCS and SE actors that were together arguing for government support to enable a "spectrum" of financial products within social policy. But the more policymakers followed the argument of equity proponents, the more they undermined the 2002 SE settlement. Although this did happen at the fringes of the field, the settlement only changed after a new government came into power in 2010. Although SII proponents' success remained limited here, they were much more successful in capitalizing upon their alliance with VCS actors by exploiting a resonance space in the field of public service delivery to establish the first Social Impact Bond.

7.4.3 Bridging the Disconnect: The Birth of Social Impact Bonds

When Gordon Brown became Prime Minister virtually all of the ideas making up Social Impact Bonds had already been firmly established in social policy. Building on this resonance space, SII proponents set up an organizational vehicle, Social Finance Ltd., by which the increasingly convoluted network of policy advisors on SII, SE, VCS, and public service delivery could propel their shared interests (and, likely, also materially benefit). Building on a resonance space, very high status positions, and a shared organizational vehicle, SII proponents were then able to break resistance from civil servants and establish the first Social Impact Bond.

By the time Gordon Brown became Prime Minister, his view on public services—the model of "constrained discretion"—had become dominant in public service reform. Core to this model was that central government (and HM Treasury in particular) would fixate specific outcomes while subjugated public bodies were granted the authority to select means for the delivery of these outcomes. This meant that the government's view on public goods became largely independent from public ownership and profit distribution. As such, central government increased the contracting-out of public service delivery. Some of these contracts, such as the Private Finance Initiative, were oriented to the achievement of particular outcomes and paid private investors a fixed return for their achievement. Here, another tenet of the Treasury view came into play: the hope to transfer risk from the Treasury to the contracted party.

But while PFIs aimed at construction projects, similar ideas of payment by results (PbR) began to be incorporated into social service contracts around 2006. As described above, VCS organizations such as ACEVO, as well as Labour-associated think-tanks such as the New Economics Foundation argued for outcomes as the basis for service delivery contracts. They emphasized that PbR would be a means to adequately price the "value added" of VCS service providers, while ensuring their "full-cost recovery." Indeed, it was VCS executives around ACEVO who began arguing for the introduction of private finance into such contracts.

> The scope for private/third sector finance initiatives and joint ventures is undeveloped. However the opportunity for a long term finance initiative between commercial and third sector bodies could open up a new way of providing services and enable expansion especially where capital investment is needed [...] Short-term contracts have effectively excluded third sector organisations from accessing investment capital. The Government could kick start this as it did with the PFI programme. (2006_ACEVO Choice and Voice, pp. 17–18)

The combination of contract proponents, Brown's outspoken support for the VCS in public service delivery, and the Treasury view emphasizing constrained discretion and value for money has led to the development of first PbR contracts in 2006 as part of the Department of Work and Pension's "Employment Zone" and "Jobcentre Plus" programs.[28] According to the DWP, these contracts should feature a consortium of local "private and voluntary sector providers to deliver additional investment and employment support under contract" (2006_DWP, p. 77). Note that in these PbR contracts, outcomes and classifications (such as "NEETs") had already been used as policy objects (2007_Treasury_Budget, p. 99). PbR contracts were grounded in a problematization that saw public services as neither offering "local solutions to local problems," nor requiring delivery organizations to "tailor their services to meet individual needs" (2006_DWP, p. 77). Likewise, unemployed individuals (rather than structural factors) were framed as a social problem (2006_DWP, p. 74).

Apart from PbR and VCS contracting, prevention increasingly became part of central government's public service reform framing. This development has been driven not only by prevention proponents in the VCS, but particularly by the Treasury: The Treasury's "Invest to Save Budget" was a funding program "aimed at promoting partnership, efficiency and innovation" particularly with "with a focus on the third sector's role in delivering public services within local communities" (2007_Treasury_CCR, p. 68). One of the key goals of the ISB was "taking preventative approaches to social problems with the aim of reducing the pressures and costs of recourse to statutory services" (p. 68). By 2007, the ISB had granted over £100 million to third sector service providers, particularly in the areas of "health and social care services, children and family services, employment and skills" (p. 68)—the prime commissioning areas of Social Impact Bonds.

Together this means that the strategic action frame of public service reform, as well as the institutional reality of the policymaking and reform processes already showed an extremely high consistency with SIB proponents' arguments (see Chap. 6). According to a member of the Council on Social Action, ideas such as SIBs were "certainly a strand [of thinking] that Gordon Brown, not least from his Chancellor of Exchequer experience, was keen to encourage" (C: 16:56). Moreover, SIBs were very similar to other CoSA ideas, such as the desire to create "willing

[28]Note that already before, the Prince's Trust was contracted by DWP and paid according to its success in integrating unemployed in the labor market (2003_ACEVO).

citizens" (2007_COSA_01) and "one-to-one" models of public service delivery (2007_COSA_03).

However, in terms of their institutional set-up, SIBs were indeed novel in two regards. First, because they contracted a SII intermediary, rather than a service provider, and second, because they paid a *variable* return that could range from minus 100% to more than 10% per year (see Chap. 5). For the first innovation to be validated by policymakers, SIB proponents needed to establish the value of intermediaries on the discursive level through framing. Here, they could build on the overlapping network structures between CoSA and Social Finance. Bridging the second disconnect, however, was far more difficult as it violated Treasury accounting principles.

As a Social Finance employee who held a key position in establishing the first SIB noted "it is the accounting issue that was the challenge" (F: 29:15):

> The piece that we needed Treasury approval, which was, now, it was an accounting complexity, not a legislative complexity, between, how they allocate, how they accounted for their spending year by year versus how they accounted over a period of time. And the problem with an impact bond was that they may or may not have a future liability to pay. So government knows how to account into the future for certain payments. What it didn't know how to do was how to account into the future for payments that were, if the program went well they'd have to pay, but if the program didn't go well they wouldn't. [...]. A decision was made that actually they could put this contingent liability year by year into their accounting process. (F: 25:37)

Despite support for the SIB idea from the Prime Minister as well as a key Treasury minister (A: 28:05), civil servants at the Treasury opposed the change in institutional rules the SIB required. Although the Treasury was generally supportive of the role of private capital in public services, directly translating tax funds into a speculative financial asset was strongly opposed by Treasury civil servants—in contrast to elected politicians. A CoSA member describes the situation as follows:

> Ahm... a stack of reasons would be the ones that we would try to deal with at that time. Running underneath that all was, I think, just a cultural resistance, ahm, born out of a... 'this isn't the way government does its business'-kind-of view of the world. It's not what... the way Treasury thinks about how we should do this kind of work. (C: 26:30)

This disconnect was resolved through the formal authority of the Treasury minister who was convinced of the SIB idea and had the Prime Minister's support.

> I have a very clear recollection of one meeting early on a Monday morning with the team of officials. And, ehm.. [Treasury minister] rang me on the Sunday afternoon and said 'I've got the papers in front of me and there is just a list of reasons from the officials here, why this isn't going to work, and...' you know, 'I go into the meeting tomorrow unable to find a way though all of this, and it is likely that from the Treasury perspective we will say, you know, that this is gonna stop, we can't do this. Can you convince me these are not significant obstacles?' And we talked that afternoon, with Social Finance people talking to the Minister, too, and at the end of it he said 'Well the only way I can see through this is to get a different team of officials. Cause they're not gonna change their minds. I'll do what I can.' And then next morning we went into the meeting and there was an entirely different team of officials. And what he had done was shift responsibility for this.. the development of the policy from one division to another. [...]He had to change people in order to deliver the PM's wishes.

> But he only did that because he felt convinced that there was a robust argument. So it was the combination of the robust argument and the political leadership that got us what we were after, I think. (C: 38:29)

Besides the Prime Ministerial and Treasury minister support for the SIB idea, it was furthermore important that the first SIB built on resonance with the Ministry of Justice where it was commissioned (F: 14:10). This is because the behavioral intervention contracted in the SIB from charity St. Giles (whose CEO was a CoSA member) followed not only the CoSA's "personalisation" approach to public service delivery, but a particular Labour Manifesto commitment of the 2005 election:

> We will tackle reoffending. By 2007 every offender will be supervised after release; [...] Voluntary organisations and the private sector will be offered greater opportunities to deliver offender services [...] (2005_Labour_Manifesto, p. 24)

Together, this means that the first SIB built on significant frame resonance between policymakers, VCS and SII actors regarding public service reform. Moreover, the network structure of these actor groups became convoluted and, with the creation of the CoSA, linked to an extremely privileged position: the UK Prime Minister himself. Based on this resonance space, SII proponents established an organizational vehicle that put the frame resonance into practice and allowed key network members to personally benefit from the SIB project. This very strong resonance space then provided enough legitimation to break resistance through the use of formal authority. With the first SIB in place, today's SII field came into existence as the role structure proposed by the SII field frame was accepted by all relevant field-level actor groups. However, the momentum of the field-level frame grew considerably only during the Cameron administration, which was also when, following a shift in policy advisory networks, the SII frame became increasingly successful in challenging the 2002 settlement.

7.5 2010–2016: Field Expansion

Early during the Coalition government, a new settlement emerged. Under Labour, the settlement was centered around the 2002 DTI social enterprise definition, despite increased boundary blurring regarding legitimate profit extraction in the third sector and the public service policy field. The goal of the Labour government had been to grow SE, while financial products increasingly became a focal point for policymakers hoping to achieve these goals. With the Cameron government, however, the primary policy goal shifted from growing social enterprise to growing private, for-profit SII.

Thus, the following segment will describe how a new settlement was forged between 2010 and 2012. My argument is that a resonance space existed between SII proponents' arguments and the electoral strategy of the Conservative party. While under Labour *both* VCS and SII proponents built on a resonance space and dense network ties, VCS proponents lost government access during the Conservative austerity regime. This allowed SII proponents to undermine previous boundaries and mobilize government support. In the second segment, I will describe how, with increased resources, the SII settlement was further entrenched. However, boosting SII through public resources has for the first time created a challenge to the financialization as welfare frame that has been spearheaded by VCS and SE proponents. However, as these challengers did not develop an alternative frame, government maintained the SII frame and followed investors in arguing that, for SII to be successful, investees would need to become "investment ready."

7.5.1 Conservatives and the Emergence of a New Settlement

The 2010 general election resulted in a hung parliament where none of the parties won a majority of seats. In the days following the election, Conservatives and Liberal Democrats, who came in third at the election, agreed on forming the first British coalition government in the post-war period. The decision of the Lib Dems not to form a coalition with Labour was not only born out of their recognition that they shared more beliefs with the Conservative "Big Society" idea than with what was portrayed as Gordon Brown's centralist desire to control and micro-manage. It also was partially a result of David Cameron's campaigning who, for example by creating the platform "LibDems4Cameron", began addressing Lib Dem voters and members shortly after becoming leader of the Conservative party in 2005 (Finn 2015). Despite entering a coalition government, the influence of Liberal Democrats on the policies regarding SE and SII remained negligible. This was not only due to the five-to-one dominance of Conservative-held positions in government (Riddel 2015), but also because these policies were at the heart of the Conservative Big Society idea. Although the Big Society rhetoric faded with a change in Cameron's policy advisors by 2012 (Seldon 2015), SE and SII policy remained in the Conservative policy portfolio throughout the Coalition, as both, the Minister for Civil Society (head of the Office for Civil Society, OCS, formerly OTS) and the Minister for the Cabinet Office were Conservative members. This is why I will restrict my analysis of party-political processes to the Conservative party.

Following his election as leader of the Conservative party in 2005, David Cameron and his key aides such as later Chancellor George Osbourne attempted to "modernize" the Conservative party in a similar fashion to what Labour did a decade earlier (Finn 2015, p. 35). This meant accepting key ideas of the "Third Way" as well as a commitment to social mobility and equality of opportunity—at least on a discursive level. In the years leading to the 2010 general election, the Conservatives forged an electoral strategy that sought to defeat Labour on its very own grounds. In particular, Conservatives accepted social problem definitions, categorizations, and imagined solutions of New Labour's framing. This can be seen, for example, in criminal justice, where the Conservative manifesto strikingly mirrored the arguments Labour put forward in developing the first SIB at Peterborough Prison:

At the moment, many prisoners leave jail and lapse back into a life of drink, drugs and re-offending. We will never bring our crime rate down or start to reduce the costs of crime until we properly rehabilitate ex-prisoners. So, with a Conservative government, when offenders leave prison, they will be trained and rehabilitated by private and voluntary sector providers, under supervision. We will use the same approach that lies behind our welfare reform plans—payment by results—to cut re-offending, with organisations paid using savings made in the criminal justice system from the resulting lower levels of crime (2010_Conservative Manifesto, p. 69)

Thus, the Conservatives not only adopted social categorizations, such as ex-prisoners at risk of re-offending, from Labour. Moreover, key institutional changes regarding the architecture of government had been overtaken, as well. These included an emphasis on value for money, the idea of social ventures' inherent impact and "added value" in public service delivery, a focus on preventative services, as well as the policy tool of payment-by-results contracts—all of which are manifestations of the Treasury view in social policy. Indeed, all of these ideas are related to achieving a reduction in public expenses—or what Dowling and Harvie (2014) called the "political economy of the Big Society" (p. 870). Yet crucially, all of these ideas had been advanced by Labour in times of fiscal expansion, and accepted by the Conservatives *before* they turned to austerity in the aftermath of the financial crisis. For example, in 2008 Francis Maude argued for an increased role of SEs in public service delivery by ascribing innovation as one of their core properties and noting that a Conservative government would advance their interests through the following actions:

So constant alertness to the need to minimise burdens. Then some real stress on making the Compact a reality. Especially on full cost-recovery [. . .]. Without the ability to cover your outgoings your ability to invest in growth is plainly hamstrung. Then we will need to be much better commissioners. More imaginative, more technically proficient, understanding better the quantum leaps in progress that can be achieved when the ability to innovate is unconstrained. (2008_Maude)

But Conservatives significantly differed from Labour (and the Conservatives of the 1980s and 1990s) in theorizing causes of both social problems and problems in public services. Where Labour focused on market failure and advocated "constrained discretion" as a solution, Conservatives established "big government" as the root cause of these problems and argued for Localism as a motivational frame in their "Big Society" program. This meant that the state should aim at galvanizing the delivery of social services in the "community" (another category taken over from Labour). David Cameron laid out this principle already in 2006:

Instead of expanding the supply of state services, as the Old Left wants, I believe we should strive to expand the supply of social services—services provided by society itself. And rather than cutting the supply of state services, as the Old Right wants, I believe we should strive to cut the demand for them [. . .]. (2006_Cameron)

For SII this meant that, where Labour required a distinct justification for private service delivery, the Conservatives openly embraced the provision of social services by community groups and SEs. Moreover, Conservatives began to increasingly follow the arguments of finance proponents and widened their definition of "social organizations" towards SII proponents' "social ventures" category. I argue that this was due to the second key difference in Conservative framing—namely the idea of "boosterism" (Harvey 1989; McCann 2013; Wiggan 2017)[29] by which Conservatives aimed at establishing themselves as the only party to credibly pursue progressive goals.

The notion of boosterism has been developed in economic geography, where it is closely related to entrepreneurialism (Harvey 1989). Policy boosterism studies "how urban policies, as well as places, are constructed as commodities to be marketed" (McCann 2013, p. 6). It is understood as "a mode of engaging with policy and with the world that has been internalized by a range of policy actors" (p. 7). Policy boosterism is not a neutral concept of doing things more quickly, but "ideological, political projects that seek to create a general sense of local common purpose in order to naturalize the notion that certain types of development and growth are good for everyone, [. . .] and to marginalize any group or individual that questions this myth" (p. 8).

In his analysis of Coalition and Conservative government discourse on the creation of an SII market, Wiggan found that "the boosterist depiction of [SII] as the future of welfare obfuscates and legitimates the recuperation and insertion of finance capital into new areas of welfare provision by weaving a problem-solution representation of [SII] within a conservative domestic and international policy narrative built around Broken Britain and the Big Society" (Wiggan 2017 p. 1). While these findings are confirmed by my own empirical analysis, my point is that boosterism is, on the one hand, an argument put forward by and materially benefitting SII proponents (and equity proponents in particular), while on the other hand, represents the Conservative approach to third sector and public service policy more generally. I argue that the Conservatives' decision to apply boosterism in order to electorally defeat Labour on its very own grounds created a resonance space for the boosterist arguments of finance proponents, and that this was of critical importance to shift from the 2002 DTI social enterprise settlement to the new Conservative SII settlement.

As a discursive strategy of financial actors, boosterism aims at legitimizing the practice of venture capital by stressing the "public benefit" of rapid organizational growth of equity-backed start-up firms. Boosterism resonates with the Treasury view that sees finance-led organizational growth as a means to achieve public goals. As such, it had already been part of Labour's 2001 election manifesto which pledged £1.7 billion annual public funding to "develop venture capital funds to boost wealth-creating capacity" (2001_Labour, p. 14). As the Treasury view expanded into social policy, Labour policymakers began to accept finance proponents' boosterist frame in that field, too. For example, the 2007 Budget noted:

[29]The idea to relate Conservative SII discourse to Boosterism was developed by Jay Wiggan (2017). I built on his idea here, but, using my own empirical analysis, expanded the concept.

The Government is strongly attracted to boosting social investment and is keen to find ways to develop this as part of wider third sector policy over the 2007 CSR years. The Government will commit resources to boost social investment. (2007_Treasury_Budget, p. 81)

In parallel, the Conservatives under Cameron began to incorporate boosterism as part of what became their "Big Society" agenda. Repeatedly, senior Conservative politicians such as David Cameron and Francis Maude expressed their support for social enterprise—while describing Labour as not doing enough to boost its development. This was particularly the case for the social investment bank, which Conservatives saw as the key opportunity to accelerate the growth of social enterprises. For example, in 2008 Francis Maude said:

what a pity it seems that the government rejected the imaginative and through work undertaken by Sir Ronnie Cohen's Commission on Unclaimed Assets, so that the scope for establish the Social Investment Bank that could make a huge contribution to the growth of the sector is to take third place behind two undoubtedly worthy and deserving causes. The reality is that there is likely to be little left for any kind of serious financial institution. And that's a massive missed opportunity. [. . .] A fast-growing role for social enterprise we think is central to a future Britain that is whole and successful (2008_Maude).

As noted above, one key difference between Labour and Conservative programs on social and public services was Conservatives' larger indifference regarding the origins of funding. Here, the ability of social ventures to "lever in" private finance strongly resonated with the Conservative boosterist electoral strategy. Already in 2006, David Cameron noted that:

If we can harness James Dyson's passion for engineering, Philip Green's knowledge of retailing and Frank Lowe's expertise for media and creativity, while leveraging more money for inner city schools then we should press on further and faster. [. . .] All in all, we need a vast expansion of the resources—human and financial—available to community groups: a supply side reform to help meet the enormous demand which is out there. (2006_Cameron)

Closer to the 2010 election the Conservatives stepped up their boosterist agenda. While previously, the Conservative focus had been somewhat more on community groups, now the rapid scale-up of social innovations, particularly through the use of equity financial products, became more important for their electoral frame. For example, in his 2009 Hugo Young Lecture, David Cameron noted:

At the moment, the work of social entrepreneurs is disparate. For over a decade, those working in the field have complained about the challenge of growing and replicating successful social programmes. [. . .] If we find the right people, a relatively small number can make a huge difference. In America, two thirds of all new job growth is created by less than one percent of the population, the fast growth economic entrepreneurs. It can be the same with social enterprise and social wealth here. (2009_Cameron)

Building on the resonance between finance proponents' and Conservative boosertism, Cameron pledged in 2009 the creation of a social investment bank (2009_Cameron) that had been renewed, and labeled "Big Society Bank" (BSB), with the "Programme for Government" days after the 2010 general election (2010_CO_Programme).

At this stage, the field witnessed a change in network structures. Before and after the election, key VCS representatives—ACEVO in particular—had been highly supportive of the Conservative plans. In 2009, ACEVO set up a "Conservative Task Force" that presented its demands to then Shadow Minister for Civil Society, Nick Hurd. Here, ACEVO argued for the creation of a social investment bank, recommended "that any future Conservative government makes the growth of a social investment market a top priority" (p. 6) and advocated for the increased usage of PbR contracts (2009_ACEVO_Cons). ACEVO repeatedly urged the government to increase funding for the social investment bank up to a level of £1–2 billion, or about ten times more than what SII proponents had proposed with the Commission on Unclaimed Assets.[30]

But with the Coalition government increasingly turning towards austerity, VCS proponents lost their access to policy networks. By 2012, the Coalition government stopped its statutory grant funding for ACEVO of £1 million (about 30% of the organization's income).[31] In July 2013, the Coalition government introduced the Transparency of Lobbying, Non-party Campaigning and Trade Union Administration Act 2014 to the House of Commons, which, among other issues, strongly limited the VCS' ability to engage in political campaigning. This represented a U-turn from the 1998 Compact and has been strongly opposed by the VCS.[32] Later, the Conservative government attempted to further tighten these rules by adding respective clauses to central government grants.[33] In summer 2016, a leading VCS representative summarized the changes in the relationship between VCS and central government as: "we've had a very, very strong relationship with Labour under Blair, and we've had a shit relationship with the Con... well, it started going wrong during the Coalition, and now it's non-existent" (H: 45:04).

By contrast, ties between SII proponents and OCS became increasingly dense. Shortly after winning the election, the Conservative government appointed Ronald Cohen and investment banker Nick O'Donohue to lead the development of the Big Society Bank. A civil servant participating in the process described these ties as follows:

> [W]orking with Nick and Ronny in the team who were thinking about 'how do we actually make this thing work?' [...]. So it was a really... we worked as a very sort of integrated team in many ways. So we would go... they borrowed some offices from Ronnys Trust in Oxford Street, we would stay over there and work together or they would come here, we drafted documents jointly [...]. (D: 24:30)

The position of finance proponents was further strengthened with the introduction of four of the UK's biggest commercial banks as shareholders to the BSB. Following

[30]See for example Stephen Bubb's Blog in November 26th 2010, Big Society Bank, http://bloggerbubb.blogspot.de/2010/11/big-society-bank.html, accessed April 25th 2017.

[31]Source: Stephen Cook, Acevo at a crossroads, Third Sector, December 28th 2016, http://www.thirdsector.co.uk/acevo-crossroads/management/article/1418648, accessed April 25th 2017.

[32]See for example a letter by Stuart Etherington to the respective Cabinet Office Minister from August 22nd 2013, https://blogs.ncvo.org.uk/wp-content/uploads/2013/08/Chloe-Smith-non-party-campaigning-final.pdf, accessed April 25th 2017.

[33]Source: e.g. BBC News, Charities 'will be silenced' by new grant rules, January 6th 2016, http://www.bbc.co.uk/news/uk-politics-35509117, accessed April 25th 2017.

its boosterist frame, the Coalition government pledged to set up the BSB by April 2011.[34] However, due to the time-consuming mechanism through which unclaimed assets became available for distribution, only £60–100 million were estimated to be available at that point in time (2011_OCS_Growing, p. 43). This would have been only marginally more, or even less, than what Labour had pledged. To maintain Conservative boosterism, the UK's main commercial banks were asked to invest into the BSB as part of the "Merlin Agreement" which was negotiated between the Treasury and these banks following the financial crisis. Critically, however, the banks were only willing to pledge the funds to the BSB as a for-profit investment. A civil servant who held a leading role in this process noted:

> In the setup that then played quite a big role in the setup of BSC [. . .]. Because the Merlin Banks were investing and not granting, there needed to be certain, there needed to be delivering certain rates of return to the Merlin Banks. So that played a part in how Big Society Capital would be able to invest [. . .]. (D: 17:43)

As a result, Big Society Capital, the new name for the BSB, was set up as a for-profit company majority-owned by the charitable Big Society Trust (holding 80% of the voting rights), while 40% of the its shares are owned by the "Merlin Banks" (D: 18:05).

As a result of these processes, SII proponents held an increasingly central position in the social policy field. This can be seen most clearly in the new OCS strategy, which was titled "Growing the Social Investment Market: A vision and strategy" (2011_OCS_Growing). Here, the government's primary goal had shifted from growing social enterprise towards growing the SII capital market. Importantly, this implied a shift in the formal definition of investees from SEs to the broader "social venture" category. In contrast to the 2006 SE strategy, the 2011 strategy followed the frame innovation developed by finance proponents in the Commission on Unclaimed Assets and depicted the "under-capitalization" of social organizations as their most pressing need. This way, SII intermediaries' role had been established as the key growth drivers of the social services field:

> [L]ack of access to capital is still holding social ventures back. [. . .] New social ventures struggle to get going without start-up capital. [. . .] And we have only a few social ventures that operate on a large scale. This is partly because of a lack of capital for growth: without it, a social venture that is ready to grow or replicate cannot invest in the facilities it needs to generate [. . .] income. (2011_OCS_Growing, p. 14)

Taken together, the Conservative Big Society agenda took over large parts of the strategic action frame developed and institutionalized by Labour. However, Conservatives differed in their diagnostic framing and furthermore developed boosterism as a motivational frame both as an electoral and a social policy strategy. This widened the resonance space for arguments on finance-led growth. As advisory networks began to magnify SII proponents at the expense of VCS and SE representatives,

---

[34]See Cabinet Office press release from July 19th 2010, Prime Minister launches the Big Society Bank, https://www.gov.uk/government/news/prime-minister-launches-the-big-society-bank, accessed April 25th 2017.

undermining the 2002 settlement in favor of the boosterist finance frame was facilitated. These changes materialized as the newly established Big Society Capital made available an unprecedented amount of resources to for-profit SII intermediaries.

7.5.2 Maintaining Investors' Expectations Through Subsidies: The Leveraging State

In contrast to the 2002 settlement, the 2011 OCS settlement aimed at profit-distributing "social ventures" and granted significant resources to investments into financial intermediaries without limiting investors' rates of return. Thus, the field rules had shifted according to the material interests of impact investors. Moreover, SII proponents had become the new incumbents of the field that built on a cooperative tie with a government that increasingly redefined its own role according to the financialization as welfare frame. In between 2010 to 2016, government increasingly moved from a regulator of social enterprises to a "leveraging" actor aiming to grow a capital market. For example, the 2011 OCS strategy attempted to legitimize subsidies for SII by pointing out its advantages to for-profit "social ventures", as well as VCS and SEs (pp. 17f), while SII was described as *one* instrument, alongside donations and government grants, to grow social organizations:

> We want to make it easier for social ventures to access the capital and advice they need to grow, unlocking the potential to improve more lives. So at the heart of our vision is nothing less than a new 'third pillar' of finance for social ventures, to sit alongside traditional giving and funds from the state. (2011_OCS_Growing, p. 17)

By contrast, the government's revised 2016 strategy described *investments*—and not social organizations—as the cause of positive social change:

> Governments around the world are increasingly recognising the potential of social investment. It is supporting economic growth, driving the innovation needed to deliver public services in the 21st century and, ultimately, tackling some of the most difficult social challenges that we face. (2016_HMG_Social, p. 6)

Rather than supporting social organizations, the government's primary goal now was to establish the UK as a "global hub" for SII. To do so, an "international strategy" was developed, which expanded the public agencies to follow the financialization frame from OCS to include the Department for International Development and others (2016_HMG_International, p. i). Between 2011 and 2016, government's focal point shifted to capital markets as a mechanism to deliver social change "at scale." With the increasing focus on scale, it increasingly became an end in itself for government to "crowd-in commercial investors"—as had been advocated by finance proponents (14_G8_Policy_levers, p. 4). For example, OCS "explored innovative methods of using government money to raise capital from the private sector" (2016_HMG_Social, p. 8) through the set-up of the Dementia Discovery Fund and the Arts Impact Funds. Moreover, a "Social Investment Tax Relief" was introduced, motivated by the hope to "unlock £480 million worth of investment" (2016_HMG_Social, p. 8).

However, the development of the SII field far lagged behind the government's and SII proponents' boosterist projections. Rather than the $1 trillion in global impact assets envisioned by JP Morgan for 2020 (2010_JPMorgan), the size of the domestic British SII market—the world leader, according to its proponents—was far below £1 billion. For example, in 2015 Big Society Capital has only been able to invest £68 million of its resources (2016_HMG_Social, p. 15). Numerous observers have noted that "Big Society Capital are flailing around a bit at the moment, and wondering where to put their money" (H: 1:04:19). By following the demands of for-profit impact investors, government has created a situation where "there is a supply of money, and there isn't a demand for it" (H: 1:02:32), which many VCS and SE actors see as problematic (e.g. interviewees H, E, C). One of the reasons for this has been the additional layer of profit extraction created by financial intermediaries that increased the cost of capital for social organizations (E: 23:56, see also Chap. 5). Similarly, the number of commissioned SIBs has been lower than policymakers' expectations (D: 40:43).

But although they voiced critique of the financialization frame in my interviews, I found much less publicly voiced critique by VCS actors. This is particularly the case for ACEVO, which rather than maintaining the boundaries of the VCS and SE categories, has, as described above, empathetically embraced the creation of BSC without scrutinizing the boundary expansion that came with it. This is why there has been hardly any critique of the 2011 OCS settlement from VCS and SE umbrella bodies. For example, I have only found one critical article on SII in the field's main news outlet, Third Sector magazine, in 2011, the year of the new settlement.[35] Moreover, only three of all blog posts made public on the NCVO website (hundreds, if not thousands of entries) offer a critical perspective on social investment and the 2011 settlement.[36]

Only in 2015 an "Alternative Commission on Social Investment" was formed which challenged several of the key components of the OCS strategic action frame. Its report questioned the development of SII towards high-growth for-profit

---

[35]For example: Press release by the National Association for Voluntary and Community Action (NAVCA) calling social investment "over-hyped": David Ainsworth, Significance of social investment has been 'over-hyped', says Navca chief, Third Sector, December 12th 2011, http://www.thirdsector.co.uk/significance-social-investment-over-hyped-says-navca-chief/finance/article/1108757, accessed April 29th 2017.

[36]Source: Charlotte Ravenscroft, If social investment is the answer, what is the question?, NCVO (The National Council for Voluntary Organisations), November 14th 2012, https://blogs.ncvo.org.uk/2012/11/14/if-social-investment-is-the-answer-what-is-the-question/, accessed April 29th 2017.

Charlotte Ravenscroft, Social Investment: Writing the Rules of a New Game, NCVO, July 16th 2012, https://blogs.ncvo.org.uk/2012/07/16/social-investment-writing-the-rules-of-a-new-game/, accessed April 29th 2017.

Andrew O'Brien, G8 social investment report: What do you need to know?, NCVO, September 17th 2014, https://blogs.ncvo.org.uk/2014/09/17/g8-social-investment-report-what-do-you-need-to-know/, accessed April 29th 2017.

investments by holding that "[m]any Social Sector Organisations believe that SIFIs sit in their expensive London offices offering finance that is of little relevance to the rest of the UK modelled on the venture capital industry" (2015_Alternative, p. 12). Moreover, it addressed BSC and SIFIs directly by asking whether they offered "lower interest rates based on expected impact" or were "prepared to take bigger risks based on expected impact" (p. 13). Lastly, the commission urged BSC and OCS to "[a]void treating the development of the social investment market as an end itself" (p. 13) and demanded those organizations to consider breaking up BSC into two separate organizations offering finance on different terms:

> Consider splitting the investment of Unclaimed Assets and Merlin bank funds. Unclaimed Assets, allocated by law to Social Sector Organisations, could be invested on terms that better meet demand than currently, while Merlin bank funds could be invested in a wider group of organisations [...]. (p. 13)

Although a former BSC employee confirmed via email that three BSC employees were tasked with taking up recommendations from this report, from a social movement perspective, the Alternative Commission failed to develop a compelling field-level strategic action frame. Rather, it proposed a patchwork of 48 recommendations to alter the shape of the SII field. In addition, it did not attempt to organize a counter-movement of VCS and SE actors.[37]

The government responded to this challenge by further entrenching its role as a "leveraging" actor, subsidizing investors' return generation. Following finance proponents' frame, OCS included the creation of "demand" for SII capital as a goal into its strategies. Here, the government attributed the cause of lacking demand to social ventures' lacking "investment readiness". For example, the 2011 OCS strategy asserted that social ventures needed "help with developing a business plan; training in financial skills, for example help with making cash flow projections; help with building credible, rigorous business cases" (2011_OCS_Growing, p. 32). Thus, rather than limiting investors' returns via regulation and thereby making SII more affordable to social ventures (as is the case in France, see Chiapello and Godefroy (2017)), the government's proposed solution followed investors' material interests and sought to alter investees' organizational structures and processes instead (pp. 32–34).

Following this strategy, in 2012, the government set up a £14 million "Investment and Contract Readiness Fund" (ICRF) that paid for social ventures' participation in "investment readiness" training programs. Pointing to the success of the intervention, the 2016 SI strategy noted that "for every £1 of support from the fund, £18 has been generated in contracts and private investment" (2016_HMG_Social, p. 8). Thus, central government has in the field of social and public services increasingly

[37]This is not to say that VCS and SE actors were not critical of the Coalition and Conservative governments—quite the opposite. But their critique and mobilization centered around austerity, i.e. direct spending cuts to social and public sector organizations. Rejecting financial products such as SIBs during austerity would for social organizations often mean losing access to public funds altogether.

become a "leveraging" actor: its economic actions aim to subsidize investors' creation of a financial return, justified by theorizing a causal link between the subsidy and the "mobilization" of private investments. The result of the 2012 ICRF has served as an important legitimation to further entrench this strategy of leverage by financing "investment readiness" interventions in the subsequent years. In 2013, a £10 million "Social Incubator Fund" has been set up, followed in 2014 by a £20 million "Big Potential" fund using lottery revenues, as well as the creation of the "Access" foundation for investment readiness, using £60 million of repaid futurebuilders loans.

To "scale" Social Impact Bonds, central government followed a similar strategy of subsidizing investors' financial returns. Again, central government followed the financialization as welfare frame to legitimize the use of public funds for their expansion. For example, the Conservative 2015 election manifesto understood SIBs as an "innovative" means to deliver "high-quality public services" and pledged to "scale these up in the future, focusing on youth unemployment, mental health and homelessness" (2015_Conservative_Manifesto, p. 46). However, due to the complexities of the SIB commissioning process as well as the high levels of financial returns that need to be paid to investors, local government commissioners are often hesitant to develop and commission new SIB projects.[38] To increase SIB commissioning, central government has set up numerous "outcome funds" that cover parts of the outcome payments. This means that only if local authorities commission SIBs, they will be provided with additional funds from central government (usually around 20% of the contract volume). Between 2012 and 2016, a total of £200 million was spent by central government departments as outcome payment subsidies (see Fig. 5.4).

Thus, although VCS and SE actors challenged the new settlement, they neither put into question the financialization frame on a general level, nor did they develop and propel an alternative field-level frame. Moreover, the challenge only occurred after VCS and SE proponents had lost their direct ties to government at the expense of SII proponents. In addition, the Cameron governments have been firmly committed to their boosterist frame—in particular by rapidly creating BSC as a flagship project. Since BSC was, due to the 2008 Dormant Accounts Act, legally required to only invest into SII intermediaries, withdrawing their support would have been equal to concede failure of one of the government's flagship boosterist projects. Thus, by responding to the VCS-led challenge in accordance to the financialization frame, central government maintained its own legitimacy. Thus, the financialization as welfare frame has become institutionalized in the social policy field.

My observation period ended with the British vote to leave the European Union on June 23rd, 2016. If any event in modern British history qualifies as an external rupture in the sense of strategic action fields and new institutional theory, this has been a prototype of such a jolt as it fundamentally altered the problem situation

[38]Source: Meeting notes from "Widening perspective on Social Impact Bonds" conference, London, September 13th 2016.

virtually any British policymaker saw her/himself confronted with. With the resignation of David Cameron and his Chancellor George Osbourne ended not only the normative program of "compassionate conservatism", but also the tenure of politicians who strongly advocated the Treasury view and its authority in domestic social policy. Just days after Theresa May became Prime Minister on July 13th 2016, the OCS was moved to a peripheral position in the Department of Culture, Media and Sports. In the 2017 general election, the OCS minister Rob Wilson lost his parliamentary seat, and subsequently the OCS minister rank was abolished and its functions merged with the (junior) minister for sports. The consequences of this rupture for the SII field remain to be seen. If financial intermediaries will lose access to central government funds, then my argument would predict a profound crisis in the SII field. However, this crisis might be buffered by the fact that BSC still holds a significant amount of resources which it is obliged to only invest into SII. Moreover, via SIBs, impact investors' government-finance ties have increasingly shifted to a local level that is not only much more fragmented but also remains somewhat resilient to these international ruptures.

Chapter 8
Financialization, Resonance, and the Emergence of Cross-Field Ties

In this book, I understand financialization as a field-level social process that transforms social orders to serve the material interests of financial intermediaries. In contrast to existing theories, I have argued for a view that is somewhat detached from the structuring force of the institutions of capitalist economies. Rather, I follow strategic action fields theory (Fligstein and McAdam 2012) and view financialization as a successful attempt of financial intermediaries to develop cooperative ties with nonfinancial actors in which their privileged field position is reproduced. That being said, my theoretical discussion has shown that SAF theory does not provide us with explanatory tools to understand the emergence of such cooperative cross-field ties. I hypothesized that this is because the question of cooperation falls on the wielding seam of the theory's two main components: the social skill perspective developed by Fligstein (2001b), and the movement and contention perspectives advanced by McAdam et al. (2001). I have argued that, to close this void, we need to look for a pragmatist mechanism (Gross 2009) that specifies the conditions under and process through which skilled social actors develop such cooperative ties.

In the preceding empirical chapters, I have studied the emergence of social impact investing in the UK as such a process of financialization. Making use of the temporal and situational variation the empirical material offered, I developed through abductive analysis (Tavory and Timmermans 2014) a guiding hypothesis of such a mechanism. Based on rigorous casing and testing of the empirical material, I developed *resonance spaces* as skilled actors' structured opportunities, and *resonance* as the underlying structuring mechanism as theoretical generalizations that accounted for a substantial amount of the empirical variance regarding the emergence of cooperative ties. As a working hypothesis, I defined resonance spaces as situations where the emergence of a new cross-field tie was preceded by a change in either of those fields such that a strategic action frame motivating a cooperative tie between those fields became acceptable to actors within that field. However, in order to transcend from the descriptive empirical level to the level of causal explanations, we need to infuse sociological theory into these heuristics. This is necessary to relate

P. Golka, *Financialization as Welfare*,
https://doi.org/10.1007/978-3-030-06100-5_8

back the question of cooperative ties to research on fields and financialization. Even more, qualifying our empirical hypotheses theoretically is crucially important from an epistemological point of view: only by casing, testing, and linking our hypotheses vis-à-vis established bodies of knowledge can we claim our findings to be generalizable beyond the studied case.

To do so, the first segment synthesizes the empirical results to carve out a more fine-grained hypothesis of the resonance mechanism. The second segment then infuses social theory into this descriptive formulation in order to establish a causal account that links dynamics within fields to the emergence of ties between them. In the third segment, I show how this causal mechanism relates to resonance spaces, and how these enhance our understanding of field dynamics. In the fourth segment, I show how these new insights improve our understanding of financialization.

8.1 Pragmatist Mechanisms and Cooperation in Social Impact Investing

The main theoretical puzzle in this study is the emergence of cooperative ties across fields. Studying the emergence of social impact investing in the UK, my principal object of inquiry has been to trace and explain the amplitude of cooperation between policymakers and financial intermediaries. What became clear most generally was that subsidies followed policymakers' increasing acceptance of investors' financialization as welfare frame. This has been most clearly the case during the Coalition government, where the publication of the 2011 Social Investment strategy preceded an unprecedented increase in subsidies for investors, as well as the rapid surge in "investment readiness" support to cope with increasing criticism of these subsidies (see Fig. 5.4). Thus, an initial conclusion might be to understand SII as an innovation of the incoming Cameron administration (Dowling and Harvie 2014). However, tracing back the development of SII further in time, I found that such an explanation would miss key parts of the story. Throughout the observation period, we saw frame acceptance preceding subsidies. This began with subsidies for the rather small community finance field granted by Treasury in the early 2000s, but the same was true for the expansion of subsidies for equity financial products during the Brown premiership 2007–2010.

While under Labour, the social enterprise settlement that limited profit distribution held back policymakers from accepting a thoroughly financialized frame on social services, during the Cameron years, the rapid acceptance of a full-fledged financialization frame triggered an explosion in subsidies to financial actors. Key to this frame has been the fact that it prescribed a highly specific role to government that structured its future action patterns vis-à-vis financial intermediaries. Thus, accepting a financialized frame resulted in cooperation as it organized joint future action and demarcated positions in the field. As both Labour and Conservative policymakers have, at least to some extent, followed financial intermediaries' mobilization attempts, political party affiliation alone cannot be the structuring mechanism we are looking for.

What, then, could form the mechanism we are looking for? Let me first point to something seemingly obvious: most key turning points in the development of SII had something to do with who talked to whom. During the Labour government, a number of senior civil servants and policymakers would very regularly talk to leading SII actors. The reasons for this are beyond the scope of this work, although the fact that one of the SII movement's main figureheads, Ronald Cohen, was among the biggest donors of the Labour party certainly played a role here. The point rather is that as long as policymakers talked to both, SII proponents *and* representatives of profit-limited organizations such as the voluntary organizations and social enterprise, the 2002 settlement remained intact. But with the 2010 change of government, VCS and SE proponents rapidly lost their direct ties to government and thus found it increasingly difficult to counterbalance arguments made by financial intermediaries. The same is true outside government as well: the key frame shift in the development of SII came as finance proponents began embracing the broad category of "social ventures" as "under-invested" contributors to the solution of social problems. Key parts of this frame shift came with the Commission on Unclaimed Assets that not only included a small group of VCS representatives, but also ran an open consultation with the sector.

But despite the importance of direct communication, talk can hardly be more than a necessary condition in a structuring mechanism since not all communication triggers structural changes. Through the application of abductive analysis, I found that a particular relation between the content of the communication and the position of the communicating actors enabled the emergence of field dynamics. This link has two main features: to yield sustained action, the cooperation frame had to build upon the *problem situation* that partaking actors saw themselves confronted with. But this problem situation is inextricably linked to *actors' position in their proximate field environment.*

The emerging cooperation between financial intermediaries and the VCS during the CUA serves as a case in point here. This cross-field tie developed because financial intermediaries took up problem discourse of VCS actors such as ACEVO: as early as 2003 had ACEVO argued for full-cost recovery and strongly supported financial investment (in the form of loans) in order to improve the VCS's position in competitive tendering vis-à-vis for-profit firms. But the reverse is also true: financial intermediaries only abandoned their opposition to the VCS because they could build on a key frame innovation developed in 2004: By referring to "social ventures" rather than the VCS or social enterprise, they could enter the field of social organizations and social service delivery without limiting their profit opportunities.

However, this emerging tie did not link all of the VCS to financial intermediaries. As Stuart Etherington of the NCVO noted at the launch of the 2007 CUA report, for the wider field of the VCS, for-profit finance was a small piece in a funding environment centered on non-repayable funds. Rather, the new tie addressed the problem situation of a particular group that was itself positioned within the VCS: its executive management. This group was represented by ACEVO who had been vocal supporters of financial innovations such as full-cost recovery, service delivery contracts, and finance-led growth as these would strengthen their positions within the organization and vis-à-vis competitors. As ACEVO enjoyed close ties to large parts of the Labour core executive, while advocating for issues such as "added value" and "outcomes" that had been shared by both competing power centers (Blair and Brown), their campaign has been highly successful, partially at the expense of other VCS constituents.

The very same link between positions and problem situations furthermore accounts for the dynamics of the SII-policy cooperation after the CUA. The alliance between financial intermediaries and the VCS structurally changed policymakers' field environment. As a result, they began to see "social investment" as more than just the niche community finance product it had been a few years earlier. Rather, they began to view it as a means to grow a larger group of social organizations and to "scale" their "social impact." While such an interpretation was facilitated by the emergence of future builders that first expanded the term "social investment" into the VCS, key was that the emerging SII-VCS tie was linked to both, respective policymakers' changing positions within the core executive, as well as the emergence of new problem situations. During the later Labour years, the Treasury view on public service delivery became increasingly dominant and Treasury policymakers gained increasingly central positions. This allowed the arguments regarding "leverage" and "risk transfer" resonate with increasingly central positions and reduced opposition. Moreover, positions of SII proponents also changed after they embraced the VCS and Brown became Prime Minister: now they were working together in a very high status position at the Council on Social Action. Here, the emerging threat from Conservatives who embraced boosterism as an electoral strategy began to shift policymakers' problem situations in favor of equity proponents and the financialization frame. However, while VCS and SE proponents still featured centrally in the social services field, boosterism was counterbalanced by a plurality of voices.

The link between positions and problem situations was also key to the trajectory of the social policy field. Here, Treasury was using the tools of "cross-cutting issues" and "value for money" that were considered as legitimate Treasury problems by other government departments. Thus, the problematization and subsequent transformation of the *content of* social policy according to the "Treasury view" was inextricably linked to positioned actors' struggle over field rules.

Together, these findings point to the fact that cooperative cross-field ties emerge in situations of direct communication where one party attempts to convince the other that the proposed future action patterns are in their own interest. Their success in doing so, however, is critically dependent upon the problem situation of the actors on the "receiving" end. These are to a very large degree determined by their position in the proximate field environment.

A situation where direct communication does not lead to the emergence of a cooperative tie would therefore serve as a litmus test for such a hypothesis. Indeed, the failure of SII proponents to convince HM Treasury of a "wholesale" financial intermediary for community finance is a case in point. Here, direct communication between policymakers and SII proponents was given since the 2000 Social Investment Taskforce, which propelled the idea, was appointed by Gordon Brown. But although HM Treasury did follow the taskforce's proposals regarding tax credits and co-investments into Bridges Community Ventures, the idea regarding the "wholesale" intermediary was not followed through. While one of the reasons certainly was that here, finance proponents' motivational framing lacked the clarity of their other proposals, my perspective would emphasize a different point: the envisioned community finance wholesale intermediary addressed a rather small field that was largely unrelated to HM Treasury's key public service agenda. Thus, from the perspective of HM Treasury, establishing such an organization would be a complex solution in search of a problem of an equal scale. By 2007, however, the situation was an entirely different one as the "wholesale" proposal now addressed the much larger field of "social ventures" that could be linked to Labour's "government in partnership" agenda with the VCS and Treasury's "value for money" view on public service delivery.

In summary, this means that all actors that are partaking in communication to establish a joint future action orientation *evaluate* or *test* possible ways to cooperate vis-à-vis the accepted frames and rules in their proximate field environment, as well as their position therein. Together with other factors that need to be traced empirically (e.g. resource dependencies or informal networks), this constitutes the problem situation based on which cooperation will either make sense for or be refused by the respective parties.

Thus, institutionalized rules play a central role in determining cooperation trajectories—albeit in a somewhat different way than argued for by most strands of new institutional theory. Throughout the development of SII, institutional dynamics enabled policymakers' positive evaluation of SII proponents' cooperation offers: the boundaries regarding legitimate profit extraction of social organizations began to be blurred with the emergence of social enterprise in the late 1990s, and thus before SII proponents' made similar claims. The same temporal order holds for the redefinition of public services from public ownership to the "value for money" delivery of social outcomes. Although investors' engagement with social impact assessment can be seen as a process of isomorphism as they entered the field of service delivery governed through "outcome" metrics, such a view misses a crucial part of the story. Remember that policymakers at the Department of Trade and Industry began to ascribe an "added value" to (partially) profit-distributing social enterprises for the delivery of social services in parallel to a Treasury-led redefinition of the social service delivery field. As these two developments progressed in the policy field, they represented an opportunity for financial actors to gain access to resources *because* they allowed positioned policymakers to validate the financialization arguments vis-à-vis their own policy field environment. This can be seen even more clearly in the case of Social Impact Bonds: although similar ideas (such as the Voluntary Finance Initiative) had been floating around New Labour social policy discourse in the early 200 s, it was only SIBs that created sufficient momentum. This is because SIBs represented a potpourri of ideas, such as outcomes-management, risk transfer,

VCS contracting, prevention, and "personalized" delivery, that a group of policy-makers, who at the very same time climbed to a central position in the core executive, had been advocating for a long time.

Social impact investing in the UK was critically enabled by nonfinancial actors' acceptance of investors' field-level financialization as welfare frame and by a reproduction of the cooperative relations legitimated in this frame. The development trajectory of this strategic action frame, as well as the amplitude of its acceptance can to a large extent be explained by making explicit partaking actors' problem situations. Following strategic action fields theory, these situations are critically dependent upon actors' position in their proximate field environment. However, the perspective proposed here critically expands SAF theory by opening up this positionality to empirical research. Rather than conceptualizing actors via a strict challenger/incumbent dualism, my abductive analysis has shown that a focus on problem situations expands our explanatory horizon. While these situations are fundamentally relational as they depend upon actors' position vis-à-vis status orders, they expand such a view by introducing a more open notion of evaluation or "tests" as a structuring force. This way, the question regarding the emergence of cross-field cooperative ties fundamentally builds upon skilled social actors who need to relate future cooperation to their present proximate field environment. In the next segment, I will show how the hypothesis developed here is a pragmatist mechanism, capable of providing a causal explanation.

8.2 Resonance

The aim of this book is, on a theoretical level, to answer the question how cooperative ties across dynamic fields emerge. To address this question, I studied the emergence of social impact investing in the UK through abductive analysis (Tavory and Timmermans 2014). I used the empirical variance baked into the case in order to derive a prototheoretical heuristic to answer this question. To transcend from the specific empirical case to the more general theoretical level, abductive analysis demands us to integrate our hypothesis into extant (sociological) theory. One part of this is to "case" our material against extant theory in order to understand the significance of the empirical case for established theoretical generalizations. In Chap. 3, I argued that the present case and research question can be addressed particularly well by strategic action fields theory. However, I found that its proposed mechanism that focuses on the interaction of extant *identities* with skilled actors' attempts to motivate cooperation is a problematic one as identities are somewhat "non-situative." Instead, I proposed to open the search for such a causal mechanism up to empirical research. I argued that Gross's (2009) concept of "pragmatist mechanisms" is sufficiently general to allow for empirical findings to emerge, while being theoretically congruent with SAF theory. Thus, what remains to be done is to show how the heuristic developed above indeed qualifies as such a mechanism.

To do so, let us first take a step back and clarify what we mean by cooperation. Whether playing chamber music or forming a joint-venture in the automotive industry, cooperation always entails a *purposeful agreement to organize future actions into a particular sequence or pattern.* As it defines future action patterns through agreement, cooperation is a social relation that is culturally mediated through actors' subjective understandings of what it means to cooperate.

One particular form of cooperation is the alignment of field-level strategic action frames (Benford and Snow 2000; Snow and Benford 1988). Here, actors come to accept a particular view of a problem situation (diagnostic framing), a possible, imagined solution (prognostic framing), and a role description of what needs to be done by whom in order to get there (motivational framing). Frame alignment thus includes a shared understanding of imaginary goals and roles, as well as strategies to be deployed in the near future. Furthermore, it implies at least some consensus about the normative and "institutional" vocabulary that forms the basis of the problem description. This is because any problem description involves at least some institutionally defined objects, such as categories, groups, or rules, that—although they appear factual as part of actors' taken-for-granted social environment (i.s.o. Berger and Luckmann 1966)—are foregrounded in the act of problem construction (Schmidt 2008) and related to the imaginary of a different future (Mische 2014). To problematize aspects of their social environment, actors need to attach a normative valuation to these objects (Lamont 2012). As strategic action frames provide actors with an instruction to act, respective justifications, and a means to interpret others' actions, they form a crucial part of institutionalized social life (Cornelissen and Werner 2014).

Not least for these reasons, frame alignment plays a central role in social movement scholarship and is cited by Fligstein and McAdam (2012, p. 110) as a source for cooperation. That said, SAF theory does not give us an understanding for how frame alignment interacts with the theory's social ontology of society-as-fields and actors' positionality. Schematically, the problem of cooperation boils down to the one depicted in Fig. 8.1. We know that actors are embedded in a "dense latticework" of fields, but we do not know how this impacts the emergence of cooperation. To open this black box, I argue that it is key to merge the causal role of frames with SAF theory's field ontology. This is where pragmatist mechanisms come into play.

As described in Chap. 3, Gross (2009) understands pragmatist mechanisms as a process S that mediates between input and output. Based on pragmatist action theory, he conceptualized this process as a chain of actors A_i that face problem situations P_i to which they find, drawing on habits H_i, the responses R_i.

Following SAF theory, these actors A_i will not only be socially skilled, but also possess different field positions and hence idiosyncratic sets of frames and network ties. The key to linking SAF theory with processes of frame resonance lies in the actors' problem situations and how we expect them to cope with these. Depending on their position in the wider field environment, actors will face specific problem *situations* P_i. For example, they may act as challengers and hence oppose parts of the institutionalized reality which they perceive as disadvantageous. To forge a

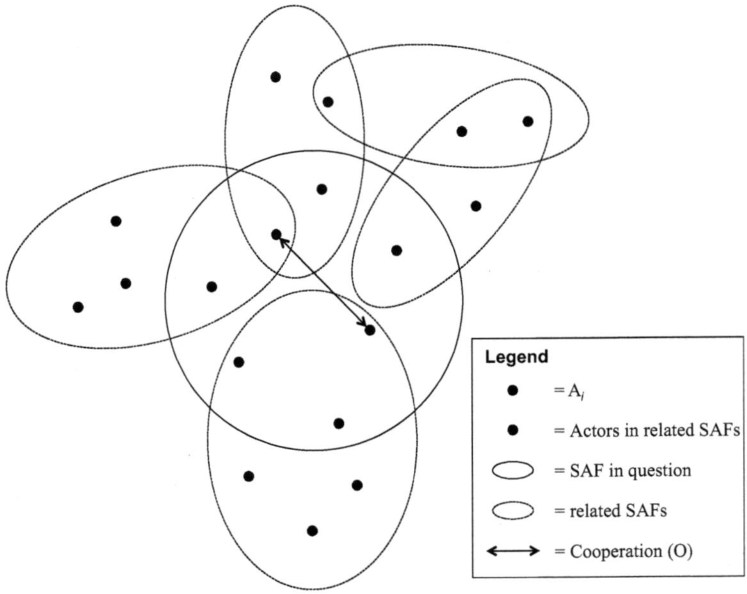

Fig. 8.1 Exemplary illustration of the problem of cooperation

cooperative tie, however, the partaking actors will need to agree on a shared strategic action frame. We know from research on social movements (Benford and Snow 2000) that one particularly effective way to do so is to build on a shared problem *description*.

As noted above, finding such an agreement is a very complex process, particularly for actors from different fields, as normative valuations and institutional vocabularies need to be aligned. At the outset, these vocabularies and justifications may profoundly differ, as for example between civil servants and financial actors. Thus, in order to achieve the outcome of a shared strategic action frame that defines a future cooperative role structure, strategic actors need to build on a habit H_i that may integrate problem situations with problem descriptions. I argue that *negotiation* is such a habit.

By negotiation, I do not primarily mean a specific set-up but rather the more general *iteration between making and testing cooperation offers*. This may take many different, culturally mediated forms, as in forming a teenage music band or an industrial joint-venture. However, the general idea is that because actors are in different positions and thus have differing environments that place idiosyncratic demands on them, they will "read" *their own* situation and evaluate whether or not, and under which conditions, a cooperation offer is acceptable from their position. This way actors' *proximate field environment* is a determining factor for the development of cooperation. But since cooperation requires a shared problem diagnosis in order to justify a shared prognostic and motivational frame, the proximate field

Table 8.1 Schematic overview of the resonance mechanism

Mechanism S	Resonance
Input I	Situated and positioned actors with divergent action frames
Outcome O	Cooperation: social relation based on a shared action frame
Actors A_i	Skilled actors in different positions with idiosyncratic field environments and frames, but communicating to each other
Problem situations P_i	Problem situation corresponding to position in proximate field environment
Habits H_i	*Negotiation:* iteration between framed cooperation *offers* and *tests* against individual frame and position in order to merge problem situations with strategic framing
Responses R_i	Prognostic and motivational frame alignment and altered social relations that affect proximate field environments

environment furthermore also structures the *trajectories* of cooperation. This A-P-H-R chain is what I call the *resonance mechanism* (see Table 8.1 for an overview).

The entrenchment of the Treasury view serves as a good example here. To subjugate other government departments to their view, policymakers at HM Treasury applied the tools of cross-cutting issues and value for money that were acceptable forms of Treasury influence from the position of other government departments. Yet critically, this also meant that the prognostic and motivational frames advanced by HM Treasury were limited to those that could be justified vis-à-vis these devices.

How is this chain of events a causal mechanism, and how does it fit to SAF theory's core assumptions? There are three causal assumptions baked into this mechanism that require theoretical clarification: How can we assume that actors communicate? Why and when will they negotiate (and not, for example, openly contest or use violence)? How does negotiation relate to frame alignment?

The relation between actors, social structures and human communication is a central albeit a contested one in sociological theory. For example, Habermas (1981) argues that social systems—capitalist ones in particular—fundamentally constrain ("colonialize") the situations in which social interactions are negotiated solely based on the "unforced force" of rational (in a Kantian sense) arguments. Luhmann (1987) sees communication structured via codes and media that are engrained in autopoietic social systems, which, although necessitating human cognition for their reproduction, do not grant humans (the systems' psychological environment) an agentic say in modifying the media provided by systems. Some have argued that capitalist structures and dynamics rest upon successful communication of imaginaries (Beckert 2016), while others have argued that they alter the form of human communication from meaning-based to consequentialist (Langenohl and Wetzel 2011). The point is that the question of how and when actors communicate directly cannot be answered objectively but rather forms a core tenet of any sociological theory.

In strategic action fields theory, the conception of social skill allows to answer this question contingently. As skilled strategic actors develop and modify strategies during the course of action, we may expect them to choose various means to achieve their goals—one of which is communication. What are, then, the conditions upon which we may expect strategic actors to communicate directly with others? As social skill includes the ability to read others' situations, we can expect that skilled actors will attempt to communicate directly when they, from imagining the likely reaction of the other, anticipate reasonable success in their efforts *and* assume that doing so will further their (fuzzy set of) aims. For example, speaking directly to extremist groups may prove successful in convincing them of a different course of action, but—depending upon position such as politician or priest—actors may fear negative repercussion from engaging with stigmatized groups. By contrast, Rosa Parks lacked the ties necessary to communicate directly with government officials—who enjoyed dense network ties with white incumbent groups and possessed strategic action frames diametrically opposed to her cause—but did have ties to black community organizations—who shared her problem diagnosis of oppression, and hence chose to communicate with these in order to achieve social mobilization (Fligstein and McAdam 2012, p. 21).

But as the latter example shows, the emergence of direct communication cannot be reduced to partaking actors' strategies. Here, again, field-level positions will play a crucial role. Actors' resources such as money or network ties will also play a central role. For example, in the case of SII, Ronald Cohen's position as a main donor of the Labour party certainly facilitated his communicative access to senior Labour policymakers. This means that the emergence of cooperation forms another chain of events that mediates between strategic actors and the outcome of direct communication—in other words, a lower-level mechanism.[1] Yet, as this is not the analytic level of interest here, I will ignore these contingencies and presuppose direct communication.

How can we assume our communicating actors to select the H_i of negotiation as spelled out above? As Gross's (2009) conception of pragmatist mechanisms suggests, this will be critically dependent upon the problem situations the actors face. In the case of SAFs, the problem situation will very often be some form of contest over field rules as strategic actors attempt to maintain or change the rules of the game according to their perspective. The problem actors face will therefore be different according to their field position. This means that the problem situation will invoke a culturally mediated interpretation of the current state of the field, i.e. its factual set-up regarding actors, rules, networks, categories, etc., as well as some kind of normative valuation of some or all of these components. If actors populate the same field, they will have a shared understanding of the factual component, but not necessarily of the normative component (Fligstein and McAdam 2012, p. 9). An alignment of partaking actors' problem understanding

[1]This implies "mechanisms all the way down," i.e. that all social processes are contingent upon other social processes. This is congruent with SAF theory, which assumes fields at all levels of analysis.

is a necessary condition for cooperation to emerge, as "directed action is contingent on identification of the source(s) of causality, blame, and/or culpable agents" (Benford and Snow 2000, p. 616).

Remember that we are talking about (at least) two skilled actors who communicate directly and aim to foster cooperation. But as the very definition of social skill means being able to "read" the situation of the other, this implies that, in communicating directly, skilled actors will translate their perception of the situation of the other into a communicated description. However, as the receiver of the communicated description is also skilled, they will "read" their own situation and assess whether the communicated description matches their own understanding of the situation. Thus, as skilled actors communicate directly, they will attempt to merge framed problem descriptions with idiosyncratic problem situations. But due to the definition of social skill this necessarily means that they engage in the habit of negotiation as defined above.

How does this form of negotiation relate to frame alignment? To answer this question, let us take a closer look at what it means to negotiate. From my perspective, negotiation is a habit of social interaction. Its goal is to reach an agreement—in our case, an agreement over the prognostic and diagnostic framing with regards to some field-level change. From a pragmatist perspective, it is a habitualized script of a sequence of actions aimed at solving a shared problem situation. It is habitualized as it builds upon taken-for-granted schemas (Emirbayer and Mische 1998; Gross 2009) that define the process of negotiation. However, as it is related to skilled actors in problem situations, its outcome may well be creative solutions.

My point is that the conception of social skill *necessarily* involves both components of negotiation. As already spelled out in SAF theory, the creative dimension of pragmatist action means that skilled actors develop, based on how they "read" the others' problem situations, proposals for alternative futures and translate those into action plans. However, as we presupposed communicative ties, this means that these future plans will need to be *accepted* by the to-be-mobilized actor. As Jürgen Habermas has shown in his discussion of speech acts (1981, Chap. 3), this acceptance is a *mechanism* for action coordination—but *only if* the transported speech acts are based on "*criticizable validity claims*" ("kritisierbare Geltungsansprüche" p. 409). Thus, to mobilize others to cooperate, it is necessary to make offers that withstand others' critical tests regarding the validity of the claims. Therefore—and this has been overlooked by Fligstein and McAdam (2012)—the process of developing cooperation, negotiation, is comprised of *two* structuring actions: *offers* and *tests*.

As Habermas points out, both making and judging validity claims in speech acts is subject to social conventions (p. 405). This is why both offers and tests are habits, because, like any convention, they need to be learned through socialization. If an offer suffices its subjected tests, this means that a "rationally motivated relation" will emerge on this basis (p. 376). Offers to engage in such a relation can be tested on three dimensions: their normative appropriateness, their factual validity, and the speaker's truthfulness (p. 411ff). Thus, to accept offers for cooperation, the senders' claims need to be validated against *what the receiver perceives as factual and appropriate.*[2] Other authors have developed different contentual models for these tests: for example, the sociology of conventions and critique (Boltanski and Chiapello 2006; Boltanski and Thévenot 2006; Chiapello 2013) distinguishes between eight different, socially constructed conventions against which claims are assessed. In contrast to Habermas, here, tests are not so much understood as binary true/false distinctions, but rather form a central component of a justificatory practice in which social orders are established through negotiated compromises between these eight "worlds."

From the perspective of pragmatist mechanisms and SAF theory, however, both of these conceptions of tests are not sufficiently specified to account for the development of cooperation because they are not related to actors' position in the proximate field environment. Based on Habermas's conception of tests, we would likely see a very large number of cooperation offers being accepted—but this is contradicted by findings from the social movement literature (Benford and Snow 2000). Certainly, factual correctness and normative appropriateness are necessary conditions for agreeing upon a joint action plan, but as we have already presupposed a shared problem diagnosis and argued that this implies a shared institutional-factual and normative-diagnostic vocabulary, a Habermasian test would mean that agreement regarding the problem diagnosis would translate into successful mobilization. Here, the conventionalist conception of compromise (Boisard and Letablier 1987; Boltanski and Thévenot 2006) would be more helpful—however, its rigid view on orders of worth is difficult to reconcile with the meso-level focus of SAF theory. Although we could conceive of such high-level orders to permeate fields, we would require theoretizations regarding the relation between the set-up of fields and the legitimate use of these conventions.

This is why it seems more appropriate to leave the contentual dimension of the test a dynamic, meso-level issue and matter for empirical research. That said, from the society-as-fields notion we can theorize tests as related to actors' *proximate field environment*. As Fig. 8.1 shows, even within a field, actors' differential positions mean that their proximate field environment is highly variable. Yet, as different fields mean different institutional rules and collective frames, we can theorize tests as *actors' assessment of cooperation claims against the rules and frames that are institutionalized in those proximate fields to which they are linked*. For skilled actors, tests mean a reading of their own idiosyncratic situation and an assessment of the cooperation demands against how they interpret their own position in the proximate field environment. This does not mean that actors engage in utility calculation as offers can be assessed against normative principles.

[2]For Habermas, this mode of action orientation through communicative rationality was threatened by strategic actions engrained in "norm-free" and nondiscursive systems of money and power. However, other scholars have shown both empirically and theoretically, how such tests form the very basis of power, economic coordination, and strategic action (Boltanski and Thévenot 2006; Forst 2015a). Here, I apply Habermas' analysis of speech acts only to show that strategic action in the sense of Fligstein and McAdam *necessitates justification vis-à-vis the receiver's idiosyncratic perspective*.

Moreover, such a view on negotiation is open towards different forms of social relations. If we take, for example, formal dependence relations, then subordinates may follow a broad set of proposed future action patterns without demanding additional justifications related to their position in the field. The steeper the formal power gradient between actors, the less will powerful actors require negotiation. However, this is precisely because subordinates will often interpret these demands as in accordance with their situation in the field. Thus, as Rainer Forst (2015a) has argued, even the most unequal power relation requires at least some legitimacy from inferiors who (in the absence of physical violence) may principally act otherwise. Maintaining future action patterns, even in dependence relations, therefore requires cooperation that rests on actors having a "good enough reason" to do so. My perspective expands the view proposed by Forst by arguing that this reason will be tied to actors' interpretation of their own position in the field.

Lastly, such a conception also does not mean that actors are fully determined by their field environment: as Gross (2009, p. 371) has argued, even collectively enacted habits such as negotiation can be infused by individual-level habits. For example, Davis and Walsh (2015) have shown how, as Treasury-trained economists took over the Department of Trade and Industry, industrial policy began to increasingly shift towards a financialization frame. Thus, arguments for different future actions have become accepted through a parallel process of shifts in proximate field environments as well as serial changes to individual-level habits.

8.3 Resonance Spaces and Field Dynamics

Resonance is a social mechanism that mediates between skilled social actors, who may or may not populate the same field, and their cooperation. Building on a pragmatist theory of action its implied causality does not emerge from a notion of "constraining and enabling" social action (such as in sociological new institutionalism or Giddens' (1984) structuration theory). Rather, resonance denotes the social process through which cooperation offers become acceptable for actors in different positions. The content of these offers takes the form of collective action frames: they propose a different future and the partaking actors' roles therein—in our case on the field level. Here, resonance assumes creativity in the development and proposition of innovative offers while linking field-level processes with individual evaluations of their validity and desirability without reducing the latter to the former.

Through resonance, we may develop a hypothetical set of all cooperation offers each actor finds principally acceptable. Since resonance is the mechanism of cooperation both between and within groups, we may develop such a set for both individual and collective actors. As the set will be dependent on actors' positions and past experience, this set will resemble an idiosyncratic "vector of positional force" that is constituent of actors in fields (Martin 2003). As such, it mirrors a recent insight from relational sociology that points to the relation between actors' network positions and their imagined futures (Mische 2009, 2014). Moreover, this set bears resemblance with Sellars's (1956) concept of a "space of reasons" that forms the basis of Forst's (2015a) social philosophical analysis of "orders of justification." However, the set's structuring importance is not derived from its relation to individual action, but rather to a specific form of social interaction. In order to materialize into sustained social relations it requires skilled strategic actors that use these sets to further their aims.

These sets therefore operate bidirectionally: they allow skilled actors to mobilize others, yet force them to phrase their goals according to these sets. As a result, strategies may profoundly shift. As these sets are tied with field-level dynamics, even the most skilled actor will have limited influence over their shape. Since these sets form the necessary condition for resonance, I will call them *resonance spaces*. As described in the first section of this chapter, resonance spaces played a key role in the development of SII. For example, they explain why finance proponents have taken over normative problem descriptions as well as the organizational outcomes discourse while in parallel shifting their strategy vis-à-vis the voluntary and community sector and public services. It would have been impossible for social policymakers, who were for a decade arguing for an increased role for the VCS in public service delivery, to accept the financialization frame if it were built in opposition to the VCS.

As resonance spaces are the structural opportunities for successful social skill that we have been looking for, it is worthwhile to explore their relation to SAFs in more detail. First, it is important to note the recursive relationship between resonance spaces and field dynamics. Resonance spaces shape field dynamics as a number of different types of ties are contingent upon (but not reducible to) them. Indeed, we may classify ties depending on the extent to which they require the acceptance of cooperation offers. For example, new ties between incumbent groups across fields—such as state and finance actors—may require much better framing because of the large discrepancy in their problem situations and habitual responses. In an accepted, formal dependence relation, however, we may assume heterogeneity of problem situations and responses such that the superior will be largely relieved from "justificatory pressure" (Forst 2015b). I will call the extent to which resonance alone determines the creation of a new tie the *reach* of a resonance space. A resonance space may thus be far-reaching for some ties but only be one of many contributing factors for the emergence of other ties. Since resonance spaces correspond to actors' positions, as fields change, resonance spaces will change accordingly. As a result, the likelihood of cooperation between different sets of actors will change accordingly. If a new cooperative tie emerges, we may expect similar cooperative ties to become more likely. By contrast, once actors have begun to engage in open contestation, the emergence of cooperation will become less likely.

The reverse is also true. As successful cooperation translates into new ties and frames, rules, alliances, and positions in fields will change accordingly—as will in some cases relations between fields. Thus, the outcome of the resonance mechanism *is* field dynamics. This means that successful cooperation at time t will alter the structure of resonance spaces in time $t + 1$. Hence, the relation between resonance spaces and field dynamics creates *trajectories* of change. However, as resonance spaces are only hypothetical opportunities that need to be used by skilled social actors, the result is not path dependence in the narrow sense, but instead a wider funnel of structured yet contingent change possibilities. Importantly, as reach is a relational property, successful cooperation may increase the reach of extant resonance spaces in the future. This means that by being successful, skilled social actors may increase the likelihood of success for future cooperation.

The relationship between resonance spaces and field dynamics has been illustrated throughout this work. For example, building on the resonance spaces "value for money" and "cross-cutting issues," the Treasury was, under Brown, able to develop ties into social policy. As this shifted the set-up of the social policy field, it also changed policymakers' resonance spaces. In particular, impact investors' arguments for financialization—which had been rejected earlier—now became principally acceptable. However, SII proponents were only able to make use of this resonance space and obtain resources after changing their view of the VCS. That social sector associations such as ACEVO failed to attribute a threat but rather cooperated with investors is partially explained by their field-level position as executive managers of social organizations. This cooperative tie helped chain policymakers' view of financial intermediaries as part of the social services field. With the 2010 transformation of government, SII proponents were furthermore able to use the resonance space of boosterism, which helped them to expand government support, particularly for equity finance.

Second, how will skilled actors use resonance spaces to forge cooperation? As argued above, forging cooperation depends on other lower- and higher-level mechanisms as well. To align problem diagnoses, skilled actors may simply be opportunistic and change their vocabulary and valuations according to the actors they communicate with. Since the pragmatist theory of social action grants actors significant amounts of creativity when dealing with problem situations, these lower-level questions are not of interest for our explanatory endeavor. As Fligstein and McAdam have noted, skilled actors "will do whatever it takes to induce cooperation" (2012, p. 47)—our question here was rather when this will be enough. My answer is that social skill will be sufficient precisely when a resonance space for the skilled actor's cooperation offers exists. Of course, resonance spaces are vast sets of possibilities. The terms of the cooperation will therefore only partially depend upon resonance spaces, but are to a large degree a question of the negotiation process. That said, resonance spaces do pose boundaries to the acceptability of terms.

For example, while both New Labour and Conservative governments gave significant subsidies to SII actors, Gordon Brown's outsourcing model of "constrained discretion" placed far more requirements upon SII actors. Under the Conservative government, investors' "financialization as welfare" frame enjoyed a much deeper (and ever-increasing) reach in social policy because it was closely linked to the government's "boosterism" frame. As a result, policymakers eventually took for granted that financial intermediaries produce "social impact." Where under Labour financialization was only one means of achieving better public services, it has, due to dynamics in the social policy field, become an end in itself under the Conservatives. As the reach of the resonance space increased and the availability of other frames decreased, SII actors required much less creativity to yield new subsidies. The policy and finance fields have thus developed a stable tie that shifted accepted frames and therefore the opportunities for other, nonfinancial social actors to win the support of the state.

Resonance spaces are closely related but not equal to actors' positions. We may conceive of rules that are taken for granted across a broad range of positions. This is for example the case for accounting standards, or accepted devices more generally. As these are used by a large set of actors, they will profoundly shape those actors' resonance spaces—while being only minimally affected by positions. That said, skilled actors may challenge these—like any—rules, but their critique may only encounter very limited resonance. Moreover, position and cognition are related but not equal. As SAF theory assumes all actors to be socially skilled at least to some extent, all actors will constantly imagine different futures that may or may not be related to their position. Thus, although actors' position shapes resonance spaces to a large degree, individual learned experience and creativity shape variance of resonance spaces across positions.

8.4 Resonance Spaces and Financialization

In this book, I aim at advancing a "third way" of financialization scholarship that rebalances the organizing force of both financial actors and the institutions of capitalist economies. I have shown how both financialization and institutionalist scholars often underestimate or oversimplify the active role of governments in explaining capitalist dynamics. This is why I have built on SAF theory in order to propose a view that centers the emergence of ties between government and financial actors. Such a view unites actors' creative social change attempts with the structuring force of their organized environments. Yet as this perspective has, to date, lacked a concept to account for the emergence of cross-field ties, I have developed the concept of resonance spaces that closes this conceptual void. In this section, I will show how this general concept may further our understanding of financialization processes beyond the case of SII.

The transformation of corporate control serves as a case in point to illustrate the explanatory potential of my perspective. As it has been shown (Lazonick and O'Sullivan 2000, Fligstein 1990), the development of Agency Theory in financial and corporate actors' shared field environment—the academic discipline of economics—has provided skilled financial investors a resonance space among corporate managers. Only after the development of Agency Theory did corporate managers come to see the "financial conception of control" as furthering their own strategic goals. Yet as the frame directed firms' actions in a particular way towards financial actors, accepting the frame inevitably meant the development of a new cooperative cross-field tie. This does not mean that the development of Agency Theory itself altered the rules of economic exchange, nor that the rules implied by the financial conception of control were uncontested. Rather, this means that the development of Agency Theory represented an opportunity for investors to enhance their position in the field of corporate governance. That said, investors had to draw on their social skill as well as other resources to make use of this resonance space and sustain the emerging cooperative ties.

In Europe, the development of Agency Theory also represented a resonance space: it was developed in managers' and investors' shared field environment, and it changed managers' sets of acceptable future-oriented frames. However, compared to the US case, it was a resonance space with much less reach. In contrast to the US, European firms' ties to proximate fields were structured differently: executives held interlocking board positions, and firms more generally held closer ties to nonfinancial fields such as labor unions (Jackson and Deeg 2012; Mizruchi 1996). However, as managers' field environment increasingly changed over the past decades, the reach of the finance resonance space increased. But to increase financialization in corporate governance, investors nevertheless have to use these new opportunities.

As these illustrative examples show, my perspective may therefore account for both: financialization in markets as well as its (partial) absence. In contrast to institutional theories of capitalist variety, it fundamentally builds upon actors' creativity in envisioning and establishing different futures. From my perspective, financialization may occur even in the most coordinated market economy, if skilled financial actors are able to build upon or create a resonance space for their frames. However, they will only succeed in doing so if they express their frames in accordance to policymakers' and managers' position in their respective proximate environments. Certainly, investors' likelihood of success will, in accordance with SAF theory, also depend on their resources such as money, network ties, and social skill. Once investors have been successful in forging such new ties, they will have changed the field and thereby created new opportunities to further alter the frames in their regard. This is why, from my perspective, distinct national or regional trajectories are as much possible as a long-term global concord. In any case, neither of these developments will occur automatically but build upon skilled actors who may succeed or fail to alter the course of things. This is why, to understand processes of financialization, we need to pay much greater attention to the position of all actors partaking in the process than current forms of new institutional theory acknowledge.

Resonance spaces furthermore expand our understanding of financialization as they widen its scope from a focus on markets. Most importantly, my view sees states not as external referees on marketplaces, but rather attempts to understand how the position of particular state actors in their field environment allows for the emergence of cooperative ties with financial actors. As such, my perspective emphasizes how the structure of the polity, for example policymakers' limited formal capacities to access public funds, creates a resonance space for financial frames. By emphasizing how the creation of new ties between financial and state actors increases the reach of policymakers' resonance spaces for financial frames, it is furthermore capable of explaining financialization trajectories on federal, state, and municipal levels (Pacewicz 2012; Quinn 2010). Being sensitive to the structure (and dynamics) of the polity, my perspective would predict a smaller likelihood for state-sponsored financialization in more complex polities, such as the federalist German state (Schmidt 2008). This is because, here, policymakers' proximate field environment consists of a host of other policy fields that reduce the depth of resonance spaces for financial frames. But this does *not* mean that the structure of the polity shapes rigid path dependencies as it does not limit the creativity of financial actors to sail, as in the empirical case presented here, on the upwinds of seemingly unrelated structural transformations.

The resonance space perspective integrates yet expands more cultural conceptions of financialization. For example, it argues that the introduction of management devices imported from finance (Chiapello 2015, see also Fligstein 1990, pp. 183–184) both presupposes and creates resonance spaces for financialization. As resonance is a pragmatist mechanism, it emphasizes that actors ought to see in financial tools a means to solve a problem situation. However, the more actors are dependent from other actors that already build on such financialization, the less will such additional justification be required. Thus, my perspective is reconcilable with a cultural view that sees financial market rationalities as a power resource in a financialized capitalism (Kädtler 2015). However, from my point of view the question of power can only be addressed on the field level: the more they can build on a resonance space, the more powerful will financial actors be. Therefore, my perspective allows us to challenge unidirectional views on financialization: as the demise of the tie between SII proponents and central government after the Brexit referendum has shown, financialization, like any social process, needs to be continuously organized for and legitimated. The power of financial actors arises from the fact that nonfinancial actors, governments in particular, see their aims advanced by drawing on financialization. With shifting problem situations, financialization loses the source of its power.

Chapter 9
Discussion and Conclusion

Are we living in a world that is increasingly dominated by financial actors? In this book, I have argued that key to answering this question is to understand the forms and processes of financial market dominance through empirical sociological research. I have shown how this question brings us right to the heart not only of the empirical debate between financialization and institutionalist scholarship, but also to the theoretical question regarding the link between structure and agency. By empirically studying the emergence of a capital market within the British welfare state, I have pointed towards the importance of cooperative ties between financial and nonfinancial actors. To the extent that financial actors are able to position themselves as an alleged solution to nonfinancial actors' problem situations, such ties will emerge. If successful, these ties cement financial actors' position and facilitate the redistribution of resources. However, financial actors' success in developing and sustaining such ties hinges not only on their social skill and resources, but also on dynamics beyond their control. To understand the balance between financial actors' capabilities and these external dynamics, I have developed through abductive analysis the concepts of resonance and resonance spaces.

In this concluding chapter, I will critically discuss the scientific value of this work. To do so, I first point to the theoretical and empirical insights that may be gained from my approach. Then, I review the methodological and epistemological limitations of this work and assess whether and how these could be addressed by future research. In the final section, I attempt to establish the value of my empirical case study for a broader audience.

9.1 Implications for Sociological Theorizing

The approach developed in this work builds on strategic action fields theory (Fligstein and McAdam 2011, 2012). Of particular interest for the question of cross-field ties are three core pillars of the theory: a situated conception of agency

P. Golka, *Financialization as Welfare*,
https://doi.org/10.1007/978-3-030-06100-5_9

based on American Pragmatism ("social skill"), a social ontology that understands society as a "dense latticework" of SAFs, as well as a relational view on institutions that combines these two by understanding actors as positioned vis-à-vis the institutionalized rules in the field ("challenger/incumbent"). But while these concepts provide the building blocks to address the question of cooperation across fields, the question itself allowed us to scrutinize the fundamentals of SAF theory. As I argued in Chap. 3, SAF theory's core mechanism of social interaction and change centers contention—although the theory fundamentally builds upon the emergence of cooperation. Fligstein and McAdam (2012, pp. 51–52) argue: "The basic problem for skilled social actors is to frame 'stories' that help induce cooperation from people by appealing to their identity, belief, and interests, while at the same time using those same stories to frame actions against various opponents."

I have argued that such a conception of cooperation is problematic in two regards. First, as the case of social impact investing has shown, not all forms of cooperative ties revolve around forging an alliance for open contestation. Sometimes, we may encounter "piecemeal" change precisely because actors who would usually openly contest begin to cooperate. This is why a mechanism—beyond the theory's "episode of contention"—to account for the emergence of cooperative ties is needed. The second point is even more fundamental. The quote above shows how cooperation in SAF theory is based on the *acceptance* of strategic action frames. However, in its current form, this acceptance is undertheorized in two important regards. On the one hand, we are left with a conception of "identity, belief, and interest" without knowing where these might come from. On the other hand, such a view runs danger of perceiving only the *construction* of frames as an agentic property without also understanding the *acceptance* of frames as a form of (potentially strategic) agency that could have repercussions on the very frame in question.

The mechanism I propose here addresses these concerns by seeing frame resonance as driven much more by actors' problem situations than by a rather "nonsituative" conception of identity. Moreover, as the mechanism builds on the habit of *negotiation*, it emphasizes how both sides partaking in such a frame resonance process hold considerable degrees of (strategic) agency. Thus, there are three key theoretical innovations in the proposed mechanism.

First, rather than grounding frame resonance on actors' identities, I follow American Pragmatism more strictly by emphasizing actors' problem situations as key to frame resonance (Gross 2009). Second, I expand SAF theory's society-as-fields ontology to the question of problem situations: I argue that actors' problem situations correspond to their position in the field. However, third, my view on field positions is a much wider one than in SAF theory. While in many cases it makes sense to analytically distinguish between the field positions of challengers and incumbents, i.e. actors' positioning vis-à-vis institutionalized rules, my empirical case has shown the limitations of such an approach. Moreover, as Jens Beckert (2010) has argued, fields are structured not only by institutionalized rules, but also by non-reducible cognitive frames and social networks. This is why I argue for a much more open view on field positions that comes to the fore as actors interpret their own position and use it as a *test* in an iterative negotiation process over strategic action frames.

How do the theoretical concepts developed here advance sociological theory? Besides the advancement of strategic action fields theory described above, they do so by allowing to answer the research question regarding the emergence of cross-field cooperation to which current sociological theories have not yet provided viable answers. Here, my conception agrees with strategic action fields theory by understanding the emergence of cooperation as a question of intra-field processes that are used by strategic actors for movement-like mobilization based on the development and acceptance of innovative frames. By emphasizing the agency of the to-be-mobilized actors and conceptualizing the role of social structures for frame acceptance through negotiation, my perspective develops a process perspective on framing and movement-like mobilization that has to date been somewhat absent in social movement scholarship (Cornelissen and Werner 2014, p. 206).

In addition to SAF theory and social movement scholarship, my approach furthermore enhances new institutional theorizing. I have argued that the structuring role of institutions is mediated through social action. In particular, I argued that institutions may serve as *tests* regarding the acceptability of institutional innovations and strategic frames that challenge the prevailing order. By doing so, the concepts developed here address two current issues in institutional theorizing. On the one hand, the Pragmatist action theory underlying my conceptions allows to circumvent the "paradox of embedded agency" (Battilana and D'Aunno 2009) that has drawn significant scholarly attention. This is because from the perspective of American Pragmatism, actors inevitably possess creative capabilities. Therefore, "institutional embeddedness" does not so much constrain the conception of novel frames or imaginaries, but rather serves as a structuring force in their interactive acceptance. By drawing on an action theory grounded in American Pragmatism, my perspective has furthermore taken up demands from institutionalist scholars who have argued for "the application of pragmatist theories of action to understand creativity within institutionalized settings" (Deeg and Jackson 2007, p. 161).

On the other hand, the perspective developed here takes into account the demands from scholars of institutional work for a more "distributed" view on agency in institutional change processes (Lawrence et al. 2011, p. 55). However, in contrast to these researchers, my perspective does not argue that such a view benefits from or necessitates a neglect of field conceptions (p. 57). To the contrary, I argue that precisely by studying such processes of "distributed" agency within and across fields, we can gain novel insights in the study of institutional change trajectories. These advantages for empirical research will be presented in the following section.

Lastly, I hope that my approach has helped integrating formerly disjointed theoretical perspectives. The scientific value of such an integration has been argued for by numerous sociologists such as Peter Berger and Arthur Stinchcombe (Cole 2001). By offering a process view that centers frame acceptance by situated actors, my approach is compatible with sociological theories that emphasize the plurality of evaluation formats, such as orders of worth theory (Boltanski and Thévenot 2006), or the institutional logics perspective (Thornton et al. 2012). At the same time, my conception chimes well with perspectives that link network structures with the development and acceptance of frame innovations (Mische 2002; Vedres and Stark 2010). Moreover, as described above, the perspective offered here also remains open towards institutionalist theories. I argue that this openness to three of the currently most important sociological theories is due to an equal attention to the concept of fields as well as a Pragmatist action theory that relates creativity and habituality of social action to structured problem situations.

9.2 Implications for Financialization Scholarship

The main implication of this work for financialization scholarship and the debate with new institutional theories is that, in many cases, it is key to financialization processes that nonfinancial actors change their way to act vis-à-vis financial intermediaries. Thus, to explain financialization, it becomes critical to understand how and why they do so. I have argued that in many cases, this change in action patterns equals the emergence of cooperative ties across fields. From such a perspective, we may understand financialization as a rather general process that neither needs to be linked to market actors, nor emerge from institutions of capitalist economies.

Through analyzing the case of social impact investing, I have shown that nonfinancial actors' acceptance of "financialized" field-level strategic action frames is absolutely central in financialization processes. For example, I have shown how SII emerged as policymakers increasingly accepted finance proponents' arguments of an "equity gap" in the field of social organizations. By doing so, policymakers have ignored evidence from the Bank of England that argued against the existence of such a "gap" and challenged the usefulness of such equity products. However, as chief executives of these social organizations, too, began to argue for such financial products *and* social policy increasingly built upon the "Treasury view," policymakers increasingly accepted finance proponents' arguments. Thus, here, corporate governance in a particular field of a "liberal market economy" had—in contrast to institutionalist predictions (Hall and Soskice 2001)—been dominated by lending, but increasingly shifted towards equity as these financial innovations were increasingly subsidized. Crucially, my perspective has shown that this was because policymakers' problem situation shifted as their position in the social policy field changed.

Thus, as a second implication for financialization scholarship, I showed the explanatory utility of strategic action fields theory. Through SAF theory, we may not only understand financial intermediaries as movement-like mobilizers for their innovative strategic action frames, but also shift our attention to how and when these frames are accepted. The key here lies in SAF theory's emphasis on actors' position in the field. However, as argued above, my expansion of SAF theory has shown that actors not only position themselves vis-à-vis institutionalized rules as challengers or incumbents, but may also position themselves by reference to cultural frames or network structures. To get a grip on such a more open view on social positioning, and how it relates to frame acceptance, my analysis has shown the utility of the concept of problem situations (Gross 2009).

For financialization research, such a view is beneficial in two domains. The concept of resonance spaces allows us to understand the structure of opportunities for financial actors in mobilizing necessary support from nonfinancial actors. Resonance spaces sensitize us for changes in the proximate field environment of nonfinancial actors that enable the acceptance of cooperative action frames vis-à-vis finance. Once we have gained an overview of the social terrain and the key events in financialization processes (or their absence), we may build on the resonance mechanism for more fine-grained research to explain the process. Here, the idea is to center transformations in the nonfinancial field in order to understand changes in nonfinancial actors' problem situations, the emergence of direct communication, as well as the process of frame enactment through the habit of negotiation.

By doing so, our understanding of institutions is transformed from a view of "constraining and enabling" towards a conception of institutions in action. Here, my conception follows criticism that new institutional theory leads us to a rather reductionist view on human communication that needs to be revised to account for the emergent properties of communicative interaction (Cornelissen et al. 2015). By understanding institutions as part of evaluative "tests" (Boltanski and Thévenot 2006) in the habit of frame negotiation, I argue for a more interpretative view on institutions. Institutions may serve as a justification for or against frame innovations for formal, normative, organizational, or many other reasons as long as these are accepted in negotiations. This allows actors significant leeway to circumvent, hollow-out, refine, or otherwise modify institutional arrangements—as long as they remain successful in achieving frame acceptance with relevant actors. Thus, institutions play a crucial role in frame dynamics, but an indirect one that builds on interpretation by actors who face particular problem situations that are linked to their position in the field.

Based on this view, I understand the causes of institutional change in the acceptance of novel frames and, in many cases, the emergence of new cooperative ties. Thus, my view invites researchers not to look for causes of change in properties of the institutions *themselves*, such as frictions within the institutional arrangement (Streeck and Thelen 2005) or institutional "voids" (Mair and Marti 2009). Rather, I argue that change attempts are a constant feature of inherently creative, strategic social actors–but that *trajectories* of change are critically mediated by interpretations that are grounded in problem situations of positioned actors. But as negotiation requires participation in the first place, respective resources form a necessary condition here, too.

As my empirical analysis has shown, it is of crucial importance to grant governments an equally central yet nuanced role in processes of financialization. Financializing actions by governments far exceed (de)regulation. Indeed, by viewing governments as a neutral referee setting and monitoring the rules of economic exchange we would have missed key parts of the SII story. Social impact investing emerged in very large parts because policymakers acted strategically with an increased interest in growing such a capital market. As the government's increased turn towards "leverage" policies has shown, changes in how governments relate to financial actors are key to understand financialization processes. Here, my perspective offers an explanatory account for such changes in action patterns that is based on a link between frame resonance and dynamic problem situations.

Lastly, the relational perspective on financialization proposed here also has implications for descriptive and analytic research. As I argued in Chap. 2, a relational view sensitizes the researcher to uncover lower-level structures that may be glossed over in categories used by field-level actors. I have applied this perspective to distinguish between two types of SII: one where investors aim at introducing nonfinancial performance criteria into market firms, and another one where investors aim at gaining a central governance position within the welfare state. Although understanding both of these cases as a "hybridization" (Battilana and Lee 2014) of financial and social "logics" is not incorrect when talking solely about investors, it still misses the point that these are two entirely different cases of institutional change.

9.3 Limitations and Future Research

In the two sections above, I have proposed how this analysis advances our understanding of sociological theorizing as well as financialization processes. That being said, the generalizability of this work remains limited in four dimensions: theory, scope, research design, and material. All of these limitations need to be addressed by future research.

On a theoretical level, this work has argued for an increased attention on processes of frame acceptance and proposed actors' problem situations as an analytical device for their study. I argued that these problem situations correspond to actors' positions in their dynamic field environment. Here, I have made the point that it is sometimes more useful to center actors' idiosyncratic positioning, rather than building on preconceived types of positions such as challengers and incumbents. However, it is legitimate to question how such an expansion of the complexity baked into the analytical terms is justified by increased conceptual clarity or empirical use. Although in the sections above I have argued for both of such justifications, I acknowledge that more needs to be done to fully address these concerns.

One particularly helpful way to discharge these demands would be to further, through empirical research, our understanding regarding the link between problem situations and actor positions. Is it possible to discern analytical roles (such as challengers and incumbents) that link positions to specific problem situations? Can we conceive of other factors that determine whether actors' problem situation will draw more strongly on either their network position, relation to institutionalized rules, or cultural values and frames of their proximate surroundings? Questions such as these could be addressed by a comparative research design that aims at developing mechanisms more detached from their immediate social context. Such a research design could also be used to address a more specific question that arises from challenging the theoretical use of the resonance mechanism for strategic action fields theory: under what conditions may we expect strategic actors to engage in more cooperative rather than openly contentious means of change? Is this more a question of the partaking actors, of the power distribution within and across fields, or of cultural or structural factors at the macro level?

Linked to these limitations on the theoretical level are those regarding the scope of this work. Although I studied the emergence of SII in the UK, I claim full validity of my results only for England. My empirical investigation of the link between government and SII was mainly confined to the core executive of the British central government, because here a particularly close tie between policymakers and SII proponents emerged, and a dramatic shift in accepted frames followed by changes in patterns of subsidies could be observed. Thus, this particular link served as the qualitatively most significant subcase and therefore legitimated my analytical focus. That being said, policymaking in the UK is a much more complicated process: in all UK nations, local administrations with partial independence from central government exist. Moreover, in Scotland, Wales, and Northern Ireland an intermediate level exists between central and local government. From a methodological point of view, these cases are particularly well-suited to test and critically refine the validity and generalizability of the claims made in this work. As the regional and local government levels are at the same time partially dependent on central government while also possessing a distinct set of ties, they could serve as embedded sub-cases for theoretical replication (Yin 2009).

A brief glimpse into the case of Scotland shows that, indeed, the relatively unchallenged acceptance of the financialization as welfare frame seems to be somewhat confined to England. For example, the Scottish social enterprise umbrella organization Senscot has been highly critical towards the introduction of for-profit organizations to the field of social organizations: in 2014, the Senscot representative on the UnLtd board resigned following the increased distribution of UnLtd grants to profit-with-purpose organizations.[1] It might have been this maintenance of the boundaries of the field of social organizations that inhibited resonance of a financialization frame focusing on equity products in social policy. This hunch is supported by the fact that the reach of Big Society Capital remains largely confined to England, while Unclaimed Assets in Scotland have been distributed to other causes. However, whether or not these differences are due to the fact that Scottish policymakers found themselves in different field positions and hence different problem situations remains an open question for future research. In this work, however, I did not attempt to address this question as the complexity of such an embedded cross-case design would have been prohibitive for my fine-grained, longitudinal research design.

---

[1]Source: Stephen Cook, 'Profit with purpose': the dispute over doing well while doing good, Third Sector, December 18th 2014, http://www.thirdsector.co.uk/profit-purpose-dispute-doing-doing-good/social-enterprise/article/1326694, accessed April 29th 2017.

The scope of this work is not only limited regarding the lower levels of local and regional government, but could furthermore be complemented and refined on the higher level of cross-national comparisons. Such a research design could investigate whether and how financial intermediaries had been successful in forging cooperative ties with government actors in other contexts as well. For example, research on SII in France has shown how the expansion of financialization has been restrained by an institutionalized rule that limits investors' profit extraction from the "social and solidarity economy" until a group of impact investors recently began to challenge this settlement (Chiapello and Godefroy 2017). Since the French polity shows an entirely different structure than the British core executive, my perspective would predict policymakers' problem situations to differ as well. Whether and how these differences in problem situations affect the resonance of impact investors' strategic action frame remains an open question for future research that could serve as a critical refinement of the predictions and claims made in this work.

Another way to increase the generalizability of my findings would be to study the emergence of cooperative government-finance ties in fields other than social welfare. Here, empirical research could first attempt to unravel other types of such relations beyond leverage. In a second step, comparative research could attempt to understand the conditions under and processes through which such different types of cooperative ties emerge. For example, in Germany, venture capitalists benefit from € 2.7 billion in public subsidies if they invest in "innovative" start-up firms (Bundesministerium für Wirtschaft und Energie 2015), while similar leverage policies are currently being developed at the EU level (European Commission 2016), too. By contrast, in German social policy, SII proponents have thus far mostly failed to take hold—despite sustained attempts of resource-rich private foundations to develop an SII capital market (Glänzel and Scheuerle 2016). If the theoretizations made in this work are correct, then such a comparative field-level research design would significantly enhance our understanding of capitalist variety and pave the way for a more nuanced and dynamic view on structural diversity.

Expanding the scope of my approach both in the micro and macro directions would furthermore be helpful to test the validity of an assumption hidden in this work. As briefly noted in Chap. 8, my approach assumes "mechanisms all the way down." Thus, I follow the fractal conception of structure baked into SAF theory that sees the same structuring mechanisms to persist on all levels of analysis. However, such a view has recently been challenged (Goldstone and Useem 2012) and thus requires further scholarly attention.

Third, my research design features one important limitation: I argued that negotiation is crucial for frame acceptance and played a central role in the emergence and development of social impact investing. However, I did not directly observe negotiation. This does pose a limitation for the validity of my claim regarding the structuring force of negotiation as an iteration between cooperation offers and situated tests. However, the material I studied clearly was the result of some kind of negotiation: this fact was not only mentioned in many of the analyzed documents, but also by my interviewees—some of whom personally participated in these very negotiations. Thus, what I did was to observe the outcome of a social process and speculate upon its cause—albeit in a highly structured manner in order to rule out interpretation biases and a number of alternative explanations. This very approach is known as abductive analysis, and Tavory and Timmermans (2014) have gone great lengths to justify the scientific validity of such a methodology. Therefore, what appears as a limitation in fact represents a core feature of my methodological approach. Moreover, since the theoretical generalizations I make fundamentally draw upon the historically contingent social context as an explanatory device, direct observation methods such as focus groups would have been inappropriate for addressing my specific research question. That being said, such methods would prove highly useful to investigate the generalizability of my negotiation model more generally.

Lastly, the empirical material also limited the generalizability of my findings. To a large degree, my analysis rested upon published documents. Although I did triangulate my findings with information obtained from a small number of expert interviews, the material was not sufficient to rule out some degree of decoupling in my findings. For example, it may well be the case that private networks played a larger role in structuring policymakers' problem situations than what I was able to account for. Unfortunately, I was not able to access data to account for such private organizing besides the few examples mentioned in Chap. 7. However, even if such private factors accounted for policymakers' motivation to develop such changes, it is only through their justification vis-à-vis a larger group of individuals that these changes gain significant momentum (Vaisey 2009; Forst 2015a).

Where the selected material did pose some limitations on generalizability was regarding the exact levels of redistribution towards financial actors. On the one hand, my analysis of central government subsidies to impact investors relied exclusively on those subsidies mentioned in the (relatively large set of) government publications analyzed. I did not cross-check whether all of these earmarked funds were actually transferred to investors, nor to what extent they might have been paid back by them. On the other hand, there were most likely other forms of subsidies distributed towards investors that I was unable to access. For example, I did not quantify non-outcome payments related to social impact bonds, or private donations to investors. That being said, the material analyzed did provide sufficient evidence both for the claim that impact investors extract funds from a variety of sources, as well as for the explanation that sees subsidies as the consequence of an increasingly cooperative relation between financial intermediaries and central government actors. Additional empirical analyses to gain a more complete picture of these financial flows are, however, welcome—not least to understand from a political economy perspective to what extent these new cooperative relations represent a qualitative transformation of statehood.

9.4 Is Social Impact Investing a Bad Thing?

I have spent a good deal of this work for challenging some of the core assumptions behind social impact investing (SII), pointing to its limitations, and showing how it may produce a more unequal world. However, this does neither mean that I think that SII is all bad, nor that it is the product of bad intentions. My point is a different one: its success in the UK and, to an extent, globally shows how SII proponents succeeded in setting the agenda and generating significant attention for the promises of impact investing. However, this work has clearly shown that SII in its current form comes with a number of important pitfalls that need to be taken into account if impact investing is to fulfill its promise of a better world for everyone. Pointing to the pitfalls of SII, I attempt to follow a common moral imperative that publicly funded research projects should at least try to achieve some kind of public value besides purely sufficing the needs of the academic system.

To do so, I follow the idea of "public sociology" that has been proposed by Michael Burawoy (2005). One of its core goals is to establish communicative action (in the sense of Habermas 1981) between the sociologist and a public (Burawoy 2005, p. 9). As communicative action means that the "forceless force" of the better argument prevails, i.e., that acceptance is free from power differentials between those communicating, such a form of public sociology is genuinely empowering. Thus, my goal in this final section is to point towards issues that, in my opinion, are often overlooked by those working in or otherwise supporting impact investing, as well as by those who research it. My hope is that increasing awareness for the pitfalls of impact investing will allow for creative solutions to become thinkable and acceptable.

I first became interested in social impact investing in 2011 and have worked in, near, and with the field ever since. Throughout, it struck me how the vast majority of people I encountered took for granted that they were changing the world for the better. Although there were lots of debates around metrics or the meaning of "social impact," I hardly encountered objections to for-profit organizational forms or advocacy for increased regulation or taxation of financial investments. This rather narrow form of critical engagement should not come to surprise: as I have shown in Chap. 6, the very idea of measuring and maximizing "social impact" is an attempt to prove that SII is the very edge of what is possible in achieving effective social change for the better. Moreover, the second core idea of SII, scale, promises that SII affects these changes not only widely, but also very rapidly. Combined with highly emotional accounts of, very often, marginalized people who are described to have, seemingly against all odds, achieved some kind of change for the better, SII produces a seductive narrative. Moreover, the thrust of innovativeness allows SII actors to position themselves vis-à-vis both "mainstream" business as well as governments and public authorities, thereby creating a strong sense of community. None of this means that SII is inherently "bad". However, there are three dimensions—key to any vision of a better future—that I suggest for further reflection. I call those the politics, the polity, and the political economy of social impact investing (see Table 9.1).

Table 9.1 Public sociology and dimensions of reflexive knowledge for SII stakeholders

Reflexive knowledge	SII proponents	Researchers
SII politics	Ensure plurality in problem descriptions and theorized causes	Understand SII politics in its specific social relations
SII polity	Formalize means to integrate all stakeholder voices, enable pluralist metric construction and accountability	Consider strategies of nonfinancial actors, too, when analyzing financial markets
SII political economy	Consider economic inequalities arising from financial intermediation and organizational change	Include research on field-level redistribution to studies of institutional change

As I attempted to show throughout this work, the very notion of "social impact" is inherently political. From a perspective of social constructivism, social impact is what those who argue for it understand as a good or better world. This is political in that it proposes a particular form of social order that may be beneficial to some but disadvantageous for others. Thus, alternative views may very well exist. As I have shown in Chap. 6, the understanding of "social impact" in a representative sample of SII proponents' discourse showed a rather one-sided view. For example, in the case of social impact bonds, a good social world was portrayed as one in which individuals cause as little as possible expenses in public budgets through the use of social services. I am not arguing that such a view is not or cannot be justified—rather, I point to the fact that such a view does not give beneficiaries of social interventions a say over their fate. Instead, beneficiaries are expected to conform to prevailing social norms without asking them whether they can or want to do so. The absence of alternative voices can furthermore be seen in the behavioral interventions of most social impact bonds. Very often, these are disciplinary interventions that aim at changing the behavior of these "disadvantaged" individuals and thus place the main burden upon those at the bottom of stratified societies.

An alternative view could emphasize the structural causes of these social problems, or simply evaluate other social situations as problematic. In most cases, beneficiaries of SII are poor—but these economic inequalities are hardly ever seen as causes of social problems, nor do they form important parts of the proposed solution. To date, there are no social impact bonds that see excessive wealth or tax avoidance as a social problem, nor are taxes or regulation—or even fair wages—proposed as a solution. One way to explain this is by taking seriously the material interests of SII actors: regulation or taxation do not allow these organizations to earn money. However, as I have shown in Chap. 7, there is another explanation for the current shape of SII politics: the very idea of "social impact" was born out of the New Labour project of fiscal prudence and "inclusive" economic growth that was established as an alternative to the "Old Labour" idea of wealth redistribution.

The polity of SII refers to the way how social impact is organized. As the politics of SII tend to emphasize the voices of financial investors over those of beneficiaries and public regulators, it should come to no surprise that these actors do not find sufficient representation in the polity of SII, either. In SII, intermediaries become the organizations to decide upon what counts and does not count as social impact. These intermediaries may either be financial investors themselves, such as Big Society Capital or Bridges Ventures, who are particularly prone to vested interests in the definition of social impact. But intermediaries also include organizations such as Social Finance or the Global Impact Investing Network who do not invest significant funds themselves. However, neither investees, nor beneficiaries, nor governments have an important—and formalized—say over the definition of social impact.

By contrast, the ability of investors to navigate social impact according to their interests is virtually unlimited. In the case of social impact bonds, they may redefine "output" metrics to "outcomes" if this serves their financial interests (see Chap. 5). In other cases, investors may commensurate their impact score across a broad set of investees and thereby circumvent particularly costly changes to organizational practices, or they may simply define the metrics altogether. As investors also decide upon the distribution of key resources, this may have profound effects on the field structure. Moreover, hardly any control structures exist that demand legitimation of the proposed impact metrics or enable pluralist access to metric construction. Thus, despite SII proponents' talk of empowerment, the SII polity in its current shape does not suffice emancipatory demands. The SII polity does not yet possess formalized means through which dominant actors can be held to account or through which marginalized voices can be made heard. To the extent this SII polity penetrates governments and public organizations, it therefore undermines democratic legitimation.

But also with regards to social organizations, the polity of SII shows a rather unilateral form of organizing. As most impact investors aim at being "active" investors, they attempt to increase their say in the governance of social organizations. This may mean that norms and interests of financial investors are introduced to professional ethics of social work and social service.

The political economy of SII is concerned with understanding the distribution of money between partaking actors. As I have shown in Chap. 5, financial intermediaries are the main beneficiaries of the SII economy. They are enabled to directly or indirectly access government funds, private donations, and social organizations' turnover, while distributing a significant part of these to asset owners as well as a very small group of limited partners. For example, in social impact bonds significant parts of (real or fictitious) savings to the public purse are redistributed to financial investors, while at best marginal "success payments" are being made to social workers in addition to their salaries. In none of the cases I analyzed are payments made to beneficiaries—even though it is them who actually change their behavior.

The SII economy may increase economic inequalities: taxes are paid by virtually all actors in a given country, but financial investments are made only by those who can afford them, and an even smaller group of individuals acts as fund managers. This means that to the extent that SII redirects public funds, it transfers funds from a very large to a very small and rather affluent group of individuals. SII may also increase economic inequalities without penetrating the state. On the one hand, as Piketty (2014) has argued, inequalities rise when the rate of return on financial investments exceeds the rate of economic growth. On the other hand, as I have argued in Chap. 5, there are instances where financial intermediaries exploit the polity of SII in order to redistribute incomes from labor towards returns on capital.

Lastly, the political economy of SII furthermore distributes significant resources towards actors that are engaged with measuring and reporting social impact. While this form of redistribution might not necessarily increase inequalities of wealth and income, it nevertheless poses the question regarding the effectiveness of these payments. A large number of studies have shown that the introduction of performance metrics may lead to unintended consequences or even effects opposite to their intention (Crouch 2015; Espeland and Sauder 2007).

The idea of public sociology is to develop reflective knowledge for different publics. Since SII proponents have already been very successful in globally raising attention to their perspective, my hope is that by providing pointed contrasts to proponents' discourse, we could move towards a more balanced discussion that equally embraces the promises and pitfalls of social impact investing. But as social scientists increasingly take up the topic of social impact investing, they, too, become a public worth addressing in a similar fashion.

I hope that this work encourages reflection upon the politics, polity, and political economy of SII in the academic sphere, too. Depending on the field set-up of SII, all three of these dimensions will be entirely different. I hope that critical sociologists will pay far more attention to how the politics of SII differ, for example, between impact investors that aim at promoting ecological practices in material goods production and those who promote social impact bonds. For financialization scholars, I hope to have shown that to understand and explain the polity of SII, we need to be more sensitive to the strategic role played by nonfinancial actors, and to how these strategies emerge from problem situations. Lastly, I hope to have sensitized scholars of organization and management theory that not all "sustainable" and "hybrid" innovations may actually mean a reduction of financial "logics." The political economy of social impact investing has shown how such "hybrid" innovations may further entrench capitalist accumulation. Therefore, different groups of researchers would benefit from applying a field approach to the study of social impact investing and other social innovations.

Appendix A: Central Government Subsidies

Name	Volume (£ mn)	Start Date	Goals	Department	Source
UnLtd. Endowment	100	2000	Set up of UnLtd. to provide capacity building grants for social entrepreneurs	Millenium Commission	https://fundraising.co.uk/2003/03/06/100-million-millennium-awards-trust-launched/
Phoenix Support for CDFIs	42	2000	Investment into CDFIs	DTI	http://webarchive.nationalarchives.gov.uk/20050301194456/http://www.sbs.gov.uk/finance/phoenix_cdfi_r3.php
Phoenix Development Fund	29	2001	Support community entrepreneurs	DTI	http://webarchive.nationalarchives.gov.uk/20040722012352/http://sbs.gov.uk/content/phoenix/leading_lights_download.pdf
Adventure Capital	3	2002	Support "enterprising culture" in poor neighborhoods	Home Office	Sustainable futures: investing in community-based organisations. New Economics Foundation (2004)
Community Development Venture Fund co-investment	20	2002	Co-investment into bridges ventures fund	DTI	http://webarchive.nationalarchives.gov.uk/20040722012352/sbs.gov.uk/phoenix/
Community Investment Tax Relief	18	2002	Income tax relief for investments into CDFIs (usage 2012 = 72m x 25% relief)	HMT	https://www.ncvo.org.uk/images/documents/practical_support/public_services/ncvo_commission_on_tax_incentives_for_social_investment.pdf
Futurebuilders	155	2004	Support non-profits in public service delivery	Treasury	Futurebuilders Evaluation: Final Report (2010)

(continued)

P. Golka, *Financialization as Welfare*,
https://doi.org/10.1007/978-3-030-06100-5

Name	Volume (£ mn)	Start Date	Goals	Department	Source
Financial Inclusion Growth Fund	36	2005	Support for third sector lenders	DWP	https://www.publications.parliament.uk/pa/cm200607/cmselect/cmtreasy/53/53.pdf
Risk Capital Investment Fund	10	2008	Matched funding for social enterprises seeking equity finance	OTS	http://webarchive.nationalarchives.gov.uk/20130128101412/http://www.cabinetoffice.gov.uk/third_sector/news/news_stories/080227_riskcapital.aspx
Capital for Enterprise Ltd Co-Investment	10	2008	Co-investment into funds for social enterprise equity investments	OTS	http://webarchive.nationalarchives.gov.uk/20130128101412/http://www.cabinetoffice.gov.uk/third_sector/news/news_stories/081001_rcf.aspx
Communitybuilders	70	2009	Capacity building for community organizations	OTS	communitybuildersfund.org.uk
Social Enterprise Investment Fund	100	2009	Support social enterprises in health	DoH	birmingham.ac.uk/generic/tsrc/documents/tsrc/reports/SEIF/SEIFevaluationreport-December2012.pdf
Bridges Social Entrepreneurs Fund Co-Investment	5	2009	Co-investment into bridges social entrepreneurs fund	OTS	http://webarchive.nationalarchives.gov.uk/20130128101412/http://www.cabinetoffice.gov.uk/third_sector/news/news_stories/090915_socialinvestmentannouncement.aspx
Community Assets and Services Fund	4	2012	Support for "Community Takeover" of public assets and services	CLG	socialenterprise.org.uk/news/grant-funding-available-for-those-looking-purchase-community-asset
Big Society Capital	400	2012	Invest into SIFIs	Legislation and PM	bigsocietycapital.com
Investment and Contract Readiness Fund	13	2012	Investment and contract readiness for social enterprises	OCS	dev-wfm-sib.pantheonsite.io/sites/default/files/files/ICRF%20Evaluation.pdf
DWP Innovation Fund	28	2012	10 Social impact bonds	DWP	https://data.gov.uk/sib_knowledge_box/department-work-and-pensions-innovation-fund
Social Incubator Fund	10	2013	Support incubators for social enterprises	OCS	https://www.gov.uk/government/news/new-social-enterprises-to-receive-jump-start-from-government-investment
Big Potential	20	2014	Investment readiness for social enterprises	Big Lottery Fund	http://www.sibgroup.org.uk/big-potential
Commissioning Better Outcomes	40	2014	SIB development	Big Lottery Fund	biglotteryfund.org.uk/sioutcomesfunds

(continued)

Name	Volume (£ mn)	Start Date	Goals	Department	Source
Social Outcomes Fund	20	2014	SIB outcome payments	OCS	https://biglotteryfund.org.uk/sioutcomesfunds
Impact Readiness Fund	4	2014	Performance management for social enterprises	OCS	https://www.gov.uk/government/news/impact-readiness-fund-round-2-15-million-funding-announced
Youth Engagement Funds	16	2014	SIB development and outcome payments	OCS	https://www.gov.uk/government/publications/youth-engagement-fund-prospectus
Social Investment Tax Relief	3	2014	Tax relief for social investments	OCS	http://www.bigsocietycapital.com/sites/default/files/attachments/Social%20Investment%20Tax%20Relief%20-%20Two%20Years%20On.pdf
Fair Chance Fund	15	2014	Social impact bonds	CLG/ OCS	https://www.gov.uk/government/publications/fair-chance-fund-full-bid-specification-and-application
Access Foundation	60	2015	Investment readiness for social enterprises	OCS (repaid futurebuilders loans)	access-socialinvestment.org.uk/
Local Sustainability Fund	20	2015	Capacity building for social enterprises	OCS	https://www.gov.uk/government/news/charitable-organisations-given-20-million-boost-by-government
Dementia Discovery Fund Co-Investment	15	2015	Co-investment into private funds investing into dementia cure companies	DoH	https://www.gov.uk/government/news/health-secretary-announces-100m-dementia-discovery-fund
Arts Impact Fund Co-Investment	<7	2015	Loans to arts organizations	Nesta	https://www.gov.uk/government/news/pioneering-investment-fund-brings-social-finance-to-the-arts
Life Chances Fund	80	2016	SIB outcome payments	OCS	gov.uk/government/publications/life-chances-fund

Appendix B: Cited Material

In referring to empirical material, I used the following denotation logic:

YY_Author_Title/ first word or keyword

In some cases, the authors are abbreviated as indicated in the according list. In cases where YY_Author denoted the respective source unambiguously, the title reference may have been omitted.

Interviews

Ref.	Position at the time of interview	Length
A	Labour MP and Treasury minister in Labour governments	39:22
B	Former senior civil servant, HM Treasury and Office of the Third Sector	86:12
C	Executive of voluntary organization, member of the Council on Social Action and other advisory roles under Gordon Brown	49:47
D	Senior civil servant in Office for Civil Society, key role in Big Society Capital creation and Social Impact Bond interventions	69:55
E	Former civil servant in Office of Third Sector	71:51
F	Senior manager at Social Finance Ltd. and part of the team working on the first Social Impact Bonds	40:38
G	Former senior civil servant at Department of Trade and Industry and Office of the Third Sector	88:34
H	Former senior executive of a voluntary sector association during most of the observation period, member of Commission on Unclaimed Assets	69:33

P. Golka, *Financialization as Welfare*,
https://doi.org/10.1007/978-3-030-06100-5

Sample 1

Date	Author	Title
Oct-00	Social Investment Taskforce	Enterprising Communities: Wealth beyond welfare
Mar-07	Commission on Unclaimed Assets	The Social Investment Bank, U.K. Commission on Unclaimed Assets
Mar-10	Social Finance	Towards a new social economy: blended value creation through Social Impact Bonds
Nov-10	JP Morgan	Impact Investments: An emerging Asset Class
Mar-11	Social Finance	A technical guide to developing social impact bonds
Sep-12	ClearlySo/ New Philanthropy Capital	Investment Readiness in the UK
Oct-12	JP Morgan	A portfolio approach to impact investment: A practical guide to building, analyzing and managing a portfolio of impact investments
Oct-12	Social Finance	Enabling long term recovery from addiction
Oct-12	Nesta	Standards of evidence for impact investing
Jan-13	Bridges Ventures	Bridges Impact Report: A spotlight on our methodology
Jan-13	Bridges Ventures	Bridges ventures ten year report
Apr-13	Schwab Foundation/ World Economic Forum	Breaking the binary: policy guide to scaling social innovation
Jun-13	Young Foundation	Social investment in education
Aug-13	UKSIF	The future of investment: impact investing
Jan-14	Big Lottery Fund	Social investment explained
May-14	Social Finance	Technical guide: building a business case for prevention
Sep-14	G8 Social Impact Investment Taskforce	Building a social impact investment market: the UK experience
Sep-14	G8 Social Impact Investment Taskforce	Building the capacity for impact: a report on the capacities needed by the social sector to deliver the aim of the social investment market
Sep-14	Social Finance	Recommendations on procurement
Sep-14	G8 Social Impact Investment Taskforce	Impact Investment: The invisible heart of markets
Dec-14	Big Society Capital	Financial inclusion and social investment
Dec-14	Big Society Capital	Health and social care and Social investment
Dec-14	Big Society Capital	Long-term unemployment and social investment
Jan-15	Big Society Capital	Criminal justice and social investment
Feb-15	OECD	Social Impact Investment: Building the evidence base
Feb-15	Big Society Capital	Social investment in education
Feb-15	Social Finance	Technical guide: designing outcome metrics
Mar-15	Big Society Capital	Communities and social investment

Sample 2

Year	Author	Title
1997	Demos/ Charles Leadbeater	The rise of the social entrepreneur
1997	Labour Party	New Labour: Because Britain deserves better. Britain will be better with new Labour.
1998	HM Treasury	Modern Public Services for Britain: Investing in Reform Comprehensive Spending Review
1998	Home Office	Compact on Relations between Government and the Voluntary and Community Sector in England
1999	Home Office/ Active Communities Unit	Grants to Voluntary Organisations: Active Community Unit Main Grants Programme
1999	HM Treasury	PAT 3: Enterprise and Social Exclusion: National Strategy for Neighbourhood Renewal
1999	ACEVO	Who pays for core cost?
2001	Labour Party	Ambitions for Britain: Labour's manifesto 2001
2002	DTI	Social Enterprise: a strategy for success
2002	HM Treasury	The Role of the Voluntary and Community Sector in Service Delivery: A Cross Cutting Review
2002	Cabinet Office	Creating Public Value: An analytical framework for public service reform
2003	ACEVO	Replacing the State? The case for third sector public service delivery
2003	Bank of England	The Financing of Social Enterprises: A Special Report by the Bank of England
2003	DTI	A progress report on Social Enterprise: a strategy for success
2004	HM Treasury	Microeconomic Reform in Britain
2004	Bridges Community Ventures	Equity-like capital for social ventures
2004	NCVO	The UK Voluntary Sector Almanac 2004: 5th edition
2004	Home Office	Firm Foundations: The Government's Framework for Community Capacity Building
2004	Charity Commission	Investment of Charitable Funds: Basic Principles (CC14)
2005	Social Investment Task Force	Enterprising Communities: Wealth beyond welfare – Update 2005
2005	Futurebuilders	Eligibility Checklist
2005	HM Treasury	Exploring the role of the third sector in public service delivery and reform: A discussion document
2005	Labour Party	Britain forward not back: The Labour party manifesto 2005
2006	HM Treasury	Value for money assessment guidance
2006	CUA	A social investment bank: consultation paper
2006	OTS	Social enterprise action plan: Scaling new heights
2006	ACEVO	Choice and Voice – The unique role of the third sector
2006	DWP	A new deal for welfare: Empowering people to work
2006	David Cameron	Chamberlain Lecture on Communities

(continued)

Year	Author	Title
2007	Gordon Brown	Speech at "Britain's Everyday Heroes" Book Launch
2007	NCVO	The UK Voluntary Sector Almanac: The State of the Sector
2007	HM Treasury/OTS	Unclaimed assets distribution mechanism: a consultation
2007	OTS	Consultation on the risk capital investment fund for social enterprise
2007	OTS	Research on Third Sector Access to Finance: Report to the Office of the Third Sector
2007	HM Treasury	Budget 2007: Building Britain's long-term future: Prosperity and fairness for families
2007	HM Treasury	The future role of the third sector in social and economic regeneration: final report
2007	CUA	The social investment bank: its organisation and role in driving development of the third sector
2007	CoSA	Willing Citizens and the making of the good society: the ideas underpinning the practical work of the Council on Social Action
2007	CoSA	Side by side and implications for Public Services
2008	Francis Maude	Speech on Social Enterprise
2008	CoSA	Council on social action: commentary on year one
2008	OTS	Risk Capital Investment Fund for Social Enterprise Government Response
2008	OTS	Social Investment Pilots: Action research final report
2009	OTS	Social Investment Wholesale Bank: A consultation on the functions and design
2009	OTS	Social Investment Wholesale Bank: Summary of responses to the consultation
2009	David Cameron	Hugo Young Lecture
2009	ACEVO	ACEVO Conservative Taskforce: A Response to "A Stronger Society
2009	Monitor Institute	Investing for Social and Environmental Impact
2010	HM Treasury	Spending Review 2010
2010	Conservative Party	Invitation to join the Government of Britain: The Conservative Manifesto 2010
2010	Cabinet Office	The Coalition: our programme for government
2011	OCS	Growing the Social Investment Market: a vision and strategy
2012	McKinsey & Company	From Potential to Action: Bringing Social Impact Bonds to the US
2014	G8 SII Taskforce	Policy levers and objectives: explanatory note for governments
2015	The Alternative Commission on Social Investment	After the Gold Rush: The Report of the Alternative Commission on Social Investment
2015	BSC	Report and Financial Statements

(continued)

Year	Author	Title
2015	The Gym Group	Annual Report and Accounts 2015
2016	HM Gov't	Social investment: the UK as a global hub 2016 international strategy
2016	HM Gov't	Social investment: a force for social change 2016 strategy

Appendix C: Analyzed Material

The text files for the material listed below can be found on the attached CD. This CD furthermore includes MaxQDA exports of my actual coding schemes that are slightly broader than the synthesized overview presented in the text as they include a number of codes that I ended up not using for further analysis. Moreover, the disk includes a justification for the inclusion or exclusion into the core set for every single report of data set 1 listed below. Interview guidelines and transcripts as well as MaxQDA files are available upon request.

Data Set 1

Date	Title	Author	Source
Oct-00	Enterprising Communities: Wealth beyond welfare	Social Investment Taskforce	Social Investment Taskforce
Jul-03	Enterprising Communities: Wealth beyond welfare – Update 2003	Social Investment Taskforce	Social Investment Taskforce
Mar-04	Unleashing Entrepreneurship: Making business work for the poor.	UNDP	GIIN
Jul-05	Enterprising Communities: Wealth beyond welfare – Update 2005	Social Investment Taskforce	Social Investment Taskforce
Jan-06	Blended Value Investing	WEF	GIIN
Jan-06	Microfinance: Building domestic markets in developing countries	Citigroup	GIIN

(continued)

P. Golka, *Financialization as Welfare*,
https://doi.org/10.1007/978-3-030-06100-5

Date	Title	Author	Source
Jan-07	From Fragmentation to Function	Said School of Business	GIIN
Mar-07	The Social Investment Bank, U.K. Commission on Unclaimed Assets	Commission on Unclaimed Assets	GIIN
Jun-07	Reflections on the Compartamos IPO	CGAP	GIIN
Nov-07	Compounding Impact: Mussion Investing by U.S. Foundations	FSG Social Impact Advisors	GIIN
Jan-08	2007 Report on Socially Responsible Investing Trends in the US	Social Investment Forum	GIIN
Jan-08	Handbook on Responsible Investment Across Asset Classes	Institute for Responsible Investing	GIIN
Jan-08	Innovative financing for sustainable small and medium enterprises in Africa	UNEP Finance Initiative	GIIN
Jan-08	Mission-Related Investing: Philanthropy's New Passing Gear	Rockefeller Philanthropy Advisors	GIIN
Mar-08	Banana Skins 2008: Risk in a Booming Industry	Center for the Study of financial innovation	GIIN
Mar-08	Quasi-equity: Case study in using revenue participation agreements	CAF Venturesome	Big Society Capital
May-08	Approach to Assessing Social Impact	CAF Venturesome	Big Society Capital
Sep-08	Financing civil society: a practitioner's view of the UK social investment market	CAF Venturesome	Big Society Capital
Oct-08	A Brief guide to the law of mission investing for U.S. foundations		GIIN
Oct-08	Risk, Return and Social Impact: Demystifying the Law of Mission Investing by US Foundations		GIIN
Jan-09	Emerging Models for Market-Based Solutions to Poverty	Monitor Inclusive Markets	GIIN
Jan-09	Investing for Social and Environmental Impact	Monitor Institute	GIIN
Jan-09	The Next Billions: Business Strategies to Enhance Food Value Chains and Empower the Poor	WEF and BCG	GIIN
Apr-09	The Nature and Type of Social Investors	Acumen Fund	GIIN
Jul-09	Business Linkages: Enabling Access to Markets at the BoP	CSR Initiative at Harvard Kennedy School	GIIN
Aug-09	Social Impact bonds: rethinking finance for social outcomes	Social Finance	Social Finance

(continued)

Date	Title	Author	Source
Aug-09	Responsible Investing – A Paradigm Shift from Niche to Mainstream	Robeco, Booz & Co	GIIN
Sep-09	Access to capital: a briefing paper	CAF Venturesome	Big Society Capital
Sep-09	Good Deals 2009: the social investment almanach	Social Enterprise	GIIN
Sep-09	Addressing Climate Risk: Financial Institutions in Emerging Markets	DEG, CERES, Riskmetrics Group	GIIN
Oct-09	Charity mergers: tackling the issues in practice	Social Finance	Social Finance
Nov-09	Solutions for Impact Investors: From Strategy to Implementation	Rockefeller Philanthropy Advisors	GIIN
Dec-09	Viewpoint 2010: What is ahead for Social Investment?	IJ Partners	GIIN
Jan-10	Stretching the Fabric of MFI Networks	Monitor Inclusive Markets	GIIN
Mar-10	Towards a new social economy: blended value creation through Social Impact Bonds	Social Finance	Big Society Capital
Mar-10	All Eyes on Microfinance Asset Quality: Microfinance Global Valuation Survey 2010	JP Morgan	GIIN
Mar-10	Investing for Impact: Case Studies Across Asset Classes	The Parthenon Group, Bridges Ventures	GIIN
Apr-10	Learning for Social Impact	McKinsey & Company	GIIN
Apr-10	Social investment: ten years on	Social Investment Taskforce	Big Society Capital
May-10	$650 Million Ain't what it used to be: The Meyer Memorial Trust considers Mission Related Investing	Harvard Kennedy School	GIIN
Jun-10	Maximizing Impact: An integrated strategy for grantmaking and mission investing in Climate Change	FSG Social Impact Advisors	GIIN
Jul-10	Money for Good: The US Market for Impact Investments and Charitable Gifts from individual donors and investors	Hope Consulting	GIIN
Jul-10	Building Houses, Financing Homes	NHB	GIIN
Aug-10	Rising Global Interest in Farmland	World Bank	GIIN
Sep-10	A shared vision for the future of the BME voluntary & community sector	Voice4change	Big Society Capital
Sep-10	Financing the big society – why social investment matters	CAF Venturesome	Big Society Capital
Sep-10	Social Impact bonds: unlocking new investment in rehabilitation	Social Finance	Social Finance

(continued)

Date	Title	Author	Source
Sep-10	Impact Investing in Commercial African Agriculture		GIIN
Oct-10	Global Microscope on the Microfinance Business Environment 2010	Economist Intelligence Unit	GIIN
Oct-10	Power to the People: Investing in Clean Energy for the Base of the Pyramid	World Resource Institute	GIIN
Oct-10	Indian Microfinance Crisis of 2010: Turf War or a Battle of Intentions	Intellecap	GIIN
Oct-10	Scaling-Up SME Access to Financial Services in the Developing World	IFC	GIIN
Nov-10	Establishing a venture philanthropy organisation in Europe	EVPA	Big Society Capital
Nov-10	Water & Wastewater: Profiting from the next big wave	Equilibrium Capital Group	GIIN
Nov-10	From Faith to Faith consistent investing: Religious Institutions and their investment Practices	3IG	GIIN
Nov-10	Global Financial Inclusion: Achieving full financial inclusion at the intersection of social benefit and economic sustainability	McKinsey & Company	GIIN
Nov-10	Impact Investments: An emerging Asset Class	JP Morgan	GIIN
Dec-10	Impact Investing: A special report from This is Africa	This is Africa Magazine	GIIN
Dec-10	Inside out: the state of community development finance	CDFA	Big Society Capital
Dec-10	Mobilizing Private Capital for Public Good	Canadian Task Force on Social Finance	GIIN
Dec-10	Over-indebtedness and Microfinance: Constructing an early warning index	ResponsAbility, Triodos	GIIN
Dec-10	Impact Finance Survey 2010	Alphamundi Group	GIIN
Dec-10	More than Money: Impact investing for development	Center for global development	GIIN
Dec-10	Community equity capital: the opportunities and challenges of growth	Pacific Ventures Community	GIIN
Jan-11	Just finance: manifesto for growth and support of the community finance sector	CDFA	Big Society Capital
Jan-11	State of the sector survey	Social Enterprise Yorkshire and the Humber	Big Society Capital
Jan-11	Impact Investing: A framework for policy design and analysis	Pacific Ventures Community, Initiative for responsible investing at Harvard University	GIIN

(continued)

Date	Title	Author	Source
Feb-11	Growing social ventures: the role of intermediaries and investors	Young Foundation	Big Society Capital
Feb-11	The impact investor's handbook: lessons from the world of microfinance	CAF Venturesome	Big Society Capital
Feb-11	Risky Business: An empirical analysis of foreign exchange risk exposure in microfinance	Microfinance Analytics	GIIN
Mar-11	A technical guide to developing social impact bonds	Social Finance	Big Society Capital
Mar-11	The practitioners' guide to community shares	Cooperatives UK	Big Society Capital
Apr-11	A new approach to banking: extending the use of jam jar accounts in the UK	Social Finance	Social Finance
Apr-11	Investing for the good of society: why and how wealthy individuals respond	NESTA	Big Society Capital
Apr-11	Twenty catalytic investments to grow the social investment market	NESTA	Big Society Capital
Apr-11	Understanding the demand and supply of social finance	NESTA	Big Society Capital
Apr-11	KL Felicitas Foundation IRIS Case Study	KL Felicitas Foundation, IRIS	GIIN
Apr-11	Sustainable Value Chain Finance Workshop Report	Rainforest Alliance	GIIN
Apr-11	Impact Investing in West Africa	Dalberg Global Development Advisors	GIIN
May-11	360 Degrees for Mission: How leading European foundations use their investments to support their mission and the greater good	Mistra, Onvalues	GIIN
May-11	Promise and Progress: Market-based solutions to poverty in Africa	Monitor Inclusive Markets	GIIN
May-11	Grantmakers in Health: Guide to Impact Investing	Grantmakers in Health	GIIN
May-11	Impact Investing in Emerging Markets	Responsible Research	GIIN
Jun-11	Subsidies as an instrument in agriculture finance: a review	World Bank	GIIN
Jul-11	Investor perspectives on social enterprise financing	Clearlyso	Big Society Capital
Jul-11	The RBS SE100 Data Report 2011	RBS (Royal Bank of Scotland)	GIIN
Jul-11	Opportunities and obstacles to financial inclusion	Accion's Center for financial inclusion	GIIN
Jul-11	Impact Investing Field Scan: Landscape overview and group profiles	Tides Foundation	GIIN
Aug-11	Introducing Impact Investing	UBS	GIIN

(continued)

Date	Title	Author	Source
Aug-11	UBS-INSEAD Study on Family Philanthropy in Asia	UBS, INSEAD	GIIN
Aug-11	Beyond the margin: redirecting Asia's capitalism	Avantage Ventures	GIIN
Sep-11	A new way to invest in better healthcare		Social Finance
Sep-11	Review of Allia's charitable bonds	New Philanthropy capital	Big Society Capital
Sep-11	Social Investment Manual: An introduction for social entrepreneurs	TU München	GIIN
Sep-11	Data Driven: A performance analysis for the Impact investing industry	GIIN	GIIN
Sep-11	Accelerating inclusive business opportunities: business models that make a difference	IFC	GIIN
Oct-11	Making good in social impact investing: opportunities in an emerging asset class	The social investment business	GIIN
Oct-11	Sustainability trends in US alternative investments	US SIF	GIIN
Oct-11	Charities and investment matters: a guide for trustees	The charity commission	GIIN
Nov-11	Best to borrow? A charity guide to social investment	New Philanthropy capital	Big Society Capital
Nov-11	Lighting the touchpaper: growing the market for social investment in England	BCG, Young Foundation	Big Society Capital
Nov-11	Technical guide to commissioning social impact bonds	Social Finance	Big Society Capital
Nov-11	The One Service. One year on. Reducing reoffending among short sentenced male offenders from Peterborough prison	Social Finance	Big Society Capital
Nov-11	2011 highlights from the center for health market innovations	Center for health market innovations	GIIN
Nov-11	Impact Capital Measurement	Robert Wood Johnson Foundation	GIIN
Nov-11	Counter(imp)acting austerity	JP Morgan	GIIN
Nov-11	Improving livelihoods, removing barriers: investing for impact in Mtanga farms	GIIN	GIIN
Dec-11	Cost-benefit analysis and social impact bond feasibility analysis for the Birmingham Be Active scheme	Social Finance	Social Finance
Dec-11	Impact-based incentive structures: aligning fund manager compensation with social and environmental performance	GIIN	GIIN

(continued)

Date	Title	Author	Source
Dec-11	Learning from leaders in a fast-growing field	Dalberg	GIIN
Dec-11	Insight into the Impact Investment Market	JP Morgan	GIIN
Jan-12	Social investment: an overview of the landscape for VCSEs in the youth sector	Social Enterprise UK	Big Society Capital
Jan-12	Advancing social impact investments through measurement	Federal Reserve Bank of San Francisco	GIIN
Jan-12	Taking stock of microfinance	Credit Suisse	GIIN
Jan-12	Investing for Impact	Credit Suisse	GIIN
Jan-12	Paying for success: investing in what works	Nonprofit finance fund	GIIN
Feb-12	Financially inclusive ecosystems: the roles of government today	CGAP	GIIN
Feb-12	A new tool for scaling social impact: how social impact bonds can mobilize private capital to advance social good	Social Finance	GIIN
Feb-12	Sustainable capitalism	Generation investment management	GIIN
Feb-12	Impact at Scale: policy innovation for institutional investment with social and environmental benefit	Pacific Ventures Community	GIIN
Feb-12	Credit Unions, Community Development Finance and the great recession	National federation of community development	GIIN
Mar-12	The good Analyst	Investing for good	GIIN
Mar-12	Bridging the gap: the business case for financial capability	Citi Foundation	GIIN
Mar-12	Strong, straightforward and sustainable banking	Global Alliance for Banking on Values	GIIN
Mar-12	Cracking the Conundrum	Ckinetics	GIIN
Mar-12	The impact investor: the need for evidence and engagement	Pacific Ventures Community	GIIN
Apr-12	Understanding human resource challenges in the Indian Social Enterprise Sector	Intellecap	GIIN
Apr-12	From Blueprint to Scale: The case for philanthropy in impact investing	Monitor Inclusive Markets	GIIN
Apr-12	Insights and Innovations	Correlation Consulting	GIIN
May-12	A technical guide to financing new employee mutuals	Social Finance	Social Finance
May-12	From Potential to Action: Bringing social impact bonds to the U.S.	McKinsey & Company	GIIN
Jun-12	Diverse perspectives, shared objective	GIIN	GIIN

(continued)

Date	Title	Author	Source
Jun-12	Gateways to impact	Calvert Foundation	GIIN
Jun-12	The CDFI Banking Sector: 2011 Annual report	National Community Development Fund	GIIN
Jun-12	A framework for action: social enterprise and impact investing	Rockefeller Foundation and UN Global Compact	GIIN
Jun-12	Generating Impact and Returns	Arabella Advisors	GIIN
Jun-12	The power of advice in the UK sustainable and impact investing market	Bridges Ventures	GIIN
Jun-12	New economics for impact investing	NEF consulting	GIIN
Jul-12	Market for social impact investing by private equity funds stands at $4 billion in the United States	Pacific Ventures Community	GIIN
Jul-12	Environmental, Social and Governance investing by College and University Endowments in the US	IRRC Institute	GIIN
Sep-12	Investment Readiness in the UK	Clearlyso, NPC	Big Society Capital
Sep-12	Accelerating Impact: Achievements, Challenges and what's next in building the impact investing industry	E.T. Jackson and Associates	GIIN
Sep-12	A brief handbook on social investment	City of London Corporation	GIIN
Sep-12	Investing in social franchising	International centre on social franchising	GIIN
Sep-12	The first billion: a forecast of social investment demand	BCG	GIIN
Sep-12	Community development loan funds, September 2012	Altrushare Securitues and cars	GIIN
Oct-12	A market emerges: the six dynamics of impact investing	Pacific Ventures Community, Case at Duke, ImpactAssets	GIIN
Oct-12	A portfolio approach to impact investment: A practical guide to building, analyzing and managing a portfolio of impact investments	JP Morgan	GIIN
Oct-12	Enabling long term recovery from addiction	Social Finance	Social Finance
Oct-12	Microfinance, Impact investing and pension fund investment policy survey	Finethic	GIIN
Oct-12	Payment by results in the Youth Sector	Social Finance	Social Finance
Oct-12	Standards of evidence for impact investing	Nesta	GIIN
Nov-12	2011 Underbanked market sizing study	CFSI	GIIN
Nov-12	Advising clients on social investments and deciding on suitability	Big Society Capital, Bates Wells Braithwaite	Big Society Capital

(continued)

Date	Title	Author	Source
Nov-12	Collaborating to harmonize standardized metrics for impact investors	NCIF, IRIS	GIIN
Nov-12	UK Giving 2012	CAF, NCVO	Big Society Capital
Nov-12	IRIS Use Case: Accion's frontier investments	GIIN	GIIN
Nov-12	Strong and straightforward: the business case for sustainable banking	Global Alliance for Banking on Values	GIIN
Dec-12	2012 Highlights from the Center for Health Market Innovations	Center for health market innovations	GIIN
Dec-12	Building a healthy & sustainable social impact bond market: the investor landscape	Godeke Consulting	GIIN
Dec-12	The U.K. Social investment market: the current landscape and a framework for investor decision making	Cambridge Associates	GIIN
Jan-13	Analysis of evidence for local impact funds	Social Investment Business	Big Society Capital
Jan-13	Bridges Impact Report: A spotlight on our methodology	Bridges Ventures	Bridges Ventures
Jan-13	Does social finance understand social need?	Can Cook CIC	Big Society Capital
Jan-13	Rebuilding the relationship between affordable housing and philanthropy	Social Finance	Social Finance
Jan-13	Research briefing: charitable trusts and foundations' engagement in the social investment market	Association of Charitable Foundations	Big Society Capital
Jan-13	The people's business	Social Enterprise UK	Big Society Capital
Jan-13	Perspectives on Progress	JP Morgan	GIIN
Jan-13	Bridges ventures ten year report	Bridges Ventures	GIIN
Jan-13	IRIS Use Case: IDB Group's OMJ Initiative	GIIN	GIIN
Jan-13	Small and medium sized enterprises in MENA	Citi Foundation	GIIN
Feb-13	Measuring Social Impact in Social Enterprise: the state of thought and practice in the UK	E3M	Big Society Capital
Feb-13	The good investor	Investing for good	GIIN
Feb-13	Guidebook for impact investors: impact measurement	Purpose capital	GIIN
Feb-13	PIIF Signatories' Report on Progress	PRI Initiative	GIIN
Mar-13	Charities and social investment: a research report for the Charity Commission	Charity Commission	Big Society Capital

(continued)

Date	Title	Author	Source
Mar-13	Identifying new ways to engage with savers in defined contribution pensions	Defined contribution investment forum	GIIN
Mar-13	The role of tax incentives in encouraging social investment	City of London Corporation	GIIN
Mar-13	Keystone performance survey: impact investment 2013	Keystone	GIIN
Mar-13	Funding industry growth: going beyond numbers	Pakistan Microfinance Network	GIIN
Apr-13	Social Impact Bonds: Using Impact Investment to Expand Effective Social Programs	Federal Reserve Bank of San Francisco	GIIN
Apr-13	IMPACT-Australia: Investment for social and economic benefit		GIIN
Apr-13	A practical guide to measuring and managing impact	EVPA	GIIN
Apr-13	Accelerating Entrepreneurship in Africa	Omidyar Network	GIIN
Apr-13	Breaking the binary: policy guide to scaling social innovation	Schwab Foundation	GIIN
May-13	Supply chains for social impact	Harvard Kennedy School	Big Society Capital
May-13	Achieving social impact at scale: case studies of seven pioneering co-mingling social investment funds	UK Cabinet Office	GIIN
May-13	Accelerating impact enterprises	Case I3	GIIN
May-13	IRIS Use Case: New Ventures Mexico	GIIN	GIIN
Jun-13	Social investment in education	Young Foundation	Big Society Capital
Jun-13	Spin out, step up	Social Enterprise UK	Big Society Capital
Jun-13	The challenges of build to rent for UK housing providers	Social Finance, Resolution Foundation	Social Finance
Jun-13	Unlocking the power of creative capitalism through social investment	CAF, Legal & General	Big Society Capital
Jun-13	IRIS Data Brief: Focus on Employment	GIIN	GIIN
Jun-13	Collecting Impact Data using mobile technology	GIIN	GIIN
Jun-13	ANDE 2012 Impact Report	ANDE	GIIN
Jul-13	Best to invest? A funders' guide to social investment	NPC	Big Society Capital
Jul-13	Growing the social investment market: the landscape and economic impact	Social Investment Research Council	Big Society Capital

(continued)

Date	Title	Author	Source
Jul-13	Investing in shared lives	Social Finance	Social Finance
Jul-13	Soft finance, hard choices: a review of the finance market for public service mutuals	BCG	Big Society Capital
Jul-13	Making Impact Investible	Impact Economy	GIIN
Aug-13	Expanding the Market for community investment in the US	US SIF Foundation	GIIN
Aug-13	The future of investment: impact investing	UKSIF	GIIN
Sep-13	Angles in the architecture	Common capital	Big Society Capital
Sep-13	Getting started with IRIS	GIIN	GIIN
Sep-13	Bringing Impact Investing from the margins to the mainstream	WEF	GIIN
Sep-13	Community foundation field guide to Impact Investing	Mission Investors Exchange	GIIN
Sep-13	Growth and Opportunity: The land-scape of organizations that support small and growing businesses in the developing world	ANDE	GIIN
Oct-13	Building homes for generation rent: can institutional investment meet the challenge?	Social Finance	Social Finance
Oct-13	Social investment compendium	Big Society Capital	Big Society Capital
Oct-13	Catalytic first-loss capital	GIIN	GIIN
Oct-13	Evolution of an impact portfolio	Sonen Capital	GIIN
Oct-13	Investing for change: An analysis of the impacts of agricultural investments	FAST	GIIN
Nov-13	Investing in Social Outcomes: Devel-opment Impact Bonds	Social Finance	GIIN
Nov-13	Impact Investing 2.0: The way forward	Pacific Ventures Community, Case at Duke, ImpactAssets	GIIN
Nov-13	E-guide to early-stage global impact investing	Toniic	GIIN
Dec-13	Impact Investing: A framework for decision making	Cambridge Associates	GIIN
Dec-13	From ideas to practice, pilots to strategy	WEF	GIIN
Jan-14	European Venture Philanthropy and Social Investment 2013/2014	EVPA	Big Society Capital
Jan-14	Social investment explained	Big Lottery Fund	Big Society Capital
Jan-14	Shifting the Lens: A de-risking toolkit for impact investment	Bank of America Merril Lynch, Bridges Ventures	GIIN

(continued)

Date	Title	Author	Source
Jan-14	Unleashing the potential of US Foundation endowments	US SIF Foundation	GIIN
Jan-14	Social and environmental Due diligence	Root Capital	GIIN
Mar-14	Foundations for Social Impact Bonds	Social Finance	GIIN
Mar-14	IRIS Data Brief: Focus on Beneficiaries	GIIN	GIIN
Apr-14	Beyond the Pioneer: Getting inclusive industries to scale	Monitor Deloitte	GIIN
Apr-14	Exploration of Social Impact Bonds for SME development	Social Finance	Social Finance
Apr-14	Market Baseline Study	UKAID	GIIN
Apr-14	New specialist sources of capital for the social investment market	Social Investment Research Council	Big Society Capital
Apr-14	Ready, willing and able: an interim review of the investment and contract readiness fund	BCG	Big Society Capital
Apr-14	The Impact Programme: Annual Report 2013	UKAID	GIIN
Apr-14	The art of the responsible exit in microfinance equity sales	CGAP	GIIN
Apr-14	Phase 2 report from the payment by results Social Impact Bond pilot	Rand Europe	GIIN
May-14	Marketing social investments	Social Investment Research Council	Big Society Capital
May-14	Social Impact bonds: supporting vulnerable 14-16 year olds	Social Finance	Social Finance
May-14	Spotlight on the market: the impact investor survey	JP Morgan	GIIN
May-14	Technical guide: building a business case for prevention	Social Finance	Social Finance
May-14	Serving client demand for impact investing: a hands-on guide for financial advisors and senior management	Impact Economy	GIIN
Jun-14	Financing social ventures and the demand for social investment	Third sector research centre	Big Society Capital
Jun-14	Growing social enterprise through the holding company model	Big Society Capital	Big Society Capital
Jun-14	Insights on program-related investing	Arabella Advisors	GIIN
Jun-14	Mapping the social impact investing market in Germany: An overview of opportunities in the Education space	Rockefeller Foundation	GIIN
Jun-14	Social impact bonds: lessons learned	Big Society Capital	Big Society Capital

(continued)

Date	Title	Author	Source
Jun-14	Private capital, public good: how smart federal policy can galvanize impact investing – and why it's urgent	US NAB	GIIN
Jun-14	Align your portfolio with your values	RBC Asset Management	GIIN
Jun-14	Going beyond good intentions: measuring impact investment and social performance in microfinance	University of Sassari	GIIN
Jul-14	Growing the market for charity bonds	Big Society Capital	Big Society Capital
Jul-14	Invest. Catalyze. Mainstream: The Indian impact investing story	Intellecap	GIIN
Aug-14	Harnessing the Power of the Purse: Female investors and global opportunities for growth	Center for talent innovation	GIIN
Aug-14	Housing and social investment	Big Society Capital	Big Society Capital
Sep-14	A short guide to impact investing	Case Foundation	Big Society Capital
Sep-14	Applying a gender lens to agriculture		GIIN
Sep-14	Building a social impact investment market: the UK experience	Social Impact Investment Taskforce	Big Society Capital
Sep-14	Building the capacity for impact: a report on the capacities needed by the social sector to deliver the aim of the social investment market	Social Impact Investment Taskforce	Big Society Capital
Sep-14	Charting the course: how mainstream investors can design visionary and pragmatic impact investing strategies	WEF	Big Society Capital
Sep-14	Recommendations on procurement	Social Finance	Big Society Capital
Sep-14	Returns policy? What the next decade holds for social investment	CAF	Big Society Capital
Sep-14	Smart money: understanding the impact of social investment. What NPC has learned so far	NPC	Big Society Capital
Sep-14	The invisible heart of markets	Social Impact Investment Taskforce	Social Impact Investment Taskforce
Sep-14	The social business frontier: a report that investigates how to recognise and protect the social impact that business delivers in the UK	Social Impact Investment Taskforce, Big Society Capital, Bridges Ventures	Big Society Capital
Sep-14	Measuring Impact	Social Impact Investment Taskforce	GIIN
Oct-14	A practical guide to planning and executing an impactful exit	EVPA	Big Society Capital

(continued)

Date	Title	Author	Source
Oct-14	Housing first social impact bond feasibility study	Social Finance	Social Finance
Oct-14	Scaling up solutions to social care	London Economics	Big Society Capital
Oct-14	Social investment compendium – 2014 update	Big Society Capital	Big Society Capital
Oct-14	Supporting homelessness prevention and alleviation through investment in the private rental sector	Social Finance	Social Finance
Oct-14	European SRI Study	EUROSIF	GIIN
Oct-14	Choosing social impact bonds: a practitioners guide	Bank of America Merril Lynch, Bridges Ventures	GIIN
Nov-14	Social impact bonds: supporting adolescents on the edge of care	Social Finance	Social Finance
Nov-14	Tackling financial exclusion: data disclosure and area-based lending data	Coventry university, Newcastle university	Big Society Capital
Nov-14	Winterbourne view & Social investment	Resonance	Big Society Capital
Nov-14	Investing in conservation: a landscape assessment of an emerging market	Eko Asset Management	GIIN
Nov-14	Growing prosperity: developing repeatable models to scale the adoption of agricultural innovations	Acument, Bain & Company	GIIN
Dec-14	Financial inclusion and social investment	Big Society Capital	Big Society Capital
Dec-14	Growing pains: getting past the complexities of scaling social impact	NPC	Big Society Capital
Dec-14	Health and social care and Social investment	Big Society Capital	Big Society Capital
Dec-14	Long-term unemployment and social investment	Big Society Capital	Big Society Capital
Dec-14	Supporting the demand and supply side of the market for social enterprise finance	Social Investment Scotland	Big Society Capital
Dec-14	Impact Investing: A primer for family offices	WEF	GIIN
Jan-15	Criminal justice and social investment	Big Society Capital	Big Society Capital
Jan-15	Scaling community lenders: the role of social investment	Cabinet Office	Big Society Capital
Jan-15	What if we wan it ourselves? Getting the measure of Britain's emerging community business sector	Social Finance	Big Society Capital
Jan-15	Report on Progress in Inclusive Finance 2014	PRI Initiative	GIIN

(continued)

Date	Title	Author	Source
Jan-15	Tracking reach to the Base of the Pyramid through impact investing	DFID Impact Programme	GIIN
Feb-15	Delivering the promise of social outcomes: the role of the performance analyst	Impetus-PEF, Social Investment Lab, Think Impact	Big Society Capital
Feb-15	Social Impact Investment: Building the evidence base	OECD	GIIN
Feb-15	Social investment in education	Big Society Capital	Big Society Capital
Feb-15	Technical guide: designing outcome metrics	Social Finance	Social Finance
Feb-15	What do charity leaders think about social investment?	Big Society Capital	Big Society Capital
Mar-15	Communities and social investment	Big Society Capital	Big Society Capital
Mar-15	Social investment for family, friends and relationships	Big Society Capital	Big Society Capital
Mar-15	Tackling financial exclusion through community investment: how should the UK strengthen its community investment sector? Lessons from the US experience	Harvard Kennedy School	Big Society Capital
Mar-15	ImpactBase Snapshot: An analysis of 300+ Impact Investing funds	GIIN	GIIN
Apr-15	Conservation of the natural environment and social investment	Big Society Capital	Big Society Capital
Apr-15	Social Investment in the arts, heritage and sport	Big Society Capital	Big Society Capital
Apr-15	The Landscape for Impact Investing in South Asia	GIIN, Dalberg	GIIN
Apr-15	Impact Investing in Africa	KPMG	GIIN
Apr-15	Impact Investing Private Equity Fund Industry: Legal considerations	Clifford Chance	GIIN
Apr-15	Industry Snapshot: aligning development impact and commercial success	KPMG	GIIN
Apr-15	Risk, Return... and Impact?	Bertelsmann Stiftung, University of Stuttgart	GIIN
May-15	Future opportunities for social investment	Big Society Capital	Big Society Capital
May-15	Eyes on the Horizon: The impact investor Survey	JP Morgan	GIIN
May-15	Investing and Social Impact: Practices of Private Foundations	Center for Effective Philanthropy	GIIN
May-15	Investing in Africa's small and growing businesses	Investisseurs & Partnaires	GIIN
Jun-15	Food, Farms, Fish and Finance	J.W. McConnell Family Foundation	GIIN

(continued)

Date	Title	Author	Source
Jun-15	Investing to tackle loneliness: a discussion paper	Social Finance	Social Finance
Jun-15	Oranges & Lemons: The state of play of impact measurement among UK social investment finance intermediaries	Investing for good	Big Society Capital
Jun-15	Portuguese Social Investment Taskforce: A blueprint for Portugal's emerging social investment market	Social Finance	Social Finance
Jun-15	The social investment market through a data lens	Social Investment Research Council	Big Society Capital
Jun-15	Bringing Impact Investing down to earth: insights for making sense, managing outcomes and meeting client demands	Money Management Institute	GIIN
Jun-15	Introducing Impact Investing Benchmark	GIIN, Cambridge Associates	GIIN
Jul-15	Breaking the deadlock: a social impact investment lens on reducing costs of road trauma and unlocking capital for road safety	Social Finance	Social Finance
Jul-15	Developing a Global Financial Centre for Social Impact Investment	City of London Corporation	GIIN

Data Set 2

Government Strategy Documents (Labour Government)

Author	Year	Title
Home Office	1998	Compact on Relations between Government and the Voluntary and Community Sector in England
HM Treasury	1998	Modern Public Services for Britain: Investing in Reform Comprehensive Spending Review: New Public Spending Plans 1999-2002
Home Office	1999	Grants to Voluntary Organisations: Active Community Unit Main Grants Programme
HM Treasury	1999	Enterprise and Social Exclusion: National Strategy for Neighbourhood Renewal: Policy Action Team 3
Cabinet Office	2001	A New Commitment to Neighbourhood Renewal: National Strategy Action Plan
Cabinet Office	2001	National Strategy for Neighbourhood Renewal: Policy Action Team Audit
Cabinet Office	2002	Creating Public Value: An analytical framework for public service reform

(continued)

Author	Year	Title
Cabinet Office	2002	Private Action, Public Benefit: A Review of Charities and the Wider Not-For-Profit Sector
DTI	2002	Social Enterprise: a strategy for success
HM Treasury	2002	The Role of the Voluntary and Community Sector in Service Delivery: A Cross Cutting Review
HM Treasury	2002	Reforming Britain's Economic and Financial Policy: Towards Greater Economic Stability
DTI	2003	A progress report on Social Enterprise: a strategy for success
Home Office	2004	Firm Foundations: The Government's Framework for Community Capacity Building
Office of the Deputy PM	2004	Jobs and Enterprise in Deprived Areas: Social Exclusion Unit Report
HM Treasury	2004	Microeconomic Reform in Britain
HM Treasury	2005	Exploring the role of the third sector in public service delivery and reform: A discussion document
DWP	2006	A new deal for welfare: Empowering people to work
OTS	2006	Social enterprise action plan: Scaling new heights
HM Treasury	2006	Pre-Budget Report: Investing in Britain's potential: Building our long-term future
HM Treasury	2006	Value for Money Assessment Guidance
DWP	2007	Reducing dependency, increasing opportunity: options for the future of welfare to work: An independent report to the Department for Work and Pensions by David Freud
OTS	2007	Consultation on the risk capital investment fund for social enterprise
OTS	2007	Research on Third Sector Access to Finance: Report to the Office of the Third Sector
OTS	2007	Unclaimed assets distribution mechanism: a consultation
HM Treasury	2007	Budget 2007: Building Britain's long-term future: Prosperity and fairness for families
HM Treasury	2007	The future role of the third sector in social and economic regeneration: final report
HM Treasury	2007	Service Transformation Agreement
Dept. for Communities and Local Government	2008	Communities in control Real people, real power
Cabinet Office	2008	Excellence and fairness: Achieving world class public services
DWP	2008	Raising expectations and increasing support: reforming welfare for the future
OTS	2008	Risk Capital Investment Fund for Social Enterprise Government Response
OTS	2008	Social Enterprise Fund – Request for proposals
OTS	2008	Social Investment Pilots: Action research final report
HM Gov't	2009	Putting the frontline first: smarter government

(continued)

Author	Year	Title
OTS	2009	Social Investment Wholesale Bank: A consultation on the functions and design
OTS	2009	Social Investment Wholesale Bank: Summary of responses to the consultation
HM Treasury	2010	Budget 2010: Securing the recovery

Government Strategy Documents (Coalition Government)

Author	Year	Title
Cabinet Office	2010	The Coalition: our programme for government
HM Gov't	2010	The Compact
HM Gov't	2010	Building the Big Society
HM Treasury	2010	Spending Review 2010
No 10	2010	Government puts Big Society at heart of public sector reform: press release
OCS	2010	Better Together: Preparing for local spending cuts to the voluntary, community and social enterprise sector
Cabinet Office	2011	Open Letter from Francis Maude to Sir Ronald Cohen and Nick O'Donohoe
OCS	2011	The Big Society Bank ("BSB") Outline Proposal
HM Gov't	2011	Open Public Services White Paper
OCS	2011	Modernising Commissioning: Increasing the role of charities, social enterprises, mutuals and cooperatives in public service delivery
OCS	2011	Growing the Social Investment Market: a vision and strategy
Cabinet Office, BSC, Nesta	2012	The Social Investment Readiness Charter Supporting the Investment Readiness Ecosystem
Lord Young	2012	Make Business your business: supporting the start-up and development of small business
OCS	2012	Making it easier for civil society to work with the state: Progress update
OCS	2012	Open Letter Stephen Lloyd
Cabinet Office	2013	G8 Social Impact Investment Forum Outputs and Agreed Actions
ICF for HM Government	2013	Growing the Social Investment Market: The Landscape and Economic Impact
OCS	2013	News Story: Cooperation to grow Social Investment Market
OCS	2013	Open Letter to Stephen Bubb
HM Treasury	2013	Consultation on social investment tax relief
Cabinet Office	2014	Social Investment Tax Relief guide

(continued)

Author	Year	Title
HM Gov't	2014	Making it easier for civil society to work with the state: Progress update
HM Gov't	2014	Growing the social investment market: 2014 progress update
OCS	2014	News Story: Government unveils major boost to social investment sector
Cabinet Office	2014	Brief Background note to UK government's approach to social investment
OCS	2015	2010 to 2015 government policy: social investment
OCS	2015	Open Letter to Sir Ronald Cohen

Government Strategy Documents (Conservative Government)

Author	Year	Title
UK Trade and Investment	2015	What is social impact investment? What it is, what it's not and how it works.
DWP	2016	Growing the social investment market: update on SIFI social investment
HM Gov't	2016	Social investment: the UK as a global hub 2016 international strategy
HM Gov't	2016	Social investment: a force for social change 2016 strategy

Speeches

Speaker	Date	Title or Venue
Gordon Brown	07/11/2007	Legislative programme statement
Gordon Brown	07/24/2007	Speech at "Britain's Everyday Heroes" Book Launch
David Cameron	07/14/2006	Chamberlain Lecture on Communities
Francis Maude	02/28/2008	Speech on Social Enterprise
David Cameron	02/10/2009	Speech on Social Enterprise
Francis Maude	10/05/2009	Speech on Ready to Deliver Change
David Cameron	11/10/2009	Hugo Young Lecture
David Cameron	04/19/2010	Speech on Big Society versus Big Government
David Cameron	04/20/2010	Speech on New Welfare Contract
Francis Maude	10/03/2010	Speech on Efficiency Savings
David Cameron	06/06/2013	Speech at G8 Social Impact Investing Event
Justine Greening	06/06/2013	Speech at G8 Social Impact Investing Event: Social Impact Investing in international development
Ian Duncan-Smith	06/06/2013	Speech at G8 Social Impact Investing Event
David Gauke	10/22/2013	Speech on Social Investment Tay Relief
Rob Wilson	10/28/2014	Speech on Grant Fund for Social Ventures

(continued)

Speaker	Date	Title or Venue
Ian Duncan-Smith	10/29/2014	Speech on The role of government in social impact investing
Rob Wilson	01/20/2015	Speech at the Social Investment and Public Services Conference
Rob Wilson	02/06/2015	Speech at Launch of OECD Social Investment Report
Francis Maude	03/05/2015	Speech at Chivas Strathisla distillery
Rob Wilson	03/15/2015	Speech at Launch of Access Foundation
Rob Wilson	12/01/2015	Speech on Giving Tuesday
Rob Wilson	12/04/2015	Speech at Fundraising Summit
Rob Wilson	03/02/2016	Speech at the Social Investment Academy

Election Manifestos (winning parties)

Party	Year	Title
Labour Party	1997	New Labour: Because Britain deserves better. Britain will be better with new Labour.
Labour Party	2001	Ambitions for Britain: Labour's manifesto 2001
Labour Party	2005	Britain forward not back: The Labour party manifesto 2005
Conservative Party	2010	Invitation to join the Government of Britain: The Conservative Manifesto 2010
Liberal Democrats	2010	Liberal Democrat Manifesto 2010
Conservative Party	2015	Strong Leadership, a clear economic plan, a brighter, more secure future

Government-related Commissions

Author	Year	Title
G8 Social Impact Investing Taskforce	2014	Impact Investment: The invisible heart of markets
G8 Social Impact Investing Taskforce	2014	Policy levers and objectives: explanatory note for governments
G8 Social Impact Investing Taskforce: UK National Advisory Board	2014	Building a social impact investment market: The UK experience
Social Investment Taskforce	2000	Enterprising Communities: Wealth beyond welfare
Social Investment Taskforce	2003	Enterprising Communities: Wealth beyond welfare – Update 2003
Social Investment Taskforce	2005	Enterprising Communities: Wealth beyond welfare – Update 2005
Social Investment Taskforce	2010	Social investment: ten years on

(continued)

Author	Year	Title
CoSA	2008	Willing Citizens and the making of the good society: the ideas underpinning the practical work of the Council on Social Action
CoSA	2008	Side by side: a report setting out the Council on Social Action's work on one-to-one
CoSA	2008	Side by side and implications for Public Services
CoSA	2008	'Collaborative Commitments': A think-piece by Professor David Grayson
CoSA	2008	Council on social action: commentary on year one
CoSA	2009	Heart of the City: Building stronger communities through business collaboration
CoSA	2009	Introducing the National Talent Bank: a briefing from the Council on Social Action Prepared by Professor Alex Linley
CoSA	2009	People of Influence: A progress report on the Council on Social Action's work on one-to-one
CoSA	2009	Time well-spent: The importance of the one-to-one relationship between advice workers and their clients.
CoSA	2009	Means and ends: a concluding commentary on the work of the Council on Social Action

Public Bodies and Regulators (alphabetically)

Author	Year	Title
Bank of England	2000	Finance for Small Businesses in Deprived Communities
Bank of England	2003	The Financing of Social Enterprises: A Special Report by the Bank of England
Bank of England	2003	The Financing of Social Enterprises: News Release
Charity Commission	2004	CC14 – Investment of Charitable Funds: Basic Principles
Charity Commission	2014	Charities and investment matters: a guide for trustees
CIC Regulator	2006	Memorandum of Understanding between the Office of the Third Sector (Cabinet Office) and the Regulator of Community Interest Companies
CIC Regulator	2013	Changes to the Dividend and Interest Caps for Community Interest Companies: Response to the CIC consultation on the dividend and interest caps
Futurebuilders	2005	Eligibility Checklist
Futurebuilders	2010	Futurebuilders evaluation: final report
National Audit Office	2009	Building the Capacity of the Third Sector
National Audit Office	2015	Outcome-based payment schemes: government's use of payment by results

Legislation and directives

Author	Year	Title
HM Gov't	2006	Charities Act 2006: What Trustees need to know
HM Gov't	2008	Dormant Bank and Building Society Accounts Act 2008
HM Gov't	2012	Public Services (Social Value) Act 2012
HM Gov't	2012	Procurement Policy Note: The Public Services (Social Value) Act 2012 – advice for commissioners and procurers
HM Gov't	2012	Welfare Reform Act 2012
HM Gov't	2014	Finance Act 2014

House of Commons

Author	Year	Title
House of Commons Treasury Committee	2007	Unclaimed assets within the financial system: Eleventh Report of Session 2006–07
House of Commons Library	2009	Special Advisers: SN/PC/03813
House of Commons Library	2011	Unclaimed financial assets / dormant accounts: Briefing paper 03027
House of Commons Library	2013	Delivering public services: The growing use of Payment by Results: SN/HA/6621
House of Commons Library	2015	The voluntary sector and the Big Society: Briefing paper 5883
House of Commons Library	2015	Big Society Bank/Capital: Briefing paper 05876

Other Commissions

Author	Year	Title
CUA	2006	A social investment bank: consultation paper
CUA	2007	The social investment bank: its organisation and role in driving development of the third sector
The Unclaimed Assets Charity Coalition	2007	The Unclaimed Assets Charity Coalition Briefing Dormant Bank and Building Society Accounts Bill – Committee Stage
The Unclaimed Assets Charity Coalition	2007	A response from the Unclaimed Assets Charity Coalition to 'A UK Unclaimed Assets Scheme: a consultation'
UKSIF	2012	Response to the Cabinet Office Red Tape Challenge Civil Society – Social Investment
The Alternative Commission on Social Investment	2015	After the Gold Rush: The Report of the Alternative Commission on Social Investment
The Alternative Commission on Social Investment	2015	After the Gold Rush: Conclusions and Recommendations
Early Action Taskforce	2011	The triple dividend: Thriving lives. Costing less. Contributing more.
Early Action Taskforce	2012	The deciding time: prevent today or pay tomorrow
Early Action Taskforce	2014	Towards Effective Prevention: Practical steps for the next Government

Social Organizations Discourse (alphabetically)

Author	Year	Title
ACEVO	2003	Replacing the State? The case for third sector public service delivery
ACEVO	2006	Choice and Voice – The unique role of the third sector
ACEVO	2009	ACEVO Third Sector Taskforce: Welfare to Work reform: the third sector's role
ACEVO	2009	ACEVO Conservative Taskforce: A Response to "A Stronger Society – Voluntary Action in the 21st Century"
ACEVO	2010	The Big Society: moving from romanticism to reality
ACEVO	2010	Understanding Social Investment
ACEVO	2013	The prevention revolution: transforming health and social care
ACEVO	2013	Refinement or reinvention: The future role of the Work Programme and the role of the Third Sector
ACEVO	2014	Good with money: Why Charity Investments Matter
ACEVO	2015	Remaking the State: Commission Briefing Paper One
ACEVO	2015	Remaking the state: Research report
NCVO	2004	The UK Voluntary Sector Almanac 2004: 5th edition
NCVO	2005	Civil renewal and active citizenship: a guide to the debate
NCVO	2007	The UK Voluntary Sector Almanac: The State of the Sector
NCVO	2011	NCVO Policy Analysis: Open Public Services White Paper
NCVO	2012	NCVO Commission on Tax Incentives for Social Investment: Analysis and Recommendations
NCVO	2014	Payment by results and the voluntary sector
NCVO	2016	Understanding the capacity and need to take on investment within the social sector
Social Enterprise Coalition	2003	There's more to business than you think: a guide to social enterprise
Social Enterprise UK	2012	Response to the Cabinet Office's Red Tape Challenge on Social Investment
Social Enterprise UK	2012	The Shadow state: a report about outsourcing public services
Social Enterprise UK	2015	Leading the world in social enterprise: State of social enterprise survey 2015

Social Impact Investing Actors

Author	Year	Title
BSC	2013	Big Society Capital's Investment Policy
BSC	2015	Report and Financial Statements
BSC		For-Profit Social Sector Organisations (SSO) – Governance Agreement
Bridges Community Ventures	2004	Equity-like capital for social ventures

(continued)

Author	Year	Title
New Philanthropy Capital	2010	Scaling up for the Big Society
Social Finance	2014	The Essex Social Impact Bond: a year in review
The Gym Group	2015	Annual Report and Accounts 2015
GIIN	2016	Annual Impact Investor Survey

Think Tanks

Author	Year	Title
Demos	1995	The other invisible hand: Remaking charity for the 21st century
Demos	1997	The rise of the social entrepreneur
New Economics Foundation	2001	The Mutual State: How local communities can run public services
New Economics Foundation	2004	Sustainable futures: investing in community-based organisations

Unions

Author	Year	Title
UNISON	2013	Branch guide to social impact bonds
Trade Union Congress and New Economics Foundation	2015	Outsourcing public services

EU Organizations

Author	Year	Title
European Parliament	2013	P7_TA(2013)0266: Social investment for growth and cohesion: European Parliament resolution of 12 June 2013 on the Commission Communication 'Towards Social Investment for Growth and Cohesion – including implementing the European Social Fund 2014-2020' (2013/2607(RSP))
European Parliament	2014	Briefing: Social impact bonds: Private finance that generates social returns

References

Aguilera, R. V., & Jackson, G. (2003). The cross-national diversity of corporate governance: Dimensions and determinants. *Academy of Management Review, 28*(3), 447–465.

Aitken, R. (2007). *Performing capital: Toward a cultural economy of popular and global finance*. New York: Palgrave Macmillan.

Alvesson, M., & Sandberg, J. (2011). Generating research questions through problematization. *Academy of Management Review, 36*(2), 247–271.

Ansell, C. K. (2001). *Schism and solidarity in social movements: The politics of labor in the French third republic*. Cambridge: Cambridge University Press.

Aoki, M. (2001). *Towards a comparative institutional analysis*. Cambridge, MA: MIT Press.

Arrighi, G. (1994). *The long twentieth century: Money, power, and the origins of our times*. London: Verso.

Ball, S. J., & Exley, S. (2010). Making policy with 'good ideas': Policy networks and the 'intellectuals' of new labour. *Journal of Education Policy, 25*(2), 151–169.

Barman, E. (2015). Of principle and principal: Value plurality in the market of impact investing. *Valuation Studies, 3*(1), 9–44.

Barman, E. (2016). *Caring capitalism: The meaning and measure of social value*. Cambridge: Cambridge University Press.

Baron-Cohen, S. (2002). The extreme male brain theory of autism. *Trends in Cognitive Sciences, 6* (6), 248–254.

Battilana, J., & D'Aunno, T. (2009). Institutional work and the paradox of embedded agency. In R. Suddaby & B. Leca (Eds.), *Institutional work: Actors and agency in institutional studies of organizations* (pp. 31–58). Cambridge: Cambridge University Press.

Battilana, J., & Dorado, S. (2010). Building sustainable hybrid organizations: The case of commercial microfinance organizations. *Academy of Management Journal, 53*(6), 1419–1440.

Battilana, J., & Lee, M. (2014). Advancing research on hybrid organizing: Insights from the study of social enterprises. *Academy of Management Annals, 8*(1), 397–441.

Battilana, J., Leca, B., & Boxenbaum, E. (2009). How actors change institutions: Towards a theory of institutional entrepreneurship. *Academy of Management Annals, 3*(1), 65–107.

Baud, C., & Durand, C. (2012). Financialization, globalization and the making of profits by leading retailers. *Socio-Economic Review, 10*(2), 241–266.

Beckert, J. (1996). What is sociological about economic sociology? Uncertainty and the embeddedness of economic action. *Theory and Society, 25*(6), 803–840.

Beckert, J. (2003). Economic sociology and embeddedness: How shall we conceptualize economic action? *Journal of Economic Issues, 37*(3), 769–787.

Beckert, J. (2010). How do fields change? The interrelations of institutions, networks, and cognition in the dynamics of markets. *Organization Studies, 31*(5), 605–627.

P. Golka, *Financialization as Welfare*,
https://doi.org/10.1007/978-3-030-06100-5

Beckert, J. (2011). Die sittliche Einbettung der Wirtschaft. Von der Effizienz-und Differenzierungstheorie zu einer Theorie wirtschaftlicher Felder. *Berliner Journal für Soziologie, 22* (2), 247–266.

Beckert, J. (2016). *Imagined futures. Fictional expectations and capitalist dynamics*. Cambridge, MA: Harvard University Press.

Beech, M., & Lee, S. (Eds.). (2015). *The conservative-liberal coalition. Examining the Cameron-Clegg government*. Basingstoke: Palgrave Macmillan.

Belfrage, C. (2008). Towards 'universal financialisation' in Sweden? *Contemporary Politics, 14*(3), 277–296.

Benford, R. D., & Snow, D. A. (2000). Framing processes and social movements: An overview and assessment. *Annual Review of Sociology, 26*(1), 611–639.

Berger, P. L., & Luckmann, T. (1966). *The social construction of reality: A treatise in the sociology of knowledge*. London: Penguin Books.

Blyth, M. (2010). On setting and upsetting agendas. In A. Gofas & C. Hay (Eds.), *The role of ideas in political analysis: A portrait of contemporary debates* (pp. 167–186). New York: Routledge.

Blyth, M. (2013). *Austerity: The history of a dangerous idea*. Oxford: Oxford University Press.

Boisard, P., & Letablier, M.-T. (1987). Le camembert: Normand ou normé. Deux modèles de production de l'industrie fromagère. In F. Eymard-Duvernay (Ed.). Paris: PUF.

Boltanski, L., & Chiapello, E. (2006). *Der neue Geist des Kapitalismus*. Konstanz: UVK Verlagsgesellschaft.

Boltanski, L., & Thévenot, L. (2006). *On justification: Economies of worth*. Princeton, NJ: Princeton University Press.

Botzem, S., & Dobusch, L. (2017). Financialization as strategy: Accounting for inter-organizational value creation in the European real estate industry. *Accounting, Organizations and Society, 59*, 31–43.

Bourdieu, P. (1998). *The state nobility: Elite schools in the field of power*. Stanford, CA: Stanford University Press.

Bourdieu, P., & Wacquant, L. J. (1992). *An invitation to reflexive sociology*. Chicago, IL: University of Chicago Press.

Bundesministerium für Wirtschaft und Energie. (2015). *INVEST – Zuschuss für Wagniskapital: Ein Programm für junge innovative Unternehmen und private Investoren*. Retrieved from http://www.bmwi.de/BMWi/Redaktion/PDF/Publikationen/invest-zuschuss-fuer-wagniskapital,property=pdf,bereich=bmwi2012,sprache=de,rwb=true.pdf

Burawoy, M. (2005). For public sociology. *American Sociological Review, 70*(1), 4–28.

Chiapello, E. (2013). Capitalism and its criticisms. In P. Du Gay & G. Morgan (Eds.), *New spirits of capitalism? Crises, justifications, and dynamics* (pp. 60–81). Oxford: Oxford University Press.

Chiapello, E. (2015). Financialisation of valuation. *Human Studies, 38*(1), 13–35.

Chiapello, E., & Godefroy, G. (2017). The dual function of judgment devices. Why does the plurality of market classifications matter? *Historical Social Research, 42*(1), 152–188.

Chiapello, E., & Medjad, K. (2009). An unprecedented privatisation of mandatory standard-setting: The case of European accounting policy. *Critical Perspectives on Accounting, 20*(4), 448–468.

Chiapello, E., & Walter, C. (2016). The three ages of financial quantification: A conventionalist approach to the financiers' metrology. *Historical Social Research, 41*(2), 155–177.

Coates, J. M., & Herbert, J. (2008). Endogenous steroids and financial risk taking on a London trading floor. *Proceedings of the National Academy of Sciences, 105*(16), 6167–6172.

Cole, S. (Ed.). (2001). *What's wrong with sociology?* New Brunswick, NJ: Transaction Publishers.

Connell, A. (2010). *Welfare policy under new labour: The politics of social security reform*. London: I.B. Tauris.

Coombs, N. (2016). What is an algorithm? Financial regulation in the era of high-frequency trading. *Economy and Society, 45*(2), 278–302.

Cornelissen, J. P., & Werner, M. D. (2014). Putting framing in perspective: A review of framing and frame analysis across the management and organizational literature. *Academy of Management Annals, 8*(1), 181–235.

Cornelissen, J. P., Durand, R., Fiss, P. C., Lammers, J. C., & Vaara, E. (2015). Putting communication front and center in institutional theory and analysis. *Academy of Management Review, 40* (1), 10–27.

Crotty, J. (2005). The neoliberal paradox: The impact of destructive product market competition and 'modern' financial markets on nonfinancial corporation performance in the neoliberal era. In G. A. Epstein (Ed.), *Financialization and the world economy* (pp. 77–110). Cheltenham: Edward Elgar.

Crotty, J. (2008). If financial market competition is intense, why are financial firm profits so high? Reflections on the current 'golden age'of finance. *Competition & Change, 12*(2), 167–183.

Crouch, C. (2011). *The strange non-death of neo-liberalism.* Cambridge: Polity Press.

Crouch, C. (2015). *The knowledge corrupters: Hidden consequences of the financial takeover of public life.* Cambridge: Polity Press.

Davies, S. (2008). Contracting out employment services to the third and private sectors: A critique. *Critical Social Policy, 28*(2), 136–164.

Davis, A., & Walsh, C. (2015). The role of the state in the financialisation of the UK economy. *Political Studies, 64*(3), 666–682.

De Tocqueville, A. (1856). *L'ancien Régime et la Révolution.* Paris: Michel Lévy.

Deakin, N., & Parry, R. (2000). *The treasury and social policy: The contest for control of welfare strategy.* Basingstoke: Macmillan Press.

Deeg, R., & Jackson, G. (2007). Towards a more dynamic theory of capitalist variety. *Socio-Economic Review, 5*(1), 149–179.

Deutschmann, C. (2008). Finanzmarkt-Kapitalismus und Wachstumskrise. In C. Deutschmann (Ed.), *Kapitalistische Dynamik: Eine gesellschaftstheoretische Perspektive* (pp. 151–174). Wiesbaden: VS Verlag für Sozialwissenschaften.

Dewey, J. (1922). *Human nature and conduct: An introduction to social psychology.* New York: Henry Holt and Company.

Diaz-Bone, R. (2015). *Die "Economie des conventions": Grundlagen und Entwicklungen in der neuen französischen Wirtschaftssoziologie.* Wiesbaden: Springer VS.

DiMaggio, P. (1988). Interest and agency in institutional theory. In L. G. Zucker (Ed.), *Institutional patterns and organizations* (pp. 1–21). Cambridge, MA: Ballinger.

DiMaggio, P. (1991). Constructing an organizational field as a professional project: U.S. art museums, 1920-1940. In M. Powell & P. DiMaggio (Eds.), *The new institutionalism in organizational analysis.* Chicago, IL: University of Chicago Press.

DiMaggio, P., & Powell, W. (1983). The iron cage revisited: Institutional isomorphism and collective rationality in organizational fields. *American Sociological Review, 48*, 147–160.

Dobbin, F. (2009). *Inventing equal opportunity.* Princeton, NJ: Princeton University Press.

Dobrowolsky, A., & Lister, R. (2008). Social investment: The discourse and the dimensions of change. In M. Powell (Ed.), *Modernising the welfare state: The Blair legacy.* Bristol: Policy Press.

Dore, R. (2008). Financialization of the global economy. *Industrial and Corporate Change, 17*(6), 1097–1112.

Dowling, E. (2016). In the wake of austerity: Social impact bonds and the financialisation of the welfare state in Britain. *New Political Economy, 22*(3), 294–310.

Dowling, E., & Harvie, D. (2014). Harnessing the social: State, crisis and (big) society. *Sociology, 48*(5), 869–886.

Du Gay, P., & Pryke, M. (2002). *Cultural economy: Cultural analysis and commercial life.* Thousand Oaks, CA: Sage.

Duménil, G., & Lévy, D. (2004). *Capital resurgent: Roots of the neoliberal revolution.* Cambridge, MA: Harvard University Press.

Dünhaupt, P. (2012). Financialization and the rentier income share–evidence from the USA and Germany. *International Review of Applied Economics, 26*(4), 465–487.

Edelman, L. B. (1992). Legal ambiguity and symbolic structures: Organizational mediation of civil rights law. *American Journal of Sociology, 97*(6), 1531–1576.
Eisenegger, C., Haushofer, J., & Fehr, E. (2011). The role of testosterone in social interaction. *Trends in Cognitive Sciences, 15*(6), 263–271.
Eisenhardt, K. M. (1989). Building theories from case study research. *Academy of Management Review, 14*(4), 532–550.
Eisenstadt, S. N. (1980). Cultural orientations, institutional entrepreneurs, and social change: Comparative analysis of traditional civilizations. *American Journal of Sociology, 85*(4), 840–869.
Eisinger, P. K. (1973). The conditions of protest behavior in American cities. *American Political Science Review, 67*(1), 11–28.
Emirbayer, M., & Mische, A. (1998). What is agency? *American Journal of Sociology, 103*(4), 962–1023.
Espeland, W. N., & Sauder, M. (2007). Rankings and reactivity: How public measures recreate social worlds. *American Journal of Sociology, 113*(1), 1–40.
Esping-Andersen, G. (1990). *The three worlds of welfare capitalism.* Princeton, NJ: Princeton University Press.
European Commission. (2016). *Capital markets union: New rules to support investment in venture capital and social enterprises* [Press release]. Retrieved from http://europa.eu/rapid/press-release_IP-16-2481_en.htm
Feist, M., & Fuchs, D. (2014). Was heißt hier nachhaltig? In M. Heires & A. Nölke (Eds.), *Politische Ökonomie der Finanzialisierung* (pp. 225–240). Wiesbaden: Springer.
Finlayson, A. (2009). Financialisation, financial literacy and asset-based-welfare. *British Journal of Politics and International Relations, 11*(3), 400–421.
Finn, M. (2015). The coming of the coalition and the coalition agreement. In A. Seldon & M. Finn (Eds.), *The coalition effect, 2010–2015* (pp. 31–58). Cambridge: Cambridge University Press.
Fischer, G. (In Preparation). *Urheberrecht und Kreativität in der Sampling-basierten Musikproduktion.* (PhD), Technische Universität Berlin, Berlin.
Fiss, P. C., & Zajac, E. J. (2004). The diffusion of ideas over contested terrain: The (non) adoption of a shareholder value orientation among German firms. *Administrative Science Quarterly, 49* (4), 501–534.
Flaherty, E. (2015). Top incomes under finance-driven capitalism, 1990–2010: Power resources and regulatory orders. *Socio-Economic Review, 13*(3), 417–447.
Fligstein, N. (1990). *The transformation of corporate control.* Cambridge, MA: Harvard University Press.
Fligstein, N. (2001a). *The architecture of markets: An economic sociology of twenty-first-century capitalist societies.* Princeton, NJ: Princeton University Press.
Fligstein, N. (2001b). Social skill and the theory of fields. *Sociological Theory, 19*(2), 105–125.
Fligstein, N. (2008). Fields, power and social skill: A critical analysis of the new institutionalisms. *International Public Management Review, 9*(1), 227–253.
Fligstein, N. (2013). Understanding stability and change in fields. *Research in Organizational Behavior, 33*, 39–51.
Fligstein, N., & Goldstein, A. (2012). A long strange trip: The state and mortgage securitization, 1968-2010. In K. Knorr Cetina & A. Preda (Eds.), *The Oxford handbook of the sociology of finance* (pp. 339–356). Oxford: Oxford University Press.
Fligstein, N., & McAdam, D. (2011). Toward a general theory of strategic action fields. *Sociological Theory, 29*(1), 1–26.
Fligstein, N., & McAdam, D. (2012). *A theory of fields*. Oxford: Oxford University Press.
Fligstein, N., & Shin, T.-J. (2004). The shareholder value society: A review of the changes in working conditions and inequality in the United States, 1976 to 2000. In K. Neckermann (Ed.), *Social inequality* (pp. 401–432). New York: Russell Sage Foundation.
Forst, R. (2013). *Justification and critique: Towards a critical theory of politics*. Cambridge: Polity Press.

Forst, R. (2015a). *Normativität und Macht. Zur analyse sozialer Rechtfertigungsordnungen*. Frankfurt am Main: Suhrkamp.

Forst, R. (2015b). Noumenal power. *The Journal of Political Philosophy, 23*(2), 111–127.

Fourcade, M. (2007). Theories of markets and theories of society. *American Behavioral Scientist, 50*(8), 1015–1034.

Friedland, R., & Alford, R. R. (1991). Bringing society back in: Symbols, practices and institutional contradictions. In W. Powell & P. DiMaggio (Eds.), *The new institutionalism in organizational analysis* (pp. 232–263). Chicago, IL: University of Chicago Press.

G-8. (2014). *Impact Investing: The invisible heart of markets*. Retrieved from http://www.socialimpactinvestment.org

Gamson, W. A. (1975). *The strategy of social protest*. Homewood, IL: Dorsey Press.

Geertz, C. (1973). *The interpretation of cultures: Selected essays*. New York: Basic Books.

Giddens, A. (1984). *The constitution of society: Outline of the theory of structuration*. Cambridge: Blackwell, Polity Press.

Giddens, A. (1998). *The third way: The renewal of social democracy*. Cambridge: Polity Press.

Gioia, D. A., & Chittipeddi, K. (1991). Sensemaking and sensegiving in strategic change initiation. *Strategic Management Journal, 12*(6), 433–448.

Gioia, D. A., Corley, K. G., & Hamilton, A. L. (2013). Seeking qualitative rigor in inductive research notes on the Gioia methodology. *Organizational Research Methods, 16*(1), 15–31.

Glänzel, G., & Scheuerle, T. (2016). Social impact investing in Germany: Current impediments from investors' and social entrepreneurs' perspectives. *Voluntas: International Journal of Voluntary and Nonprofit Organizations, 27*(4), 1638–1668.

Glaser, B. G., & Strauss, A. L. (1967). *The discovery of grounded theory*. New York: Aldine.

Godechot, O. (2015). Financialization is marketization! A study on the respective impact of various dimensions of financialization on the increase of global inequality. *Sociological Science, 3*, 495–519.

Goffman, E. (1959). *The presentation of self in everyday life*. Garden City, NY: Doubleday.

Goffman, E. (1973). *Frame analysis: An essay on the organization of experience*. Cambridge, MA: Harvard University Press.

Goldstone, J. A. (2004). More social movements or fewer? Beyond political opportunity structures to relational fields. *Theory and Society, 33*(3), 333–365.

Goldstone, J. A., & Useem, B. (2012). Putting values and institutions back into the theory of strategic action fields. *Sociological Theory, 30*(1), 37–47.

Golka, P. (2015). *Impact Investing: Ein Begriff, zwei Handlungsfelder*. Unpublished manuscript.

Goodwin, J., & Jasper, J. M. (1999). *Caught in a winding, snarling vine: The structural bias of political process theory*. Paper presented at the Sociological forum.

Greenwood, R., & Hinings, C. R. (1996). Understanding radical organizational change: Bringing together the old and the new institutionalism. *Academy of Management Review, 21*(4), 1022–1054.

Gross, N. (2009). A pragmatist theory of social mechanisms. *American Sociological Review, 74*(3), 358–379.

Habermas, J. (1981). *Theorie des kommunikativen Handelns band 1: Handlungsrationalität und gesellchaftliche Rationalisierung*. Frankfurt am Main: Suhrkamp.

Hall, P. A., & Soskice, D. (2001). *Varieties of capitalism: The institutional foundations of comparative advantage*. Oxford: Oxford University Press.

Hardy, C., & Maguire, S. (2010). Discourse, field-configuring events, and change in organizations and institutional fields: Narratives of DDT and the Stockholm convention. *Academy of Management Journal, 53*(6), 1365–1392.

Harvey, D. (1989). From managerialism to entrepreneurialism: The transformation of urban governance in late capitalism. *Geografiska Annaler, 71*(B), 3–17.

Harvey, D. (2005). *A brief history of neoliberalism*. Oxford: Oxford University Press.

Hebb, T. (2013). Impact investing and responsible investing: What does it mean? *Journal of Sustainable Finance & Investment, 3*(2), 71–74.

Hedström, P., & Swedberg, R. (1998). *Social mechanisms: An analytical approach to social theory*. Cambridge: Cambridge University Press.

Hiß, S. (2006). *Warum übernehmen Unternehmen gesellschaftliche Verantwortung?* Frankfurt am Main: Campus.

Hiß, S. (2013). The politics of the financialization of sustainability. *Competition & Change, 17*(3), 234–247.

Hiß, S. (2014). Was bleibt von der Nachhaltigkeit nach ihrer Finanzialisierung? In M. Heires & A. Nölke (Eds.), *Politische Ökonomie der Finanzialisierung* (pp. 211–224). Wiesbaden: Springer.

Ho, K. (2009). *Liquidated: An ethnography of wall street*. Durham, NC: Duke University Press.

Hoffman, A. J. (1999). Institutional evolution and change: Environmentalism and the US chemical industry. *Academy of Management Journal, 42*(4), 351–371.

Höpner, M., & Jackson, G. (2006). Revisiting the Mannesmann takeover: How markets for corporate control emerge. *European Management Review, 3*(3), 142–155.

Jackson, G., & Deeg, R. (2012). The long-term trajectories of institutional change in European capitalism. *Journal of European Public Policy, 19*(8), 1109–1125.

James, W. (1907/1975). *Pragmatism: A new name for some old ways of thinking*. Cambridge, MA: Harvard University Press.

Jessop, B. (2010). Cultural political economy and critical policy studies. *Critical Policy Studies, 3* (3–4), 336–356.

Jessop, B. (2011). *Imagined recoveries, recovered imaginaries: A cultural political economy perspective*. Retrieved from http://www.lancs.ac.uk/cperc/docs/E-2012 Jessop-CPE-SwanseaRecovery.pdf

Joas, H. (1996). *The creativity of action* (J. Gaines & P. Keast, Trans.). Chicago, IL: University of Chicago Press.

JP Morgan. (2010). *Impact investments: An emerging asset class*. Retrieved from https://thegiin.org/knowledge/publication/impact-investments-an-emerging-asset-class

JP Morgan. (2014). Spotlight on the market: The impact investor survey. Retrieved from https://thegiin.org/knowledge/publication/spotlight-on-the-market-the-impact-investor-survey

Jung, J. (2015). A struggle on two fronts: Labour resistance to changing layoff policies at large US companies. *Socio-Economic Review, 15*(1), 213–239.

Jung, J., & Dobbin, F. (2012). Finance and institutional investors. In K. Knorr Cetina & A. Preda (Eds.), *The Oxford handbook of the sociology of finance* (pp. 52–74). Oxford: Oxford University Press.

Kädtler, J. (2011). Financialisation of capitalist economies: Bargaining on conventional economic rationalities. *Historical Social Research, 36*(4), 169–191.

Kädtler, J. (2015). Macht und Machtverhältnisse im Rahmen und außerhalb des konventionenökonomischen Programms. In L. Knoll (Ed.), *Organisationen und Konventionen: Die Soziologie der Konventionen in der Organisationsforschung*. Wiesbaden: Springer VS.

Kelly, J. (2007). Reforming public services in the UK: Bringing in the third sector. *Public Administration, 85*(4), 1003–1022.

Kendall, J. (2000). The mainstreaming of the third sector into public policy in England in the late 1990s: Whys and wherefores. *Policy & Politics, 28*(4), 541–562.

Khurana, R. (2007). *From higher aims to hired hands: The social transformation of American business schools and the unfulfilled promise of management as a profession*. Princeton, NJ: Princeton University Press.

Kingdon, J. (1995). *Agendas, alternatives, and public policies*. New York: HarperCollins College Publishers.

Kluttz, D. N., & Fligstein, N. (2016). Varieties of sociological field theory. In S. Abrutyn (Ed.), *Handbook of contemporary sociological theory* (pp. 185–204). Cham: Springer.

Knoll, L. (2012). *Über die Rechtfertigung wirtschaftlichen Handelns: CO2-Handel in der kommunalen Energiewirtschaft*. Wiesbaden: Springer VS.

Knorr-Cetina, K. (2009). What is a financial market? In J. Beckert & C. Deutschmann (Eds.), *Wirtschaftssoziologie* (Kölner Zeitschrift für Soziologie und Sozialpsychologie 49) (pp. 326–342). Wiesbaden: VS-Verlag für Sozialwissenschaften.

Konings, M. (2009). The construction of US financial power. *Review of International Studies, 35* (01), 69–94.

Krippner, G. R. (2005). The financialization of the American economy. *Socio-Economic Review, 3* (2), 173–208.

Krippner, G. R. (2011). *Capitalizing on crisis*. Cambridge, MA: Harvard University Press.

Kurzman, C. (1996). Structural opportunity and perceived opportunity in social-movement theory: The Iranian revolution of 1979. *American Sociological Review, 61*(1), 153–170.

Lake, R. W. (2015). The financialization of urban policy in the age of Obama. *Journal of Urban Affairs, 37*(1), 75–78.

Lamont, M. (2012). Toward a comparative sociology of valuation and evaluation. *Annual Review of Sociology, 38*(1), 201–221.

Langenohl, A., & Wetzel, D. (2011). Finanzmärkte und ihre Sinnformen: Handlungskoordination und Signalkommunikation. *Berliner Journal für Soziologie, 21*(4), 539–559.

Langley, P. (2006). Securitising suburbia: The transformation of Anglo-American mortgage finance. *Competition & Change, 10*(3), 283–299.

Langley, P. (2008). Financialization and the consumer credit boom. *Competition & Change, 12*(2), 133–147.

Larsen, T. P., Taylor-Gooby, P., & Kananen, J. (2006). New labour's policy style: A mix of policy approaches. *Journal of Social Policy, 35*(4), 629–649.

Lawrence, T. B., Suddaby, R., & Leca, B. (Eds.). (2009). *Institutional work: Actors and agency in institutional studies of organization*. Cambridge: Cambridge University Press.

Lawrence, T. B., Suddaby, R., & Leca, B. (2011). Institutional work: Refocusing institutional studies of organization. *Journal of Management Inquiry, 20*(1), 52–58.

Lazonick, W. (2014). Profits without prosperity. *Harvard Business Review, 92*(9), 46–55.

Lazonick, W., & O'Sullivan, M. (2000). Maximizing shareholder value: A new ideology for corporate governance. *Economy and Society, 29*(1), 13–35.

Lee, S. (2006). Gordon Brown and the 'British way'. *The Political Quarterly, 77*(3), 369–378.

Lee, S. (2008). *Best for Britain? The politics and leagcy of Gordon Brown*. Oxford: Oneworld Books.

Leifer, E. M. (1995). *Making the majors: The transformation of team sports in America*. Cambridge, MA: Harvard University Press.

Lewis, J. (2005). New labour's approach to the voluntary sector: Independence and the meaning of partnership. *Social Policy and Society, 4*(02), 121–131.

Lin, K.-H., & Tomaskovic-Devey, D. (2013). Financialization and US income inequality, 1970–20081. *American Journal of Sociology, 118*(5), 1284–1329.

Lister, R. (1998). From equality to social inclusion: New labour and the welfare state. *Critical Social Policy, 18*(2), 215–225.

Luhmann, N. (1987). *Soziale Systeme: Grundriss einer allgemeinen Theorie*. Frankfurt am Main: Suhrkamp.

MacKenzie, D. (2008). *An engine, not a camera: How financial models shape markets*. Cambridge, MA: MIT Press.

MacKenzie, D. (2016). A material political economy: Automated trading desk and price prediction in high-frequency trading. *Social Studies of Science, 47*(2), 172–194.

MacKenzie, D., & Millo, Y. (2003). Constructing a market, performing theory: The historical sociology of a financial derivatives exchange1. *American Journal of Sociology, 109*(1), 107–145.

Macmillan, R. (2010). *The third sector delivering* public *services: An evidence review*. Working Paper. Birmingham: University of Birmingham.

Mader, P. (2015). *The political economy of microfinance: Financialising poverty*. London: Palgrave Macmillan.

Mader, P. (2016). *Questioning three fundamental assumptions in financial inclusion* (IDS evidence report, 176). Brighton: IDS.
Maguire, S., Hardy, C., & Lawrence, T. B. (2004). Institutional entrepreneurship in emerging fields: HIV/AIDS treatment advocacy in Canada. *Academy of Management Journal, 47*(5), 657–679.
Mair, J., & Hehenberger, L. (2014). Front-stage and backstage convening: The transition from opposition to mutualistic coexistence in organizational philanthropy. *Academy of Management Journal, 57*(4), 1174–1200.
Mair, J., & Marti, I. (2006). Social entrepreneurship research: A source of explanation, prediction and delight. *Journal of World Business, 41*(1), 36–44.
Mair, J., & Marti, I. (2009). Entrepreneurship in and around institutional voids: A case study from Bangladesh. *Journal of Business Venturing, 24*(5), 419–435.
Martin, R. (2002). *Financialization of daily life*. Philadelphia, PA: Temple University Press.
Martin, J. L. (2003). What is field theory? *American Journal of Sociology, 109*(1), 1–49.
Martin, J. L. (2011). *The explanation of social action*. Oxford: Oxford University Press.
Mayring, P. (2015). *Qualitative Inhaltsanalyse: Grundlagen und Techniken*. Weinheim: Beltz.
McAdam, D. (1982). *Political process and the development of black insurgency*. Chicago, IL: University of Chicago Press.
McAdam, D., Tarrow, S., & Tilly, C. (2001). *Dynamics of contention*. Cambridge: Cambridge University Press.
McCann, E. (2013). Policy boosterism, policy mobilities, and the extrospective city. *Urban Geography, 34*(1), 5–29.
McGoey, L. (2012). Philanthrocapitalism and its critics. *Poetics, 40*(2), 185–199.
McGoey, L. (2015). *No such thing as a free gift: The gates foundation and the price of philanthropy*. London: Verso Books.
Mead, G. H. (1934). *Mind, self, society*. Chicago, IL: University of Chicago Press.
Merriam, S. B. (2009). *Qualitative research: A guide to design and implementation*. San Francisco, CA: Jossey-Bass.
Meyer, A. D. (1982). Adapting to environmental jolts. *Administrative Science Quarterly, 27*, 515–537.
Meyer, J. W., & Rowan, B. (1977). Institutionalized organizations: Formal structure as myth and ceremony. *American Journal of Sociology, 83*, 340–363.
Meyer, J. W., & Scott, W. R. (1991). The organization of societal sectors: Propositions and early evidence. In M. Powell & P. DiMaggio (Eds.), *The new institutionalism in organizational analysis* (pp. 108–140). Chicago, IL: University of Chicago Press.
Milberg, W. (2008). Shifting sources and uses of profits: Sustaining US financialization with global value chains. *Economy and Society, 37*(3), 420–451.
Mische, A. (2002). Cross-talk in movements: Reconceiving the culture-network link. In M. Diani & D. McAdam (Eds.), *Social movement and networks: Relational approaches to collective action* (pp. 258–280). Oxford: Oxford University Press.
Mische, A. (2009). Projects and possibilities: Researching futures in action. *Sociological Forum, 24* (3), 694–704.
Mische, A. (2014). Measuring futures in action: Projective grammars in the Rio+ 20 debates. *Theory and Society, 43*(3–4), 437–464.
Mizruchi, M. S. (1996). What do interlocks do? An analysis, critique, and assessment of research on interlocking directorates. *Annual Review of Sociology, 22*(1), 271–298.
Morin, F. (2000). A transformation in the French model of shareholding and management. *Economy and Society, 29*(1), 36–53.
Mortensen, J. L., & Seabrooke, L. (2008). Housing as social right or means to wealth? The politics of property booms in Australia and Denmark. *Comparative European Politics, 6*(3), 305–324.
Mulderrig, J. (2011). The grammar of governance. *Critical Discourse Studies, 8*(1), 45–68.
Mulgan, G., Tucker, S., Ali, R., & Sanders, B. (2007). *Social innovation: What it is, why it matters and how it can be accelerated*. Oxford: Oxford University Skoll Centre for Social Entrepreneurship.

Newman, J. (2001). *Modernising governance: New labour, policy, and society*. London: Sage.
Nicholls, A. (2010). The institutionalization of social investment: The interplay of investment logics and investor rationalities. *Journal of Social Entrepreneurship, 1*(1), 70–100.
Nölke, A., & Perry, J. (2007). The power of transnational private governance: Financialization and the IASB. *Business Power and Global Governance, 9*(3), 1–25.
Pacewicz, J. (2012). Tax increment financing, economic development professionals and the financialization of urban politics. *Socio-Economic Review, 11*(3), 413–440.
Peirce, C. (1934). *Collected papers of Charles Sanders Peirce* (C. Hartshorne & P. Weiss Eds. Vol. 5). Cambridge, MA: Harvard University Press.
Piketty, T. (2014). *Capital in the twenty-first century*. Cambridge, MA: Harvard University Press.
Podolny, J. M. (1993). A status-based model of market competition. *American Journal of Sociology, 98*(4), 829–872.
Polanyi, K. (1944). *The great transformation: The political and economic origins of our time*. Boston, MA: Beacon Press.
Powell, M. (2000). New labour and the third way in the British welfare state: A new and distinctive approach? *Critical Social Policy, 20*(1), 39–60.
Powell, M. (Ed.). (2008). *Modernising the welfare state: The Blair legacy*. Bristol: Policy Press.
Quinn, S. L. (2010). *Government policy, housing, and the origins of securitization, 1780–1968*. (PhD), Berkeley, CA: University of California.
Ragin, C. C., & Becker, H. S. (1992). *What is a case? Exploring the foundations of social inquiry*. Cambridge: Cambridge University Press.
Reay, T., & Hinings, C. R. (2005). The recomposition of an organizational field: Health care in Alberta. *Organization Studies, 26*(3), 351–384.
Riddel, P. (2015). The coalition and the executive. In A. Seldon & M. Finn (Eds.), *The coalition effect, 2010–2015* (pp. 113–136). Cambridge: Cambridge University Press.
Rule, J., & Tilly, C. (1975). Political process in revolutionary France: 1830-1832. In J. M. Merriman (Ed.), *1830 France* (pp. 41–85). New York: New Viewpoints.
Schelkle, W. (2012). A crisis of what? Mortgage credit markets and the social policy of promoting homeownership in the United States and in Europe. *Politics and Society, 40*(1), 59–80.
Schmidt, V. A. (2008). Discursive institutionalism: The explanatory power of ideas and discourse. *Annual Review of Political Science, 11*, 303–326.
Schwartz, H. (2012). Housing, the welfare state, and the global financial crisis: What is the connection? *Politics and Society, 40*(1), 35–58.
Scott, W. R. (1987). The adolescence of institutional theory. *Administrative Science Quarterly, 32* (4), 493–511.
Scott, W. R. (1991). Unpacking institutional arguments. In W. Powell & P. DiMaggio (Eds.), *The new institutionalism in organizational analysis* (pp. 164–182). Chicago, IL: University of Chicago Press.
Scott, W. R. (1995). *Institutions and organizations*. Thousand Oaks, CA: Sage.
Scott, W. R. (2001). *Institutions and organizations*. Thousand Oaks, CA: Sage.
Seabrooke, L. (2007). Everyday legitimacy and international financial orders: The social sources of imperialism and hegemony in global finance. *New Political Economy, 12*(1), 1–18.
Seabrooke, L. (2010). Everyday legitimacy and institutional change. In A. Gofas & C. Hay (Eds.), *The role of ideas in political analysis: A portrait of contemporary debates* (pp. 78–93). New York: Routledge.
Seldon, A. (Ed.). (2007). *Blair's Britain, 1997–2007*. Cambridge: Cambridge University Press.
Seldon, A. (2015). David Cameron as prime minister, 2010–2015: The verdict of history. In A. Seldon & M. Finn (Eds.), *The coalition effect, 2010–2015* (pp. 1–30). Cambridge: Cambridge University Press.
Seldon, A., & Finn, M. (Eds.). (2015). *The coalition effect, 2010–2015*. Cambridge: Cambridge University Press.
Sellars, W. (1956). Empiricism and the philosophy of mind. *Minnesota Studies in the Philosophy of Science, 1*, 253–329.

Siggelkow, N. (2007). Persuasion with case studies. *Academy of Management Journal, 50*(1), 20–24.
Smith, A. (2010). The third sector, regeneration and sustainable communities: "Rolling" with the new labour agenda. *International Journal of Sociology and Social Policy, 30*(1/2), 48–65.
Snow, D. A., & Anderson, L. (1991). Researching the homeless: The characteristics and virtues of the case study. In J. R. Feagin, A. M. Orum, & G. Sjoberg (Eds.), *A case for the case study* (pp. 148–173). Chapel Hill, NC: University of North Carolina Press.
Snow, D. A., & Benford, R. D. (1988). Ideology, frame resonance, and participant mobilization. *International Social Movement Research, 1*, 197–217.
Snow, D. A., & Trom, D. (2002). The case study and the study of social movements. In B. Klandermans & S. Staggenborg (Eds.), *Methods of social movement research* (pp. 146–172). Minneapolis, MN: University of Minnestoa Press.
Social Finance. (2011). *Social impact bonds: The one* service. One year on.* Retrieved from https://www.bigsocietycapital.com/sites/default/files/attachments/The One Service One Year On.pdf
Social Finance. (2012). *Enabling long-term recovery from addiction.* Retrieved from http://www.socialfinance.org.uk/wp-content/uploads/2014/05/SF_DRUGS_REPORT.pdf
Social Finance. (2014). *Technical guide: Building a business case for prevention.* Retrieved from http://www.socialfinance.org.uk/wp-content/uploads/2014/07/BLF_Tech_Guideprevention.pdf
Sparsam, J. (2014). *Wirtschaft in der new economic sociology: Eine Systematisierung und Kritik.* Wiesbaden: Springer VS.
Stark, D. (2011). *The sense of dissonance: Accounts of worth in economic life.* Princeton, NJ: Princeton University Press.
Stinchcombe, A. L. (1998). Monopolistic competition as a mechanism: Corporations, universities, and nation-states in competitive fields. In P. Hedström & R. Swedberg (Eds.), *Social mechanisms: An analytical approach to social theory* (pp. 267–305). Cambridge: Cambridge University Press.
Stockhammer, E. (2004). Financialisation and the slowdown of accumulation. *Cambridge Journal of Economics, 28*(5), 719–741.
Strauss, A. L., & Corbin, J. (1990). *Basics of qualitative research.* Newbury Park, CA: Sage.
Streeck, W. (2013). *Gekaufte Zeit. Die vertagte Krise des demokratischen Kapitalismus.* Frankfurt/Main: Suhrkamp.
Streeck, W., & Thelen, K. A. (2005). *Beyond continuity: Institutional change in advanced political economies.* Oxford: Oxford University Press.
Sturm, R. (2009). *Politik in Großbritannien.* Wiesbaden: Springer VS.
Swartz, D. (1997). *Culture and power: The sociology of Pierre Bourdieu.* Chicago, IL: University of Chicago Press.
Tarrow, S. (2011). *Power in movement: Social movements and contentious politics* (3rd ed.). Cambridge: Cambridge University Press.
Tavory, I., & Timmermans, S. (2014). *Abductive analysis: Theorizing qualitative research.* Chicago, IL: University of Chicago Press.
Teasdale, S. (2011). What's in a name? Making sense of social enterprise discourses. *Public Policy and Administration, 27*(2), 99–119.
Thomas, G. (2011). A typology for the case study in social science following a review of definition, discourse, and structure. *Qualitative Inquiry, 17*(6), 511–521.
Thornton, P. H., Ocasio, W., & Lounsbury, M. (2012). *The institutional logics perspective: A new approach to culture, structure, and process.* Oxford: Oxford University Press.
Tilly, C. (1978). *From mobilization to revolution.* Reading, MA: Addison-Wesley.
Tilly, C. (2001). Mechanisms in political processes. *Annual Review of Political Science, 4*(1), 21–41.
Timmermans, S., & Tavory, I. (2012). Theory construction in qualitative research: From grounded theory to Abductive analysis. *Sociological Theory, 30*(3), 167–186.

Tolbert, P. S., & Zucker, L. G. (1983). Institutional sources of change in the formal structure of organizations: The diffusion of civil service reform, 1880-1935. *Administrative Science Quarterly, 28*, 22–39.
Tomaskovic-Devey, D., & Lin, K.-H. (2011). Income dynamics, economic rents, and the financialization of the US economy. *American Sociological Review, 76*(4), 538–559.
Turk, H. (1977). *Organizations in modern life*. San Francisco, CA: Jossey-Bass.
Vaisey, S. (2009). Motivation and justification: A dual-process model of culture in action. *American Journal of Sociology, 114*(6), 1675–1715.
Van de Ven, A. H., & Poole, M. S. (2005). Alternative approaches for studying organizational change. *Organization Studies, 26*(9), 1377–1404.
Van Den Bos, W., Golka, P. J., Effelsberg, D., & McClure, S. M. (2013). Pyrrhic victories: The need for social status drives costly competitive behavior. *Frontiers in Neuroscience, 7*, 1–11.
Van der Zwan, N. (2014). Making sense of financialization. *Socio-Economic Review, 12*(1), 99–129.
Vaughan, D. (1997). *The challenger launch decision: Risky technology, culture, and deviance at NASA*. Chicago, IL: University of Chicago Press.
Vaughan, D. (2004). Theorizing disaster: Analogy, historical ethnography, and the challenger accident. *Ethnography, 5*(3), 315–347.
Vedres, B., & Stark, D. (2010). Structural folds: Generative disruption in overlapping groups. *American Journal of Sociology, 115*(4), 1150–1190.
Vitols, S. (2002). Shareholder value, management culture and production regimes in the transformation of the German chemical-pharmaceutical industry. *Competition and Change, 6*(3), 309–325.
Walsh, C. (2013). *Financialization and UK chancellor rhetoric, 1976–2013*. (PhD), London: Goldsmiths, University of London.
Warren, R. L. (1967). The interorganizational field as a focus for investigation. *Administrative Science Quarterly, 12*, 397–419.
Weber, M. (1921/2002). *Wirtschaft und Gesellschaft: Grundriss der verstehenden Soziologie*. Tübingen: Mohr Siebeck.
White, H. C. (1970). *Chains of opportunity: System models of mobility in organizations*. Cambridge, MA: Cambridge University Press.
Widmer, F. (2011). Institutional investors, corporate elites and the building of a market for corporate control. *Socio-Economic Review, 9*(4), 671–697.
Wiggan, J. (2017). *Selling financialised welfare futures: The social impact investment market and the policy boostering discourse of UK Governments*. Paper presented at the Social Finance, Impact Investing and the Financialisation of the Public Interest Conference, Hamburg, Germany.
Windolf, P. (2005). *Finanzmarkt-Kapitalismus: Analysen zum Wandel von Produktionsregimen*. Wiesbaden: VS Verlag für Sozialwissenschaften.
Windolf, P. (2008). Eigentümer ohne Risiko. *Zeitschrift für Soziologie, 37*(6), 516–535.
Wooten, M., & Hoffman, A. J. (2017). Organizational fields: Past, present and future. In R. Greenwood, C. Oliver, T. Lawrence, & R. Meyer (Eds.), *The Sage handbook of organizational institutionalism* (pp. 55–76). Thousand Oakes, CA: Sage.
Worley, C. (2005). It's not about race. It's about the community': New labour and 'community cohesion. *Critical Social Policy, 25*(4), 483–496.
Yin, R. K. (2009). *Case study research: Design and methods*. Los Angeles, CA: Sage.
Zorn, D. (2004). Here a chief, there a chief: The rise of the CFO in the American firm. *American Sociological Review, 69*(3), 345–364.
Zorn, D., Dobbin, F., Dierkes, J., & Kwok, M.-S. (2005). Managing investors: How financial markets reshaped the American firm. In K. Knorr Cetina & A. Preda (Eds.), *The sociology of financial markets* (pp. 269–289). Oxford: Oxford University Press.
Zucker, L. G. (1977). The role of institutionalization in cultural persistence. *American Sociological Review, 42*(5), 726–743.

MIX
Papier aus verantwortungsvollen Quellen
Paper from responsible sources
FSC® C105338

If you have any concerns about our products,
you can contact us on
ProductSafety@springernature.com

In case Publisher is established outside the EU,
the EU authorized representative is:
Springer Nature Customer Service Center GmbH
Europaplatz 3, 69115 Heidelberg, Germany

Printed by Libri Plureos GmbH
in Hamburg, Germany